CADOGAN
guides

Dana Facaros & Michael Pauls

110665466

FRANCE:
PROVENCE

Cadogan Books plc
London House, Parkgate Road, London SW11 4NQ, UK
e-mail: guides@cadogan.demon.co.uk

Distributed in North America by The Globe Pequot Press
6 Business Park Road, PO Box 833, Old Saybrook,
Connecticut 06475–0833

Copyright © Dana Facaros and Michael Pauls 1992, 1994, 1996
Updated by Nicky O'Hara 1996
Illustrations © Pauline Pears 1992, 1994, 1996

Design by Animage
Cover illustration by Povl Webb
Maps © Cadogan Guides, drawn by Map Creation Ltd

Editor: Dominique Shead
Series Editors: Rachel Fielding and Vicki Ingle

Proofreading: Lorna Horsefield
Indexing: Ann Hudson
Production: Book Production Services

A catalogue record for this book is available from the British Library
Library of Congress Cataloguing and Publication data available
ISBN 1–86011–046–0

The author and publishers have made every effort to ensure the accuracy of the information in this book at the time of going to press. However, they cannot accept any responsibility for any loss, injury or inconvenience resulting from the use of information contained in this guide.

Output to bromide by Dorchester Typesetting. Printed and bound in Great Britain by Page Brothers.

About the Authors

Dana Facaros and Michael Pauls have written over 20 books for Cadogan Guides, including four on France. They live in a farmhouse in southwest France with their two children and assorted animals.

Acknowledgements

The updater, Nicky O'Hara, would like to acknowledge the Magentas at Château de Sully (especially worth a visit). The publishers would like to thank Lorna Horsefield for proof-reading, Simon Brockbank for extra research and editorial work, Animage for the design, Ann Hudson for indexing, and Andrew Gordon, sales director of Corney & Barrow wine-merchants (established 1780), for updating the wine sections.

Please help us to keep this guide up to date

We have done our best to ensure that the information in this guide is correct at the time of going to press. But places and facilities are constantly changing, and standards and prices in hotels and restaurants fluctuate. We would be delighted to receive any comments concerning existing entries or omissions. Authors of the best letters will receive a copy of the Cadogan Guide of their choice.

Attention!

On 18 October 1996 France is changing its telephone numbers from 8 digits to 10 digits. All the phone numbers in the Provence and Côte d'Azur areas should be preceded by 04 from this date. Similarly, any Paris phone numbers should be preceded by 01 instead of 1.

Les Baux.

Contents

Travel   1–10

Practical A–Z   11–34

History   35–44

Art and Architecture 45–52

Topics 53–64

Down the Rhône: Orange to Tarascon 65–98

Down the Rhône: Alpilles, Crau and Camargue 99–136

Introduction

The sun-drenched landscapes of Provence seduce like few others—the days shot through with the colour of silvery olives, purple mountains, yellow sunflowers, black cypresses and lavender, the nights thrilling, dry and clear and boiling with stars. Vincent Van Gogh, who saw more clearly into the heart of this extravagant world than anyone else, painted these landscapes, and especially those cypresses, as if they were churning and alive, with a lyrical and passionate intensity. Come to the hills around St-Rémy when the mistral is up, and you'll see nature imitating art.

We outsiders have had an on-off love affair with the south of France ever since the Romans colonized it and spent their decline lounging around their heated pools. Even the medieval popes and cardinals in Avignon succumbed to its worldly temptations, its wines and the scents of the *maquis*, its roses and violets, the droning hum of the cicadas. The painters in the papal court, including some of the greatest artists of the 14th century, lent their radiant Madonnas something of the voluptuous Mediterranean light and colour that would one day inspire Van Gogh and Cézanne, Braque and Picasso; painters whose works have changed the way our eyes see not only the south of France, but the rest of our world as well.

These days, our world has decided on Provence as its possible paradise. Millions come here every year, hoping to catch a glimpse of it, wishing it didn't have so many second homes, holiday flats, trinket shops and traffic jams. To see the region at its best the delicate question of when to go becomes as crucial as where: in August, the sacred month of French holidays, even the dullest town in Provence can be as frantic as the monkey pit in a zoo. At other times, Provence's essentially classical spirit is easier to grasp—in the lovely countryside around Aix-en-Provence and Cézanne's fetish Mont Ste-Victoire, or the flame-like peaks of the Alpilles or Cubist tile-roofed *villages perchés* in the Lubéron, the cliffs and fjord-like *calanques* off the coast of Marseille, the secret valleys by Mercantour National Park in the Alps, the bullring of Arles and the Roman theatre of Orange, like molten gold in the last rays of the sun. Colourful markets, wild mountains, abandoned Brigadoons or beautifully restored art towns, and restaurants that rival Paris' finest beckon, but perhaps best of all is the leisure in doing as the Romans did and spending the day lounging around the pool, surrounded by perfumed gardens, idly dreaming about what's for lunch. No wonder that Pope Gregory XI, who returned the papacy to Rome in 1377, took one look at the Eternal City and immediately decided to pack his bags to return to the comforts and delights of Avignon. Much to the relief of the Italians, he died before he could go.

The Best of Provence

Castles: Château du Roi René, Tarascon; Citadelle des Baux-de-Provence; Château d'If.

Curiosities: world's first concrete canoe, Musée du Pays Brignolais, Brignoles; Cathedral, Vaison-la-Romaine.

Follies: Mausoleum Sec, Aix.

Gardens: L'Harmas, northeast of Orange.

Markets: Arles, Apt, Carpentras.

Medieval art and architecture: Avignon, the Abbaye de Sénanque.

Natural wonders: Grand Canyon du Verdon, Garagaï chasm on Mt Ste-Victoire, Fontaine-de-Vaucluse.

Regions of picturesque villages: Vallée de la Roya, Comtat Venaissin, eastern Lubéron, country north of Draguignan.

Roman monuments: Orange, St-Rémy, Vaison-la-Romaine, Arles, Riez.

Traditional festivals: Gipsy pilgrimage, Stes-Maries-de-la-Mer.

Wine touring: Châteauneuf-du-Pape; Dentelles de Montmirail (Gigondas); east of Draguignan (Côtes de Provence).

Travel

A little preparation will help you get much more out of your holiday in the south of France. Check the list of festivals (*see* p.15) to help you decide where you want to be and when, and book accommodation early: if you plan to base yourself in one area, write ahead to the local tourist offices listed in the text for complete lists of self-catering accommodation, hotels, and campsites in their areas, or else contact one of the many companies in the UK or USA (*see* p.32). For more general information and a complete list of tour operators, get in touch with a French Government Tourist Office:

UK: 178 Piccadilly, London, W1V OAL, ✆ (0171) 629 2869, ✉ (0171) 493 6594.

Ireland: 35 Lower Abbey St, Dublin 1, ✆ (1) 703 4046, ✉ (1) 874 7324.

Australia: BWP House, 12 Castlereagh St, Sydney NSW 2000, ✆ (612) 231 5244.

USA: 444 Madison Avenue, NY 10022, ✆ (212) 838 7800, ✉ (212) 838 7855; 676 N. Michigan Av., Chicago, IL 60611, ✆ (312) 751 7800, ✉ (312) 357 6339; 9454 Wilshire Blvd, Suite 715, Beverly Hills, CA 90212, ✆ (310) 271 2358, ✉ (310) 276 2835. Nationwide information ✆ freephone (1900) 990 0040.

Canada: 1981 Av. McGill College, No. 490, Montreal, Quebec H3A 2W9, ✆ (514) 288 4264, ✉ (514) 845 4868; 30 St Patrick St, Suite 700, Toronto MST 3A3, ✆ (416) 593 4723, ✉ (416) 979 7587.

Getting There

By Air

The main international airports in the south are at Nice, Marseille, and Montpellier. Unfortunately, with the exception of Nice, these airports serve mainly business travellers and don't get enough holiday volume to make international fares competitive. Prices are highest in the summer and during the Easter holidays, but those who book several months in advance can usually save money. Check with your travel agent or your major Sunday newspaper for bargains or packages. There are a number of charters from London to Nice, but from most other points of departure—the rest of the UK, Ireland, North America, Australia, etc.—it's usually cheaper to fly to Paris and from there catch a cheap Air Inter flight or TGV train to the south. Check out Air France's Air and Rail scheme, which may save you money.

From Orly Airport in Paris, there are Air Inter flights to Nice, Cannes, Toulon, Montpellier, Nîmes and Marseille; discounts exist if you fly in low 'blue' periods (in the UK, Nouvelles Frontières, 2/3 Woodstock St, London, W1R 1HE, ✆ (0171) 629 7772 have all the Air Inter details). Students who equip themselves with the relevant ID cards are eligible for considerable reductions, not only on flights, but on trains and admission fees to museums, concerts, and more. Agencies specializing in student and youth travel can help in applying for the cards, as well as filling you in on the best deals. Try STA, ✆ (0171) 937 9921, and Campus Travel, ✆ (0171) 730 3402, in London or branches throughout the UK; STA, ✆ (03) 347 4711, in Australia; STA, ✆ (800) 777 0112, in the US; CUTS, ✆ (416) 979 2406, in Canada.

Air prices and airport hassles make France's highspeed TGVs (*trains à grande vitesse*) a very attractive alternative. TGVs shoot along at the average of 170 mph when they're not breaking world records, and the journey from Paris' Gare de Lyon to Marseille takes only 4 hours and 44 minutes; to Avignon 3 hours and 45 minutes; and to Nice 7 hours. Train fares are only minimally higher on a TGV. Some weekday departures require a supplement (30–40F) and seat reservations (20F), which you can make when you buy your ticket or at the station before departure. Another pleasant way of getting there is by overnight sleeper after dinner in Paris, although a recent spate of robberies in the compartments at night suggests that you should take extra precautions. People under 26 are eligible for a 30 per cent discount on fares (*see* the travel agencies above) and there are other discounts if you're over 65 available from major travel agents. For the TGV, reservations are compulsory.

If you plan some long train journeys, look into the variety of rail passes: France's national railway, the SNCF, offers a *France Railpass* that gives you either four days (they don't have to be consecutive) of unlimited travel in a 15-day period, or nine days of travel within 30 days. It includes extras like a day's free travel in Paris (from the airport, the metro, etc.), TGV supplements (except the seat reservation), and discounts on car rentals and Channel crossings. Get it before you leave from travel agents or SNCF offices: at 179 Piccadilly, London W1, ✆ 'The Rail Shop' (0990) 300003 for bookings. For simple information SNCF has created a new number whereby you pay for the pleasure of asking for train times: the 0891 number costs 48p a minute peak time, ✆ 0891 515 477. In the USA contact 610 Fifth Av., New York, NY 10020, ✆ (212) 582 2816 (or ✆ (800) 848 7245). Other alternatives include the well-known InterRail pass for European residents under age 26, which offers a month's unlimited travel in Europe and 50 per cent reductions on Channel ferries, and various Eurail passes for non-Europeans, valid for 15 days to three months.

By Coach

The cheapest way to get from London to the south of France is by National Express Eurolines coach, ✆ (0990) 80 80 80; tickets available from any National Express office. There are two journeys a week: to Aix and Marseille (19 hours); and to Avignon and Nîmes (19 hours approximately, allow an extra 45 minutes to Nîmes).

By Car

A car entering France must have its registration and insurance papers. If you're coming from the UK or Ireland, the dip of the headlights must be adjusted to the right. Carrying a warning triangle is mandatory, and this should be placed 50m behind the car if you have a breakdown. Drivers with a valid licence from an EU country, Canada, the USA or Australia don't need an international licence. If you're driving down from the UK, going through or around Paris is almost inevitable, a task best tackled on either side of the rush hour. The various *autoroutes* will get you south the fastest but be prepared to pay some 500F in tolls; the N7 south of Paris takes much longer, but costs nothing and has great scenery.

A fairly comfortable but costly option is to put your car on the train. Motorail accommodation is compulsory, in a 4-berth (1st class) or 6-berth (2nd class) carriage. Linen is provided, along with washing facilities at the end of each carriage. Compartments are not segregated by sex. Services run from both Boulogne and Dieppe to Avignon and Fréjus/St Raphaël, and from Boulogne to Nice.

Taking 'Le Shuttle' is the most convenient and fastest way to travel by car to France. It takes half an hour on the train, while you remain in your car (although you can get out to stretch your legs). Prices are around £260 return. Ring for further information on ✆ (0990) 353535.

If you plan to hire a car, look into air and holiday package deals as well as combination 'Train and Auto' rates to save money, or consider leasing a car if you mean to stay three weeks or more. Prices vary widely from firm to firm, and beware the small print about service charges and taxes: three firms to try in the US are France Auto Vacances, ✆ (800) 234 1426; Europe by Car Inc, ✆ (800) 223 1516; or Renault, ✆ (800) 221 1052.

Entry Formalities

Passports and Visas

Holders of EU, US, and Canadian passports do not need a visa to enter France for stays of up to three months, but everyone else still does. Apply at your nearest French Consulate: the most convenient visa is the *visa de circulation*, allowing for multiple stays of three months over a three-year period. If you intend on **staying longer**, the law says you need a *carte de séjour*, a requirement EU citizens can easily get around as passports are rarely stamped. On the other hand, non-EU citizens had best apply for an extended visa at home, a complicated procedure requiring proof of income, etc. You can't get a *carte de séjour* without this visa, and obtaining this is a trial run in the *ennuis* you'll undergo in applying for a *carte de séjour* at your local *mairie*.

Health and Travel Insurance

Citizens of the EU who bring along their E-111 forms are entitled to the same health services as French citizens. This means paying up front for medical care and prescriptions, of which costs 75–80 per cent are reimbursed later—a complex procedure for the non-French. As an alternative, consider a travel insurance policy, covering theft and losses and offering 100 per cent medical refund; check to see if it covers your extra expenses in case you get bogged down in airport or train strikes. Beware that accidents resulting from sports are rarely covered by ordinary insurance. Canadians are usually covered in France by their provincial health coverage; Americans and others should check their individual policies.

By Train

The **SNCF** runs a decent and efficient network of trains through the major cities of the south, with an added service called the *Métrazur* that links all the resorts of the Côte d'Azur from Menton to St-Raphaël as often as every half-hour in the peak summer season. There is one journey worth taking for its mountain scenery: from Nice to Digne, the narrow-gauge *Train des Pignes* is run by the **Chemin de Fer de la Provence**, *see* p.235 (French rail passes are valid, other passes are granted a 50% discount).

Prices have recently gone up but are still reasonable. If you plan on making only a few long hauls the France Railpass (*see* above) will save you money. Other possible discounts hinge on the day of your departure. The SNCF has divided the year into blue, white, and red days, based on demand. If you depart in a *Période Bleue* (off-peak) with a return ticket and travel over 1000km you'll get a 25% discount (*Billet Séjour*). Married couples are eligible for a free *Carte Couple* which entitles one to pay half-fare when travelling together on blue days. People over 65 can purchase a *Carte Vermeille*, valid for a year of half-price blue-period travel; under 26-year-olds can buy a *Carte Jeune* for half-price blue-day travel from June to September. The more children you have, the more economical an expensive *Carte Kiwi* becomes: the card is in the name of one child, and family members each purchase complimentary cards. The child then pays full fare, and everyone else half.

Tickets must be **stamped** in the little orange machines by the entrance to the lines that say *Compostez votre billet* (this puts the date on the ticket, to keep you from using the same one over and over again). Any time you interrupt a journey until another day, you have to re-compost your ticket. Long-distance trains (**Trains Corails**) have snack trolleys and bar/cafeteria cars; some have play areas for small children. Nearly every station has large computerized lockers (*consigne automatique*) which take about half an hour to puzzle out the first time you use them, so plan accordingly.

By Bus

Do not count on seeing any part of rural France by public transport. The bus network is barely adequate between major cities and towns (places often already well-served by rail) and rotten in rural areas, where the one bus a day fits the school schedule, leaving at the crack of dawn and returning in the afternoon; more remote villages are linked to civilization only once a week or not at all. Buses are run either by the SNCF (replacing discontinued rail routes) or private firms. Rail passes are valid on SNCF lines and they generally coincide with trains. Private bus firms, especially when they have a monopoly, tend to be a bit more expensive than trains; some towns have a *gare routière* (coach station), usually near the train stations, though many lines start from any place that catches their fancy. The posted schedules are not to be trusted. The tourist office or shopkeepers near the bus stop have a more accurate inkling of when a bus is likely to appear. Services improve in relation to the size of the town—bigger is most definitely better.

Unless you plan to stick to the major cities or the coast, a car is unfortunately the only way to see most of Provence. This has its drawbacks: high car rental rates and petrol, and an accident rate double that of the UK (and much higher than the US). The vaunted French logic and clarity break down completely on the asphalt. Go slowly and be careful—although in cities such as Nice, you're a danger to everyone if you do not adopt the local policy of putting your foot down and going with the flow.

Roads are generally excellently maintained, but anything of less status than a departmental route (D-road) may be uncomfortably narrow. Mountain roads are reasonable except in the vertical department of Alpes-Maritimes, where they inevitably follow old mule tracks. Shrines to St Eloi, patron of muleteers, are common here, and a quick prayer is a wise precaution. Throughout the summer, on the coast, avoid using your car after 9am or before late evening because everyone else will want to go where you do. Petrol stations are rare in rural areas, so consider your fuel supply while planning any forays into the mountains. If you come across a garage with petrol-pump attendants, they will expect a tip for oil, windscreen-cleaning or air. The French have one delightfully civilized custom of the road; if oncoming drivers unaccountably flash their headlights at you, it means the *gendarmes* are lurking just up the way.

Always give **priority to the right** (*priorité à droite*) at any intersection—anywhere, unless you're on a motorway or on a road with a yellow diamond 'priority route' sign. This French anachronism is a major cause of accidents; most people only follow the rule when they're feeling generous. If you are new to France, think of every intersection as a new and perilous experience.

When you are looking to park, the blue 'P' signs will infallibly direct you to a village's or town's car park. Watch out, though, for the tiny signs that indicate which streets are meant for pedestrians only (with complicated schedules in even tinier print), and for Byzantine street parking rules (which would take pages to explain—do as the natives do, and especially be careful about village centres on market days). Many towns have car parks underneath their very heart, spectacularly so in Avignon and Nice, and even in smaller towns such as Vence. Although expensive, these car parks are safe and secure. There are even plans to build one under France's no.2 tourist attraction, Les Baux.

Unless sweetened in an air or holiday package deal, car hire in France is an expensive proposition (350–400F a day, without mileage, for the cheapest cars; *see* p.4 for hiring a car). Petrol (*essence*) at the time of writing is 6.09F a litre for leaded, 5.84F or 5.91F for unleaded. Speed limits are 130km/80mph on the *autoroutes* (toll motorways); 110km/69mph on dual carriageways (divided highways); 90km/55mph on other roads; 50km/30mph in an 'urbanized area'—this starts as soon as you pass a white sign with a town's name on it and lasts until you pass another sign with the town's name barred. Fines for speeding, payable on the spot, begin at 1300F and can be astronomical if you fail the breathalyzer. If you wind up in an accident, the procedure is to fill out and sign a *constat aimable*. If your French isn't sufficient to deal with this, hold off until you find someone to translate for you so you don't accidentally incriminate yourself. If you have a breakdown and are a member of a motoring club affiliated with the Touring Club de France, ring the latter; if not, ring the police (✆ 17).

By Boat

The major towns, as well as the islands, along the Côte d'Azur are linked by regular boat services. These come in handy especially in the summer when travelling by road is hot purgatory; just look for signs near the port for the *gare maritime*.

By Bicycle

Cycling spells more pain than pleasure in most French minds, and one of the hazards of driving in the foothills of the Alps and Pyrenees is suddenly coming upon bands of uniformed cyclists pumping up the kinds of inclines that most people require escalators for. If you mean to cycle in the summer, start early and stop early to avoid heatstroke. French drivers, not always courteous to fellow motorists, usually give cyclists a wide berth; and yet on any given summer day, half the patients in a French hospital are from accidents on two-wheeled transport. Consider a helmet. Also beware that bike thefts are fairly common, especially along the Côte d'Azur, so make sure your insurance covers your bike—or the one you hire.

Getting your own bike to France is fairly easy: Air France and British Airways carry them free from Britain. From the US or Australia most airlines will carry them as long as they're boxed and are included in your total baggage weight. In all cases, telephone ahead. Certain French trains (called *Autotrains*, with a bicycle symbol in the timetable) carry bikes for free; otherwise you have to send it as registered luggage, and pay a 40F fee, with delivery guaranteed within 5 days. The best maps, based on ordnance surveys, are put out by the Institut Géographique National (1:50,000 or 1:100,000), available in most French bookshops.

You can hire bikes of varying quality (most of them 10-speed) at most SNCF stations and in major towns. The advantage of hiring from a station means that you can drop it off at another, as long as you specify where when you hire it. Rates run at around 50F a day, with a deposit of 300–400F or credit card number. Private firms hire mountain-bikes (VTTs in French) and racing bikes.

On Foot

A network of long-distance paths or *Grandes Randonnées*, GRs for short (marked by distinctive red and white signs), take in some of the most beautiful scenery in the south of France. Each GR is described in a *Topoguide*, with maps and details about camping sites, *refuges*, and so on, available in area bookshops or from the Comité National des Sentiers de Grande Randonnée, 8 Ave Marceau, 75008 Paris, ✆ (1 16) 47 23 62 32.

There are 5000km of marked paths in the Alpes-Maritimes alone. Of special interest are: **GR 5** from Nice to Aspremont, the Gorges de la Vésubie and St-Dalmas-Valdeblore—and thence to Amsterdam; **GR 52** from Menton up to Sospel, the Vallée des Merveilles to St-Dalmas-Valdeblore; **GR 52a** and **GR 5** through Mercantour National Park, both of which are open only from the end of June to the beginning of October.

In Provence, **GR 9** begins in St-Tropez and crosses over the region's most famous mountains: Ste-Baume, Ste-Victoire, the Lubéron and Ventoux. **GR 4** crosses the Dentelles de Montmirail and Mont Ventoux en route to Grasse. **GR 6** crosses much of the area in this book, from the Alps through the Vaucluse and Alpilles, to Beaucaire and the Pont du Gard before veering north up the River Gard on to its final destination by the Atlantic. **GR 42** descends the west bank of the Rhône from near Bagnols-sur-Cèze to Beaucaire.

Special-interest Holidays

There are a number of ways to combine a holiday with study or a special interest. For information, contact the French Centre on ✆ (0171) 792 0337 or the Cultural Services of the French Embassy: 23 Cromwell Road, London SW7 2DQ, ✆ (0171) 838 2055, or at 972 Fifth Av., New York, NY 10021, ✆ (212) 439 1400. French universities—Aix for the humanities, Marseille for the sciences, Montpellier for law, agriculture and medicine—are easy to enter if you're already enrolled in a similar institution at home; tuition fees are nominal but room and board are up to you. The Cultural Services can send a prospectus and tell you what paperwork is required.

in France

Alliance Française, 2 Rue Paris, 06000 Nice, ✆ 93 62 67 66, ✉ 93 85 28 06: French classes at all levels. Courses last a month but they can and will tailor to your needs.

Association Neige et Merveilles, La Minière de Vallauria, 06430 St-Dalmas-de-Tende, ✆ 93 04 62 40: courses in archaeology and restoration.

Centre d'Etudes Linguistiques d'Avignon, 16 Rue Sainte Catherine, ✆ 90 86 04 33, ✉ 90 85 92 01: for French courses at all levels.

Direction des Antiquités Préhistoriques et Historiques of each *département* has summer openings for volunteers who are invited to assist at archaeological digs. Write to them in early spring. The address in Provence is 21–23 Blvd du Roy René, 13617 Aix-en-Provence; in Languedoc, it is 5 bis Rue de la Salle l'Evêque, 24000 Montpellier.

L'Ecole de Moulin, Restaurant L'Amandier, Mougins 06250, ✆ 93 75 35 70, and Hôtel Beau Rivage, Rue Brea, 06300 Nice, ✆ 93 75 35 70: year-round *Cuisine du Soleil* cookery courses lasting a week under the auspices of Roger Vergé Inc.

from the UK

Abercrombie & Kent, Sloane Square House, Holbein Place, London SW1W 8NS, ✆ (0171) 730 9600: hotel accommodation and tailor-made holidays to the Var, Vaucluse, Côte d'Azur and Bouches-du-Rhône.

Allez France, 27 West St, Storrington, West Sussex, RH20 4DZ, ✆ (01903) 742 345: city breaks in Nice, wine tours, short breaks in Antibes, Juan-les-Pins and Gorges du Verdon.

Alternative Travel Group, 69–71 Banbury Road, Oxford OX2 6PE, ✆ (01865) 310 399: walking and cycling holidays in Provence; wine tours.

Andante, Grange Cottage, Winterbourne Dauntsey, Salisbury, Wiltshire SP4 6ER, ✆ (01980) 610 555, ✉ (01980) 610 002: archaeological and historical study tours.

Arblaster & Clarke, Clarke House, Farnham Road, West Liss GU33 6JQ, ✆ (01730) 893 344, ✉ (01730) 892 888: wine tours of the Rhône region, escorted by a wine expert.

Artscape Painting Holidays, 7 Clifftown Parade, Southend-on-Sea, Essex, SS1 1DP, ✆ (01702) 435 990: painting courses in Provence.

Belle France, Bayham Abbey, Lamberhurst TN3 8BG, ✆ (01892) 890 885: walking holidays in Provence; cycling holidays in Provence and the Camargue.

CV Travel, 43 Cadogan Street, London SW3 2PR, ✆ (0171) 581 0851, ✉ (0171) 584 5229: country-house accommodation and tailor-made holidays.

Headwater Holidays, 146 London Road, Northwich CW9 5HH, ✆ (01606) 48699: cycling for 10 or 6 nights; walking in the Gorges du Verdon.

Hoseasons Holidays, Sunway House, Lowestoft NR32 2LW, ✆ (01502) 500 555: canal tours of the Camargue, with a base at Beaucaire.

InnTravel, Hovingham, York YO6 4JZ, ✆ (01653) 628811: walking and cycling holidays.

LSG Theme Holidays, 201 Main Street, Thornton LE67 1AH, ✆ (01509) 231 713 or (01509) 239 857 (24 hrs): a French-run company offering painting courses; language classes at all levels; cultural discovery; photography; cooking; horseriding in Provence.

Martin Randall, 10 Barley Mow Passage, London W4 4PH, ✆ (0181) 742 3355, ✉ (0181) 742 1066: lecturer-accompanied cultural tours of Provence, including 'The Romans in Provence'.

Plantagenet Tours, 85 The Grove, Moordown, Bournemouth BH9 2TY, ✆ (01202) 521895: cultural tours, including 'The Provence Tour'.

Susi Madron's Cycling for Softies, 2 and 4 Birch Polygon, Rusholme, Manchester M14 5HX, ✆ (0161) 248 8282, ✉ (0161) 248 5140: easy cycling in Provence and the Camargue.

Waymark Holidays, 44 Windsor Road, Slough SL1 2EJ, ✆ (01753) 516 477, ✉ (01753) 517 016: walking tours, centre-based in Provence.

from the USA

Abercrombie & Kent, 1520 Kensington Road, Oakbrook, IL 60521, ✆ (708) 954 2944, ✉ (708) 954 3324: barge holidays, walking and rail tours.

Adventure Center, 1311 63rd Street, Suite 200, Emeryville, CA 94608, ✆ (510) 654 1879, ✉ (510) 564 4200: walking and camping in Provence.

Baumeler Tours, 10 Grand Avenue, Rockville Centre, NY 11570, ✆ (516) 766 6160: cycling in Provence.

Le Boat Inc., 215 Union Street, Hackensack, NJ 07601, ✆ (201) 342 1838, 🖷 (201) 342 7498: canal boat holidays.

Practical A–Z

Provence has a basically Mediterranean climate, one wafted by winds that give it a special character. The most notorious is the **mistral** (from the Provençal *mistrau*, or master) supposedly sent by northerners jealous of the south's climate—rushing down the Rhône and gusting east as far as Toulon and west to Narbonne, sparing the hot-house of the Côte d'Azur. On average the mistral blows 100 to 150 days a year, nearly always in multiples of three, except when it begins at night. It is responsible for the dryness in the air and soil (hence its nickname, *mangio fango*, or mud-eater). Houses in its line of fire are built *pointes en avant*, at an angle, the north side blank and in the shade, protected by cypresses, while on the south side plane trees protect the house from the strong sun. It blows so hard that it can drive people mad: an old law in Provence acquitted a murderer if it could be proved that he killed his victim while the mistral was blowing. But the mistral has its good points: it blows away harmful miasmas and pollution from the Rhône and makes the stars radiantly clear, as alive as Van Gogh's *Starry Night*. Besides the Master, there are twenty-two other winds: most importantly, the east wind, or **levant**, or south-easterly 'Greek' wind which brings the much desired rain; the **pounent**, or west wind; and the suffocatingly hot **sirocco** from Africa.

Rainfall varies widely across the south. The Camargue barely gets 500mm a year, the least rainfall in France. In the average year, it rains as much in Nice (750mm per year) as Brest and more in Marseille than Paris. In the heart of Provence it rains much less frequently—not at all in the summer, and violently in spring and autumn (up to 135mm in an hour)—hence the *restanques* or terraces carved in the hills by the farmers to prevent erosion. Recent years have been even drier than average, turning the forests of the south into tinder-boxes.

Each season has its pros and cons. In January all the tourists are in the Alps; in February the mimosa and almonds bloom on the Côte d'Azur. In April and May you can sit outside at restaurants and swim, and after an hour's drive ski at Auron or Isola 2000. By June, the mistral slows down and the resorts begin to fill up; walking is safe in the highest mountains. July and August are bad months, when everything is crowded, temperatures and prices soar and tempers flare, but it's also the season of the great festivals in Avignon and Aix. Things quieten down considerably once French school holidays end in mid-September. In October the weather is traditionally mild on the coast, although in 1992 and 1993 the month was marked by torrential downpours and floods; the first snows fall in the Alps. November is another bad month; it rains and many museums, hotels, and restaurants close down. December brings Christmas holiday tourists and the first skiers.

Average Temperature Chart in °C (°F)

	Jan	Feb	Mar	Apr	May	June	July	Aug	Sept	Oct	Nov	Dec
Nice	11(52)	12(54)	14(56)	17(62)	20(69)	22(72)	24(75)	26(79)	25(77)	20(69)	16(61)	13(55)
Avignon	7(44)	7(44)	11(52)	15(59)	17(62)	21(70)	23(73)	25(77)	23(73)	16(61)	10(50)	8(45)

Consulates

UK:

Nice: 12 Rue de France, ☎ 93 82 32 04

Marseille: 24 Ave du Prado, 6e, ☎ 91 53 43 32, ✆ 91 37 47 06

USA:

Nice: Rue Maréchal Joffre, ☎ 93 88 89 55

Marseille: 12 Blvd Paul Peytral, near the Préfecture, ☎ 91 54 92 00

Canada:

Marseille: 24 Ave du Prado, 6e, ☎ 91 37 19 37

Ireland:

Marseille: 148 Rue Sainte, 1er, ☎ 91 54 92 29

Antibes: Villa les Chênes Verts, 152 Blvd Kennedy, Antibes, ☎ 93 61 50 63

Crime and the Police

Everyone in Marseille seemed most dishonest. They all tried to swindle me, mostly with complete success.

Evelyn Waugh

There is a fair chance that you will be had in the south of France, though probably not in Marseille; thieves and pickpockets go for the flashier fish on the Côte d'Azur. Road pirates prey on motorists blocked in traffic, train pirates prowl the overnight compartments looking for handbags and cameras, car bandits just love the ripe pickings in cars parked in isolated scenic areas or tourist car parks. Although violence is rare, the moral of the story is to leave anything you'd really miss at home, carry traveller's cheques and insure your property, especially if you're driving—and try always to leave bicycles inside and out of sight. Report thefts to the nearest *gendarmerie*, not a pleasant task but the reward is the bit of paper you need for an insurance claim. If your passport is stolen, contact the police and your nearest consulate for emergency travel documents. Carry photocopies of your passport, driver's licence, etc.; it makes it easier when reporting a loss. By law, the police in France can stop anyone anywhere and demand an ID; in practice, they only tend to do it to harass minorities, the homeless, and scruffy hippy types. If they really don't like the look of you they can salt you away for a long time without any reason.

The drug situation is the same in France as anywhere in the west: soft and hard drugs are widely available, and the police only make an issue of victimless crime when it suits them (your being a foreigner just may rouse them to action). Smuggling any amount of marijuana into the country can mean a prison term, and there's not much your consulate can or will do about it.

Disabled Travellers

When it comes to providing access for all, France is not exactly in the vanguard of nations; many Americans who come over are appalled. But things are beginning to change, especially in newer buildings. Access and facilities in 90 towns in France are covered in *Touristes quand même! Promenades en France pour les voyageurs handicapés*, a booklet usually available in the tourist offices of large cities, or write ahead to the Comité National Français de Liaison pour la Réadaptation des Handicapés, 30–32 Quai de la Loire, 75019 Paris. Hotels with facilities for the handicapped are listed in Michelin's *Red Guide to France*.

RADAR (The Royal Asociation for Disability and Rehabilitation), 12 City Forum, 250 City Road, London EC1V 8AF, ✆ (0171) 250 3222: publishes *Holidays and Travel Abroad: A Guide for Disabled People*.

Mobility International USA, PO Box 10767, Eugene, OR 97403, USA, ✆ (503) 343 1248: all aspects of travel information covered.

Environment

As elsewhere in the Mediterranean, a sad litany of forest fires heads the television news in summer. Especially in Provence, most of the herbs and trees are xerophytes, able to thrive in dry hot conditions on poor rocky soils. Most forests are pine—Aleppo pines in limestone, maritime pines in the Maures. Here they often close roads in summer to decrease the chance of fires. Most are caused by twits with matches (you'll be more careful, won't you?), though many fires are deliberately instigated by speculators who burn off protected forests to build more holiday villas and suchlike. Fires often lead to erosion and flooding, though the local governments now do a good job of reforestation. The weird wasteland of Blausasc, in a valley north of Nice (caused by greedy logging in the 1800s), shows what Provence would soon look like if they didn't.

Since the war there has simply been too much money involved for governments to act responsibly. Paris bureaucrats are as responsible as local politicians; in public transport, for example, they insist on pushing a new TGV route around the coast, bringing down even more people, instead of improving local transport that might cut down on the ferocious traffic they already have. The new route is a monster, cutting across scores of scenic areas and wine regions.

Other enemies of the Midi include: the army, which has commandeered enormous sections of wilderness (Plan de Canjuers and parts of the Crau) and regularly blows them to smithereens in manoeuvres and target practice; the nuclear industry, with France's nuclear research centre at Cadarache and most of its nuclear missiles hidden away on the Plateau de Vaucluse; the *chancre coloré*, a fungus that, like phylloxera, came from the US (on wooden crates during the Second World War) and now threatens the lovely plane trees of Provence; and finally the truly villainous national electric company, EDF, which once tried to flood the Grand Canyon du Verdon. The one genuine contemporary ecological disaster is the Etang de Berre, now entirely surrounded by the industrial and suburban sprawl of Marseille, a ghastly horror of power pylons, pollution and speculative development. Here too the EDF is involved; heated water, pumped from its giant power plant into the lagoon, is killing off the few remaining fish; local groups are fighting hard to make it stop.

Festivals

The south of France offers everything from the village fête, with a pilgrimage or religious procession, bumper cars, a *pétanque* tournament, a feast (anything from sardines to *cassoulet* to paella) and an all-night dance, sometimes to a local band but often a travelling troupe playing 'Hot Music' or some other electrified cacophony. A *bravade* entails some pistol- or musket-shots; a *corso* is a parade with carts or floats. St John's Day (24 June) is a big favourite and often features bonfires and fireworks.

In the southern Rhône valley people still like to celebrate with a *farandole*, a dance in 6/8 time with held hands or a handkerchief, which may be as old as the ancient Greeks. One-man musical accompaniment is provided by a little three-holed flute called a *galoubet* played with the left hand, and a *tambourin*, a drum played with the right. Both *farandoles* and flamenco enliven the proceedings of the 24 May pilgrimage at Saintes-Maries-de-la-Mer, by far the best attended of all popular festivities in the south.

Note: dates change every year. For complete listings and precise dates of events in Provence, pick up a copy of the annual lists, available in most tourist offices.

Calendar of Events

January

Throughout month	International Exhibition of Ornamental Figures, Arles
Sunday nearest the 17th	*Fête de St-Marcel*, folkdancing and singing at **Barjols**; every four years (next 1998) Barjols does an ox roast as well

February

2	*Fête des Chandelles*, **Marseille**
3	Festival of olives and late golden Servan grapes, **Valbonne**
First week	*Fête des Oursins*, sea urchin festival at **Carry-le-Rouet**
10 days at Carnival	*Fête du Citron*, **Menton**
Carnival	**Nice** has the most famous festivities in France
Ash Wednesday	*Les Pailhasses* at **Cournonterral**, a 14th-century parade of boys in straw and turkey feathers, who try to squirt wine on passers-by

March

Throughout month	Carnivals at **Aix-en-Provence** and **Marseille**

April

Good Friday–Easter	Bullfights in **Arles**
25	Winegrowers' festival and blessing of the vines, **Châteauneuf-du-Pape**; *Fête de St-Marc*, **Villeneuve-lès-Avignon**
Last Sunday	*Fête des Gardians*, traditional rodeo in **Arles**
April to May	Comedy Festival, **Cavaillon**

May

1	*Gardians* Day with religious ceremony, *Gardians* parade, entertainment in arenas at **Arles**
Sunday after the 15th	*Fête de St-Gens*, costumes, pistol shots, etc., at **Monteaux**
Third Sunday	Cherry Festival, **Le Luc-en-Provence**
24–25	Gypsy pilgrimage at **Saintes-Maries-de-la-Mer**
10 days at Pentecost	*Cavalcade*, music festival at **Apt**

June

1	*Cérémonie du St-Vinage*, benediction of wines with Provençal mass, **Boulbon**
Last half of June	Jazz and chamber music, in **Aix**
23–24	*Fête de St-Jean*, with processions, **Entrevaux**
Sunday after the 24th	*Fête Provençal*, with blessings of animals, in **Allauch** (near Marseille)
End of June	Folklore parades, horsemanship shows, concerts and *abrivados*, **Tarascon**

July

Throughout month	*Rencontres Internationales de la Photographie*, **Arles**; film festival, **La Ciotat**; *Festival de la Sorgue*, music, theatre and dance at **Fontaine-de-Vaucluse** and around; Festival of Côtes-du-Ventoux Wine, **Caromb**; *Dance On The Port* by the Roland Petit National Ballet, **Marseille**; International Festival of Lyrical Art and Music, **Aix-en-Provence**
First Sunday	*Fête de St-Eloi*, bullfights and a decorated cart pulled by 40 horses in **Châteaurenard**
First two weeks	Dance Festival, **Aix**; International Folklore Festival, **Marseille**

Mid-July	*Corso de nuit* for Notre-Dame-de-Santé, **Carpentras**; *Soirées Musicales*, **St-Maximin-la-Ste-Baume**; *Féria du cheval*, horse fair at **Saintes-Maries-de-la-Mer**
14	Fireworks in many places for Bastille Day; **Avignon** puts on an excellent show
Last three weeks	Music festival, **Aix**; *Festival de Radio France*
Last Saturday	Folklore festival of St Jean, **Les Baux**; *Fête de la Tradition*, **Arles**
Last Sunday	*Fête de la Tarasque*, **Tarascon**
July–August	Festival of Early Music, **Entrevaux**; *Nuits de l'Empéri*, theatre festival in **Salon**; island festival, **Marseille**; Festival of Dance, Music and Theatre, **Vaison-la-Romaine**; *Nuits de la Citadelle*, music and theatre at **Sisteron**; *Rencontres Internationales d'Eté à la Chartreuse*, concerts, dance and theatre at **Villeneuve-lès-Avignon**
Mid-July–mid-Aug	International theatre festival, **Avignon**; *Festival Passion*, operettas, ballet, and music at **Carpentras**
21–22	*Fête de Ste-Madeleine*, **St-Maximin-la-Ste-Baume**
Last two weeks	Music festival, **Orange**; fête in **Martigues**, with theatre, seafood, music and dancing
Last Sunday	Donkey races and village fête, **Lacoste**
July–Aug	La Falaise Theatre Festival, **Cotignac**

August

Throughout month	World folklore festival, **Martigues;** music and dance festival, **Arles**, culminating around the 25th
Early August	Medieval festival, **Entrevaux**
First two weeks	Music and theatre festival, **Gordes**
1st weekend	*Fête de la Veraison*, marking colour change of grapes, **Châteauneuf du Pape**
First Sunday	Lavender Festival, **Digne**; *Fête de la Madeleine*, with parade of flowered carts, **Châteaurenard**
2nd week	Festivals and dancing at the Windmill, **Fontvielle**
9 and 11	*Fête de St-Laurent*, with bullfights, at **Eygalières**
15	Village *fête* and operettas, **Le Thor**
Third week	Provençal festival with processions, *bravades* and drama, **Séguret**
First Sunday after the 20th	*Fête du Traou*, dancing and *polenta* feasts at **Tende**

Third week	Provençal wine festival, **Séguret**
End of August	*Fête de St-Louis*, with historical re-enactment, at **Aigues-Mortes**
29–29	*Fête de Notre-Dame-de-Grâce*, **Maillane**

September

Throughout month	Festival of the first harvest of rice, **Arles**
Early September	Wine festival, **Cassis**
8	Village fête and pilgrimage to **Notre-Dame-des-Fontaines**, **Brigue**
3rd Sunday	Wine harvest festival with sale of country produce in 19th-century costumes and free grapejuice-tasting, **Coustellet**
End of month	Festival of the Green Olives, **Mouries**; *Féria des Vendanges*, fairs with bull-fights at **Arles** and **Nîmes**

October

Throughout month	Regional music festival, **Fayence**
Mid-October	*Fête-Votive*, with Provençal bullfights, at **Aigues-Mortes**
22	*Fête de Ste-Marie-Jacobe*, **Saintes-Maries-de-la-Mer**
End of October	String Quartet Festival, **Fayence**

November

All Saints' Day	Festival of spiritual games, with tarot and belote, **Avignon**
All Saints' Weekend	Festival of science fiction, **Fayence**
Last Friday	*Foire St-Siffrein*, with truffle market, **Carpentras**
Last Sunday	*Foire des Santons*, until Epiphany, at **Marseille**

December

All month	Music festival, **Marseille**
2nd weekend	Festival of the Shepherds, seasonal migration of livestock through the streets, **Istres**
24	Provençal midnight mass at **Ste-Baume**, **Séguret** and **Fontvieille**, with shepherds at **Allauch** (near Marseille); *Fête des Bergers* and midnight mass, **Les Baux**; torchlight and wake, **Séguret**

... and south of Valence, Provincia Romana, the Roman Provence, lies beneath the sun. There there is no more any evil, for there the apple will not flourish and the Brussels sprout will not grow at all.

Ford Madox Ford, *Provence*

Eating is a pleasure in the south, where seafood, herbs, fruit and vegetables are often within plucking distance of the kitchen and table. The high quality of these fresh native ingredients demands minimal preparation—Provençal cooking is perhaps the least fussy of any regional French cuisine, and as an added plus neatly fits the modern definition of a healthy diet. For not only is the south a Brussels sprout-free zone, but the artery-hardening delights of the north—the rich creamy sauces, butter, cheese and egg dishes, mega-calorie desserts—are rare birds in the land of olives, apricots, and almonds.

Some of the most celebrated restaurants in the world grace the south of France, but there are plenty of stinkers, too. The most tolerable are humble in their mediocrity while others are oily with pretensions, staffed by folks posing as Grand Dukes and Duchesses fallen on hard times, whose exalted airs are somehow supposed to make their clients feel better about paying an obscene amount of money for the eight *petits pois à la graisse de yak* that the chef has so beautifully arranged on a plate. These places never last more than a year or two, but may just be in business as you happen by.

Just as intimidating for the hungry traveller are France's much ballyhooed gourmet bibles, whose annual awarding or removing of a star here, a chef's hat there, grade food the way a French teacher grades a *dictée* in school. Woe to the chef who leaves a lump in the sauce when those incognito pedants of the perfect palate are dining, and whose guillotine pens will ruthlessly chop off percentage points from the restaurant's final score. The less attention you pay them, the more you'll enjoy your dinner.

Restaurant Basics

Restaurants generally serve food between 12 noon and 2pm and in the evening from 7 to 10pm, with later summer hours; *brasseries* in the cities generally stay open continuously. All post menus outside the door so you know what to expect; if prices aren't listed, you can bet it's not because they're a bargain. If you have the appetite to eat the biggest meal of the day at noon, you'll spend a lot less money. Almost all restaurants have a choice of set-price menus; many offer a cheaper lunch special—the best way to experience some of the finer gourmet temples. Eating *à la carte* will always be much more expensive, in many cases twice as much; in most average spots no one ever does it.

Menus in inexpensive places sometimes include the house wine (*vin compris*); if you choose a better wine anywhere, expect a scandalous mark-up. Don't be dismayed, it's a long-established custom (as in many other lands); the French wouldn't dream of a meal without wine, and the arrangement is a simple device to make food prices seem lower. If service is included it will say *service compris* or *s.c.*, if not *service non compris* or *s.n.c.* Some restaurants offer a set-price gourmet *menu dégustation*—a selection of chef's specialities, which can be a great treat. At the other end of the scale, in the bars and brasseries, is the *plat du jour* (daily special) and the no-choice *formule*, which is more often than not steak and *frites*.

A full French meal may begin with an apéritif, hors d'oeuvres, a starter or two, followed by the *entrée*, cheese, dessert, coffee and chocolates, and perhaps a *digestif* to finish things off. If you order a salad it may come before or after, but never with your main course. In everyday eating, most people condense this feast to a starter, main course, and cheese or dessert. Vegetarians will have a hard time in France, but most establishments will try to accommodate them somehow.

When looking for a restaurant, homing in on the one place crowded with locals is as sound a policy in France as anywhere. Don't overlook hotel restaurants, some of which are absolutely top notch even if a certain red book refuses on some obscure principle to give them more than two stars. To avoid disappointment, call ahead in the morning to reserve a table, especially at the smarter restaurants, and especially in the summer. One thing you'll soon notice is that there's a wide choice of ethnic restaurants, mostly North African (a favourite for their economical *couscous*—spicy meat and vegetables served with a side dish of *harisa*, a hot red pepper sauce on a bed of steamed semolina); Asian (usually Vietnamese, sometimes Chinese, Cambodian, or Thai); and Italian, the latter sometimes combined with a pizzeria, although beware, quality very much depends on proximity to Italy, i.e. the pasta and pizza are superb in Nice and tolerably good in Marseille.

Don't expect to find many of these outside the big cities; country cooking is French only (though often very inventive). But in the cosmopolitan centres, you'll find not only foreign cuisine, but specialities from all over France. There are Breton *crêperies* or *galetteries* (with whole-wheat pancakes), restaurants from Alsace serving *choucroute* (sauerkraut and sausage), Périgord restaurants featuring *foie gras* and truffles, Lyonnaise *haute cuisine* and *les fast foods* offering *basse cuisine* of chips, hot dogs, and cheese sandwiches.

There are still a few traditional French restaurants that would meet the approval of Auguste Escoffier, the legendary chef (and a native of Provence); quite a few serve regional specialities (*see* below) and many feature *nouvelle cuisine*, which isn't so *nouvelle* any more, and has come under attack by devoted foodies for its expense (only the finest, freshest and rarest ingredients are used), portions (minute compared to usual restaurant helpings, because the object is to feel good, not full), and especially because many *nouvelle cuisine* practitioners have been quacks.

For it is a subtle art, to emphasize the natural flavour and goodness of a carrot by contrasting or complementing it with other flavours and scents; disappointments are inevitable when a chef is more concerned with appearance than taste, or takes a walk on the wild side, combining oysters, kiwis and cashews or some other abomination. But *nouvelle cuisine* has had a strong influence on attitudes towards food in France, and it's hard to imagine anyone going back full time to smothering everything on the plate in a *béchamel* sauce.

The Cuisine of Provence

Thanks to the trailblazing work of writers and chefs like Elizabeth David and Roger Vergé, Provençal cooking no longer sends the average Anglo-Saxon into paroxysms of garlic paranoia as it did a hundred years ago. Many traditional dishes presage *nouvelle cuisine*, and their success hangs on the quality of the ingredients and fragrant olive oil, like the well-known *ratatouille*—aubergines (eggplant), tomatoes, garlic and courgettes (zucchini) cooked separately to preserve their individual flavour, before being mixed together in olive oil—or *bagna cauda*, a dish of the southern Alps, consisting of raw vegetables dipped in a hot fondue of garlic, anchovies and olive oil.

Among the starters, a refreshing summertime favourite is *salade niçoise*, interpreted in a hundred different ways even in Nice. Most versions contain most of the following: tomatoes, cucumbers, hard-boiled eggs, black olives, onions, anchovies, radishes, artichokes, green peppers, croutons, green beans, and sometimes tuna and even potatoes. In Nice pasta dishes come in all sorts of shapes, but the favourites are *ravioli* and *gnocchi* (potato dumplings), two forms served throughout Italy and invented here when Nice was still *Nizza*. Another dish that tastes best in the summer, *soupe de pistou* is a thick minestrone served with a fresh basil, garlic, and pine-nut sauce similar to Italian *pesto*. *Tian* is a casserole of rice, spring vegetables and grated cheese baked in the oven; *tourta de blea* is a sweet-savoury Swiss chard pie. *Mesclum* is a salad of dandelion and other green leaves, and a favourite hors d'oeuvre is *tapenade*, a purée of olives, olive oil and capers.

Aïoli, a kind of mayonnaise made from garlic, olive oil and egg yolks, served with codfish, snails, potatoes or soup, is for many the essence of the region (*see* recipe on p.64); Mistral even named his nationalist Provençal magazine after it. In the same spirit Marseille named its magazine *Bouillabaisse*, for its world-famous soup of five to twelve kinds of Mediterranean fish, flavoured with saffron; the fish is removed and served with *rouille*, a sauce of fresh red chilli peppers crushed with garlic, olive oil, and the soup broth. Because good saffron costs money and the fish, especially the gruesome *racasse* are rare, a proper *bouillabaisse* will run to at least 200F. A less expensive but delicious alternative is *bourride*, a soup made from white-fleshed fish served with *aïoli*, or down a gastronomical notch or two, *baudroie*, a fish soup with vegetables and garlic. A very different kettle of fish is the indigestible Niçoise favourite, *estocaficada*, stockfish (and stockfish guts) stewed with tomatoes, olives, garlic, and eau-de-vie. Less adventurous, and absolutely delicious is *loup aux fenouille*, sea bass grilled over fennel stalks.

Lamb is the most common meat dish; real Provençal lamb (becoming increasingly rare) grazes on herbs and on special salt-marsh grasses from the Camargue and Crau. Beef usually comes in the form of a *daube*, slowly stewed in red wine and often served with ravioli. A Provençal cook's prize possession is the *daube* pan, which is never washed, but wiped clean and baked to form a crust that flavours all subsequent stews. Rabbit, or *lapin à la provençal*, is simmered in white wine with garlic, mustard, tomatoes and herbs. A more daunting dish, *pieds et paquets* is tripe stuffed with garlic, onions and salt pork, traditionally (although rarely in practice) served with calf's trotters. Stuffed courgette (zucchini) flowers, tarts of Swiss chard, and grilled tomatoes with garlic and breadcrumbs are popular vegetable dishes. Local cheeses are invariably goat—*chèvre*—little roundlets flavoured with thyme, bay, and other herbs. *Lou Pevre*, *Banon* and *Poivre d'Ain* are among the best.

Markets, Picnic Food and Snacks

The food markets of Provence are justly celebrated for the colour and perfumes of their produce and flowers. They are fun to visit, and become even more interesting if you're cooking for yourself or are just gathering the ingredients for a picnic. In the larger cities they take place every day, while smaller towns and villages have markets on one day a week, which double as a social occasion for the locals. Most markets finish around noon.

Other good sources for picnic food are the *charcuteries* or *traiteurs*, both of which sell prepared dishes sold by weight in cartons or tubs. You can also find counters at larger supermarkets. Cities are snack-food wonderlands, with outdoor counters selling pastries, crêpes, pizza slices, *frites*, *croque-monsieurs* (toasted ham and cheese sandwiches) and a wide variety of sandwiches made from *baguettes* (long thin loaves of bread).

Drink

You can order any kind of drink at any bar or café—except cocktails, unless it has a certain cosmopolitan savoir-faire or stays open into the night. Cafés are also a home away from home, places to read the papers, play cards, meet friends, and just unwind, sit back, and watch the world go by. You can sit hours over one coffee and no one will try to hurry you along. Prices are listed on the *Tarif des Consommations*: note they are progressively more expensive depending on whether you're served at the bar (*comptoir*), at a table (*la salle*) or outside (*la terrasse*).

French coffee is strong and black, and lacklustre next to the aromatic brews of Italy or Spain (you'll notice an improvement in the coffee near their respective frontiers). If you order *un café* you'll get a small black *express*; if you want milk, order *un crème*. If you want more than a few drops of caffeine, ask them to make it *grand*. For decaffeinated, the word is *déca*. Some bars offer *cappuccinos*, but again they're only really good near the Italian border; in the summer try a *frappé* (iced coffee). The French only order *café au lait* (a small coffee topped off with lots of hot milk) when they stop in for **breakfast**, and if what your hotel offers is expensive or boring, consider joining them. There are baskets of *croissants* and pastries, and some bars will make you a *baguette* with butter, jam or honey. If you want to go native, try the Frenchman's Breakfast of Champions: a *pastis* or two, and five non-filter *Gauloises*. *Chocolat chaud* (hot chocolate) is usually good; if you order *thé* (tea), you'll get an ordinary bag. An *infusion* is a herbal tea—*camomile, menthe* (mint), *tilleul* (lime or linden blossom), or *verveine* (verbena). These are kind to the all-precious *foie*, or liver, after you've over-indulged at the table.

Mineral water (*eau minérale*) can be addictive, and comes either sparkling (*gazeuse* or *pétillante*) or still (*non-gazeuse* or *plate*). If you feel run down, *Badoit* has lots of peppy magnesium in it—it's the current trendy favourite. The usual international corporate soft drinks are available, and all kinds of bottled fruit juices (*jus de fruits*). Some bars also do fresh lemon and orange juices (*citron pressé* or *orange pressée*). The French are also fond of fruit syrups—red *grenadine* and ghastly green *diabolo menthe*.

Beer (*bière*) in most bars and cafés is run-of-the-mill big brands from Alsace, Germany, and Belgium. Draft (*à la pression*) is cheaper than bottled beer. Nearly all resorts have bars or pubs offering wider selections of drafts, lagers, and bottles.

The strong spirit of the Midi comes in a liquid form called *pastis*, first made popular in Marseille as a plague remedy; its name comes from the Latin *passe-sitis*, or thirst quencher. A pale yellow 90 per cent nectar flavoured with anis, vanilla, and cinnamon, pastis is drunk as an apéritif before lunch and in rounds after work. The three major brands, *Ricard, Pernod,* and *Pastis 51*, all taste slightly different; most people drink their '*pastaga*' with lots of water and ice (*glaçons*), which help make the taste more tolerable. A thimble-sized *pastis* is a *momie*, and you may want to try it mixed: a *tomate* is with grenadine, a *mauresque* with orgeat (almond and orange flower syrup), and a *perroquet* is with mint.

Other popular apéritifs come from Languedoc-Roussillon, including *Byrrh* 'from the world's largest barrel', a sweet wine mixed with quinine and orange peel, similar to *Dubonnet*. Spirits include the familiar Cognac and Armagnac brandies, liqueurs and *digestifs* made from walnuts, cherries, pears, and herbs (these are a specialty of the Alps), and fiery *marc*, the grape spirit that is the same as Italian *grappa* (but usually better).

Wine

One of the pleasures of travelling in France is drinking great wines for a fraction of what you pay at home, and discovering excellent labels you've never seen in your local shop. The south holds a special place in the saga of French wines, with a tradition dating back to the Greeks, who are said to have introduced an essential Côtes-du-Rhône grape variety called *syrah*, originally grown in Shiraz, Persia. Nurtured in the Dark and Middle Ages by popes and kings, the vineyards of Provence and Languedoc-Roussillon still produce most of France's wine—certainly most of it is plonk, graded only by its alcohol content.

Some of Provence's best-known wines grow in the ancient places near the coast, especially its quartet of tiny AOC districts—*Bellet, Bandol, Cassis* and *Palette*. But the best-known wines of the region come from the Rhône valley, under the general heading of *Côtes-du-Rhône*, including *Châteauneuf-du-Pape, Gigondas*, the famous rosé *Tavel*, and the sweet muscat apéritif wine, *Beaumes-de-Venise*. Elsewhere, winemakers have made great strides in boosting quality in the past 30 years, recognized in new AOC districts. Even greater strides have been made in Languedoc-Roussillon, the rising star on the French wine charts. Corbières, the fourth AOC district in France, and Minervois are only the two best known, while seldom-exported delights like *La Clape* and *Faugères* await the wine explorer. Languedoc is also the home of *Blanquette de Limoux*, the world's oldest sparkling wine, *Banyuls*, France's answer to port, and *Rivesaltes*, a sweet muscat good Catalans drink all the live long day.

'If rules inhibit your enjoyment of wines, there should be no rules,' Alexis Lichine wrote in the 1950s, and it still holds true today. The innocent drinker has to put up with even more words and snootery than the beleaguered eater. Confronting a wine list makes a lot of people nervous, while an obsequious *sommelier* can ruin their entire meal. Equally ruinous is the way some smart restaurants mark up AOC wines to triple or quadruple the retail price. If you love wine but have to watch expenses (and who doesn't these days?), buy it direct from the producers, or *vignerons*. In the text we've included a few addresses for each wine to get you started.

If a wine is labelled AOC (*Appellation d'Origine Contrôlée*) it means that the wine comes from a certain defined area and is made from certain varieties of grapes, guaranteeing a standard of quality. *Cru* on the label means vintage; a *grand cru* is a great, noble vintage. Down the list in the vinous hierarchy are those labelled VDQS (*Vin de Qualité Supérieure*), followed by *Vin de Pays* (guaranteed at least to originate in a certain region), with *Vin Ordinaire* (or *Vin de Table*) at the bottom, which may not send you to seventh heaven but is usually drinkable and cheap. In a restaurant if you order a *rouge* (red) or *blanc* (white) or *rosé* (pink), this is what you'll get, either by the glass (*un verre*), by the quarter-litre (*un pichet*) or bottle (*une bouteille*). *Brut* is very dry, *sec* dry, *demi-sec* and *moelleux* are sweetish, *doux* sweet, and *méthode champenoise* sparkling.

If you're buying direct from the producer (or a wine co-operative, or *syndicat*, a group of producers), you'll be offered glasses to taste, each wine older than the previous one until you are feeling quite jolly and ready to buy the oldest (and most expensive) vintage. On the other hand, some sell loose wine à la petrol pump, *en vrac*; many *caves* even sell the little plastic barrels to put it in.

Health and Emergencies

Local hospitals are the place to go in an emergency (*urgence*). If you need an ambulance (SAMU) dial ℂ 15; police and ambulance, ℂ 17; fire, ℂ 18. Doctors take turns going on duty at night and on holidays even in rural areas: *pharmacies* will know who to contact or telephone *SOS Médecins*—if you don't have access to a phone book or Minitel, dial directory enquiries, ℂ 12. To be on the safe side, always carry a phone card (*see* telephones, below). If it's not an emergency, the *pharmacies* have addresses of local doctors, or visit the clinic at a *Centre Hospitalier*. Pharmacists are also trained to administer first aid, and dispense free advice for minor problems. *Pharmacies* themselves open nights on a rotating basis. Addresses are posted in their windows and in the local newspaper.

Doctors will give you a brown and white *feuille de soins* with your prescription; take both to the pharmacy and keep the *feuille* for insurance purposes at home. British subjects who are hospitalized and can produce their E-111 forms (*see* p.4) will be billed later at home for 20 per cent of the costs that French social insurance doesn't cover.

Money and Banks

The franc (abbreviated with an F) consists of 100 centimes. Banknotes come in denominations of 500, 200, 100, 50 and 20F; coins in 20, 10, 5, 2 and 1F, and 50, 20, 10, and 5 centimes. You can bring in as much currency as you like, but by law are only allowed to take out 5000F in cash. Traveller's cheques or Eurocheques are the safest way of carrying money; the most widely recognized credit card is VISA (*Carte Bleue* in French) which is accepted almost everywhere and will allow you to draw from most cash dispensers. If you plan to spend a lot of time in rural areas, where banks are few and far between, you may want to opt for International Giro Cheques, exchangeable at any post office.

Banks are generally open 8.30am–12.30pm and 1.30–4pm; they close on Sunday, and most close either on Saturday or Monday as well. Exchange rates vary, and nearly all take a commission of varying proportions. *Bureaux de change* that do nothing but exchange money (and exchanges in hotels and train stations) usually have the worst rates or take out the heftiest commissions, so be careful. It's always a good bet to purchase some francs before you go, especially if you arrive during the weekend.

Opening Hours, Museums and National Holidays

While many shops and supermarkets in Marseille, Nice and other large cities are now open continuously Tuesday–Saturday from 9 or 10am to 7 or 7.30pm, businesses in smaller towns still close down for lunch from 12 or 12.30pm to 2 or 3pm, or in the summer until 4pm in the afternoon. There are local exceptions, but nearly everything closes down on Mondays, except for grocers and *supermarchés* that open in the afternoon. In many towns Sunday morning is a big shopping period. Markets (daily in the cities, weekly in villages) are usually open mornings only, although clothes, flea and antique markets run into the afternoon. On the coast, it is common for tourist attractions and shops to be open daily on week-days, but always check.

Most museums close for lunch as well, and often on Mondays or Tuesdays, and sometimes for all of November or the entire winter. Hours change with the season: longer summer hours begin in May or June and last until the end of September—usually. Some change their hours every darn month. We've done our best to include them in the text, but don't sue us if they're not exactly right. Most give discounts if you have a student ID card, or are an EU citizen under 18 or over 65 years old; most charge admissions ranging from 10F upwards. Churches are usually open all day, or closed all day and only open for mass. Sometimes notes on the door direct you to the *mairie* or priest's house (*presbytère*) where you can pick up the key. There are often admission fees for cloisters, crypts, and special chapels.

On French **national holidays**, banks, shops, and businesses close; some museums do, but most restaurants stay open. They are: 1 January, Easter Sunday, Easter Monday, 1 May, 8 May (VE Day), Ascension Day (40 days after Easter), Pentecost (7th Sunday after Easter) and the following Monday, 14 July (Bastille Day), 15 August (Assumption of the BVM), 1 November (All Saints'), 11 November (First World War Armistice) and Christmas Day.

Post Offices and Telephones

Known as the *PTT* or *Bureau de Poste*, easily discernible by a blue bird on a yellow background, French post offices are open in the cities Mon–Fri 8am–7pm, and Saturdays 8am until 12 noon. In villages offices may not open until 9am, break for lunch, and close at 4.30 or 5pm. You can receive mail *poste restante* at any of them; the postal codes in this book should help your mail get there in a timely fashion. To collect it, bring some ID. You can purchase stamps in some tobacconists as well as post offices.

Post offices offer free use of a Minitel electronic directory, and they usually have at least one telephone booth with a meter—the easiest way to phone overseas. Most other public telephones have switched over from coins to *télécartes*, which you can purchase at any post office for 40F for 50 *unités* or 96F for 120 *unités*. The French have eliminated area codes, giving everyone an eight-digit telephone number, which is all you have to dial within France (though see below for further changes in October 1996). For international calls, first dial 19, wait for the change in the dial tone, then dial the country code (UK 44; US and Canada 1; Ireland 353; Australia 61; New Zealand 64), and then the local code (minus the 0 for UK numbers) and number (again, see below for changes). The easiest way to reverse the charges is to spend a few francs ringing the number you want to call and giving them your number in France, which is always posted in the box; alternatively ring your national operator and tell him or her that you want to call reverse charges (for the UK dial ✆ 19 00 44; for the US ✆ 19 00 11). France's international dialling code is 33. For directory enquiries, dial ✆ 12; international directory enquiries is ✆ 19 33 12 followed by the country code, but note that you'll have to wait around the telephone for them to ring you back with your requested number.

change of telephone numbers

On 18 October 1996 France is changing its telephone numbers from 8 digits to 10 digits. All the phone numbers in the Provence and Côte d'Azur areas should be preceded by 04 from this date. Similarly, any Paris phone numbers should be preceded by 01 instead of 1. When calling abroad from France, dial 00 instead of 19.

Racism

Unfortunately in some parts of the south of France the forces of bigotry and reaction are strong enough to make racism a serious concern. We've heard some horror stories, especially about Marseille and Nice, where campsites and restaurants suddenly have no places if the colour of your skin doesn't suit the proprietor; the bouncers at clubs will inevitably say it's really the cut of your hair or trousers they find offensive. If any place recommended in this book is guilty of such behaviour, please write and let us know; we will not only remove it from the next edition, but forward your letter to the regional tourist office and relevant authorities in Paris.

Shopping

All in all, this is not a brilliant region for the holiday shopper. Traditional handicrafts have died out almost completely, and attempts to revive them—inevitably in the tourist areas of Provence—produce little you'd be proud to show the neighbours. Typical items are the *santons*, terracotta Christmas crib figures dressed in 18th-century Provençal costumes, usually as artful as the concrete studies of the Seven Dwarfs sold at your local garden centre.

Every town east of the Rhône has at least one boutique specializing in Provençal skirts, bags, pillows and scarves, printed in intense colours (madder red, sunflower yellow, pine green) with floral, paisley or geometric designs. Block-print fabrics were first made in Provence after Louis XIV, wanting to protect the French silk industry, banned the import of popular Indian prints. Clever entrepreneurs in the papal-owned Comtat Venaissin responded by producing cheap imitations still known in French today as *indiennes*. The same shops usually sell the other essential bric-a-brac of the South—dried lavender pot-pourris, sachets of *herbes de Provence* (nothing but thyme and bay leaves), perfumed soaps.

Moustiers has hand-made ceramics, and in Provence at least a million artists wait to sell you their productions. Fontaine-de-Vaucluse has a traditional paper and stationery industry.

The sweet of tooth will find western Provence heaven. Nearly every town has its own speciality: candied fruits in Apt, the chocolates and *calissons* (almond biscuits) of Aix, *berlingots* (mint-flavoured caramels) in Carpentras, *marrons glacés* in Collobrières, and orange-flavoured chocolates called *papalines* in Avignon.

Sport and Leisure Activities

bicycling

See 'Getting Around', p.7.

bullfights

The Roman amphitheatres at Nîmes and Arles had hardly been restored in the early 1800s when they once again became venues for *tauromachie*. Attempts to abolish the sport in the 1900s fell flat when the poet Frédéric Mistral, the self-appointed watchdog of all things Provençal intervened; and if anything, bullfights are now more popular than ever.

Provence is so long in the tooth that not only does it put on regular bullfights with pica-dors and matadors, ultimately derived from the amphitheatres of ancient Rome, but also *courses provençales* (or *courses libres*), a sport descending from the bull games of ancient

Thessaly as described by Heliodorus. Played by daring young men dressed in white called *razeteurs*, the sport demands grace, daring, and dexterity, especially in leaping over the barriers. The object is to remove a round cockade from between the horns of the bull by cutting its ribbons with a blunt razor comb—a sport far more dangerous to the human players than the animals. The bulls used for the *courses provençales* are the small, lithe, high-horned breed from the Camargue; good sporty ones retire with fat pensions.

You will see three other types of bullfight advertised: the *corrida*, or traditional Spanish bullfight where the bull is put to death (*mise à mort*). The bullfighters are usually Spanish as well, and the major festivals, or *ferias,* bring some of the top *toreros* to France, although beware that the already expensive tickets tend to be snapped up by touts. A *novillada*, pitting younger bulls against apprentice *toreros* (*novilleros*), is less expensive, but much more likely to be a butchery void of *arte*. In a *corrida portuguaise* the bullfighter (*rejoneador*) fights from horseback, and only kills the bull during selected *corridas*.

canoeing and kayaking

Fédération Française de Canoe-Kayak, BP 58, Joinville Le Pont 94340, ✆ 48 89 39 89, is the national centre for information. Some of the most dramatic rafting and canoeing in this book is down the Grand Canyon du Verdon, but the journey requires considerable experience and considerable portage. Another disadvantage is that the electric company may be playing with the water. Contact Verdon Plus, 4 Allée Louis Gardiol, Riez, ✆ 92 77 76 36, ✉ 92 77 75 73, for group excursions.

fishing

You can fish in the sea without a permit as long as your catch is for local consumption; along the Riviera captains offer expeditions for tuna and other denizens of the deep. Freshwater fishing requires an easily obtained permit from a local club; tourist offices can tell you where to find them.

football

Professional football in Provence is dominated by L'Olympique de Marseille, 1993 winners of the European Cup now stripped of their crown following match-rigging allegations (Monaco replaced them as the French entry in the 1994 European Cup).

gambling

If you're over 21, every big resort along the coast comes equipped with a **casino** ready to take your hard-earned money. Or you can do as the locals do and play for a side of beef, a lamb, or a VCR in a **Loto**, in a local café or municipal *salle de fête*. Loto is just like bingo, although some of the numbers have names: 11 is *las cambas de ma grand* (my grandmother's legs) and 75, the number of the *département* of Paris, is *los envaïsseurs* (the invaders). Everybody plays the horses, at the local bar with the *PMU* (off-track betting) outlet.

Increasingly popular in France, there are courses near most of the major resorts on the Côte d'Azur, and almost as many under construction. Cannes offers golfers the most choice, with three courses in Mandelieu and three in Le Cannet. The most spectacular course is Monaco's, which was laid out around the turn of the century, high over Monte Carlo.

horse-riding

Every tourist office has a list of *centres hippiques* or *centres equestres* that hire out horses. Most offer group excursions, although if you prove yourself an experienced rider you can usually head down the trails on your own. The Camargue, with its many ranches, cowboy traditions and open spaces, is the most popular place to ride, and there is an increasing number of stables in the Alps for those who want to follow lonesome mountain trails. Most of the posher country inns can also find you a horse.

pétanque

Like pastis and olive oil, *pétanque* is one of the essential ingredients of the Midi, and even the smallest village has a rough, hard court under the plane trees for its practitioners— nearly all male, although women are welcome to join in. Similar to *boules*, the special rules of *pétanque* were according to tradition developed in La Ciotat (*see* p.139). The object is to get your metal ball closest to the marker (*bouchon* or *cochonnet*). Tournaments are frequent and well attended.

sailing

Most of the resorts have sailing schools and boats to hire. Get the complete list from the Fédération Française de Voile, 55 Ave Kléber, 75084 Paris Cedex 16, ℰ (16 1) 45 53 68 00.

skiing

If the weather ever decides to settle down to what's expected of it (in 1990–1 Nice had as much snow as some of the Alps), you can do as in California: ski in the morning and bake on the beach in the afternoon. The biggest resorts in the Alpes-Maritimes are Isola 2000, Auron, and Valberg, and closest to Nice, Gréolières-les-Neiges. For the Alpes-Maritimes, contact the Comité Régional de Tourisme Provence Alpes Côte d'Azur, Immeuble C.M.C.I., 2 Rue Henri Barbusse, 13241 Marseille, ℰ 91 39 38 00, ✆ 91 56 66 61.

walking

See 'Getting Around', p.7.

water sports and beaches

For the best beaches around Marseille, *see* p.138.

Tourist Information

Every city and town, and most villages, has a tourist information office, usually called a *Syndicat d'Initiative* or an *Office de Tourisme*. In smaller villages this service is provided by the town hall (*mairie*). They distribute free maps and town-plans, hotel, camping, and self-catering accommodation lists for their area, and can inform you on sporting events, leisure activities, wine estates open for visits, and festivals. Addresses and telephones are listed in the text, and if you write to them, they'll post you their booklets to help you plan your holiday before you leave.

Where to Stay

Hotels

 In the south of France you can find some of the most splendid hotels in Europe and some genuine scruffy fleabags of dubious clientele, with the majority of establishments falling somewhere between. As in most countries in Europe, the tourist authorities grade them by their facilities (not by charm or location) with stars from four to one, and there are even some cheap but adequate places undignified by any stars at all.

We would have liked to put the exact prices in the text, but in France this is not possible. Almost every establishment has a wide range of rooms and prices—a very useful and logical way of doing things, once you're used to it; in some hotels, every single room has its own personality and the difference in quality and price can be enormous; a large room with antique furniture, a television or a balcony over the sea and a complete bathroom will cost much more than a poky back room in the same hotel, with a window overlooking a car park, no antiques, and the WC down the hall. Some proprietors will drag out a sort of menu for you to choose the level of price and facilities you would like. Most two-star hotel rooms have their own showers and WCs; most one-stars offer rooms with or without.

The following guide will give you an idea of what prices to expect; away from major tourist areas, accommodation will be nearer to the bottom of each category.

Note: all prices listed here and elsewhere in this book are for a double room.

★★★★	400–2300F
★★★	240–700F
★★	150–500F
★	130–300F

Hotels with *no stars* are not necessarily dives; their owners probably never bothered filling out a form for the tourist authorities. Their prices are usually the same as one-star places.

Although it is, alas, impossible to be more precise, we can add a few more generalizations. **Single rooms** are rarer than doubles, usually two-thirds of the price, but rarely will a hotelier give you a discount if only doubles are available (again, because each room has its own price); on the other hand, if there are three or four of you, a **triple or quad** or adding extra beds to a double room is usually cheaper than staying in two rooms. Prices are posted at the reception desk and in the rooms to keep the management honest. Flowered wallpaper, usually beige, comes in all rooms with no extra charge—it's an essential part of the French experience.

Breakfast (usually coffee, a croissant, bread and jam for 20F or 30F) is nearly always optional: you'll do as well for less in a bar. As usual rates rise in the busy season (holidays and summer, and in the winter around ski resorts), when many hotels with restaurants will require that you take **half-board** (*demi-pension*—breakfast and a set lunch or dinner). Many hotel restaurants are superb and described in the text; non-residents are welcome. At worst the food will be boring, and it can be monotonous eating in the same place every night when there are so many tempting restaurants around. Don't be put off by obligatory dining. It's traditional; French hoteliers think of themselves as innkeepers, in the old-fashioned way. In the off-season board requirements vanish into thin air.

Your holiday will be much sweeter if you **book ahead**. The few reasonably priced rooms are snapped up very early across the board. In Provence, July and August are the only really impossible months; otherwise it usually isn't too difficult to find something. Phoning a day or two ahead is always a good policy, although beware that hotels will only confirm a room with the receipt of a cheque covering the first night (not a credit card number). Tourist offices have complete lists of accommodation in their given areas or even *département*, which come in handy during the peak season; many will even call around and book a room for you on the spot for free or a nominal fee.

Chain hotels (Sofitel, Formula One, etc.) are in most cities, but always dreary and geared to the business traveller more than the tourist, so you won't find them in this book. Don't confuse chains with the various **umbrella organizations** like *Logis et Auberges de France*, *Relais de Silence*, or the prestigious *Relais et Châteaux* which promote and guarantee the quality of independently owned hotels and their restaurants. Many are recommended in the text. Larger tourist offices usually stock their booklets, or you can pick them up before you leave from the French National Tourist Office. If you plan to do a lot of driving, you may want to take the English translation of the French truckers' bible, *Les Routiers*, an annual guide with maps listing reasonably priced lodgings and food along the highways and byways of France (£8.99, Routiers Limited, 25 Vanston Place, London SW6 1AZ).

Bed and breakfast: in rural areas, there are plenty of opportunities for a stay in a private home or farm. *Chambres d'hôtes*, in the tourist office brochures, are listed separately from hotels with the various *gîtes* (*see* below). Some are connected to restaurants, others to wine estates or a château; prices tend to be moderate to inexpensive.

Youth Hostels, Gîtes d'Etape, and Refuges

Most cities and resort areas have youth hostels (*auberges de jeunesse*) which offer simple dormitory accommodation and breakfast to people of any age for around 40–70F a night. Most offer kitchen facilities as well, or inexpensive meals. They are the best deal going for people travelling on their own; for people travelling together a one-star hotel can be just as cheap. Another down-side is that many are in the most ungodly locations—in the suburbs where the last bus goes by at 7pm, or miles from any transport at all in the country. In the summer the only way to be sure of a room is to arrive early in the day. Most require a Youth Hostels Association membership card, which you can usually purchase on the spot, although regulations say you should buy them in your home country (UK: from YHA, 14 Southampton Street, London WC2; USA: from AYH, P.O. Box 37613, Washington DC 20013; Canada: from CHA, 1600 James Maysmyth Dr, 6th floor, Gloucester, Ottawa, Ont K1B 5N4; Australia: from AYHA, 60 Mary St, Surrey Hills, Sydney, New South Wales 2010.) Another option in cities are the single-sex dormitories for young workers (*foyers de jeunes travailleurs et de jeunes travailleuses*) which will rent out individual rooms if any are available, for slightly more than a youth hostel.

A *gîte d'étape* is a simple shelter with bunk beds and a rudimentary kitchen set up by a village along GR walking paths or a scenic bike route. Again, lists are available for each *département*; the detailed maps listed under 'Walking' above mark them as well. In the mountains similar rough shelters along the GR paths are called *refuges*, most of them open summer only. Both charge around 40F or 50F a night.

Camping

Camping is a very popular way to travel, especially among the French themselves, and there's at least one campsite in every town, often an inexpensive, no-frills place run by the town itself (*camping municipal*). Other campsites are graded with stars like hotels from four to one: at the top of the line you can expect lots of trees and grass, hot showers, a pool or beach, sports facilities, and a grocer's, bar and/or restaurant, and on the coast, prices rather similar to one-star hotels (although these, of course, never have all the extras). You'll find more living space inland. If you want to camp outside official sites, it's imperative to ask permission from the landowner first, or risk a furious farmer, his dog and perhaps even the police.

Tourist offices have complete lists of campsites in their regions, or if you plan to move around a lot pick up a *Guide Officiel Camping/Caravanning,* available in French bookshops. A number of UK holiday firms book camping holidays and offer discounts on Channel ferries: Canvas Holidays, © (0383) 621 000; Eurocamp Travel, © (0565) 62 62 62; Keycamp Holidays, © (081) 395 4000. The French National Tourist Office has lists.

Gîtes de France and Other Self-catering Accommodation

Provence offers a vast range of self-catering: inexpensive farm cottages, history-laden châteaux with gourmet frills, flats in modern beach resorts or even on board canal boats.

The *Fédération Nationale des Gîtes de France* is a French government service offering inexpensive accommodation by the week in rural areas. Lists with photos arranged by *département* are available from the French National Tourist office, or in the UK from the official rep: **Gîtes de France**, 178 Piccadilly, London W1V 9DB, ✆ (071) 493 3480. Prices range from 1000F to 2000F a week. Other options are advertised in the Sunday papers or contact one of the firms listed below. The accommodation they offer will nearly always be more comfortable and costly than a *gîte*, but the discounts holiday firms can offer on the ferries, plane tickets, or car rental can make up for the price difference.

in the UK

Air France Holidays, Gable House, 18–24 Turnham Green Terrace, London W4 1RF, ✆ (0181) 742 3377: apartments.

Allez France, 27–29 West Street, Storrington, West Sussex RH20 4DZ, ✆ (01903) 742345: wide variety of accommodation from cottages to châteaux.

Apartment Service, 5–6 Francis Grove, London SW19 4DT, ✆ (0181) 944 1444, ✆ (0181) 944 6744: selected apartment accommodation in Nice and Marseille for short or extended stays.

Bowhills, Mayhill Farm, Swanmore, Southampton SO32 2QW, ✆ (01489) 877627: luxury villas, farmhouses, mostly with pools.

Brittany Ferries, The Brittany Centre, Wharf Road, Portsmouth PO2 8RU, ✆ (01705) 827701: gîtes.

Dominique's Villas, 13 Park House, 140 Battersea Park Road, London SW11 4NB, ✆ (0171) 738 8772: large villas and châteaux with pools etc. in Provence.

French Life Holidays, 26 Church Street, Horsforth, Leeds LS18 5LG, ✆ (0113) 239 0077: apartments and gîtes in the south of France.

French Villas, 175 Selsdon Park Road, Croydon CR2 8JJ, ✆ (0181) 651 1231: gîtes, villages de vacances, and villas near the coast and in the Var and Vaucluse.

Gîtes de France, 178 Piccadilly, London W1V 9DB, ✆ (0171) 493 3480: gîtes.

InnTravel, Hovingham, York YO6 4JZ, ✆ (01653) 628811: apartments with pools.

International Chapters, 102 St. John's Wood Terrace, London NW8 6PL, ✆ (071) 722 9560: farmhouses, châteaux, and villas.

LSG Theme Holidays, 201 Main Street, Thornton, Coalville LE67 1AH, ✆ (01509) 231713: seaside gîtes.

Meon Villas, Meon House, College Street, Petersfield GU32 3JN, ✆ (01730) 268411: villas with pools.

Owners Abroad, Second Floor, Astral Towers, Betts Way, Crawley RH10 2GX, ✆ (01293) 560777.

Palmer and Parker Villa Holidays, The Beacon, Penn HP10 8ND, ✆ (0494) 815 411: upmarket villas with pool, in the Var and the Alpes-Maritimes.

Unicorn Holidays, 2 Place Farm, Wheathampstead, AL4 8SB, ✆ (01582) 834400: fly-drive and tailor-made holidays to châteaux-hotels.

Vacances en Campagne, Bignor, Pulborough, West Sussex RH20 1QD, ✆ (01798) 869433: farmhouses, villas and gîtes.

VFB Holidays, Normandy House, High Street, Cheltenham GL50 3FB, ✆ (01242) 240310: from rustic gîtes to luxurious farmhouses.

in the USA

At Home Abroad, 405 East 56th St, New York, NY 10022, ✆ (212) 421 9165: châteaux and farmhouses in Provence.

Hideaways International, P.O. Box 1464, Littleton, MA 01460, ✆ (508) 486 8955: farmhouses and châteaux.

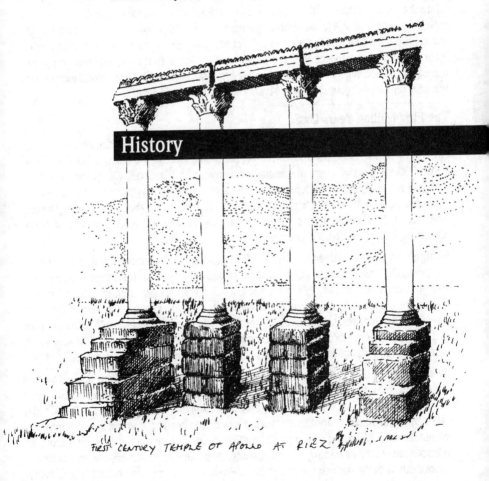

FIRST CENTURY TEMPLE OT APOLLO AT RIEZ

History

The names of French regions can be maddeningly fluid, and one of the biggest problems with writing a history of Provence is that its boundaries change all the time. The Romans called Gaul's southern coast their dear 'province', their first conquest outside Italy. Specifically, this was the province of *Gallia Narbonnensis*, stretching from Toulouse to Geneva, although its heartland was always the rich coast between Narbonne and Marseille. In the early Middle Ages, Gaul was evolving its linguistic north-south division between the *langue d'oc* and the *langue d'oeil* (two words for saying 'yes', from the Latin *hoc* and *hoc ille*). Provence then came to mean the southern third of what is now France, stretching north to the Dordogne and Lyon.

At the same time, the political boundary of the Rhône river was redefining the terminology, between lands subject to the Holy Roman Emperors and those claimed by the kings of France. 'Provence' came to mean the semi-independent county east of the Rhône, while the rest, as far as Toulouse, came to be known as Languedoc. Today, southerners use the word *Occitania* (a word only invented in the 18th century) to describe all of the old *langue d'oc*. Old regional names fell out of official use during the Revolution, when France was divided into standardized *départements*. But with the regional autonomy laws passed by the Socialists in 1981, the five departments east of the Rhône were formed into the new region of *Provence-Côte d'Azur*. There, got it?

The First Million Years Or So

It seems that Provence's charms were lost on the earliest inhabitants of the Mediterranean. On the Côte d'Azur, tools and traces of habitation around Monaco go back as far as 1,000,000 BC. To the west, in Languedoc, remains of 'Tautavel Man' date to at least 450,000 BC, and perhaps as far back as 680,000. Someone may have been in Provence through all this, but evidence is rare. Neanderthal Man turns up about 60,000 BC. The first evidence of the Neanderthalers' nemesis, that quarrelsome and unlovable species *Homo Sapiens*, appears some 20,000 years later.

Neolithic civilization arrived as early as 3500 BC, and endured throughout the region for the next 2000 years. People knew agriculture and raised sheep, traded for scarce goods, and built dry-stone houses. The Neolithic era left few important monuments: an impressive but little-known temple complex at Castellet, near Arles, and some large dolmens in the Massif des Maures. Of succeeding ages we know more about technology than culture and changes in population: the use of copper began about 2000 BC, iron *c.* 800 BC. In both cases the region was one of the last parts of the Mediterranean basin to catch on.

By now, at least, the inhabitants have a name, even if it is a questionable one applied by later Greek and Roman writers: the Ligurians, who occupied most of Provence in addition to northwestern Italy. From about 800 BC, they begin building their first settled villages, today called by the Latin name *oppidum*, a word you will see often in the south; it even survives in village names (Oppedette). It is a small, fortified village, usually on a hilltop, built around a religious sanctuary or trading centre. Already, more advanced outsiders were coming to make deals with the natives: the Phoenicians, Etruscans, and most importantly the Greeks.

A major event of this same era was the arrival of the Celts, Indo-European cousins of the

Ligurians and Iberians from the north. Beginning in coastal Languedoc in the 8th century BC, they gradually spread their conquests eastwards until the 4th century at the expense of the Ligurians. At the same time, Greek merchant activity was turning into full-scale colonization. The Ionian city-states of Asia Minor had become over-populated, agriculturally exhausted and politically precarious, and their citizens sought to reproduce them in new lands. The first was *Massalia*—Marseille, c. 600 BC. Soon Massalia was founding colonies of its own: Nice and Hyères were among the most important. Greek influence over the indigenous peoples was strong from the start; as with everywhere else they went, they brought the vine (wild stocks were already present, but the Celts hadn't worked out what to do with them) and the olive, and also their art. The Celts loved Greek vases, and had metals and other raw materials to offer in return. Increased trade turned some of the native *oppida* into genuine cities, such as Arles.

Roman Provincia

From the start, the Greeks were natural allies of the young city of Rome—if only because they had common enemies. Besides the strong Etruscan federation, occupying the lands in between the two, there were their trade rivals, the Phoenicians (later Carthaginians), and occasionally the Celts and Ligurians. As Rome gobbled up Etruria and the rest of Italy, the area became of increasing importance; a fact Hannibal demonstrated when he marched his armies along the coast towards Italy in 218 BC, with the full support of the Celts (historians still argue over how and where he got the elephants across the Rhône).

When the Romans took control of Spain in the Second Punic War (206), the coasts of what they called Gaul became a logical next step. In 125, Roman troops saved Marseille from a Celtic attack. This time, though, they had come to stay. The reorganization of the new province—'Provincia'—was quick and methodical. Domitius Ahenobarbus, the vanquisher of the Celts, began the great Italy–Spain highway that bears his name, the Via Domitia, in 121. New cities were founded, most importantly Aix (122). Dozens of other new foundations followed over the next century, many of them planned colonies with land grants for veterans of the legions. The Celts were not through yet, though. Two northern tribes, the Cimbri and Teutones, mounted a serious invasion of Gaul and Italy in 115. They raided those areas continuously until 102, when they were destroyed by a Roman army under Marius near Mt-Ste-Victoire, near Aix. Marius, later populist dictator in Rome, became a folk hero and the subject of legends ever after (Provençal parents still name their children after him). Celtic-Ligurian resistance continued intermittently until 14 BC; the great monument at La Turbie, on the border of Gaul, commemorates the defeat of the last hold-outs in the Alps.

The downfall of Marseille, still the metropolis of Provence and still thoroughly Greek in culture and sympathies, came in 49 BC. Always famed for its diplomacy, the city made the fatal mistake of supporting Pompey over Julius Caesar in the Roman civil wars. A vengeful Caesar crippled its trade and stripped nearly all its colonies and dependencies. Thereafter, the influence of Marseille gave way to newer, more Romanized towns: Aix, Arles, and Fréjus.

Throughout all this, Provence had been easily assimilated into the Roman economy, supplying food and raw materials for the insatiable metropolis. With Caesar's conquest of the rest of Gaul, the Rhône trade route (which had always managed to bring down a little Baltic amber and tin from Cornwall) became a busy river highway and military route. Under the good government and peace bestowed by Augustus (27 BC–AD 14) and his successors, Provence blossomed into an opulence never before seen. The cities, especially those of the Rhône valley, acquired theatres, amphitheatres for the games, aqueducts, bridges and temples. Provence participated in the political and cultural life of the empire, even contributing one of the better emperors, Antoninus Pius (from Nîmes, AD 138–61), only obscure because his reign was so peaceful and prosperous.

Large areas of Roman towns have been excavated at Glanum and Vaison-la-Romaine, and both have turned up a preponderance of wealthy villas. This is the dark side of Roman Provence; from the beginning of Roman rule, wealthy Romans were able to grab up much of the land, forming large estates and exploiting the indigenous population. This trend was magnified in the decadent, totalitarian and economically chaotic late empire, when, throughout Roman territory, the few remaining free farmers were forced to sell themselves into virtual serfdom to escape crushing taxes. After AD 200, in fact, everything was going wrong: trade and the cities stagnated while art and culture decayed; the first of the barbarian raids brought Germans into Provence in the 250s, when they destroyed Glanum.

Constantine, while yet emperor of only the western half of the empire (312–23), often resided at Arles and favoured that city; his baths there were probably the last big Roman building project in Provence. His pro-Christian policy gave the cult its first real influence in Gaul, at least in the cities; under his auspices, the first state-sponsored Church council was held at Arles in 314. Before that Christianity does not seem to have made much of an impression (later, to make up for it elaborate mythologies were constructed to place Mary Magdalene and other early saints in Provence after the Crucifixion; *cf.* the towns of Stes-Maries-de-la-Mer and St-Maximin-la-Ste-Baume).

600 Years of Uninvited Guests

French historians always blame the barbarian invaders of the 5th century for destroying the cities of Provence, as if Teutonic warriors enjoyed pulling down temple colonnades on their days off. In fact, few armies passed through Provence; the Visigoths, in the early 400s, were the most notable. Though government collapsed in chaos, business went on much as usual, with the Roman landowners (and their new German colleagues) gradually making their transition to feudal nobles. Arles, untouched by the troubles, became the most important city of the west, and briefly the capital, under Constantius III in 412. The weakness of the central power brought some long-due upheavals in the countryside, with guerrillas and vigilante justice against the landlords. The old and new rulers soon found common cause. For a while, a clique of a hundred of the biggest landowners took over administration in Gaul, even declaring one of their own as 'emperor' in Arles (455), with the support of the Visigoths.

The Visigoths soon tired of such games, and assumed total control in 476, the year the Western Empire formally expired. They had to share it, however, with the Ostrogoths, who had established a strong kingdom in Italy and seized all of Provence east of the Rhône—the beginnings of a political boundary that would last in various forms for a thousand years. When the Eastern Empire under Justinian invaded Italy, the Franks were able to snatch the Ostrogoths' half (535). They were never able to hold it effectively, and the area gradually slipped into virtual independence.

The Visigoths kept the western half (now Languedoc), a distant zone of their Spanish kingdom, until the Arab invasion of the early 700s rolled over the Pyrenees. In 719 the Arabs took Narbonne. The next two centuries are as wonderfully confused as anything in prehistory. There is the legend of the great Spanish Caliph Abd ar-Rahman, defeated in battle and leaving a treasure buried somewhere in the Alpilles. Charles Martel, the celebrated Frankish *generalissimo* who stopped the Arab wave at Poitiers in 732, made an expedition to the southern coast in 737–9, brutally sacking Marseille, Avignon and Aix. His mission was hardly a religious crusade—rather taking advantage of the Visigothic defeat to increase Frankish hegemony in the south; the cities of Provence are recorded as petitioning the Arabs at Córdoba to help them keep the nasty Franks out.

The Arabs couldn't help; the climate was too eccentric and the pickings too slim for them to mount a serious effort in Gaul. The nascent Franks gained control everywhere, and the entire coast was absorbed by Charlemagne's father, Pépin the Short, in 759. Under Charlemagne (768–814), Occitania seems to have shared little in the Carolingian revival of trade and culture, and after the break-up of the empire (at the Treaty of Verdun in 843) its misery was complete. The 9th- and 10th-century invasions were the real Dark Age in many parts of Europe. Provence suffered constant and destructive raids by the Normans, the Arabs again, who held the Massif des Maures and St-Tropez until the 970s, and even the Hungarians, who sacked what was left of Nîmes in 924.

The Beginnings of the Middle Ages

Even in this sorry period, the foundations were being laid for recovery. Monastic reformers in Charlemagne's time, men such as Benedict of Aniane (in the Hérault) helped start a huge expansion of Church institutions. The Abbey of St-Victor in Marseille took the lead in this, founding hundreds of new monasteries around Occitania; hard-working monks reclaimed land from forests and swamps—later they sat back and enjoyed the rents, while always keeping up the holy work of education and copying books. Pilgrimages became an important activity, especially to Arles (St-Trophime), getting a sleepy and locally bound society moving again and providing an impetus to trade.

The Treaty of Verdun (*see* above) had confirmed the Rhône as a boundary, and politically Provence and Languedoc went their separate ways. The Kingdom of Provence (or 'Kingdom of Arles'), proclaimed by a great-grandson of Charlemagne in 879, was little more than a façade for a feudal anarchy. Though the Kingdom was united with the Kingdom of Burgundy in 949, and formally passed to the Holy Roman Empire in 1032, the tapestry of battling barons and shifting local alliances continued without interference from the overlords.

Provençal Medieval Civilization

As elsewhere in Europe, the year 1000 is the rough milestone for the sudden and spectacular development of the medieval world. Towns and villages found the money and energy to build impressive new churches. The end of the foreign raiders made the seas safe for merchants, from Genoa, Pisa and Barcelona mostly, but also a few from Marseille. In 1002, the first written document in Occitan appears. The great pilgrimage to Santiago de Compostela, in Spain, made what was left of the old Roman roads into busy highways once more; along the main southern route the first of the medieval trade fairs appeared, at the new town of St-Gilles-du-Gard.

Things were on the upswing throughout the 11th century, and the trend was given another boost by the Crusades, which began in 1095. With increased prosperity and contact with a wider world, better manners and the rudiments of personal hygiene were not slow to follow. Feudal anarchy began to look quite genteel—maintaining a delicate balance of power, with feudal ties and blood relations keeping the political appetites of rulers from ever really getting out of hand. From the more civilized east, and from nearby Muslim Spain, came new ideas, new technologies and a taste for luxury and art. As an indication of how far Occitania had come, there are the troubadours, with modern Europe's first lyric poetry. Almost every court of the south was refined enough to welcome and patronize them.

The growing cities began to assert themselves in the 12th century, often achieving a substantial independence in *communes* governed by consuls: Avignon in 1129, Arles in 1132. In the countryside, successive waves of monastic reform spawned a huge number of new institutions: first the movement from Cluny in the 11th century, and in the 12th the Cistercians, who started a score of important monasteries. Efficiently exploiting the lands bequeathed by noblemen made them rich, and also did much to improve the agricultural economy.

By 1125 the Counts of Barcelona controlled much of Provence south of the Durance. The other leading power in the region, Toulouse, contended with the Catalans for Provence while being overlords of all Languedoc, excepting Carcassonne and Béziers, ruled by the Trencavel family, and Narbonne, with its independent Viscounts. It was a great age for culture, producing not only the troubadours but an impressive display of Romanesque architecture, and an original school of sculpture at Arles. Perhaps the most remarkable phenomenon of the times was a widespread religious tolerance, shared by rulers, the common people and even many among the clergy. Religious dissenters of various persuasions sprang up everywhere. Most of the new sects soon died out, and are little known today—like the extremist 'Petrobrusians' of St-Gilles, who didn't fancy churches, sacraments, relics or priests, and who even had their doubts about the crucifixion of Jesus.

One sect, however, made startling inroads into every sector of society in 11th- and 12th-century Languedoc—the Cathars, or Albigensians. This Manichaean doctrine, obsessed with Good and Evil, had in its upright simplicity a powerful attraction for industrious townspeople and peasants. The Cathars were never a majority in any part of the south; in most places they never made up more than 10 per cent of the population. They might have passed on as only a curious footnote to history, had they not provided the excuse for the biggest and most flagrant land grab of the Middle Ages. The 'Albigensian Crusade', arranged after the 1208 murder of a papal legate, was a cynical marriage of convenience between two old piratical enemies, the papacy and the crown of France. Diplomacy forced King Philip Augustus to disclaim any part in the affair, but nevertheless a big army of knights from the Ile-de-France, led by the redoubtable Simon de Montfort, occupied most of Languedoc, while committing vicious massacres of the heretics everywhere. Montfort won battle after battle and took every town he attacked, save only Beaucaire.

In a last attempt to save their fortunes, Count Raymond VI of Toulouse and King Peter II of Aragon combined to meet the northerners. With an overwhelmingly superior force, they blundered their way to crushing defeat at the Battle of Muret in 1213. Four centuries after the fall of the Carolingian Empire, the French once again had their foothold in the south. Languedoc was finished, its distinctive culture quickly snuffed out.

The Coming of French Rule

Provence was still free, enjoying a prosperous era under its Catalan counts, though still troubled by incessant feudal struggles waged by such local powers as the *seigneurs* of Les Baux and Forcalquier. Count Raymond Berenger V (1209–45) was usually strong enough to keep them in check; under him Provence did very well, and developed a constitutional government on the Catalan model. Provence managed temporarily to avert French aggression in a roundabout way. In 1246, Raymond Berenger's daughter and heir married Charles of Anjou, St Louis' brother. The ambitious Angevin used Provence as a springboard to create an empire that at its height, in the 1280s, included southern Italy and parts of Greece.

The city of Avignon and its hinterlands, the Comtat Venaissin, loyal possessions of Toulouse, had suffered greatly at the hands of Louis VIII after the Albigensian Crusade. In 1274 Charles and Louis arranged to give the Comtat to the papacy—its discreetly delayed share of the Albigensian booty. In 1309 Pope Clement V, fleeing anarchy in Rome, installed himself at Carpentras in the Comtat. Politically, the popes found Provence a convenient new home and decided to stay—the 'Babylonian Captivity' (as jealous Italians called it) that would last over a century. They soon moved to Avignon, purchasing the city in 1348 and conducting a worldly court that to many seemed a Babylon indeed.

The late 14th century brought hard times to Provence: first the Black Death in 1348, and then political instability under the hapless Queen Jeanne (1343–82). Once more the Seigneurs of Les Baux and their imitators raged over the land, with bands of unscrupulous mercenaries (the *Grandes Compagnies*) to help them ravage town and country. The popes returned to Rome in 1377; they kept control of Avignon and the Comtat, though French-supported anti-popes held Avignon as late as 1403. After 1434, peace had returned and Provence was ruled by Good King René (Count of Provence, and only 'king' from his claim to Sicily, in which the Angevins had been replaced by the Aragonese after the 'Sicilian Vespers' revolution of 1282). The 'Good' is equally spurious. René was open-handed to courtiers, and a patron of artists, but his futile dream of recapturing Sicily and Naples led him to wring the last penny out of everyone else.

René's successor, Charles III, lasted only a year and died without an heir (1481), bequeathing Provence to the French crown. It was intended to be a union of equals, maintaining Provençal liberties and institutions. As such, the Provençal Estates-General ratified the agreement. The French immediately went back on their word, attempting to govern through royal commissioners, but their attempts to swallow Provence whole had to wait.

Louis XI and Charles XII needed a peaceful Provence as a bridge for their invasions of Italy; the region paid for this, with two destructive invasions in the 1520s and '30s by France's arch-enemy Charles V, Holy Roman Emperor and King of Spain. This era also saw a landmark in the cultural effacement of Occitania, the 1539 Edict of Villars-Cotterets that decreed French as the official language throughout the kingdom.

The Wars of Religion

Meanwhile, the new Protestant heresy was floating down the Rhône from Calvin's Geneva. The Occitans received it warmly, and soon there were large Protestant communities in all towns. Though this seems a repeat of the Cathar story, the geographical distribution is fascinating—the old Cathar areas in Languedoc now were loyally Catholic, while the orthodox regions of the 1300s now came out strongly for the dissenters. Tolerance was still out of fashion, and the opening round of a pointless half-century of religious wars came with the 1542 massacres in the Lubéron mountains. The perpetrator was the Aix *Parlement* (pre-Revolution *parlements* were not parliaments, but powerful judicial bodies appointed by and responsible to the king); the victims mostly Waldensians (Vaudois), pre-Reformation heretics who had migrated to Provence before the union with France, to escape oppression there.

In the open warfare that followed across the south, there were massacres and atrocities enough on both sides. Protestants distinguished themselves by the wholesale destruction of churches and their art (as at St-Gilles); churches were often converted into fortresses. Henry IV's 1598 Edict of Nantes acknowledged Protestant control of certain areas (Orange and Lourmarin in Provence). The French monarchy had been weakened by the wars, but as soon as it recovered new measures were introduced to keep the south in line. Under Cardinal Richelieu in the 1630s, the laws and traditions of local autonomy were swept away; after 1639 the Etats-Généraux of Provence was not allowed to meet until the eve of the Revolution. As insurance, scores of feudal castles (such as Beaucaire and Les Baux) were demolished to eliminate possible points of resistance.

Louis XIV's revocation of the Edict in 1685 caused more troubles. Thousands of Protestants, the south's most productive citizens, simply left; most of the community in Orange went off to colonize new lands in Prussia. Louis' long and oppressive reign continued the impoverishment of the south, despite well-intentioned economic measures by his brilliant minister Colbert. The 18th century witnessed the beginnings of an important textile industry—usually promoted by the remaining Protestants: silk around Nîmes and parts of Provence (where farmers gave up their bedrooms to raise the delicate silkworms in them), and linen and cotton goods in Orange. In the rest of Provence, though, the century told a miserable tale: economic stagnation, deforestation of mountain areas that has still not been entirely repaired today, and plagues. The biggest plague, in 1720, carried off almost half the population of Marseille. The one bright spot was the growing naval town of Toulon.

An Unwanted Revolution

The French Revolution was largely a Parisian affair, though southerners often played important roles (the Abbé de Sieyes and Mirabeau), while bourgeois delegates from the manufacturing towns fought along with the Girondins in the National Assembly for a respectable, liberal republic. Unfortunately, the winning Jacobin ideology was more centralist and more dedicated to destroying any taint of regional difference than the *ancien régime* had ever dreamed of being. Whatever was left of local rights and privileges was soon decreed out of existence, and when the Revolution divided France into homogenous departments in 1790, terms like 'Provence' and 'Languedoc' ceased to have any political meaning.

In 1792 volunteers from Marseille had brought the *Marseillaise* to Paris, while local mobs wrecked hundreds of southern churches and châteaux. Soon, however, the betrayed south became counter-revolutionary. Incidents occurred like the one in Bédoin, near Carpentras, in 1793; when someone cut down the 'liberty tree', French soldiers burned the town and shot 63 villagers to 'set an example'. The Catalans raised regiments of volunteers against the Revolution. The royalists and the English occupied Toulon after a popular revolt, and were only dislodged by the brilliant tactics of a young commander named Bonaparte in 1793.

The south managed little enthusiasm for Napoleon or his wars. The Emperor called the Provençaux cowards, and said theirs was the only part of France that never gave him a decent regiment. Today the tourist offices promote the 'Route Napoléonienne', where Napoleon passed through from Elba in 1815 to start the Hundred Days—but he had to sneak along those roads in an Austrian uniform to protect himself from the Provençaux.

After Waterloo, the restored monarchy started off with a grisly White Terror and tried to turn the clock back to 1789. After the Revolution of 1830, the 'July Monarchy' of King Louis Philippe brought significant changes. The old industrious Protestant strain of the south finally got its chance with a Protestant Prime Minister from Nîmes, François Guizot (1840–8); his liberal policies and his slogan—*enrichissez-vous!*—opened an age where there would be a little Protestant in every Frenchman. Guizot's countrymen were rapidly demanding more; radicalism and anti-clericalism (except in the lower Rhône and Vaucluse) increased throughout the century.

Southerners supported the Revolution of 1848 and the Second Republic, and many areas, especially in the Provençal Alps, put up armed resistance to Louis Napoleon's 1851 coup. Under the Second Empire (1852–70), France picked up yet another territory: Nice and its hinterlands (now the *département* of Alpes-Maritimes), with a mixed population of Provençaux and Italians. This was the price exacted by Napoleon III in 1860 for French aid to Vittorio Emanuele II in Italy's War of Independence.

Rural Decay and Recovery

The second half of the century saw the beginnings of a national revival in Occitania. While in Languedoc it was political, largely involved with modern France's first agricultural movements, in Provence it tended to be all cultural and apolitical: a linguistic and literary revival bound up with Nobel Prize-winning poet Frédéric Mistral and the cultural group called the *Félibrige* (*see* p.55), founded in 1854. To counter these advances, the post-1870 Third Republic pursued French cultural oppression to its wildest extremes. History was rewritten to make Occitania seem an eternal part of the 'French nation'. The Occitan languages were lyingly derided as mere *patois*, bastard 'dialects' of French; children were punished for speaking their own language in school, a practice that lasted until the 1970s.

After 1910, economic factors conspired to defeat both the political and cultural aspirations of the Midi; rural depopulation, caused by the break-up of the pre-industrial agricultural society, drained the life out of the villages—and decreased the percentage of people who spoke the native languages. The First World War decimated a generation—go into any village church in the south and look at the war memorial plaques; from a total population of a few hundred, you'll see maybe 30 names of villagers who died for the 'Glory of France'. By 1950, most villages had lost at least half their population; some died out altogether.

After the French débâcle of 1940, Provence found itself under the Vichy government. German occupation came in November 1942, after the American landings in North Africa, provoking the scuttling of the French fleet in Toulon to keep it out of German hands. After 1942, the Resistance was active and effective in the Provençal Alps and the Vaucluse—not to mention Marseille, where the Germans felt constrained to blow up the entire Vieux Port area. Liberation began two months after D-Day, in August 1944. American and French troops hit the beaches around St Tropez, and in a remarkably successful (and little-noticed) operation they had most of Provence liberated in two weeks. In the rugged mountains behind Nice, some bypassed German outposts held out until the end of the war.

The post-war era has brought momentous changes. The overdeveloped, ever more schizophrenic Côte d'Azur has become the heart of Provence—the tail that wags the dog. Besides its resorts it has the likes of IBM and the techno-paradise of Sophia-Antipolis. Above all, the self-proclaimed 'California of Europe' has money, and will acquire more; in two or three decades it will be the first province in centuries to start telling Paris where to get off. In rural Provence waves of Parisians and foreigners (mostly British) have come looking for the good life and a cheap stone house to fix up. They have brought life to many areas, though the traditional rural side suffers a bit. The increasingly posh Vaucluse has the highest rural crime and suicide rates in France.

The greatest political event has been the election of the Socialist Mitterrand government in 1981, followed by the creation of regional governments across France. Though their powers and budgets are extremely limited, this represents a major turning point, the first reversal of a thousand years of increasing Parisian centralism. Its lasting effects will not be known for decades, perhaps centuries; already the revival of Occitan language and culture is resuming; indicators include such things as new school courses in the language, and some towns and villages changing the street signs to Provençal.

Politics, quietly Socialist in most of the south, can still be primaeval in Provence. Jean-Marie Le Pen and his tawdry pack of adolescent bigots find their biggest following here, riding a wave of resentment against immigrants (200,000 North Africans since 1945—but this is a Provençal tradition; there were anti-Italian pogroms in Marseille and other towns in the 1870s). The other notable figure in recent years has been Le Pen's arch-enemy, the liberal Marseille industrialist, Bernard Tapie. Tapie became embroiled in scandals involving (among other affairs) game-fixing for his soccer club, L'Olympique de Marseille. At the time of writing he is bankrupt and possibly heading for jail; he is still widely popular though. Le Pen, meanwhile, putters along with 10 per cent or more national support in each election, enough to be a permanent thorn in the side of the French political class.

VAUCLUSE
CHURCH IN LACOSTE

Art and Architecture

Great art and architecture in Provence coincides neatly with its three periods of prosperity: the Roman, the Middle Ages, and the mid-19th and early 20th centuries, when railways opened up the coast not only to aristocrats, but to artists as well.

Prehistoric and Pre-Roman

Back in the Upper Palaeolithic era, the first known inhabitants of Provence decorated at least one cave, the recently discovered Grotte Cosquer; its awkward submerged entrance in the *calanques* near Marseille suggests that others may have been lost in the rising sea level. Their Neolithic descendants left few but tantalizing traces of their passing: dolmens (there's a good one near **Draguignan**), a few menhirs and a tomb-temple complex at **Castellet** near Arles. The first shepherds may well have put up the dry-stone, corbel-roofed huts called *bories*, rebuilt since countless times and still a feature of the landscape (especially at the 18th-century '*village des bories*' outside **Gordes**). In the Iron Age (1800–1500 BC), the Ligurians or their predecessors covered the Vallée des Merveilles under Mont Bégo with extraordinary rock incisions of warriors, bulls, masked figures and inexplicable symbols.

The arrival of the Celts around 800 BC coincided with an increase in trade; Greek, Etruscan and Celtic influences can be seen in the artefacts of this age. The Celts had talents for jewellery and ironwork—and a bizarre habit of decapitating enemies and making images of the heads (atavistically surviving in the little grotesque heads that pop up all over Romanesque buildings). The best of the originals are in the Musée Granet in **Aix**, the Musée d'Archéologie Méditerranée in **Marseille** and in the Lapidary Museum of **Avignon**.

Gallo-Roman: 3rd Century BC–AD 4th Century

Archaeologically the Greeks are the big disappointment of Provence—the only remains of their towns are bits of wall at **Marseille** and at **St-Blaise** on the Etang de Berre. But what the Romans left behind in their beloved *Provincia* makes up for the Greeks: the theatre of **Orange**, with the only intact stage building in the West; the amphitheatre and crypto-porticus in **Arles**; the elegant 'Antiques' of **St-Rémy**; the Pont Flavien at **St-Chamas**; the excavated towns at **Vaison-la-Romaine** and **Glanum** (St-Rémy).

Thanks to a lingering Celtic influence, Provence was the one province of the western Roman empire that developed a definite style of its own, characterized by vigorous, barbaric reliefs emboldened by deeply incised outlines. Battle scenes were the most popular subject, or shields and trophies arranged in the exotic, uncouth style you see on the triumphal arches of **Orange** and **Carpentras**, or in the Musée Archéologique in **Arles**. Roman landowners lived in two-storey stone houses, with their farm buildings forming an enclosed rectangular courtyard known as a *mansio*, the ancestor of the modern Provençal farmhouse, the *mas*.

Early Christian and Dark Ages: 5th–10th Centuries

Very few places had the resources to create any art at all during this period; the meagre attempts were nearly always rebuilt later. The oldest Christian relics are a remarkable sarcophagus from the 2nd century in **Brignoles**, and a large collection of 4th-century sarcophagi in the Musée Archéologique, at **Arles**, both close to Roman pagan models. Octagonal baptistries from the 5th and 6th centuries survive in **Aix** and **Riez**. Many church crypts are really the foundations of original Dark Age churches.

Romanesque: 11th–14th Centuries

When good times returned in the 11th century, people began to build again, inspired by the ancient buildings they saw around them. There is a great stylistic continuity not only from Roman to Romanesque (rounded arches, barrel vaults, rounded apses), but also in the vigorous Celtic-inspired decoration of Roman Provence. At the same time, the enduring charm of Romanesque is in its very lack of restrictions and codes, giving architects the freedom to improvise and solve problems in highly original and sophisticated ways. Although parish and monastic churches were usually in the basilican form (invented for Roman law courts, and used in Rome's first churches), masons also created extremely esoteric works, often built as funeral chapels in pre-Christian holy sites: **Notre-Dame-du-Groseau** and **Montmajour** are two in Provence.

Of the four distinct styles of Romanesque that emerged in southern France, the Provençal is the most austere and heaviest, characterized by simple floor plans, thick-set proportions, few if any windows, minimal if any decoration, and façades that are often blank. Churches that could double as fortresses were built along the pirate-plagued coast, most notably the church of **Saintes-Maries-de-la-Mer**. In the mid-12th century, the Cistercians founded three important new abbeys in a sombre and austere style, known as the 'Three Sisters': **Le Thoronet**, **Sénanque**, and **Silvacane**. An octagonal dome at the transept crossing is a common feature of more elaborate churches, especially **Avignon** cathedral, the Ancienne-Major in **Marseille**, **Vaison-la-Romaine**, **Le Thor** and **Carpentras** (the ruined original). The finest of the few paintings that survive from this epoque is the 13th-century fresco cycle at the Tour Ferrande, in **Pernes-les-Fontaines**. **Ganagobie** has the only floor mosaics from the period, as well as good sculpture.

In general, churches in the Rhône valley are more ornate, thanks to a talented group of sculptors known as the School of Arles. The wealth of ruins inspired them to adapt Roman forms and decorations to the new religion, complete with triumphal arches, gabled pediments, and Corinthian columns. The saints on the façade of St-Trophime in **Arles** seem direct descendants of Gallo-Roman warriors. Arlésien artists also created the remarkable façade of **St-Gilles-du-Gard**, portraying the New Testament—the true dogma in stone for all to see, perhaps meant as a refutation of the Cathar and other current heresies. Yet other Romanesque sculpture in the area, as at **Vaison-la-Romaine**, seems nothing but heretical.

Gothic and Renaissance: 14th–16th Centuries

Although Gothic elements first appear in Provence in 1150 (the façade of St-Victor in **Marseille**), the style's ogival vaulting and pointy arches belonged to a foreign, northern style that failed to touch southern hearts. The only place where it really found a home was in **Avignon**, when the 14th-century popes summoned architects from the north to design the flamboyant Papal Palace, St-Pierre, the Convent des Célestines and St-Didier (other isolated examples include the basilica of **St-Maximin-la-Ste-Baume**).

Painting in the south of France took a giant leap forward when the papal court in Avignon hired some of Italy's finest *trecento* artists, especially Simone Martini of Siena and Matteo Giovannetti of Viterbo. Their frescoes combined the new Italian naturalism with the courtly, elongated grace of medieval French art to create the fairy-tale style known as International Gothic (see **Avignon** and its Petit Palais museum).

From International Gothic, and from the precise techniques of the Flemish painters favoured by the last popes, a new local style developed in the early 15th century, the *School of Avignon*. The school's greatest masters were from the north: the exquisite Enguerrand Quarton (or Charton, *c.* 1415–66) from Laon (**Villeneuve-lès-Avignon**), and Nicolas Froment (Cathedral, **Aix**); also see Aix's church of the Madeleine and the Petit Palais museum in **Avignon**. Their most interesting native contemporaries were a pair of Piedmontese painters, Giovanni Canavesio (*c.* 1430–1500) and Giovanni Baleison (*c.* 1425–95), who would be better known had they not left their charming fresco cycles in remote, out-of-the-way churches up in Provence's alpine valleys, most notably **Notre-Dame-des-Fontaines** in the Roya Valley, and others in the valleys of the Vésubie and Tinée. This was also the time when King René, the great patron of the artists, built himself a fine chivalric castle in **Tarascon** and had a hand in the evolution of French sculpture when he invited the Italian Renaissance master **Francesco Laurana** (*c.* 1430–1502) to Provence. Laurana, a Dalmatian trained in Tuscany, is best known for his precocious geometrical softening of features and forms, especially in his portrait busts (in St-Didier, **Avignon**; Ancienne Major, **Marseille**; Cathedral, **Aix**).

Despite this promising start, subjugation by the French and the Wars of Religion made the Renaissance a non-event in Provence. The few buildings of the day are imitative, mostly of the heavy, classicizing Roman style, as in the palace of the Cardinal Legate in Avignon. The best Renaissance building, the once delightful Château La Tour d'Aigues in the Lubéron, is only a burnt-out shell.

The Age of Bad Taste: 17th–18th Centuries

The French prefer to call this their *époque classique* and even in the poor, benighted south admittedly many fine things were done. Towns laid out elegant squares, fountains and promenades as in **Pernes-les-Fontaines, Aix, Barjols**; trees were planted on a grand scale, on market squares, and along roads, where many (mostly out-of-the-way ones) are still lined with majestic 18th-century avenues of plane trees. **Moustiers** has a collection from its thriving faïence industry of the day (as does **Marseille's** Musée Cantini). Southerners went ape for organs, gargantuan works sheathed in ornate carved wood.

But nearly everything else is all wrong. People took the lovely churches left to them by their ancestors and tricked them out like cat-houses in pink and purple and tinkered so much with the architecture that it's often difficult to tell the real age of anything. Aix, the capital of Provence and self-proclaimed arbiter of taste, knocked over its magnificently preserved Roman mausoleum and medieval palace of the counts of Provence just before the Revolution. Although the 17th- and 18th-century palaces that replaced them lend Aix a distinctive urbanity and ostentation, they are rarely first-rate works of architecture in their own right, but rather eclectic jumbles with touches from Gothic, Renaissance, and Baroque style-books.

The one great Baroque sculptor and architect Provence produced, **Pierre Puget** (1620–94), suffered the usual fate of a prophet in his own land. Puget began his career painting ships' figureheads before he went on to study in Rome under Bernini; snubbed at home, he spent much of his career sculpting enormous saints in Genoa but left his native **Marseille** the striking Vieille Charité and a handful of sculptures in its Musée des Beaux Arts. In painting, the south produced two virtuoso court painters, Hyacinthe Rigaud and Fragonard, whose portrayals of happily spoiled, rosy-cheeked aristocrats were enough in themselves to provoke a Revolution. The most sincere paintings of the age are the naive ex votos in many churches (some of the best are from sailors, as at Notre-Dame-de-la-Garde, in **Marseille**). Then there are the works of Avignon native **Claude Joseph Vernet** (1714–89), a landscape painter best known for his seascapes and ports, in which he showed himself to be one of the first French artists interested in the play of light and water, if in a picturesque manner (Musée Calvet, **Avignon**; Musée des Beaux Arts, **Marseille**).

France's Little Ice Age: Late 18th–mid-19th Centuries

If the last era lacked vision, taste in the Neoclassical/Napoleonic era had all the charm of embalming fluid. The Revolution destroyed more than it built; the wanton devastation of the region's greatest Romanesque art (begun in the Wars of Religion) was a loss matched only by the mania for selling it off in the next century to the Americans. The greatest monuments of the Napoleonic era include the paintings in many museums by David, Ingres, and Hubert Robert, the latter of whom specialized in scenes of melancholy Roman ruins in Provence and Italy, capturing the taste of the day (it was also a great age for cemeteries). **Jacques-Louis David** (1748–1825) deserves special mention as Napoleon's favourite painter, as cold and perfect as ice, who portrayed the Frenchies of his day in kitsch-Roman heroic attitudes and costumes (Musée Granet, **Aix**; Musée Calvet, **Avignon**). David's pupil, **François Marius Granet** (1775–1849) was a native of Aix; although his canvases are run-of-the-mill academic, his watercolours and sketches reveal a poetic observation of nature that became the hallmark of the Provençal school (Musée Granet, **Aix**).

Another current in French painting at the time is represented by **Jean Baptiste Camille Corot** (1796–1875), a landscape painter of ineffable charm, who made the typical French sojourn in Rome to discover the calm and tranquillity of classical landscapes. Although not a southerner, he spent time in Provence, and his smaller, spontaneous sketches and private portraits that remain here show him off as a precursor of the impressionists (Musée Calvet, **Avignon**; Musée des Beaux-Arts, **Marseille**). In his lifetime, Corot was known for his kindness, and one who benefited the most was **Honoré Daumier** (1808–79), whom Corot supported in his impoverished blind old age. Born in Marseille, Daumier began his career risking jail terms as a political caricaturist for a magazine. But he was also a highly original pre-expressionist painter in the Goya mould, best known for his hypnotic, violently lit scenes based on the inherent tragedy of the human condition—a precursor of Toulouse-Lautrec, Degas, and Picasso (Musée des Beaux Arts, **Marseille**).

For the first time, however, there was a reaction to purposeful destruction of the past. Ruskin's contemporary, Viollet-le-Duc (1814–79), restored architecture, rather than just wrote about it (the walls of **Avignon**). Thanks to the Suez Canal, **Marseille** suddenly had money to burn and tried to revive the past in its own way, with monstrous neo-Byzantine basilicas and the overripe Baroque Palais Longchamp. It also produced **Adolphe Monticelli** (1824–86), perhaps Van Gogh's most important precursor, especially in his technique. Obsessed with light ('*La lumière, c'est le ténor,*' he claimed), Monticelli conveyed its effects with pure unmixed colour applied with hard brushes; subjects dissolve into strokes and blobs of paint (Musée des Beaux Arts and Musée Cantini, **Marseille**).

Revolutions in Seeing: 1850–the Present

> *A lady once came to look at Matisse's paintings and was horrified to see a woman with a green face. 'Wouldn't it be horrible to see a woman walking down the street with a green face?' she asked him. 'It certainly would!' Matisse agreed. 'Thank God it's only a painting!'*

In the 1850 Paris Salon, hanging amongst the stilted historical, religious, and mythological academic paintings were three large canvases of everyday, contemporary scenes by **Gustave Courbet** (1819–77). Today it's hard to imagine how audacious his contemporaries found Courbet's new style, which came to be called realism—almost as if it took the invention of photography by Louis Daguerre (1837) to make the eye see what was 'really' there. 'Do what you see, what you want, what you feel,' was Courbet's advice to his pupils. A keen student of luminosity in nature, one thing Courbet felt like doing was painting in the south, where his art revelled in the bright colour and light; his seascapes are awash in atmosphere (Musée des Beaux Arts, **Marseille**). Courbet's visit and fresh luminous style was a major influence on the 19th-century painters of Provence, especially **Paul Guigou** (1834–71). Born in Villars in the Vaucluse, Guigou sought out the most arid parts of Provence, especially the banks of the Durance, for his subjects, illuminating them with scintillating light and colour. Unable to make a living in the south, he took teaching jobs in the north, where he died at age 37, just as his career began to take off (Musée des Beaux Arts, **Marseille**; Musée Granet, **Aix**).

In the 1860s, physicists made the discovery that colour derives from light, not form. The idea inspired a new kind of art known as impressionism. Pissarro, Renoir, Manet and company made it their aim to strip Courbet's new-found visual reality of all subjectivity and to simply record on canvas the atmosphere, light, and colour the eye saw, all according to the latest scientific theories. The crucial role Provence was to play in modern art came later, in the 1880s, thanks to the careers of the two great post-impressionist painters: Vincent Van Gogh and Paul Cézanne. Not only did they change the history of art, but they produced, albeit in wildly different styles, the most loved images the outside world has of Provence.

A failed Dutch minister, **Vincent Van Gogh** (1853–90) was inspired by the impressionists and Japanese prints in Paris, but the most astonishing revolution in his art occurred when he moved to Arles in 1888 in search of 'a different light, in the belief that to look at nature under a clearer sky could give us a better idea of the way the Japanese see and draw; finally, I seek a stronger sun'. He responded to the heightened colour and light on such an emotional level that colour came less and less to represent form in his art (as it did for the impressionists), but instead took on a symbolic value, as the only medium Van Gogh found powerful enough to contain his extraordinary moods and visions: 'Instead of trying to reproduce exactly what I have before my eyes, I use colour more arbitrarily so as to express myself more forcibly.' The result was an intense lyricism that has never been equalled, a 'research into the infinite' that ended with suicide. He sold only one painting in his 37 years, and ironically not a single one of the 800 or so canvases he painted around Arles remains in Provence.

Van Gogh's revolutionary liberation of colour from form was taken to an extreme by a group of painters that the critic Louis Vauxcelles nicknamed the **Fauves** ('wild beasts') for the violence of their colours. The Fauves used colour to express moods and rhythms to the detriment of detail and recognizable subject matter. As a movement the Fauves lasted from 1904 until 1908, but in those few years revolutionized centuries of European art. Nearly all the Fauves—André Derain, Matisse, Maurice Vlaminck, Raoul Dufy, Kees Van Dongen—painted in the south, along the Riviera, and at La Ciotat, Cassis, and L'Estaque. Their work paved the way for expressionism, cubism, and abstractionism—avenues few of the Fauvists themselves ever explored. For after 1908 the collective new vision these young men had shared in the south of France vanished as if they had awoken from a mass hypnosis; all went their separate ways, leaving others to carry their ideas on to their logical conclusions. 'Fauve painting is not everything,' Matisse explained. 'But it is the foundation of everything.'

Unlike Van Gogh, **Paul Cézanne** (1839–1906) was a native of Provence, born in Aix, where fellow schoolmate Emile Zola was his best friend, until Zola published his autobiographical *L'Oeuvre* that thinly disguised Cézanne as the failed painter Lantier. Cézanne never forgave him, and anyway, compared to poor Van Gogh, Cézanne enjoyed a certain amount of success in his lifetime. His response to Provence was analytical rather than emotional, his interest not so much in depicting what he saw, but in the contradiction between the eye and mind, between the permanence of nature and the ephemeral qualities of light and movement. 'Nature is always the same, but none of it lasts beyond what we perceive,' he wrote. His goal was 'to make impressionism solid and enduring, like the art of the museums'. His painting went through several distinct periods: a sombre romantic stage (1861–71); an impressionistic manner, inspired by Pissarro (1872–82); a period of synthesis (1883–95), combining elements of impressionism with an interest in volume, surface planes, and the desire to represent perspective by nuances of colour and tonality only; and lastly, his lyric period (1896–1906), where singing rhythms of colour and form are intellectually supported by the basic tenets of cubism, splitting planes and volumes into prisms to express the tension between seeing and knowing. A handful of his paintings are on disply in the Musée Granet, in **Aix**.

In 1908, Georges Braque and the Fauvist Dufy went to paint together at L'Estaque in homage to Cézanne. The beginnings of the prismatic splitting of forms are in their respective works, and when the same critic Vauxcelles saw Braque's paintings, he came up with a new name: **cubism**. In 1912 Braque and Picasso worked together in Sorgues, near Avignon, where they produced canvases that verge on abstraction. **Pablo Picasso** (1881–1973), the 20th century's most endlessly inventive and prolific artist, returned to the south of France for good in 1948. Living here heightened the Mediterranean and pagan aspects of his extraordinarily wide-ranging work; when he felt nostalgic for his native Spain he would attend the bullfights at **Arles** and left a collection of drawings to the town's Musée Réattu.

Although a long list of other 20th-century artists, including Renoir, Matisse, and Chagall, settled in the south, like Picasso they usually chose to live on the Côte d'Azur. One exception in Provence is Hungarian-born founder of Op Art and experimenter in kinetic art, Victor Vasarély (b. 1908), whose foundation in **Aix-en-Provence** waits to make your eye balls squirm. Modern architecture has also left most of Provence alone: the one notable exception is Le Corbusier's idealistic *Unité d'Habitation* in **Marseille** (1952), part of a large housing project that was to consist of a row of rectangular slabs built on stilts. The rest were cancelled by the horrfied Marseillais after the first building was finished. Other architects thought it was the future, however, and it's hard to think of any city in the world that escaped a copy since.

Roussillon

Topics

Beyond the glamorous life in the villas and *résidences secondaires*, the cycle of the seasons goes on in the south of France as it has since Hector was a pup. A few crops have changed—silk, madder and a dozen different varieties of wheat have vanished, while flowers and early garden vegetables have become more important. Some corners are warm enough to produce three crops a year.

The calendar begins with two months of repose: *l'ivèr a ges d'ouro*, 'winter has no hours', is an old saying in the country. The mistral and tramontane winds howl away, and it snows, sometimes even in Nice. In **January** the Three Kings are fêted with crown-shaped brioches studded with candied fruit. Fattened geese and ducks are turned into *confits* and pigs into sausages and raw ham. In early **February** the mimosas bloom and olives are squeezed into oil; traditional presses are still used in many villages. Flaky tarts filled with jam or cream are baked for Carnival. By the end of February the almonds burst into lacy bloom.

The real work begins in **March**, when farmers prune their olives and vines and sow wheat and oats, and plant potatoes and melons. In **April** two things must be cut: hay and fleece, much of the work done by itinerant sheep shearers who travel from farm to farm. Plums, apricots, cherries, and pears spring into blossom; and everyone prays the mistral doesn't blow the flowers and buds off the trees. Good Friday is traditionally celebrated with an *aïoli*, or dried cod and garlic mayonnaise feast; for Easter the first roast lamb of the year is served with a salad of *romaine* lettuce, fresh onions and hard boiled eggs.

In **May** the flocks are driven to the greener pastures in the hills, following transhumance trails that date back to the Neolithic era. Early vegetables are abundant in the markets—little green artichokes called *mourre de gat* for omelettes, *fèves* (broad beans), garlic, spring onions and peas.

June brings the wheat harvest, once the most colourful event on the calendar as mountaineers descended by the thousands to provide the labour, fuelled on five meals and a barrel of wine a day. Asparagus, cherries and apricots ripen, and gourmets poke around in the woods for delectable morel mushrooms. The summer solstice and end of the harvest (St John's Day) are given a good old-fashioned Celtic send-off with bonfires and fireworks; the sun itself is said to dance and jump three times over the Alpilles. Almonds are ready to be picked in **July**, but now and throughout **August** it's too hot to work except in the early morning. Melons and peaches are everywhere, and the lavender is ready to be cut. The evenings are alive with village fêtes, for this has always been the time to eat, drink and make merry, to hoard strength for hard tasks ahead.

September brings fresh figs, and the rice is ready to be harvested in the Camargue. With the first rains mushrooms begin to poke up in the woods, especially the fragrant *cèpes*; these are tracked down with a relentlessness matched only by the hunters whose blasting advent is marked by a noticeable decline in birdsong. But the most important event of the month is the *vendange*, or grape harvest. **October**, too, is very much occupied with winemaking. The stripped vines turn red, wild boar meat appears in the markets, walnuts and chestnuts are gathered in the hills.

November marks the beginning of a new agricultural year, with the planting of wheat. Cold weather forces the shepherds and their flocks down from the mountains. Olives wait to be picked, and truffle hounds (the picturesque but uncontrollably greedy pigs have been retired) seek out the elusive *rabasso*, the black gold of the Vaucluse.

December brings Christmas, or *Calendo* in Provençal, a word resulting from an early confusion of Christ's birth with the Roman Calends. On Christmas Eve, *le réveillon*, the grandfather of each family blesses the *cacho-fió* (a Yule log from a fruit tree) and the youngest in the family lays it in the hearth; a lavish meal of fish and vegetables tradition-ally followed by thirteen desserts precedes midnight mass. This being France, the stomach dominates Christmas day as well: oysters, *foie gras*, black truffles, stuffed capon, goose with pears, and champagne, by necessity punctuated by frequent *trous provençaux*—snorts of frozen *marc* that magically make it possible to eat as much as Gargantua. And by New Year's Eve (*St-Sylvestre*) everyone's digestion has sufficiently recovered to eat it all again.

Mistral and the Félibrige

The attitude of the French was best expressed by Paul Morand's speech upon being admitted to the Académie Française: 'To write in French is to see flowing the waters of a mountain stream, next to which all languages are muddy rivers; it is to live in a crystal palace.' To someone like Morand, master of *pointu* or 'proper' French with all its mushy slushy vowel sounds, one of the muddiest rivers was *langue d'oc*. Its demise became a priority in the 19th century; after subjugating the south politically and religiously, Paris decided to finish off the job linguistically and decreed French the sole legal language in the schools, military, government and press.

One of the strategies of the *Franchimands* (as the southerners called French speakers) was to divide and conquer: *langue d'oc*, claimed the central Frenchifyers, was actually thou-sands of dialects and could never constitute a language. Even the southerners admit to seven 'grand dialects' of Occitan, two of which fall into the confines of this book: the Dauphinois of the Alpine valleys and Provençal. But it was in Provence that the reaction to the *Franchimands'* linguistic imperialism took its most curious form—in a sentimental, artificially contrived literary movement called the Félibrige.

According to legend, the idea for the Félibres was 'born of a mother's tear' when the mother of the poet Joseph Roumanille wept because she couldn't understand the French verses of her son. Not long after, on 21 May 1854, at the Château de Font Ségugne near Avignon, Roumanille, Frédéric Mistral and five other poets proclaimed the formation of a literary school to 'safeguard indefinitely for Provence its language, its colour, its easy liberty, its national honour, and its fine level of intelligence, for such as it is, we like Provence'. It was the 24-year-old Mistral who came up with the name for the school when he quoted a folk rhyme on the Seven Sorrows of Mary from his native village Maillane: *li sètt felibre de la Lèi*—the seven doctors or sages of the law. As 21 May (the day when the sun is in the constellation of the Pleiades, or seven sisters) was the feast day of Santo Estello, the seven-pointed star of the Cathars was adopted as one of the Félibres' symbols. In later years, after Mistral's epic *Miréio* gave the movement its lustre, 21 May would be celebrated with a Grand Félibre Banquet when all the fifty members or *Majoraux* and their leader, the *capoulié* (Mistral, naturally), would pass around the *Coupo Santo*, the Félibres' Holy Grail.

The Félibres' greatest moment came in 1904, when Mistral won the Nobel Prize for literature, the only writer in a minority language ever to be awarded a Nobel Prize. Thanks to him and the other Félibres Provence became conscious and proud of its separate identity; the richness of the language charmed even foreigners like Ezra Pound, who wrote and translated Provençal. But in spite of these successes, the Félibrige best serves as a lesson on how *not* to revive a language. Today only a few people in their eighties in remote areas still use Provençal as a daily tool, a sorry record compared to the subsequent revivals of Irish, Catalan, Basque, Welsh, and most successful of all, Hebrew.

Where did the Félibres go wrong? Not for lack of trying: unlike the courtly troubadours, they purposely wrote in a simple style to appeal to the *paysans*. Slipshod grammar and spelling were codified in Mistral's labour of love, the *Trésor du Félibrige* (a work accused by some of passing off the rustic dialect of Maillane as the last word in Provençal). But the Félibres' biggest mistake was confusing language and time, associating Provençal with folklore and the past, and shunning the necessary political fight with Paris in a romantic illusion that their poetry was powerful enough to revive a dying tongue. Mistral's powerful, mystical evocation of western Provence (the real hero of all his epics) was more of a swansong to a dying culture, not the foundation for a Renaissance of new troubadours.

For nearly everything Mistral celebrated in his poetry was undergoing a sea change—Italians, Corsicans, and Spaniards were moving in by the thousands, and helping to build new roads and railroads, while old farming practices, rural customs, traditions, and even villages were rapidly being abandoned. Mistral for all his art, energy, charm and influence could not turn the clock back. He had the unique honour of attending the unveiling of his own statue in Arles—a melancholy recognition that he was dead in his own lifetime.

Hocus Pocus Popes

Filling the lifeless shell of the papal palace in Avignon with the lost trappings of the medieval popes is not an easy task for the imagination. And the more you learn, the harder it gets, for besides all the harlots, speculators, gluttons, and cheats that Petrarch railed against, there seems to have been a shocking amount of voodoo. Accusations of sorcery had already sullied the name of one Occitan pope, Sylvester II (Gerbert of the Auvergne) who reigned from 999 to 1003 after studying in the Islamic schools in Toledo, where he acquired a prophetic bronze head that advised him in sticky moments. Even today, his tombstone in St John Lateran sweats and rattles before the death of each pope.

In 1309, the French pope Clement V moved the papacy from Rome to Avignon, then died from eating a plate of ground emeralds (prescribed by his doctor for a stomach ache). He was succeeded by John XXII, a native of Cahors, who owed his election to a magic knife that enchanted the conclave of cardinals. This John was also a famous alchemist, and he filled the papal treasury with gold, while King Philip V gave him a pair of *languiers*, or amulets shaped like serpents' tongues, encrusted with gems that changed colour on contact with poison. They served the pope in good stead, as plenty of rivals in the Church were trying to do him in. The most notable culprits were Clement V's doctor, caught manufacturing a diabolical homunculus, and Hughes Geraud, Bishop of Cahors, who confessed in 1317 that he had tried to assassinate the pope 'by poison and by sorcery with wax images, ashes of spiders and toads, the gall of a pig, and the like substances.' John XXII ordered him burnt at the stake.

The next pope, Benedict XII, spent hundreds of thousands of florins on a new palace, and still had enough gold and precious stones left over to top up his treasury—thanks, it is said, to an elderly woman residing in Avignon's ghetto, who told him where to find the 'treasure of the Jews' buried under her hovel. And in the bitter end, just before the anti-pope Benedict XIII was forced to flee Avignon, he sealed up a secret room in the palace with a cache of solid gold statues, confiding the secret to his friend, the Venetian ambassador. They were never found, although in Mistral's epic *Poème du Rhône*, three Venetian ladies who inherited the secret come to the palace and remove the flagstones that cover up the secret room—only to discover a bottomless abyss.

Marcel Pagnol and the Provençal Mystique

A certain part of Provence's current mystique derives from two of the best-loved French movies in recent years, *Jean de Florette* and *Manon des Sources*, directed by Claude Berri. Not only are both beautifully set in the heart of Provence, but more than that, they stick in the mind like glue: tales of mythic simplicity, of water, of a conspiracy of silence, of revenge. The stories, from *L'Eau des Collines*, were written by Marcel Pagnol and are based, according to him, on true stories that he heard as a child. The even more recent films, *La Gloire de mon Père* and *La Château de ma Mère*, were based on Pagnol's childhood memoires. They evoke a Provençal idyll from the beginning of the century; from the photography alone you can almost smell the wild herbs of the Garrigue baking in the sun.

Yet Marcel Pagnol's role in creating a universal mental image of Provence goes back to the 1930s, when he himself was a pioneer in the then new medium of 'talkies'—in fact, it's impossible to imagine a Pagnol film without sound because most of the time his characters are jawing away non-stop. Now relegated to cinematheques and the occasional late-night movie slot on television, his films, all filmed on location in Provence's villages, are often difficult to watch for modern viewers, weened on colour, constantly changing camera angles and scenes, fast-paced dialogue and action. Many families shoot better home videos. Pagnol's photography is bad, the camera angles are boring, and he never uses the slightest cinemagraphic trick, always preferring to 'say' rather than 'show'—it often seems that no one is directing the film at all. Many of Pagnol's ideas were adopted by the *nouvelle vague* directors in the 1960s.

Pagnol was a fervent believer in the power of human speech: for him the word was sacred. He was one of the first playwrights to move on to film because he was delighted to have his actors express themselves in conversational tones—with rich Provençal accents, naturally, and without using the exaggerated voices, gestures and makeup necessary in the theatre or in silent movies. No director before him gave his actors so much freedom. When filming his favourite actor, Raimu, star of *Marius, César* and *La Femme du Boulanger*, Pagnol said: 'He's so good that I just let him go on until he's tired of talking or we've run out of film.'

Most importantly, where Mistral and the Félibres failed to reach the masses through atavistic artiness (*see* above), Pagnol succeeded. There is nothing folkloric, stilted or affected in his Provence, but instead a sunny, attractive vision on a human scale and measured to a moral order, where life, as in all Mediterranean lands, revolves around the family. His stories are invariably simple—eternal fables of the human condition, planted in the fragrant soil of the Midi. An often wry sense of humour is never far, even when everything is going wrong. In 1967, French critic Jacques Lourcelles summed up the effect of Pagnol:

> *Seeing his films today, one realizes that they are a kind of classic, for which the sceneraio and creation of characters counted more than anything… His Provence is an immemorial Provence, static, hardly referred to [in the films] but profoundly linked to the destiny of his characters, underemphasized, and yet as present as the landscapes in the best westerns, with which the films of Pagnol are not without affinity. This vanished, non-touristy Provence is without doubt the most interesting feature of Pagnol's classicism.*

Troubadours

Lyric poetry in the modern Western world was born around the year 1095 with the rhymes of Count William (1071–1127), grandfather of Eleanor of Aquitaine. William wrote in the courtly language called Old Provençal (or Occitan) although his subject matter was hardly courtly ('Do you know how many times I screwed them? / One hundred and eighty-eight to be precise; / so much so that I almost broke my girth and harness . . .'). A descendant of the royal house of Aragon, William had Spanish-Arab blood in his lusty veins and had battled against the Moors in Spain on several occasions; but at the same time he found inspiration (for his form, if not his content) from a civilization that was centuries ahead of Christian Europe in culture.

The word *troubadour* may be derived from the Arabic root for lutenist (*trb*), and the ideal of courtly love makes its first appearance in the writings of the spiritual Islamic Sufis. The Sufis believed that true understanding could not be expressed in doctrines, but could be suggested obliquely in poetry and fables. Much of what they wrote was love poetry addressed to an ideal if unkind and irrational Muse, whom the poet hopes will reward his merit and devotion with enlightenment and inspiration.

Christians who encountered this poetry in the Crusades converted this ideal Muse into the Virgin, giving birth to the great 12th-century cult of Mary. But in Occitania this mystic strain was reinterpreted in a more worldly fashion by troubadours, whose muses became flesh and blood women, although these darlings were equally unattainable in the literary conventions of courtly love. The lady in question could only be addressed by a pseudonym. She had to be married to someone else. The poet's hopeless suit to her hinged, not on his rank, but on his virtue and worthiness. The greatest novelty of all was that this love had to go unrequited.

Art songs of courtly love were known as *cansos*, and rarely translate well, as their merit was in the poet's skill in inventing new forms in his rhyming schemes, metres, melodies, and images. But the troubadours wrote many other songs as well, called *sirventes*, which followed established forms but took for their subjects politics, war, miserly patrons, and even satires on courtly love itself.

The golden age of the troubadours began in the 1150s, when the feudal lords of Occitania warred amongst each other with so little success that behind the sound and fury the land enjoyed a rare political stability. Courts indulged in new luxuries and the arts flourished, and troubadours found ready audiences, travelling from castle to castle. One of their great patrons was En Barral, Viscount of Marseille, who was especially fond of the reputedly mad but charming Peire Vidal. Vidal not only wrote of his love for En Barral's beautiful wife, but in a famous incident even went beyond the bounds of convention by stealing a kiss from her while she slept (her husband, who thought it was funny, had to plead with her to forgive him). Vidal travelled widely, especially after the death of En Barral in 1192, and wrote a rare nostalgic poem for the homeland of his lady fair:

> With each breath I draw in the air
> I feel coming from Provence;
> I so love everything from there
> that when people speak well of it,
> I listen smiling, and with each
> word ask for a hundred more,
> so much does the hearing please me.

> (trans. by Anthony Bonner, in *Songs of the Troubadours*).

If nothing else, Provence will make you more aware of that sense we only remember when something stinks. The perfumeries of Grasse will correct this 'scentual' ignorance with a hundred different potions; every *village perché* has shops overflowing with scented soaps, pot-pourris and bundles of *herbes de Provence*; every kitchen emits intoxicating scents of garlic and thyme; every cellar wants you to breathe in the bouquets of its wines. And when you begin to almost crave the more usual French smells of *Gauloise* butts, *pipi* and *pommes frites*, you discover that this nasal obsession is not only profitable to some, but healthy for all.

Aromathérapie, a name coined in the 1920s for the method of natural healing through fragrances, is taken very seriously in the land where one word *sentir* does double duty for 'feel' and 'smell'. French medical students study it, and its prescriptions are covered by the national social security. For as an aromatherapist will tell you, smells play games with your psyche; the nose is hooked up not only to primitive drives like sex and hunger, but also to your emotions and memory. The consequences can be monumental. Just the scent of a madeleine cake dipped in tea was enough to set Proust off to write *Remembrance of Things Past*.

Aromatherapy is really just a fashionable name for old medicine. The Romans had a saying, *Cur moriatur homo, cui salvia crescit in horto?* (Why should he die, who grows sage in his garden?), about a herb still heralded for its youth-giving properties. Essential oils distilled from plants were the secret of Egyptian healing and embalming, and were so powerful that there was a bullish market in 17th-century Europe for mummies, which were boiled down to make medicine.

Essential oils are created by the sun and the most useful aromatic plants grow in hot and dry climates—as in the south of France, the spiritual heartland of aromatherapy. Lavender, the totem plant of the Midi, has been in high demand for its mellow soothing qualities ever since the Romans used it to scent their baths (hence its name from the Latin *lavare*, to wash). Up until the 1900s, nearly every farm in Provence had a small lavender distillery, and you can still find a few kicking about today. Most precious of all is the oil of *lavande fine*, a species that grows only above 3000 feet on the sunny side of the Alps; 150 pounds of flowers are needed for every pound of oil.

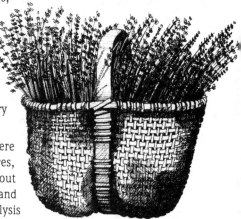

For centuries in Provence, shepherds were regarded as magicians for their plant cures, involving considerable mumbo-jumbo about picking their herbs in certain places and certain times—and indeed, modern analysis has shown that the chemical composition of a herb like thyme varies widely, depending on where it grows and when it's picked. When the sun is in Leo, shepherds make *millepertuis*, or red oil (a sovereign anaesthetic and remedy for burns and wounds) by soaking the flowers of St John's wort in a mixture of white wine and olive oil that has been exposed to the hottest sun. After three days, they boil the wine off, and let the flowers distil for another month; the oil is then sealed into tiny bottles, good for one dose each, to maintain the oil's healing properties.

Still awaiting a fashionable revival are other traditional Provençal cures: baked ground magpie brains for epilepsy, marmot fat for rheumatism, dried fox testicles rubbed on the chest for uterine disease and mouse excrement for bedwetting.

The Village Sociologist

Look up from the lavender fields for a minute, towards the typically picturesque *village perché* on the hills above. It seems a timeless place, where generation after generation of peasants have tilled the soil and lived their simple lives, until modern times came in with tractors, cars and store-bought clothes to spoil the effect. Writers such as Daudet and Giono, living in a time when rapid change was transforming villages and village life, made their careers chronicling the loss of old country ways with a sort of romantic melancholy. City people weren't discouraged, of course. The fantasy that attaches to places like Bonnieux, Les Arcs, or Lacoste has a lot to do with this image of a lost rustic paradise. Along with the lavender, it's what draws the tourists, the second-home buyers and the art schools.

This picture isn't entirely false—only nearly so. The romantic point of view can often lead to gross oversimplifications that do the little rural communities of Provence scant justice. If you look closely at a village and its past, you'll most likely find a fascinating story, with as much change and troubles as any big city. One way to do this is to read a lovely book called *Village in the Vaucluse*, written by an American sociologist named Laurence Wylie. In the '50s Wylie wangled one of the all-time sweet study grants, allowing him and his family to spend a year in Roussillon (disguised in the book as 'Peyrane') to examine the structure of village society. *Village in the Vaucluse* is hardly a dry sociological text. Wylie poked into every aspect of village life, sitting in at the local school, sifting through the archives (a bag of old papers in the mayor's closet) and gossiping with the old farmers. The result was a book written with considerable understanding and affection, one more like Marcel Pagnol than sociology.

Wylie also took the trouble to explore Roussillon's history, a tale full of ups and downs that makes a perfect illustration of the complexity of village life. In the early 1800s, as Roussillon entered the modern world, it began changing from a largely self-sufficient farming economy. Village women found good money in the exacting work of raising silkworms, while the men raised a new cash crop: madder, used in dying cloth. The Roussillonais did just fine until the disaster of the 1860s and '70s: silkworm diseases, a terrible winter that destroyed the olive trees, and the phylloxera epidemic that did in the vines. Things picked up again in the 1890s, when the ochre mines came back into production; depending on the market, these have been exploited on and off since Roman times. The First World War shut the mines off from their market in Russia, and carried away all too many of the village's sons, resulting in a steep decline not reversed until the '50s, when modern farming methods and tourism brought prosperity gradually back.

Along with the changes in the economy there have been correspondingly extreme swings in population. Roussillon has been a boom town many times over the centuries—and bust just as often, as it was in the '50s with half its houses empty and mostly old folks in the rest of them. In the first half of the 19th century, the population increased from 1195 to 1568. By 1886 it was back down to 1213. After the First World War it reached a low point of about 900, and the village has been inching its way back since. Today the population is 1300 and growing.

This population has always been more complex than just a simple collection of Provençal farmers. Even back in 1896, more than 10 per cent of Roussillon's population was made up of people from elsewhere. In the past, whenever the business cycle favoured a village new people would come from somewhere, and the natives would undoubtedly call them *étrangers*, even if they came from Marseille. In the 1890s Italian immigrants came to try their fortune. More recently it has been the Spanish, many of them Republicans exiled by the Civil War, as well as some Portuguese and a large number of *pied noirs*, French settlers chased out of Algeria when that country won its independence. Lately the 'immigrants' have been Parisian, British and American refugees from the rat race.

Another surprise Wylie found is how much internal politics, conflict and mutual dislike a village of a thousand people or so can generate. It's no surprise, really, to anyone who has ever spent time in such a village. Under a seamless veneer of French politeness, you'll always find that most of the inhabitants don't really much care for each other; life can be as intense as any soap opera, though without the glitter. To each, there's always the division between a few families whom one knows and who can be trusted, and *les autres* —those neighbours who are always peeking from behind their curtains, and who might report you to the tax man. Feuds of one sort or another are common—they may be the village's main source of entertainment. In our times these are usually expressed in politics; any French village could provide enough political news and opinions to fill a daily newspaper, if only there were enough people to read it.

Amidst all the change, these feuds sometimes provide the biggest element of stability. Wylie knew of two families in Roussillon that didn't get along, the Jouvauds and the Favres; the family heads were also among the leaders of two rival political parties in the village. Looking through the old records, he found that a Jouvaud had killed a Favre back in 1740, in a dispute that started when the victim led a band dancing the *farandole* across a square where Jouvaud had been playing an intense game of boules.

In Roussillon or any other village, there will always be something to talk about. In the *anomie* of modern life, we may forget just how complex a community of a thousand souls can be. A village is a world in itself, with enough interest and incident to satisfy all but the most jaded. Once they come to know what a rich and intricate place they have moved to, many of the city folk who seek refuge in the village find that this is the biggest attraction of all.

Wide Open Spaces

Gertrude Stein, a great fan of Provence who spent a lot of time in St-Rémy thinking inscrutable thoughts, once dropped a famous line about Oakland, California: 'There's no *there* there,' she concluded after a brief visit. Take an equally inscrutable modern-day rapper from Oakland out to the exact centre of Provence, around the Lac de Castillon, and you will get a neatly symmetrical opinion. Lac de Castillon, a big artificial lake behind a concrete dam, is a special place, surrounded by wrinkled hills of a grey so immaculately grey that it is hard to see them at all. Outside of a few dam workers and an occasional trendy hang-gliding above, the whole gigantic grey place will be eerily deserted. The Lac de Castillon is *nowhere*, and all the towns and villages for thirty miles or more in any direction are only variations on the theme. We like to imagine an advert in a London paper: '*Delightful farmhouse half-restored in the heart of the Provençal mountains, near mountain lake; 1½hr from Cannes. Must sell.*'

When you visit, take a look at the sort of Frenchman who lives in such a place: no poodles, no shades, no attitudes; even in summer, he may well be wearing a flannel shirt, which under the big moustaches will make him look entirely like one of the jolly Gaulish villagers in *Astérix*. Some of these are real frontiersmen, rough-edged, self-sufficient types whose lives revolve around hunting, gathering mushrooms and getting in wood for the winter; they grumble laconically in a tongue that is still more Provençal than French.

But we once met a picture-perfect example on the way to Draguignan. He was the baker in a village near the lake, hitch-hiking to the city with a jerry can of petrol to buy a used car (in France one never expects a used car to have any in the tank). His brother had gone off to the Harvard Business School and made it big. The baker, with his degree in cultural anthropology, preferred less stress and yeastier dough; having an assistant allowed him enough time for long scholarly vacations in the darker corners of South America and Asia.

The moral seems to be: rural France provides some of the world's most interesting hitch-hikers. It does, but the point was that the English shibboleth the 'South of France' is not always what one might expect. The toadstool growth of the Côte d'Azur in the last century has entirely eclipsed the real Provence: lonely expanses of mountain and introverted villages, shepherds who still drive their flocks up to the mountains in summer on the old transhumance paths, and a traditional rural culture that, despite a great loss of population in the last century, is not yet prepared to compromise entirely with the modern world.

One wild snapshot among many sticks in the mind: two Indian chiefs, Iron Tail and Lone Bear, sipping champagne with the Marquis de Baroncelli-Javon in 1889, while watching

Camargue *gardians* and the cowboys of Buffalo Bill's Wild West Show compare their skills at a Provençal rodeo. The men of two worlds had a great time together, and seemed to understand one another perfectly. One young Sioux, whom the French called *Pan Perdu*, chose to stay behind in Provence; Frédéric Mistral met him, and thought he might be the reincarnated soul of a troubadour.

Aïoli Recipe

This typical Provençal mayonnaise is best served with white fish such as *bourride*, or with snails, potatoes or soup.

> *Ingredients*:
>
> *1 or 2 eggs (yolks only)*
> *7–8 garlic cloves, approx.*
> *extra-virgin olive oil*
>
> *To accompany the aïoli (per person):*
> *1 potato*
> *1 carrot*
> *1 hard-boiled egg*
> *75–80g green beans*
> *2 cauliflower florets*
> *100–150g cod*
> *a few snails*

Using a mortar and pestle, crush from ½ to six cloves of garlic per person, according to taste. Reduce the garlic to a paste and add one or two egg yolks. Begin whipping the mixture with a fork or small whisk while adding good quality (extra-virgin) olive oil, first drop by drop, then in a thin stream as the mayonnaise begins to set. Add salt only once all the oil has been integrated and the mayonnaise has formed. Should the *aïoli* lack substance or the oil separate from the mixture, you can still 'save' your mayonnaise: remove the mixture and add another egg yolk to the clean mortar. Whipping constantly, reintegrate the old *aïoli* mixture and any remaining oil. This operation is called 'reconstituting' the *aïoli*. One litre of olive oil will make enough *aïoli* for at least 10 people.

Down the Rhône: Orange to Tarascon

Despite Frédéric Mistral's best efforts in the epic 1896 *Poème du Rhône*, this is not a lyrical river, neither fair of face nor full of grace. Its nickname *malabar*, the strongman, describes it well: deep and swift-flowing with muscular currents, its banks like bulging biceps, its secret depths hosting legendary man-eating monsters such as the Tarasque and Drac. For the Rhône is a Saturday's child and has to work for a living: after serving the industries and nuclear plants to the north, it does it all again in Provence, at France's biggest centre for the processing of nuclear waste, at Marcoule, at the hydro-electric plant and Satanic mills of Avignon's industrial quarter, and at the paper mills near Tarascon.

Historically most of the Rhône's traffic has come south with the current, ferrying the blond barbarians, the eaters of *frites* and drinkers of beer, down to the sultry Mediterranean. The river also divided the spoils: Provence, on the east bank, owed allegiance to the emperor and pope; Languedoc, on the west, belonged to the kingdom of France after the Albigensian crusade. Rhône boatmen called the banks not port and starboard, but Empire and Kingdom. On the empire's side are Orange, with its famous Roman theatre, Châteauneuf-du-Pape and Avignon, where 14th-century popes spent what Petrarch called their 'Babylonian exile', and Tarascon, favoured home of Provence's Good King René.

Note that on 18 October 1996 France is changing its telephone numbers from 8 digits to 10 digits. All phone numbers in Provence should be preceded by 04 from this date.

Orange

 There seems to have been a settlement of some kind around the hill of St-Eutrope in prehistoric times, and the city dates its chronicles from 35 BC—enough time for all imaginable Oranges to have come and gone. The present incarnation must be one of the sadder ones, a miasmic provincial town with a few cosy corners among the prevailing drabness. Fate, or the lack of a bypass road, has made its streets a kind of Le Mans for heavy lorries, fouling the air, menacing pedestrians and coating the old houses with a sooty film. Nevertheless you'll come, to see two ancient monuments unmatched in France, and for some surprises besides.

History

Rome took good care of its soldiers; keeping its word by them was one secret of the empire's success. Nine years after Julius Caesar's death, many veterans of the Second Gallic Legion were ready for their promised retirement. The pattern was already set. Rome would establish a colony for them in the lands they conquered, often replacing a native village they had destroyed; the veterans farmed their allocated lands, and could look forward to real wealth in their declining years as the colony grew into a town. The colony that became Orange was called *Colonia Julia Secundanorum Arausio*.

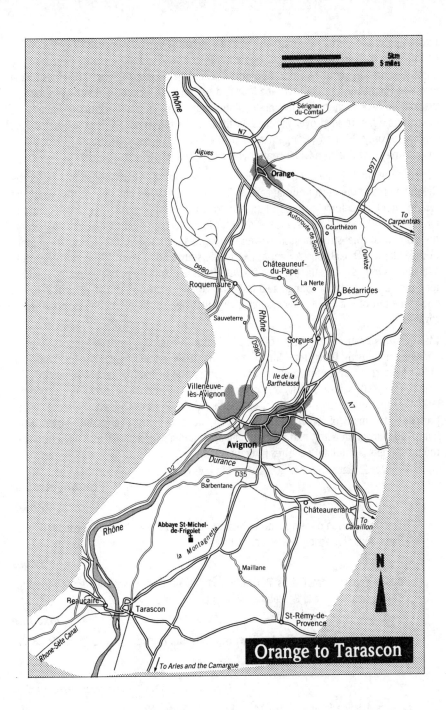

Orange to Tarascon

Exceedingly prosperous throughout Roman times, Orange survived the Visigothic conquest in 412; it was the site of two Church councils in the following decades. The chronicles are largely blank from then until the mid-12th century, when the city's feudal lord was Raimbaut d'Orange, troubadour and patron of troubadours. Even then, history was on the back-burner; the city and its hinterlands were often in hock to pay Raimbaut's debts, while he presided over the most brilliant of Provençal courts. He died in 1173, at the age of only 29, and Orange passed to the Counts of Baux. In the 1300s it was a thriving place, with a municipal charter and even a university.

In 1530, the city became the property of the German House of Nassau, just in time for the Reformation and the most unusual page of the city's history, an odd chance that would let Orange lend its colour to the Dutch, the Northern Irish, the Orange Free State and Orange, New Jersey. The Nassaus declared for Protestantism, and Orange rapidly became the dissenters' chief stronghold in Provence, a home for thousands of refugees and a thorn in the side of arch-Catholic Avignon, just to the south. Soon after, William of Nassau— William of Orange—became the first *stadhouder* of the United Provinces and led the fight for Dutch independence. Orange held fast through all the troubles of the Wars of Religion, and came out of it a Dutch possession, giving its name to the Netherlands' present-day royal family.

Maurice of Nassau, in the early 1600s, did Orange a bad turn by destroying most of its ancient ruins, using their stone for the new wall he was building against the French. It didn't keep them away for long. In 1672, during one of his frequent wars against the Dutch, Louis XIV seized the city and demolished its wall and castle. French rule, particularly after the revocation of the Edict of Nantes (*see* p.42), was a disaster; Orange lost its prosperity and many of its best citizens. The city never really recovered, but it earns a fair living today from industry, and from the big army and air force bases that make it one of the most important military centres in France.

Getting Around
by train

The train station on Av. Frédéric Mistral, ✆ 90 82 50 50, has direct connections to Paris, Avignon, Arles, Marseille, and Cannes.

by bus

Buses depart from Cours Portoules, ✆ 90 34 15 59, several times a day for Carpentras, Vaison-la-Romaine, Avignon and three daily for Séguret.

bike hire

You can hire a bike at **Cycles Lurion**, 48 Cours Aristide Briand, ✆ 90 34 08 77. Closed Sunday and Monday.

Tourist Information

Cours Aristide Briand, ✆ 90 34 70 88, ✆ 90 34 99 62

The Best-preserved Theatre of Antiquity

Open daily 9–6.30 in summer, 9–12.30 and 1.30–5 in winter, guided tours July and August only; adm; also valid for Municipal Museum; ℃ 90 51 17 60.

The architects of the **Théâtre Antique** might be distressed to hear it, but these days the most impressive part of this huge structure is its back wall. 'The best wall in my kingdom', Louis XIV is said to have called it. If the old prints in the municipal museum are accurate, this rugged, elegant sandstone cliff facing Place des Frères-Mounet was originally adorned with low, temple-like façades. In its present state, it resembles a typical Florentine Renaissance palace, without the windows. The classically minded architects of the 1400s all travelled in Provence, and perhaps this stately relic of Rome at its best had a hidden influence that would have made its architects proud.

Built in the early 1st century AD, the theatre is a testimony to the culture and wealth of Arausio. Like the Colosseum in Rome, it even had a massive awning (*velum*), a contraption of canvas and beams that could be raised to cover most of the spectators. All over the Mediterranean, theatres fell into disuse in the cultural degradation of the late empire. This one was probably already abandoned when it burned in the 4th or 5th century. In the Middle Ages other buildings grew up over the ruins; old prints show the semicircular tiers of seats (*cavea*) half-filled in and covered with ramshackle houses.

The site is typical for a Roman theatre, backed into the hill of St-Eutrope where the banks of seats could be built on the slope. These have been almost completely restored. Since 1869, Orange has used the theatre for a summer festival called *Les Chorégies*. Mistral and the Félibres (*see* p.55) were active in its early years, when Greek and Roman plays were often on the bill; today contemporary drama and opera are more common.

Unlike Greek theatres, which always opened to a grand view behind the stage, those of the Romans featured large stage buildings, serious architectural compositions of columns, arches and sculptured friezes. This is what the great exterior wall is supporting; Orange's stage building (35m high) is one of two complete specimens that remain to us (the other is at Aspendos, in Turkey), though the fragments of its decoration are mostly in the municipal museum across the street. A statue of Augustus remains, in the centre, over an inscription honouring the people of Arausio and welcoming them to the show. Outside the theatre, foundations of a temple have been excavated, along with a semicircular ruin that may have been a nymphaeum, or a gymnasium.

The Musée Municipal

Open daily 9–7 in summer, 9–12 and 1.30–5.30 in winter; adm; also valid for the Roman theatre.

Save some time for this bulging curiosity shop, directly opposite the theatre on Place des Frères-Mounet; it is one of the most fascinating town museums in Provence. As expected, the main rooms are given over to Roman art, including an exceptional frieze of satyrs and amazons from the theatre. The *plan cadastral* (land survey) is unique: a stone tablet engraved with property records for the broad Roman grid of farmland between Orange and Montélimar. The first pieces of it were discovered in 1856, though no one guessed what they were until the rest turned up, between 1927 and 1954; since then they have been a great aid to scholars in filling in some of the everyday details of Roman life and law.

Climbing the stairs into the upper levels of the museum, you'll pass rooms of Dutch portraits and relics of Nassau rule, and a collection of works by the Welsh impressionist Frank Brangwyn (who was, in fact, born in Bruges): heroic compositions among wharves and factories, along with some lovely country scenes. The most unexpected exhibit is the **Salle des Wetters**, a remarkable relic of the Industrial Revolution in France. The Wetters were a family of mid-18th-century industrialists who produced *indiennes*, printed cotton cloth much in demand at the time. They commissioned an artist named G. M. Rossetti to paint a record of their business; this he did (1764) in incredible detail, on five huge, colourful naive canvases showing every aspect of the making of *indiennes*, from the stevedores unloading the cotton on the docks to the shy, serious factory girls in the great hall—the Wetters were among the first in France to stumble on the factory system, and employed over 500 people.

Old Orange and the Triumphal Arch

Touring old Orange does not handsomely reward the visitor; you may walk up the **Hill of St-Eutrope** for a view over the town and a look at the foundations of the castle destroyed by the French. In the city centre, there is only an utterly pathetic cathedral, begun in 529 over a Temple of Diana and rebuilt to death between 1561 and 1809. One thing Orange does have is original street names—sometimes unintentionally hilarious ones, like the *Impasse de Parlement*.

THE TRIUMPHAL ARCH OF TIBERIUS, ORANGE.

Rue Victor-Hugo, roughly following the route of the ancient Roman main street, or *cardo major*, is the axis that leads to Orange's other Roman attraction. The **Triumphal Arch**, built around 20 AD, celebrates the conquests of the Second Gallic Legion with outlandish, almost abstract scenes of battling Romans and Celts. This is the epitome of the Provençal-Roman style: excellent, careful reliefs, especially in the upper frieze, portraying a naval battle, though with a touch of Celto-Ligurian strangeness in the details. Odd oval shields are a prominent feature, decorated with heraldic devices and thunderbolts. Seemingly random symbols at the upper left—a whip, a pitcher, something that looks like a bishop's crozier, and others—are in fact symbols of animal sacrifice and marine attributes (the 'crozier' is the prow of a ship). On the sides of the arch are heaps of arms—'triumphs'—that were to influence the militaristic art fostered by rulers such as Emperor Charles V in the Renaissance. A little over a half-century before this arch was built, Orange was still Rome's wild frontier, and art such as this evokes it vividly. Note the standards the legionaries are carrying: not the expected Roman eagle, but a boar.

When frontier days returned to Orange, in the Middle Ages, the arch was expanded into a castle by Raymond of Baux—typical of that haughty family. It is said that Raymond arranged it so that the battle reliefs would be a wall of his dining hall; we have his arrogance to thank for their relatively good state of preservation.

Orange ✉ *84100*   **Where to Stay and Eating Out**

The best bet in the centre of Orange is the ★★★**Hôtel Arène** on Place de Langes, ✆ 90 34 10 95, 📠 90 34 91 62: pleasant, with a good restaurant, on a quiet square where you can't hear the lorries (*closed Nov–mid-Dec*). There are a number of decent budget choices: the ★**St-Florent** at 4 Rue du Mazeau, ✆ 90 34 18 53, 📠 90 51 17 25; or the dour old **Hôtel Fréau**, near the theatre at 3 Rue Ancien Collège, ✆ 90 34 06 26.

For lunch after looking over Orange's theatre, try Rue du Pont Neuf, where there are a number of restaurants, or Place Sylvian where the pretty **Le Yaca**, ✆ 90 34 70 03, has appetizing menus at 85F and 125F (*closed Tues evenings and Wed*). **Le Pigraillet**, ✆ 90 34 44 25, on Colline St-Eutrope, a wooded park overlooking the Rhône, is an unforgettable place to spend a warm summer's night: clients may use the swimming pool before eating for a luxurious 155F.

Sérignan-du-Comtat and the 'Virgil of Insects'

A short 8km detour northeast of Orange on the D 976 will allow you to pay your respects to the great entomologist, botanist, scientist and poet Jean-Henri Fabre (1823–1915). Although born into poverty, the largely self-taught Fabre qualified as a *lycée* teacher of sciences in Avignon, only to be fired in 1870 for explicitly describing the sex life of flowers. In 1879 he bought an abandoned property here that he called **L'Harmas**, the 'fallow land' (*open daily except Tues 9–11.30 and 2–6, 2–4 winter*; ✆ *90 70 00 44*). Fabre walled in the garden and planted a thousand species of flower and herb, which have run amok as he intended and are now part of a botanical preserve. Purchased by the state in 1922, the house strongly evokes Fabre's personality and work, most extraordinarily of all in his 700 watercolours of the fungi of the Vaucluse, so real that you can hardly believe they are only two-dimensional. You can also see the harmonium Fabre liked to play and his study, where he wrote his passionate books on insects that have been translated into English (and made several children of our acquaintance into amateur entomologists) but are disgracefully out of print and hard to find, even in French.

South of Orange: Châteauneuf-du-Pape

Je veux vous chanter, mes amis,
Ce vieux Châteauneuf que j'ai mis
Pour vous seuls en bouteille:
Il va faire merveille!

Quand de ce vin nous serons gris,
Vénus applaudira nos ris:
Je prends à témoin Lise,
La chose est bien permise!

(My friends, I want to sing you / Of this old Châteauneuf that I've bottled just for you / It will work miracles! / For when this wine makes us tipsy / Venus will crown our mirth / I take Lise as my witness / No one will mind if I do!)

Pope John XXII's drinking song.

Tourist Information

Place du Portail, ✆ 90 83 71 08

You'll begin to understand why Châteauneuf's wines are so expensive when you pass through the vineyards, between Orange and Avignon. Blink, and you'll miss them. This pocket-sized wine region, tucked between the outskirts of Avignon and Orange, has become one of the most prosperous corners of France; every available square inch is covered with vineyards of a rare beauty, so immaculately precise and luxuriant they resemble bonsai trees. Such good fortune is not without its disadvantages.

Châteauneuf-du-Pape, the very attractive village that gives the wine its name, has not resisted the temptation to become the Midi's foremost oenological tourist trap; along the main street, there are few grocers or boutiques, but plenty of wine shops. In places it is hard to see the buildings for the signs, advertising other shops, or the winemakers' estates in the hinterlands.

Legend has it that one of the first things Clement V did on leaving Rome was to inspect his vineyards north of Avignon. In 1316, his successor John XXII, a celebrated imbiber, did him one better by building a castle here, which the Avignon popes used as a summer residence—a 14th-century Castel Gandolfo. Sacked by the Protestants in the Wars of Religion, it was finally blown up by the retreating Germans in 1944; two crenellated walls still stand. Even if you don't like ruins or crowds, brave the hordes anyway to see the huge plain below you, and the Rhône muscling away to the west on its way south to Avignon, or wait till dusk if you can, for a magnificent sunset. Down on the plain, on the road to Avignon, you can taste chocolate, if you're bored of wine (Chocolaterie Artisanale, ✆ 90 83 54 71).

Châteauneuf-du-Pape

An inspiration to both popes and lovers, Châteauneuf-du-Pape's reputation has remained strong through the ages; to safeguard it in 1923 its growers agreed to the guarantees and controls that formed the basis for France's modern *Appellation d'Origine* laws. Several factors combine to give the wine its unique character: the alluvial red clay and pebbly soil, brought down by a Rhône glacier in the ice age; the mistral which chases away the clouds and haze, letting the sun hit the grapes like an X-ray gun; and the wide palette of grapes that each winemaker can choose from: grenache, syrah, cinsault, mourvèdre, terret noir, vaccarèse, connoise, and muscardin for the reds; and clairette, bourboulenc, roussane, picpoul and picardan for the whites, 30 years ago dismissed as mere novelties and today celebrated as some of Provence's top wines—pale blond with greenish highlights and a fresh, floral bouquet.

Because of the complex blends that give Châteauneuf its voluptuous qualities, the grapes are sorted by hand—unique among southern wines. The end result must have the highest alcoholic minimum of any great French wine (12.5%), a level achieved by spacing the vines a good 2m apart to soak up the maximum amount of sun, and from the heat-absorbing pebbles underneath the vines that keep the grapes toasty after dark. Light, soft, and fast to mature, Châteauneuf-du-Pape red can be enjoyed much earlier (often in three years) than its Rhône rivals, and only gets better the longer you can bear to wait.

In its home town, the wine is not exactly hard to find, and even in the cellars it's not cheap, as many of the *cuvées* of the 1980s promise to be superb. Perhaps the best known of the many excellent vineyards that welcome visitors are **Château Le Nerthe**, with its fascinating ancient cellars, ✆ 90 83 70 11, or the vaulted cellars of **Château de la Gardine**, ✆ 90 83 73 20. In Bédarrides, the vineyards of **Domaine du Vieux Télégraphe**, 3 Route de Châteauneuf, ✆ 90 33 00 31, occupy a rugged promontory topped by a tower once used for optic telegraphic experiments; the '90 reds and whites are excellent buys. The three finest estates are in a class of their own and have such highly individual styles as to be unmistakable even tasted blind. **Clos des Papes**, ✆ 90 83 70 13, is run by the highly intelligent and innovative Paul Avril. Avril is alone in employing humidifiers in his cellar to alleviate the drying effects of the mistral wind in particular and the heat in general. As a consequence his wines have the best defined fruit of the region and are the most elegant. With age Avril's Châteauneuf-du-Pape can taste like expensive claret.

The wines of **Château de Beaucastel,** in Courthézon, ℂ 90 70 41 00, have been consistently among the top wines of the *appellation*—lately the superb 1990 red, and a very classy '89 white.

The most extraordinary source of Châteauneuf-du-Pape and possibly one of the country's most interesting wines is made by Jacques Raynaud at **Château Rayas.** Raynaud's cellar has been described as the most filthy and disorganized in France, and it is only fair to warn you he has a well-deserved reputation for being very inhospitable. One well-known wine merchant, and one not used to anything other than gracious hospitality when visiting growers, turned up on time for a pre-arranged rendezvous to find the place deserted. After nearly an hour's wait, the hapless fellow got back into his car and pulled out of the driveway. Looking back in his rearview mirror he caught a glimpse of Raynaud clambering out of the ditch in which he had been hiding! Raynaud may be difficult to visit but his wines are a must for all keen wine lovers. They are the product of a bygone era—wines of incredible concentration and depth with the capacity to age 20 years or more. Wines such as these are increasingly rare in an age when technology, which has helped to ensure that most wine is well made, also means that too many are sound but mediocre.

Châteauneuf-du-Pape ✉ *84230*   ***Where to Stay and Eating Out***

It's difficult to imagine how such a sweet old hotel-restaurant could survive in a tourist trap like Châteauneuf-du-Pape, but if you're passing through do stop at **La Mère Germaine,** Ave Cdt Lemaitre, ℂ 90 83 54 37, ✆ 90 83 50 27. The restaurant serves tantalizing dishes such as *pistou de morue fraîche* and the succulent *flan de chèvre au caramel de miel épicé.* Menus at 135, 210 and 350F. There are also fine rooms, adorned with antiques (*closed Sun eves and Mon, and 10–31 Jan*). For an even more luxurious stay, there is the ★★★★**Château des Fines Roches,** 2km south on the D 17, ℂ 90 83 70 23, ✆ 90 83 78 42, an imposing but entirely fake crenellated castle (19th-century) with gardens, set among the vineyards south of Châteauneuf; elegant and quite expensive, the kitchen shines in seafood dishes and elaborate desserts; menus 195F, 270F (*closed mid-Dec–Feb*).

Avignon

Avignon has known more passions and art and power than any town in Provence, a mixture of excitement whipped to a frenzy by the mistral. But even the master of winds has never caused as much trouble as the papal court, a vortex of mischief that ruled Avignon for centuries, trailing violence, corruption and debauchery in its wake. 'In Paris one quarrels, in Avignon one kills,' wrote Hugo. In Avignon Petrarch's platonic, courtly love for Laura was an aberration. 'Blood is hot there,' wrote an anonymous writer in the 1600s, 'And the most serious occupation in the land is the search for pleasure . . . even most of the husbands are accommodating in love, and allow their wives the same free-doms they enjoy themselves.'

Avignon still has a twinkle in its eye; it is alive, ebullient, and has been one of France's most innovative cities ever since the Italian Renaissance filtered through here to the rest of Europe. As the cultural and publishing centre of the south, it rocked the cradle of the Félibrige, the Provençal literary movement (*see* p.55) and since the war it has been the stage for Europe's most exciting theatre festival. Charming it's not, but as an old Provençal proverb puts it: *Quau se lèvo d'Avignoun, se lèvo de la resoun* or 'He who takes leave of Avignon takes leave of his senses'.

History

Rome, *anno domini* 1303. Anarchy reigns: popular riots, regular visits from foreign armies, and clans waging medieval gang war in the streets, turning the tombs of the Caesars into urban fortresses. The papacy, though in the thick of it all, usually kept the papal person himself in places like Viterbo and Anagni for safety's sake—as it had the arrogant intriguer Boniface VIII, now fresh in his grave. Boniface's arch-enemy, Philip the Fair of France, has just bribed the conclave to elect a Frenchman, Clement V. Philip also suggested that the new pope flee the inferno of Rome for the safer havens of the Comtat Venaissin in Provence—and Clement didn't have to be asked twice.

The Church had picked up this piece of Provence real estate as its spoils after the Albigensian Crusade. Isolated within it was the little city-republic of Avignon, belonging to the Angevin Counts of Provence—old papal allies, who welcomed their illustrious visitor. Clement V always intended to return to Rome, but when he died the French cardinals elected a former archbishop of Avignon, John XXII (1316–34), who moved the Curia into his old episcopal palace and greatly enriched the papacy (through alchemy, it was rumoured: *see* pp.56–7). Although he enlarged the palace with the proceeds, it still wasn't roomy enough for his successor, Benedict XII (1334–42), who replaced it with another palace, or for Clement VI (1342–52), who added another. It seemed that the popes meant to stay forever, especially after 1348 when Clement purchased Avignon outright from the young Angevin Countess of Provence, Jeanne I of Naples, for the sale price of 80,000 florins and an absolution for her possible involvement in the suspicious strangulation of her husband.

Meanwhile all the profits that the 14th-century papal machine generated—from tithes and the sale of indulgences, pardons, offices, and the visits of pilgrims—went to Avignon instead of Rome. Overcrowding, debauchery, dirt, luxury, plague, blackmail, and crime came with the deal—troubles exasperated by papal tolerance that admitted outcasts from everywhere else into Avignon, as long as they could pay. Such refugees included not only common criminals but also Jews and, during the Schism, heretics. The Italians, mortified at losing their cash cow during this 'Babylonian captivity', expressed their self-righteous indignation through the longtime Avignon resident Petrarch: 'Avignon is the hell of living people, the thoroughfare of vice, the sewers of the earth . . . Prostitutes swarm on the papal beds.' Yet these same popes summoned the best *trecento* artists from Italy,

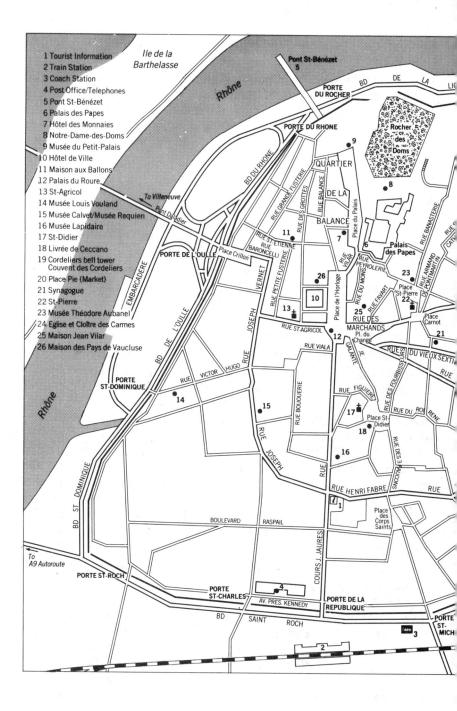

1 Tourist Information
2 Train Station
3 Coach Station
4 Post Office/Telephones
5 Pont St-Bénézet
6 Palais des Papes
7 Hôtel des Monnaies
8 Notre-Dame-des-Doms
9 Musée du Petit-Palais
10 Hôtel de Ville
11 Maison aux Ballons
12 Palais du Roure
13 St-Agricol
14 Musée Louis Vouland
15 Musée Calvet/Musée Requien
16 Musée Lapidaire
17 St-Didier
18 Livrée de Ceccano
19 Cordeliers bell tower
   Couvent des Cordeliers
20 Place Pie (Market)
21 Synagogue
22 St-Pierre
23 Musée Théodore Aubanel
24 Eglise et Cloître des Carmes
25 Maison Jean Vilar
26 Maison des Pays de Vaucluse

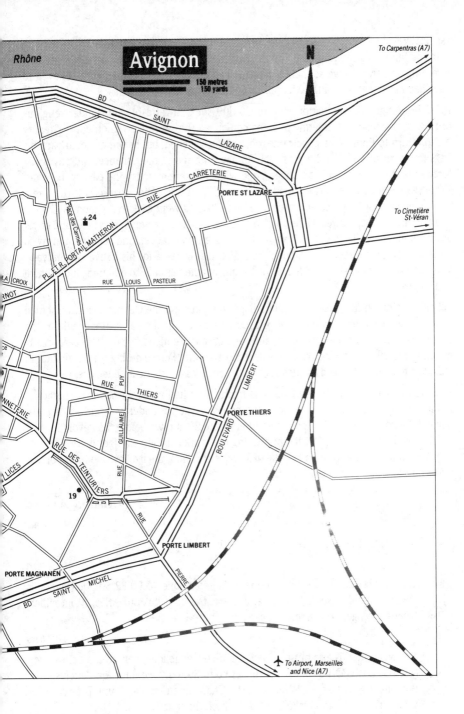

Rhône

Avignon

150 metres
150 yards

N

To Carpentras (A7)

BD SAINT LAZARE

CARRETERIE

RUE

PORTE ST LAZARE

To Cimetière
St-Véran

■24

Place des Carmes

PL. ET R. PORTAIL MATHERON

LA CROIX

RNOT

RUE LOUIS PASTEUR

ce

RUE PUY THIERS

GUILLAUME

NNETERIE

LIMBERT

BOULEVARD

PORTE THIERS

RUE DES TEINTURIERS

LICES

19●

RUE

PORTE LIMBERT

PORTE MAGNANEN

BD SAINT MICHEL

PIERRE

✈ To Airport, Marseilles
and Nice (A7)

especially from Siena, who perfected in Avignon the elegant, courtly, fairy-tale style of painting known as International Gothic. And when he wasn't being outraged, Petrarch wrote incomparable love sonnets to his beloved Laura, a mysterious figure believed to have been an ancestress of the Marquis de Sade.

In 1377, Avignon's population rose to 30,000 souls, a third of them under religious orders. In that year St Catherine of Siena convinced the seventh Avignon pope, Gregory XI, to return to Rome. The pope came, he saw, he sickened, but before he could pack his bags to return to Avignon, he died. The Roman mob seized their chance, and physically forced the cardinals to elect an Italian pope who would re-establish the papacy in Rome. When the French cardinals escaped the Romans' clutches, they sparked off the Great Schism by electing a French anti-pope, Clement VII, and went back to Avignon. A Church council, held in Pisa 30 years later to resolve the conflict, only ended in the election of yet a third pope. In 1403 the French went over to the Rome faction and sent in an army to persuade Avignon's second anti-pope, Benedict XIII, to leave for his native Catalunya— where he spent the rest of his life bitterly raining anathemas and excommunications on all and sundry.

When the Church finally settled on one pope, Avignon and the Comtat Venaissin settled in for three and a half centuries of relaxed rule by cardinal legates, under whom the debauchery and violence continued, although on a more modest level. The party really ended when the Comtat Venaissin was incorporated into France during the Revolution in a blood rite of atrocities and the destruction of centuries of art and architecture.

But even as part of France, Avignon has maintained its lively international character. Publishers who first set up shop with the popes stayed on under the cardinal legates, beyond the bounds of French censorship (there were 20 in town before the Revolution); in the 1850s they took on a new life publishing the works of the Félibrige. In 1946, actor Jean Vilar founded the Avignon Festival of Theatre and Film, the liveliest and most popular event on the entire Provençal calendar.

Getting Around

by air

Avignon's airport is at Caumont, ✆ 90 81 51 15.

by train

The train station is outside the Porte de la République, ✆ 90 82 50 50; Avignon is on the Paris–Marseille TGV line, and has frequent links to Arles, Montpellier, Nîmes, Orange, Toulon and Carcassonne.

by bus

The bus station is also outside the Porte de la République, next to the train station (Blvd St Roch, ✆ 90 82 07 35). Buses go to St-Rémy, Fontaine-de-Vaucluse, the Pont du Gard, Uzès, Châteaurenard, Châteauneuf-du-Pape and Tarascon; for Villeneuve-lès-Avignon take bus No. 10 from the train station.

Travellers of yore always approached Avignon by boat, a thrill still possible on the
tourist excursion boat *Le Cygne* from Beaucaire, ✆ 66 59 35 62, or with a
lunch or dinner cruise on *Le Miréio*, based at Allées de l'Oulle, ✆ 90 85 62 25,
✉ 90 85 61 14; the food is delicious and an afternoon's exploration of Arles is
included in the price. Or spend a week on the Rhône and Saône on the *Princesse
de Provence* (Apr–Nov), ✆ 78 39 13 06.

car and bike hire

Inexpensive car hire firms are **VEO**, 51 Ave Pierre Sémard, ✆ 90 87 53 43, and
Eurorent, 3 Ave Saint Ruf, ✆ 90 86 06 61. Bike hire shops in Avignon include
Dopieralski, 80 Rue Guillaume Puy, ✆ 90 86 32 49; **Richard Masson**, Place
Pie, ✆ 90 82 32 19; and **Transhumance** (for all-terrain and mountain bikes),
✆ 90 95 57 81.

Tourist Information

The helpful office is at 41 Cours Jean Jaurès, ✆ 90 82 65 11, ✉ 90 82 95 03 (open
Mon–Fri 9–1 and 2–6; Sat 9–1 and 2–5; and 10–6 daily during the Festival).

The **post office** is on Cours Président-Kennedy, ✆ 90 86 78 00.

market days

Covered market Tues–Sun at Les Halles in Place Pie; bric-a-brac on Sat in Place
Crillon; flower market Sat morning and flea-market Sun morning in Place des
Carmes; travelling market Sat and Sun morning at Rempart St-Michel.

The Famous Half-Bridge

From the Rhône Avignon is a brave two-tiered sight: in front rise the sheer cliffs of the
Rocher des Doms, inhabited since Neolithic times, and behind it, the sheer man-made
cliffs of the Palais des Papes, the same colour as the rock, and almost as haphazard a pile.
The ensemble includes the **walls** that the popes wrapped around Avignon: bijou, tooth-
some garden walls ever since Viollet-le-Duc re-crenellated them and filled in the moat
in 1860.

From the walls, four arches of a bridge leapfrog into the Rhône, sidle up to a waterbound
Romanesque chapel (dedicated to St Nicholas, the patron of sailors), and then stop
abruptly mid-river, long before reaching Villeneuve-lès-Avignon on the distant bank. This
is the famous **Pont St-Bénézet**, or simply the Pont d'Avignon, begun in 1185 (*open daily
Easter–Sep 9–6.30, Oct–Easter 9–1 and 2–5, closed Mon;* ✆ *90 85 60 16*). It was built
at a time when all bridges were the work of either devils or saints; in this case a shepherd
boy named Bénézet, obeying the mandates of heaven, single-handedly laid the huge foundation stones. Originally 22 arches and half a mile long, the bridge enriched Avignon with
its tolls: its presence was a major factor in the popes' decision to live here. In 1660 the

Avignonais got tired of the constant repairs it demanded, however, and abandoned it to the monsters of the Rhône.

And did they ever '*danse, tout en rond*' on their bridge, as the nursery song would have it? No, the historians say, although they may well have danced *under* it on the mid-river **Ile de la Barthelasse**, formerly a hunting reserve and headquarters for many of Avignon's prostitutes and thieves. It was here that in later years the Avignonais came for Sunday picnics. The Félibres liked to bring pretty 'Félibresses' here to recite poetry. In the summer, people still come to cool off in its Olympic-size pool. Next to the bridge, a new exhibition hall boasts a multivision show in seven languages relating the history of Avignon (*closed Jan–mid-Feb*).

The Palais des Papes

Open daily Apr–Oct 9–7, till 8 in September; Nov–Mar 9–12.45 and 2–6; adm. Last ticket 45 mins before closing time. Optional guided tours in English at 3pm; © 90 27 50 71.

For a curious sensation, park directly under the popes' palace and take the lift up to the traffic-free **Place du Palais**. Once crowded with houses, the square was cleared by anti-pope Benedict XIII to emphasize the message of the Palace's vertical, impregnable walls: 'you would think it was an Asiatic tyrant's citadel rather than the abode of the vicar of the God of peace', wrote Mérimée. But the life of a 14th-century pope justified paranoia. The entrance is up the steps, in the centre of Clement VI's façade.

What is harder to realize is that the life of a 14th-century pope and his cardinals, courtiers, mistresses and toadies, was also extremely luxurious. The palace was spared destruction in the Revolution only to end up serving as a prison and a barracks, and until 1920 its bored residents amused themselves by chipping off frescoes to sell to tourists, so that on most of the walls the only remaining decoration is an extraordinary variety of masons' marks.

Old Palace: Ground Floor

After crossing the **Cour d'Honneur**, the great courtyard dividing Benedict XII's stern Cistercian Palais Vieux (1334–42) and Clement VI's flamboyant Palais Neuf (1342–52), the tour begins in the **Jesus Hall**, so called for its decorative monograms of Christ. Once used to house the pope's treasure and account books, it now contains a hoard of maps, views of old Avignon and curios like a pair of 17th-century bell-ringing figures, or *Jacquemarts*. The most valuable loot would be stored behind walls 3m thick in the windowless bowels of the **Angels' Tower**, its ceiling supported by a single stone pillar like an enormous palm tree.

Next, the **Consistory**, where the cardinals met and received ambassadors; as its lavish frescoes and ceiling burned in 1413, it now displays 19th-century portraits of Avignon's popes and Simone Martini's fresco of the *Virgin of Humility*, detached from the cathedral porch in 1960. Under the fresco, the restorers found Martini's *sinopia*, or initial line sketch etched in the stone. As an artist could only paint a small patch of fresh, wet plaster a day, such *sinopie* were essential to maintain the composition, and these, as is often the case in Italy, give a clearer idea of the painter's intent than the damaged fresco itself. Traces of *sinopie* in situ are in the **Chapelle St-Jean**, dedicated to both Johns, the Baptist and the Evangelist. Matteo Giovannetti of Viterbo, a *trecento* charmer who left the bulk of his work in Avignon, did the frescoes for Clement VI; saints float overhead in starry blue landscapes (recall that at the time ultramarine blue paint was even more expensive than gold). On one wall, John's head is blissfully served to Herod at table, as if in a restaurant.

Old Palace: First Floor

The tour continues to the first floor and the banqueting hall, or **Grand Tinel**, hung with 18th-century Gobelin tapestries. Although big enough for a football pitch, the Grand Tinel was too small to hold all the cardinal-electors who would gather in a conclave ten days after a pope's death. Masons were brought in to accommodate them: the arches on the far end were knocked down to give the cardinals more room to manoeuvre (in both senses of the word), while the doors and windows were bricked up to keep them from bringing in more food and endlessly prolonging the conclave. The trick always worked, for the appetites of the 14th-century Curia were Pantagruelian—the adjacent **Upper Kitchen** boasts a pyramidal chimney that could easily handle a roast elephant, or the menu of Clement VI's coronation feast: 1023 sheep, 118 cattle, 101 calves, 914 kids, 60 pigs, 10,471 hens, 1446 geese, 300 pike, topped off by 46,856 cheeses and 50,000 tarts, all consumed by just 3000 guests—some 16 tarts per person, with a few thousand left over for the pope's midnight snack. Off the Grand Tinel, more delightful frescoes by Matteo Giovannetti decorate the **Chapelle St-Martial**, celebrating the French saint who came from the same Limousin village as Benedict XII.

The New Palace

The tour continues from the Grand Tinel to the pope's **Anti-chamber**, where he would hold private audiences, and continues to the **Pope's Bedroom** in the Tower of Angels, a room covered with murals of spiralling foliage, birds, and birdcages. It leads directly into the New Palace and the most delightful room in the entire palace, the **Chambre du Cerf**, Clement VI's study, where he would come 'to seek the freedom of forgetting he was pope'. In 1343 he had Matteo Giovannetti (probably) lead a group of French painters in depicting outdoor scenes of hunting, fishing, and peach-picking that not only quickened the papal gastric juices, but expressed what was then a revolutionary new interest in the natural world, where flowers and foliage were drawn from observation rather than copying a 'source'.

The arrows direct you next to the **Sacristy**, crowded with statues of kings, queens, and bishops escaped from Gargantua's chessboard, followed by Clement VI's **Great Chapel**, longer even than the Grand Tinel and just as empty, though the altar has recently been reconstructed. The **Robing Room** off the chapel contains casts of the Avignon popes' tombs. Revolutionaries bashed most of the figures that once adorned the elaborate **chapel gate**; through the bay window in front of this, the pope would bless and give indulgences to pilgrims. A grand stair leads down to the flamboyant **Great Audience Hall**, where a band of Matteo Giovannetti's *Prophets* remain intact, along with outline sketches of a *Crucifixion* that would have been splendid if it had ever been completed.

Around the Palace: Notre-Dame-des-Doms

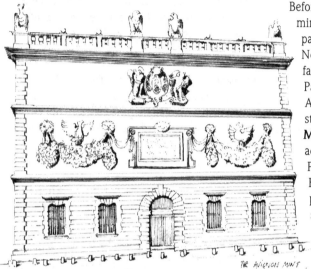

THE AVIGNON MINT

Before spray paint, the posterity-minded had to record their passing with family emblems. None did it better than the family of the Borghese pope, Paul V; his nephew, legate in Avignon, produced the striking 1619 **Hôtel des Monnaies**, or mint, just across from the Palais des Papes, where reliefs of the Borghese dragon and eagle prance in garlands of fruit salad.

To the left of the palace is Avignon's cathedral, **Notre-Dame-des-Doms**, built in 1150, its landmark square bell tower ridiculously dwarfed by a massive gilt statue of the Virgin added in 1859, an unsuccessful attempt to make the church stand out next to the overwhelming papal pile. The interior has been fuzzily Baroqued like a soft-centre chocolate, but it's worth focusing on the good bits: the dome at the crossing, with an octagonal drum pierced with light, the masterpiece of this typically Provençal conceit; the 11th- or 12th-century marble bishop's chair in the choir; and in a chapel next to the sacristy, the flamboyant *Tomb of John XXII* (d. 1334) by English sculptor Hugh Wilfred, mutilated in the Revolution, and restored in the 19th century with a spare effigy of a bishop on top to replace the smashed pope.

Next to the cathedral, ramps lead up to the oasis of the **Rocher-des-Doms**, now a garden enjoying panoramic views from the Rhône below to Mount Ventoux rising on the right. Peacocks squawk and preen in trees so crippled by the mistral they need crutches; you can tell the hour with your own shadow on a sundial called the *cadran solaire annalemmatique*, and admire a statue dedicated to an Armenian refugee named Jean Althen who 'introduced the cultivation of madder to the Midi'.

Musée du Petit Palais

Open 9.30–11.50 and 2–6, closed Tues; adm; © 90 86 44 58.

Overlooking the Rhône at the end of the Place des Papes stands the **Petit Palais**, built in 1318 and modified in 1474 to suit the tastes of Cardinal Legate Giuliano della Rovere—

one day to become Michelangelo's patron and nemesis, as Pope Julius II. In 1958, the Petit Palais became a museum to hold all the medieval works remaining in Avignon.

Although the scale of the Petit Palais can be daunting, it contains rare treats from the dawn of the Renaissance by artists hailing for the most part from Siena or Florence. But Avignon gets its say as well: the sculptures and pretty courtly frescoes from the 12th to the 14th century in the first two rooms demonstrate the city's role in creating and diffusing the late International Gothic style of the early 1400s. The third room contains some fascinating fragments of the 15m, 8-storey **Tomb of Cardinal Jean de Lagrange** (1389), which stood in Avignon's church of St-Martial before the Revolution. One bit that survived was the *transi*, or relief of the decomposing corpse that occupied the lowest level of the tomb and was carved with morbid anatomical exactitude. Such *mementi mori* would soon become popular in northern France, always used to contrast the handsome effigy of the deceased while alive. The mouldering Cardinal Lagrange is one of the earliest, perhaps the prototype of the genre.

The next six rooms glow with the gold backgrounds (the better to show up in dim churches) of 14th- and early 15th-century Italian painting. Nearly all depict the Virgin and Child, a reflection of the cult of Mariolatry and chivalric ideals of womanhood that began where the troubadours left off. Although the subject matter is repetitive, it makes it easy to trace the medieval revolution in art and seeing, back in the good old days when art was content merely to imitate nature and not try to outdo her. The iconic, Byzantine flatness of the earliest paintings (see especially Paolo Veneziano's *Virgin* (1340), remarkably never restored in its 650 years) begins to give way to a more natural depiction of space, composition and human character after the innovations of Giotto in Italy (see especially Taddeo Gaddi, Pseudo Jacopino di Francesco, Lorenzo Monaco, and Gherardo Starnina). Meanwhile, Sienese artists, following the lead of the great Duccio di Buoninsegna, took up a more elegant, stylized line and richer colours (see Simone Martini and the many works by Taddeo di Bartolo).

The taste of Avignon's popes for Sienese art made the latter the strongest influence in the International Gothic style forged at the papal court (room 8), a style which the Sienese kept at long after the Florentines had moved on to new things—see Giovanni di Paolo's *Nativity* (1470), or Pietro di Domenico da Montepulciano's kinky *Vierge de Miséricorde* (1420), a delicate portrayal of a congregation sheltered under the Virgin's mantle, while a band of flagellants whip themselves in robes with custom-cut backs. Bridal chests (*cassoni*) were often used to illustrate cautionary tales for women: in room 9, see Domenico de Michelino's *cassone* panels of 1450 on the story of Suzanna and the Elders.

Renaissance Gems, Sacred and Profane

Beyond the *salon de repos* hangs the museum's best-known work, Botticelli's *Virgin and Child*, a tender, lyrical painting of his youth inspired by his (and Leonardo da Vinci's) master, Verrocchio. The next few rooms offer nothing as striking until room 15 and its four delightful narrative panels from bridal chests (*c.* 1510) by the Maestro dei Cassoni Campana. This unknown master's meticulous, miniaturist style is as rare as the subject of his cautionary tale: *The Minotaur*, beginning with Queen Pasiphae of Crete's love for a white bull, resulting in the birth of the Minotaur. The third panel shows Ariadne, her ball of twine, and Theseus slaying the Minotaur in an exquisite labyrinth of concentric circles.

The sacred equivalent of the *cassoni* is in room 16b: the *Sagra Conversazione* by Venetian Vittore Carpaccio, lyrical master of charm, colour and incidental detail. Such 'sacred conversations' portray the Virgin and saints meditating together on matters sublime, to the accompaniment of angelic music. To this, Carpaccio has added a landscape dominated by a natural rock bridge, where episodes from the lives of SS. Jerome, Augustine and Paul the Hermit take place.

Lastly, rooms 17–19 are devoted to works by French artists in Avignon, who after 1440 formed one of the most important schools of French Renaissance art. Influenced by the realism of Flemish oil painting (introduced to Avignon by Benedict XIII) and the almost abstract, decorative lines of the Italians, it concentrates on strong, simple images, as in the altarpiece *Virgin and Child between two Saints* (1450), by the school's greatest master, Enguerrand Quarton, with a pair of luminous shutters with SS. Michael and Catherine on the reverse by Jossé Lieferinxe. Or take two works by an accomplished but unknown hand: the striking *Jacob's Dream* and the lyrical *Adoration of the Child* (c. 1500), where the well-dressed donor seems to have stumbled unexpectedly onto the divine mystery.

Place de l'Horloge and Quartier des Fusteries

Just below the Place du Palais, an antique carousel spins gaily in the Place de l'Horloge, site of the old Roman forum, now full of buskers and holiday layabouts. The timepiece of its name is in the 1363 tower of the Hôtel de Ville; this originally belonged to a Benedictine monastery on the site, but was secularized with a clock and two **jacque-marts** who sound the hours. They aren't the only archaic figures here: many first-time visitors do a double-take when they notice the windows on the east side of the square filled with *trompe-l'oeil* paintings of historic personages, who all are linked in some way to the city.

Behind the Hôtel de Ville lies the **Quartier des Fusteries**, thus named for the wood merchants and carpenters, who had their workshops here in the Middle Ages, which were replaced in the 18th century with *hôtels*: in one, the **Maison aux Ballons** (with little iron balloons on the window sills) at 18 Rue St-Etienne, Joseph de Montgolfier discovered the principle of balloon flight in 1782 when he noticed how his shirt, drying by the fire, puffed up and floated in the hot air. From the Quartier des Fusteries, the steep picturesque lanes of the **Quartier de la Balance** wind back up to the Place des Papes.

Off Place de l'Horloge and Rue St-Agricol, Rue du Collège-du-Roure leads to the fine mid-15th-century **Palais du Roure**, marked by a flamboyant gate topped by intertwining mulberry branches in memory of the Taverne de Mûrier that it replaced. Equally flamboyant was the 19th-century descendant of the Florentine family who built it, the Félibre poet Marquis Baroncelli-Javon, who preferred to spend his time as a cowboy in the Camargue and lent this town-house to Mistral as a headquarters for his Provençal-language journal *Aïoli*. It now houses a study centre and exhibits on the language (℗ 90 80 80 88, *free guided tours Tues at 3pm)*. Rue St-Agricol is named after the recently restored Gothic church of **St-Agricol** (1326); its treasure is the *Doni Retable*, a rare Provençal work from the Renaissance. At No. 19 is the **Librairie Roumanille**, founded in 1855 by the Avignon poet Joseph Roumanille, father of the Félibrige (*see* p.55). The bookshop published the movement's first masterpiece, Mistral's epic *Miréio* (1859) and continues to put out books in Provençal, while Avignon's literati chum around in the shop's atmospheric 19th-century salon.

Museums: Vouland, Calvet, Requien, Lapidaire and Mont de Piété

At the end of Rue St-Agricol curves Rue Joseph-Vernet, lined with 18th-century *hôtels*, antique shops, pricey restaurants and cafés. The kind of overly ornate, spindly furniture, porcelains, and knick-knacks that originally embellished these mansions is on display nearby in Rue Victor Hugo's **Musée Louis Vouland** (*open June–Sept 10–12 and 2–6, otherwise 2–6, closed Sun and Mon;* ℗ *90 86 03 79*).

More exciting are the contents of the handsome Hôtel de Villeneuve-Martignan, at 65 Rue Joseph-Vernet, first opened to the public as a 'cabinet of curiosities' in the late 1700s by collector Esprit Calvet. Now the **Musée Calvet** (*open 10–12 and 2–6, closed Tues; adm;* ℗ *90 86 33 84*), it offers something for every taste: 6000 pieces of wrought iron, Greek sculpture, 18th-century seascapes by Avignon native Joseph Vernet and paintings of ruins by Hubert Robert and Panini, mummies, a portrait of Diane de Baroncelli (grandmother of the Marquis de Sade), a bust of a boy by Renaissance sculptor Desiderio da Settignano, tapestries, prehistoric statue-steles, dizzy kitsch paintings of nude men (David's *Mort de Barra* and Horace Vernet's *Mazeppa and the Wolves*), as well as an excellent collection of 19th- and 20th-century paintings by Corot, Guigou, Soutine, Daumier, Dufy, Morisot, Utrillo, Seurat, Toulouse-Lautrec, Vlaminck, and Rouault. At the time of writing, the museum is undergoing a major restoration, and is due to reopen in June 1996. Although the clean-up may well destroy its delightful faded charm, it may save some of the exhibits: one Egyptian mummy began to stink so badly in 1985 that it had to be buried in the local cemetery.

Adjacent to the Calvet museum, the **Musée Requien** is Avignon's fuddy-duddy natural history collection (*open Tues–Sat 9–12 and 2–6;* ℗ *90 82 43 51*) where a 81lb beaver found in the Sorgue steals the show. Lastly, at 27 Rue de la République, in the chilly 17th-century chapel of a Jesuit College, are the sculptures of the **Musée Lapidaire** (*open 10–12 and 2–6, closed Tues;* ℗ *90 85 75 38*). It's worth popping in for the 2nd-century BC (or Merovingian) man-eating *Tarasque de Noves*, each hand gripping the head of a Gaul, while an arm dangles from its greedy jaws; or for its statues of Gallic warriors, looking much nattier in their mail than Asterix; or for the unlabelled masks in petal-like hoods. There is good Renaissance sculpture as well, but the best is in the nearby church of **St-Didier** (1359), just to the north in Place St-Didier: Francesco Laurana's polychrome **reredos** of Christ bearing the Cross, called *Notre-Dame du Spasme* for the spasm of pain on Mary's face; it was one of the first Renaissance sculptures to reach France, executed for

Good King René in 1478. Opposite, in the first chapel on the left, are Florentine frescoes c. 1360, uncovered in 1952. More 14th-century frescoes have recently been restored opposite the church in the **Livrée de Ceccano**, now the town library. The **Musée du Mont de Piété**, 6 Rue Saluces, © 90 86 53 12 (*open Mon to Fri, 8.30–11.30 and 1.30–5.30*), the oldest pawnbroker's in France, now houses not only the town archives, but the *conditions des soies*, or silk conditioning, once the wealth of Avignon.

The Eastern Quarters

From Place St-Didier, Rue du Roi René is lined with chiselled palaces, one built on the site of the church of Ste-Claire (No. 22) where Petrarch first saw his Laura on Good Friday 1327. ('It was the day when the sun darkened, as God/Himself vanished into death, when I was taken,' he wrote). Laura died, probably of the plague, in 1348, and was buried nearby in the Franciscan **Couvent des Cordeliers**, by the corner of Rue des Lices and Rue des Teinturiers; only the Gothic bell tower survived the fury of the Revolution. In 1533, a humanist from Lyon claimed to have found her tomb in the church, and such was Petrarch's reputation that François I made a special trip to Avignon to see it.

Rue des Teinturiers, the most picturesque street in Avignon, was named after the dyers and textile-makers who powered their machines on water-wheels in the Sorgue, two of which survive. Shaded by ancient plane trees, crossed by little bridges, it is a pleasant place to dawdle over a beer or dinner; it's hard to believe this Sorgue is the same stream that comes bursting like a bomb out of that other Petrarchan shrine, the Fontaine de Vaucluse.

Rue des Teinturiers turns into Rue Bonneterie on its way to Avignon's shopping district and Place Pie, home of the ugly-duckling new **market**, although the produce inside is fit for a swan. Another evocative street, Rue Vieux Sextière, once the site of the Jewish Ghetto, is the address of Avignon's 19th-century synagogue, while just beyond Place Carnot, **St-Pierre**'s flamboyant façade boasts a set of beautifully carved walnut doors (1551). Facing St-Pierre, Avignon's cosiest museum, **Musée Aubanel** (*private, free visits on request,* © *90 82 95 54*) is dedicated to printing in Avignon, and to the romantic poet and Félibre Théodore Aubanel, whose family still owns one of Avignon's oldest publishing houses.

From Place St-Pierre, Rue Carnot continues to another charming square, the Place des Carmes, dominated by the 14th-century **L'Eglise des Carmes,** or White Friars', Avignon's biggest church, with a pretty cloister refurbished as a Festival venue. Visitors in the last century would continue from here along Rue Carreterie, out of the city gate and down the Lyon road to the **Cimetière St-Véran**, a romantic, shady park where John Stuart Mill and his wife Harriet are buried. Harriet died at the Hôtel d'Europe in 1858, a loss so devastating for the philosopher of utilitarianism that he lived in a house by the cemetery until he himself died in 1873. Another celebrated tomb belongs to Maurille de Sombreuil, who became a heroine during the Revolution when, to save the life of her father, the governor of the Invalides, she drank a goblet of human blood. Contemporaries noted that she always ordered white wine with her meals after that.

In 1947 Jean Vilar with his Théâtre National Populaire founded the **Avignon Festival**, with the aim of bringing theatre to the masses. It is now rated among the top international theatre festivals in Europe, and Avignon overflows in July and August with performances by the Théâtre National in the Palais des Papes, and others throughout the city; the cinemas host films from all over the world, and churches are used for concerts (the **Maison Jean Vilar**, 8 Rue de Mons, ☏ 90 86 59 64, is the nerve centre and hosts exhibitions, films, and lectures the rest of the year). For festival bookings and information contact the **Bureau du Festival d'Avignon**, 8 bis Rue de Mons, Avignon 84000, ☏ 90 82 67 08. During the festival Avignon's squares and streets overflow with fringe (or 'Off') performers. To receive the Off programme, send a stamped envelope, with 11.50F, to Avignon Public Off, BP5 75521 Paris cedex 11, or call ☏ (1) 48 05 20 97. Otherwise, there seems to be some sort of festivity every month, whether horses are your passion (the *Cheval Passion*, January), Baroque art (April), a Triathlon (May) or of course fireworks on 14 July. The fortnightly broadsheet *Rendez–Vous*, from the tourist office, is an exhaustive map of what exactly's going on.

Shopping

Pâtisseries, especially around Rue Joseph Vernet, sell Avignon's gourmand speciality, *papalines*, made of fine chocolate and a liqueur, *d'Origan du Comtat*, distilled from 60 herbs picked from the slopes of Mont Ventoux, and said to be a sure cure for cholera. You will find all the regional specialities: *fruits confits d'Apt*, *berlingots de Carpentras*, *melon de Cavaillon*, *nougat de Sault*, *truffe de Carpentras et du Tricastin*, garlic, olives, honey, pastis, goat's cheese, *fougasse*, and the omnipresent *herbes de Provence*. If you're not going to Aix, don't fail to buy some delicious diamond-shaped almond *calissons d'Aix* here. Also there are essential oils, *santons*, bold Provençal fabrics, local pottery and soaps. Behind the Hôtel de Ville in Place des Puits-de-Boeufs, the **Maison des Pays de Vaucluse**, ☏ 90 85 55 24, has a large display of regional products and crafts, but best of all is to browse and discover more yourself at the markets (*see* p.79).

Avignon ✉ 84000   **Where to Stay**

Avignon's **hotel-finding/reservation service** is at Place Campana, ☏ 90 82 05 81, 🖷 90 86 54 77, though even that may fail you in July and August, when it's imperative to book ahead. Also note there are many other choices across the river in Villeneuve. Oldest and still classically formal with its Louis XV furnishings, the ★★★★**Hôtel d'Europe**, 12 Place Crillon, ☏ 90 82 66 92, 🖷 90 85 43 66, was built in the 1500s, and converted to an inn in the late 1700s. Napoleon stayed here, as did the eloping Browning and Barrett. Avignon's newest hotel, ★★★★**Cloître Saint-Louis**, is just within the walls near the station, at 20 Rue du Portail Boquier, ✆ 90 27 55 55, ◉ 90 82 24 01. Built in 1589 as part of the Jesuit school of theology, the beautiful cloister is an island of tranquillity. Rooms are austerely modern; meals are served under the portico or by the rooftop swimming pool. **★★Palais des Papes**, 1 Rue Gérard Philipe, ✆ 90 86 04 13, ◉ 90 27 91 17, has the best views of the Palace, modern soundproofed rooms and air conditioning; or for even more quiet, the 16th-century **★★La Ferme Jamet**, Chemin de Rhodes on the Ile de la Barthelasse (off Pont Daladier), ✆ 90 86 16 74, ◉ 90 86 17 72, has rooms ranging from traditional Provençal in style to a gypsy caravan, around tennis courts and a swimming pool. Cheaper bets include the bright and charming **★Mignon**, 12 Rue Joseph Vernet, ✆ 90 82 17 30, ◉ 90 85 78 46, with small but modernized rooms; the friendly **★★Hôtel d'Angleterre**, 29 Blvd Raspail, ✆ 90 86 34 31, ◉ 90 86 86 74 (*closed Jan*); and the quieter **★★Saint-Roch**, with a delightful garden just outside the walls of Porte St-Roch at 9 Rue Mérindol, ✆ 90 82 18 63, ◉ 90 82 78 30. The **★Innova**, near the station at 100 Rue Joseph Vernet, ✆ 90 82 54 10, ◉ 90 82 52 39, is run by a jolly family with a dog, cat, and two canaries in tow. The hotel **★Splendid** isn't, but it is cheap: 17 Rue A. Perdiguier, ✆ 90 86 14 46. Otherwise, Ile de la Barthelasse has four **camping sites**, one of which, **La Bagatelle**, ✆ 90 86 30 39, ◉ 90 27 16 23, has dormitory rooms in the summer.

Eating Out

Avignon's gourmet bastion for the past 60 years, **Hiély**, 5 Rue de la République, ✆ 90 86 17 07, ◉ 90 86 32 38, is a resolutely old-fashioned place, with a first-floor dining room. The kitchen refuses to conform to any label, but never disappoints with its *tourte* of quail and *foie gras*, a legendary *cassoulet des moules aux épinards* and for dessert, *pudding aux fruits à la crème vanille*, accompanied by carafes of Châteauneuf-du-Pape or Tavel; menus 195–300F. Its less expensive sister restaurant, **La Fourchette** at 17 Rue Racine, ✆ 90 85 20 93, ◉ 90 85 57 60, serves as good for less, with menus from 100F; a choice of 12 desserts and wine by the carafe. **Le Bain Marie**, at 5 Rue Pétramale, ✆ 90 85 21 37, serves traditional French fare from 140F, and is popular for its reasonably priced and good food. **Entrée des Artistes** has the added advantage of its location in quiet Place des Carmes, ✆ 90 82 46 90; menus 78 and 115F. **Le Petit Bedon**, 70 Rue Joseph-Vernet, ✆ 90 82 33 98, is quickly becoming an Avignon institution for well-prepared dishes seldom found elsewhere, like *lotte au Gigondas*, angler-fish cooked in wine (lunch menu 100F, more in the evening). For under 100F there's **Le Forum**, 20 Place de l'Horloge, ✆ 90 82 43 17, with more traditional French food, or **Le Tournesol**, at 64 Rue Bonneterie, ✆ 90 14 00 31, for Polynesian dishes starting at only 45F; or go global with a feast of 'world cuisine' and live music at **Woolloomoolloo,** 16 bis Rue des Teinturiers, ✆ 90 85 28 44. For lunch, pop into **Restaurant Nani** on Rue Aubanel just down from the tourist office, ✆ 90 82 60 90; salads and rosé for less than 70F. Chocolate, cake and ice cream *gourmands* should not miss Avignon's number one dessert emporium, **Le Restaurant de Desserts**, 11/13 Rue de la Balance, ✆ 90 82 32 10. The menu offers...just desserts.

Around Avignon

If your pockets are deep enough, in easy driving distance of Avignon are three exceptional hotel/restaurants: ★★★**Ermitage-Meissonnier**, 30 Ave de Verdun, 30133 Les Angles (4km west on D 900), ✆ 90 25 41 68, ✆ 90 25 11 68, which has 16 luxurious rooms and a glorious restaurant specializing in Provençal cuisine of the highest order—even the tomatoes taste better here, especially in the lovely garden (menus 140–450F); ★★★**Auberge de Cassagne**, 450 Allée de Cassagne, 84130 Le Pontet, 5km north on the N 7, ✆ 90 31 04 18, ✆ 90 32 25 09, which has a pool, tennis courts, and access to a golf course; the food (fillet of red mullet with lime, followed by pear *croquant* in bitter chocolate) and wine cellar are perfect (menus 220–380F); and 5km east, on the N 107 (follow the Ave d'Avignon), ★★★★**Le Jardin des Frênes**, 645 Ave les Vertes-Rives, 84140 Montfavet, ✆ 90 31 17 93, ✆ 90 23 95 03, which is a Relais et Châteaux member, its buildings set around a beautiful garden and pool; antiques furnish the rooms. Half-board mandatory in season, but the food, with imaginative delights like salmon with truffles in a sweet and sour sauce, is as marvellous as the setting; lunch menus from 250F.

Entertainment and Nightlife

Outside July and August, Avignon's best source of information on cultural events is the **Centre d'Action Culturelle**, Hôtel de Brantes, 2 Rue Petit Fusterie, ✆ 90 80 80 11. Try to take in a performance by one of Provence's most talented theatre companies, **Le Chêne Noir**, 8 Rue Ste-Catherine, whose range covers the classics to the avant-garde (✆ 90 86 58 11). The same theatre is also the home of the jazz club **AJMI**, ✆ 90 86 08 61, featuring live music every Thursday at 9pm (membership cards available at the door). Avignon's oldest permanent company, the **Théâtre des Carmes**, performs in the restored Gothic cloister of the Eglise des Carmes (HQ at 6 Place des Carmes, ✆ 90 82 20 47). Quality old and new films in their original language are shown at the **Cinemas Utopia** at 4 Rue Excalier Ste Anne and 5 Rue Figuière, ✆ 90 82 65 36 for both.

The young come even from Arles and Nîmes for the nightlife here. The more spontaneous is concentrated in the bars in the southeast corner of town, especially around Place des Corps Saints and Rue des Teinturiers. There are three more cinemas: **Pathé Palace**, 38 Cours Jean Jaurés, ✆ 36 68 20 22; **Capitole**, 3 Rue Pourquery de Boisserin, ✆ 90 82 24 27; and **Cinevox** at 22 Place de l'Horloge, ✆ 90 82 03 61. For rock and zebras head to **Pub Z** at 58 Rue Bonneterie, ✆ 90 85 42 84, and its bar decked out in black and white stripes. Go to **Club 5/5** at Porte St Roch, ✆ 90 82 61 32, or the **Ambassy Club**, 27 Rue Bancasse, ✆ 90 86 31 55, if you want to strut your stuff. Check your *Rendez-Vous*.

In 586, on Puy Andaon, the rock that dominates Villeneuve-lès-Avignon, Casarie, a Visigoth princess-hermit, died in the odour of sanctity (a smell like crushed violets, apparently). In the 10th century, Benedictines built the abbey of St-André to shelter her bones and lodge pilgrims on the route to Compostela. St-André soon became one of the mightiest monasteries in the south of France, and in 1226, when Louis VIII besieged pro-Albigensian Avignon, the abbot offered the king co-sovereignty of the abbey in exchange for royal privileges. And so what was once an abbey town became a frontier fortress of the king of France, a new town (*ville neuve*) and a heavily fortified one, in case the pope over the river should start feeling frisky.

But Villeneuve was soon invaded in another way; wanton, squalid Avignon didn't suit all tastes, and the pope gave permission to his cardinals who liked it not-so-hot to retreat across the Rhône into princely *livrées cardinalices* (or palaces 'freed' from their original owners by the Curia). Though a dormitory suburb these days, Villeneuve still maintains a separate peace amongst its villas, well-fed cats snoozing in the sun, leisurely afternoons at the *pétanque* court and some amazing works of art.

Getting Around and Tourist Information

From Avignon, bus No. 10 runs every half-hour from the train station or Porte de l'Oulle to Villeneuve. Place Charles-David is the best place to park and has the Tourist Information as well, © 90 25 61 55, ✆ 90 25 91 55. Note that everything is closed Tues and in February.

market day

Thursday morning on Place Charles-David

Around Town

When Philip the Fair ratified the deal that made Villeneuve royal property, he ordered a citadel to be built on the approach to Pont St-Bénézet and be named after guess who. As times grew more perilous, this **Tour Philippe-le-Bel** (*open Oct–Mar 10–12 and 2–5; Apr–Sept 10–12.30 and 3–7.30; closed Tues and in Feb; © 90 27 49 68*) was made higher to keep out the riff-raff, and now offers splendid views of Avignon, Mont Ventoux and on a clear day, the Alpilles.

From here, Montée de la Tour leads up to the 14th-century **Collégiale Notre-Dame**, once the chapel of a *livrée* and now Villeneuve's parish church. From Villeneuve's Chartreuse (Charterhouse) it has inherited an elaborate marble altar of 1745, but the church's most famous work, a beaming, swivel-hipped, polychrome ivory statue of the Virgin carved in Paris out of an elephant's tusk *c.* 1320, has been removed to safer quarters in the nearby **Musée Pierre-de-Luxembourg** (*same hours as Tour Philippe-le-Bel; adm; © 90 25 42 03*), housed in yet another *livrée*.

The museum's other prize is the masterpiece of the Avignon school: Enguerrand Quarton's 1454 *Couronnement de la Vierge*, one of the greatest works of 15th-century French painting, commissioned for the Charterhouse (*see* below). Unusually, it portrays God the Father and God the Son as twins, clothed in sumptuous crimson and gold, like the Virgin herself, whose fine sculptural features were perhaps inspired by the ivory Virgin. Around these central figures the painting evokes the spiritual route travelled by the Carthusians through vigilant prayer, to purify the world and reconcile it to God. St Bruno, founder of the Order, saints, kings, and commoners are present, hierarchically arranged, while the landscape encompasses heaven, hell, Rome and Jerusalem, and local touches like Mont Ste-Victoire and the cliffs of the Estaque.

Other notable works in the museum include a curious 14th-century *double-faced Virgin*, the 'Eve' face evoking original sin and the 'Mary' face human redemption; Simon de Châlon's 1552 *Entombment*; and amid the uninspired 17th-century fluff, Philippe de Champaigne's *Visitation*.

La Chartreuse and Fort St-André

From the museum, take Rue de la République up to No. 53, the **Livrée de la Thurroye**, the best-preserved in Villeneuve; a cardinal would maintain a household of a 100 or so people here. Further up the street and up the scale stands one of the largest charterhouses in France, the **Chartreuse du Val-de-Bénédiction** (*open Apr–Sept 9–6.30; Oct–Mar 9.30–5.30; adm*). This began as the *livrée* of Etienne Aubert who, upon his election to the papacy in 1352 as Innocent VI, deeded his palace to the Carthusians for a monastery. For 450 years it was built and rebuilt, granted immense estates on either side of the Rhône by kings and popes, and in general lived rather high, even by Carthusian standards. In 1792, the Revolution forced the monks out, and the Charterhouse was sold in 17 lots; squatters took over the cells and outsiders feared to enter the cloisters after dark. Now mostly re-purchased and restored, the buildings house the Centre International de Recherche de Création et d'Animation (CIRCA), devoted to a wide variety of arts, especially audio-visual and newer technologies; it hosts workshops, seminars, and exhibitions, both during the Avignon festival and at other times (℃ 90 25 05 46).

Still, the sensation that lingers in the Charterhouse is one of vast silences and austerity, the hallmark of an order where conversation was limited (originally) to one hour a week; monks who disobeyed the rule of prayer, work, and silence ended up in the prison cells around the Great Cloister. Much of the art that once adorned the community buildings is now in the museum (*see* above), with the exception of 14th-century frescoes by Matteo Giovannetti and his school in the refectory chapel. In the church, the star attraction is **Innocent VI's tomb**, with an alabaster effigy under a fine Gothic baldachin. A hundred years ago this tomb was used as a rabbit hutch. Popes who took the name Innocent have tended to suffer similar posthumous indignities: the great Innocent III was found stark naked in Perugia cathedral, a victim of poisoned slippers, while the corpse of Innocent X— the last of the series—was dumped in a tool-shed in St Peter's.

Gazing down into the Charterhouse from the summit of Puy Andaon are the formidable bleached walls of **Fort St-André** (*open Oct–Mar 10–12 and 2–5, Apr–Sep 9.30–12.30* *and 2–6.30; adm;* ℰ *90 25 45 35*), built around the old abbey in the 1360s, the heyday of the *Grandes Compagnies* (bands of unemployed mercenaries, who pillaged the country-side and held towns to ransom). The fort's stout round towers afford a famous vantage point over Avignon; the southwestern tower is called the Tour des Masques (sorcerers' tower), although no one seems to remember why. Jumbly ruins are all that remain of the splendid abbey of St-André, amid Italian gardens and writhing olives.

Villeneuve ✉ *30400*   **Where to Stay and Eating Out**

 Villeneuve makes an attractive and quieter alternative to Avignon, and has some notable lodgings in its own right. The exquisite ★★★★**Le Prieuré**, centrally located in Place du Chapître, ℰ 90 25 18 20, ✆ 90 25 45 29, gives you the option of sleeping in the 16th-century priory, where the rooms are furnished with antiques, or in the more comfort-able annex by the swimming-pool; gardens, tennis, and a remarkable restaurant that does delightful things with seafood and truffles—gourmet lunch menus at 195F (*closed Nov–10 Mar*). At ★★★**La Magnaneraie**, 37 Rue Camp-de-Bataille, ℰ 90 25 11 11, ✆ 90 25 46 37, you can choose between the old-fashioned rooms in a former silkworm nursery, or another modern annex; it too has been endowed with a pool, gardens, and Le Prieuré's rival for the best restaurant in town (menus 170F and up). For a less expensive sojourn into history, there's the 16th-century ★★**L'Atelier**, 5 Rue de la Foire, ℰ 90 25 01 84, ✆ 90 25 80 06, with a walled garden in the centre of town, or the 17th-century ★★**Résidence Les Cèdres**, 39 Blvd Pasteur, ℰ 90 25 43 92, ✆ 90 25 14 66, named after the ancient cedars that surround it, with a pool and a bungalow annex (*closed Nov–Mar*). Top budget choices include: ★**Beauséjour**, 61 Ave Gabriel Péri, ℰ 90 25 20 56, or the **Hostel YMCA**, by the river at 7 bis Chemin de la Justice, ℰ 90 25 46 20, with views of the Rhône and a pool to boot (*closed Nov–Mar*). For a reasonably priced meal, try **La Mamma**, in central Place Victor Bosch, ℰ 90 25 00 71, or **Restaurant La Maison**, 1 Rue Montée du Fort St. André, ℰ 90 25 20 81, where a meal will cost less than 100F.

To the north in Roquemaure (✉ 30150), large gardens, old-fashioned rooms and delicious food combine to make a restful stay in the 18th-century ★★★**Château de Cubières**, on the Route d'Avignon, ℰ 66 82 64 28 (*closed mid-Nov–mid-Mar*).

Around Villeneuve, Through Rosé-coloured Glasses

Once you cross the Rhône into the Gard, the land takes on a more arid and austere profile, its knobby limestone hills and cliffs softened by crowns of silver olives and the green pin-stripes of vines, especially in the river bend north of Villeneuve along the D 976. The landmark here is **Roquemaure**, where Pope Clement V died his peculiar death (*see* p.57) in its ruined castle, although it's not his ghost who haunts it, but that of a lovely but leprous queen who was quarantined in the tower. After she died, Rhône boatmen would see her on summer nights, flitting freely along the bank, dressed in white and sparkling with jewels. The D 976 continues west to the little village of **Tavel**, a place just as haunted—by wine fiends slaking their thirst on the pale ruby blood of the earth.

Tavel and Lirac

The sun-soaked, limestone pebbly hills on the right bank of the Rhône are as celebrated for their rosés as Châteauneuf-du-Pape is for its reds and whites. Tavel has the longest pedigree, a wine beloved of kings since the 13th century, when Philippe le Bel declared: 'It isn't good wine unless it's Tavel'. By the 1930s, the vine stocks—grenache, cinsault, bourboulenc, carignan and red clairette—were so old that Tavel nearly went the way of the dodo. Since revived to the tune of 825 healthy hectares, the French have once again crowned it as king of the rosés, the universal, harmonious summer wine that goes with everything from red meat to seafood.

Be warned, however, that Tavel may be a little strong in alcohol to less acclimatized, non-French constitutions. Some growers add syrah and mourvèdre to give their Tavels extra body and colour, including the two best-known producers in the village, whom you can visit by ringing ahead: the de Bez family at the **Château d'Aquéria**, © 66 50 04 56, ✉ 66 50 18 46, and the prize-winning **Domaine de la Mordorée**, © 66 50 00 75, ✉ 66 50 47 39, where the talented Christophe Delorme also bottles a potent red Côtes-du-Rhône, Lirac, and Châteauneuf-du-Pape.

The Lirac district begins 3km to the north of Tavel and encompasses four communes—Roquemaure, Lirac, St-Laurent-des-Arbres and St-Geniès-de-Comolas. Its pebbly hills are similar to Tavel, and the *appellation* differs in the addition of two grape varieties—white ugni and maccabéo, and the fact that everything doesn't come up rosé: Lirac is making a name for its fruity whites, with a fragrance reminiscent of the wildflowers of the nearby *garrigue*, and for its well-structured reds. Both '93 and '94 were fine years and can be sampled weekdays at **Domaine Duseigneur** at St-Laurent-des-Arbres, © 66 50 02 57, ✉ 66 50 43 57, and at **Château St-Roch** in Roquemaure, © 66 82 82 59, ✉ 66 82 83 00.

Between Avignon and Tarascon: La Montagnette

South of Avignon the Rhône curves to accommodate La Montagnette, a white mini-mountain sliced with valleys of market gardens and orchards of almonds and apricots, protected from the huffing and puffing of the mistral by hedgerows and poplars. Dominating this bijou landscape, **Barbentane** is a refined old town that so loved its *farandole* that a man who could not dance it would not be considered a fit husband. It is still defended by the 14th-century **Tour Angelica**, its medieval gates, and the arcaded **Maison des Chevaliers**, a lovely souvenir of the Renaissance. The **Château** (*open July–Sept, 10–12 and 2–6, closed Weds, other times Sun only; adm;* © *90 95 51 07*), built in 1674 by the Marquis de Barbentane, the king's ambassador to Tuscany, would not look out of place in the Ile de France: the furnishings are Louis XV and Louis XVI but the builder's acquired Italian taste permeates the other decoration. The enormous plane trees in the garden were brought over from Turkey by an earlier marquis in the 1670s.

East of Barbentane, **Châteaurenard** is one of Provence's main wholesale fruit and vegetable markets, lording over a plain known as La Petite Crau, although it looks nothing like the rocky waste of the 'big' Crau (*see* p.123). Two proud towers on its hill survive from its castle. This castle was first owned by Reinardus, a friend and ally of Charles Martel, who was killed below its walls fighting the Saracens; his wife Emma took over the command and fought bravely before dying of a broken heart, and her ghost haunts the **Tour de Griffon**. This now offers a little museum as well as great views over the Lubéron and Alpilles (*open 10–12 and 2–6, closed Jan and Feb*).

On the D 35 south of Barbentane, **Boulbon** was known as Bourbon until 1792, when the guillotine cut into the name's popularity. Still defended by 10th-century walls built into and onto the rocky escarpment overlooking the Rhône, Boulbon is best known for its unique 1 June *cérémonie du St-Vinage*, in honour of its patron saint Marcellin: the men of the village each bring a full bottle of wine to the saint's Romanesque chapel and hear the gospel in Provençal, after which the wine is blessed and God is toasted with a mighty swig. The bottle is then corked and for the rest of the year the blessed wine is used as a sovereign remedy for grave illnesses.

If you leave Barbentane by the D 35E, you'll arrive at the **Abbaye St-Michel-de-Frigolet**, founded around the year 1000 in the sheltered centre of La Montagnette (*guided tours 2.30 Mon to Sat, 4 Sun*). The word Frigolet comes from the Provençal *férigoulo*, or thyme, a healthy, invigorating herb, for here the monks of Montmajour (*see* p.110), enervated by the swamps, came for a cure—some of it in the form of a liqueur called *Le Frigolet*, on sale at the monastery. In 1632, Anne of Austria, barren after 20 years of marriage, came here to the Romanesque chapel of the Conception Immaculée to pray for a son, and soon after gave the world Louis XIV. In gratitude the queen sent the sumptuous gilt *boiseries* that frame 14 turgid Mignards. Another celebrity to pass

ABBAYE ST. MICHEL DE FRIGOLET

through was the young Frédéric Mistral, who attended an improvised school here, where lessons were bartered for food; the stories and customs of these hills were to be a great source of inspiration in his writings.

In 1830, Mistral was born in **Maillane**, just to the east, and spent as much time as possible there until he died in 1914. It's been sensibly bypassed by the main routes, and is still very pretty, but despite its quaintness it feels like a lived-in village. The house the master Félibre had built after 1876 is now the **Musée Mistral**, ✆ 90 95 74 06 (don't mistake it for the rotting concrete *Centre F. Mistral*, which is something else). It is preserved as it was the day he died in 1914, 'as sympathetic and as cosy as a coffin' as James Pope-Hennessy described it. You won't be allowed in until the tour begins, on the hour; your guide is a sinewy cockerel of a man whose high-speed spiel won't be stopped. If you do interrupt, he will forget where he is and have to start from the beginning again. No concessions if you only speak English (*closed Mon and for lunch*). Mistral's tomb, in the ghastly, gravelly graveyard over the road, is modelled after the Pavillon de la Reine Jeanne at Les Baux, and decorated with a seven-pointed star and other Félibre symbols. If you can, leave Maillane southwards by the D27, over beautiful fields and streams.

Where to Stay and Eating Out

Barbentane (✉ 13570)

★★Castel Mouisson, at the foot of the Montagnette in Quartier Castel Mouisson, ✆ 90 95 51 17, is a typical Provençal hotel, with a pool and tennis (*closed mid-Oct–Mar*), while in the centre, **★St-Jean**, 1 le Cours, ✆ 90 95 50 44, is open all year, has decent rooms from 180F, and a restaurant with a good menu.

At **St-Michel-de-Frigolet**, the Prémontrés monks run a hostel with 38 rooms for guaranteed quiet retreats for a day or two or even a month; write to the Service Hostellerie, Abbaye St-Michel-de-Frigolet, 13150 Tarascon, or call ✆ 90 95 70 07 between 9 and 11am, or ✆ 90 95 75 22.

Tarascon

Few towns in the south of France are as determinedly unglamorous as Tarascon. Most of the houses are not only unrestored but cry out for a lick of paint; garages outnumber craft shops; even the poodles look like real dogs instead of topiary hedges. Meanwhile the rival fairy-tale castles of Tarascon and Beaucaire muse at each other across the Rhône like the embodiments of a bi-communal Walter Mitty daydream, reminders of heroism, romance, international markets, man-eating monsters, and Alphonse Daudet's buffoonish anti-hero Tartarin, who never told a lie but, under the hot sun, was prone to imagine things. Provençal nationalists accuse Daudet (a native of Nîmes) of creating a stereotype that only heightened Paris's already smug attitude towards the Midi, to which Daudet replied that 'All Frenchmen have in them a touch of Tarascon'.

Nearly every east–west **train** from Provence to Languedoc stops in Tarascon (✆ 90 91 59 06). **Buses** run regularly between Beaucaire, Tarascon, and Avignon; other lines, from Tarascon's station, go to Arles, Boulbon, Nîmes, St-Rémy and Cavaillon.

Bike hire in Tarascon: **Cycles Christophe**, 70 Blvd Itam, ✆ 90 91 25 85, and **Motobécane**, 1 Rue E. Pelletan, ✆ 90 91 42 32.

59 Rue des Halles, ✆ 90 91 03 52

Tarascon and St Martha

All centuries have quirks that seem quaint to later generations: tulip-bulb speculation in the 18th, ladies' bustles in the 19th, muzak in the 20th. In the 11th and 12th centuries, it was a mania for the bodily parts of saints, a fad so passionate that a sure candidate for the inner circle, such as St Francis, had bodyguards from Assisi in his dying days to prevent rival towns from kidnapping him. If it had no fresh relics, every town with a saintly legend attached to it began digging for bones; and in Tarascon, *voilà*, in 1187 they just happened to stumble across the relics of St Martha. The pious 9th-century legend told how she found Tarascon bedevilled by a Tarasque, a man-eating amphibian whose ancestors are portrayed in Celtic sculpture chomping on human heads. Martha neatly tidied away the monster by showing it a Cross, lassoing it with her girdle, then ordering it to the bottom of the Rhône, never to return.

The new-found relics attracted so many pilgrims that the 12th-century **Collégiale Ste-Marthe** was enlarged in the 13th and 16th centuries into a curious Romanesque/Gothic hybrid. The church was badly bombed in the Second World War, but even worse mischief had been done earlier in the Revolution, when the great south portal of 1197 was shorn of its sculptures. Nowadays the chapels of the attractive five-aisled Gothic nave are filled with the lukewarm efforts of Mignard and Parrocel, masters of the Baroque fruitcake style, while in the crypt (part of the original 1197 church) there's a king-sized statue of Martha from 1400 and the slightly later and much more refined *effigy of Jean de Cossa*, Seneschal of Provence, attributed to Francesco Laurana.

The Château du Roi René

Open 9–7 summer, 9–12 and 2–5 winter; adm; ✆ 90 91 01 93.

Rooted in a limestone rock over the Rhône, Tarascon's château gleams like white satin between the sun and water, a storybook feudal castle with crenellations and moat, named after the one character in Tarascon's history actually rounded out in flesh and blood. Good King René earned the 'Good' in his name for his good appetite and fondness for the good things of life, as well as the good sense not to let troubles or sorrows, of which he had

TARASCON CASTLE.

many, get under his skin. He spent the last decade of his life (1471–80) surrounded by poets and artists in Tarascon, in this castle begun in 1401 by his father, Louis II of Anjou. After René's death and Provence's annexation to France, it underwent the usual conversion into a prison.

While the exterior is all serious business, the interior was designed with the good taste of René in mind—flamboyant and elegant and now, eloquently empty. In the courtyard there are busts of the king and his second wife, Jeanne de Laval; sculptural titbits and faded ceiling panels offer clues of the original decoration; graffiti by British sailors imprisoned here between 1754 and 1778 recall the castle's later use. And taking in the precipitous views from the top terrace, you can see why no one ever tried to sneak up on it; or why, during the Revolution, Tarascon never needed to invest in a guillotine.

Elsewhere around Town

Perhaps because they haven't been prettified to death as in some Provençal towns, the streets of Tarascon, lined with rose, lemon and ochre houses with pots of geraniums in the windows and laundry flapping in the breeze, make a delightful place to wander around. The main **Rue des Halles** is still covered by medieval arcades. Halfway up it from the tourist office you'll find the Franciscan **Cloître des Cordeliers** (1450s), now used for special exhibitions (*open 10–12 and 2–5.30, summer 3–7, closed Jan and Feb*). At the top of Rue des Halles stands the handsome **Hôtel de Ville** (1648); from here, Rue Proudhon leads to the **Musée Souleiado** (No. 39; open by appointment only, ✆ 90 91 08 80). Souleiado—a Provençal word for 'sun-ray piercing through clouds'—is Provence's leading manufacturer of block-printed textiles, founded in 1938 by Charles Deméry to revive a 200-year-old Tarascon industry. The museum holds 40,000 18th-century fruit-wood blocks—still the basis for all the company's patterns. Brought back to fashion in the 1950s on such diverse backs as Bardot's and Picasso's, Souleiado's colour-drenched prints are again a hot fashion item and can be purchased in the nearby shop.

Lastly, there's the so-called **House of Tartarin**, across from a Fiat garage at 55 bis, Boulevard Itam (*open Oct–Mar 9–12 and 1.30–5; summer Apr–Sept 9.30–12 and 2–7; ✆ 90 91 05 08*). The modern Tarasconnais say they have forgiven Daudet for making them ridiculous, for in the age of Tourist Man he has also made them famous. Daudet claimed that the character of Tartarin was derived from his cousin, a big game hunter whom Daudet accompanied on a lion hunt in Algeria, but there's another version: in the original story, published as a newspaper serial, Tartarin was named Barbarin after an old

Tarasconnais family—the head of which had rejected the author's suit for the hand of his daughter. The family threatened to sue if Daudet used their name in his novel, so he changed it to the fictional Tartarin, but got his own back by making the whole town the butt of his jokes. Inside are mementoes from the three Tartarin novels, and photos from the plays and films. The garden has been planted to fit the books' exotic flora and baobab tree, where Tartarin held court with his tall tales.

Also on display is the famous **Tarasque**, a moustachioed armadillo covered with red spikes. Scholars argue whether the monster is named after the town or vice versa; when King René founded the *Jeux et Courses de la Tarasque* in 1474, it was given a thick carapace to hide the men that made it walk, while fireworks blasted out of its nostrils and the people sang '*Lagadigadèu, la Tarasco, Lagadigadèu!*', or 'Let her pass, the Tarasque, let her dance'.

Festival

Nowadays the *Fêtes de la Tarasque* take place for five days around St John's Day (24 June), and include bonfires, costumes, bullfights, cavalcades, dances, opera (the *Miréio* of course), and—yes—someone dressed up like Tartarin.

Tarascon ✉ *13150*

Where to Stay and Eating Out

The best hotel in town, **★★★De Provence**, 7 Blvd Victor Hugo, ✆ 90 91 06 43, 🖷 90 43 58 13, offers big rooms, big baths, colour TV and breakfast on your own balcony (*closed mid-Dec–mid-Jan*). More modest, though hardly less spacious, are the rooms at **★★Le Saint-Jean**, 24 Blvd Victor Hugo, ✆ 90 91 13 87, 🖷 90 91 32 42; it is connected to one of Tarascon's best restaurants, with the best value menu at approx 100F. Of the cheapies, try the **Hôtel du Rhône**, by the station in Place de la Gare, ✆ 90 91 03 35. There are 65 beds in the well-kept **Auberge de Jeunesse** (youth hostel), 31 Blvd Gambetta, ✆ 90 91 04 08 (*open Mar–Dec*); lodgers can take advantage of the hostel's inexpensive bike hire. As for victuals, they're cheap, if not *cordon bleu*. The **★★Hôtel-Bar Le Terminus** opposite the station in Place Colonel Berrurier, ✆ 90 91 08 00, 🖷 90 91 08 00, proposes 16 different entrées and 10 main dishes, as well as inexpensive rooms.

ARLES AMPHITHEATRE

Down the Rhône: Alpilles, Crau & Camargue

The Rhône that flows so majestically from the Swiss Alps down half of France comes to a rather messy end in the Camargue, dithering indecisively through a delta of swamps, salt-pans and sand-dunes. And yet if all the chapters of this book had to compete in a talent show, this would be the one to beat. It has wild bulls, horses and pink flamingos; it has the cowboys, gypsies and the fancy dress of the Arlésiennes; it has Roman ruins, the best Romanesque art, and the most romantic stories, worthy of Sir Walter Scott; it has the sharpest mountains, a plain so uncanny that it took a myth to explain it, and the mistral-whipped landscapes painted by Van Gogh; it has the biggest bullring, France's only AOC hay (from Arles), and all the aluminium ore you could ask for.

Note that on 18 October 1996 France is changing its telephone numbers from 8 digits to 10 digits. All phone numbers in Provence should be preceded by 04 from this date.

St-Rémy-de-Provence and the Alpilles

Getting Around

Though there are no trains, St-Rémy is a crossroads, surrounded by several big towns; consequently the **coach service** is slightly better than in most places. All leave from Place de la République, across from the church: at least one a day to Arles, Tarascon, Cavaillon and Aix; more frequently to Avignon. You can easily walk to Les Antiques (*see* p.102) and Glanum, but buses from St-Rémy to Les Baux are rare and inconvenient. The latter is better connected to Arles, with four or five buses a day, stopping at Fontvieille.

The Alpilles are not too steep for **cycling** in most places; the Syndicat d'Initiative in St-Rémy has a list of bike-hire firms. You might enjoy a tour around the southern slopes of the Alpilles, near St-Rémy, looking for the spots where Van Gogh painted many of his famous landscapes.

Tourist Information

St-Rémy (✉ 13210): Place Jean-Jaurès, on the way to Les Antiques, ✆ 90 92 05 22, 🖷 90 92 38 52

Les Baux (✉ 13520): Impasse du Château, ✆ 90 54 34 39, 🖷 90 54 51 15

 Fontvieille (✉ 13990): 5 Rue Marcel Honorat, ✆ 90 54 67 49, 🖷 90 54 69 82

market day

St-Rémy: Wednesday morning

St-Rémy-de-Provence

Enclosed by a garland of boulevards lined with plane trees, St-Rémy's tranquillity has attracted its share of the famous: Nostradamus was born here, Gertrude Stein spent years here, and Princess Caroline drops in for discreet visits (St-Rémy used to belong to the

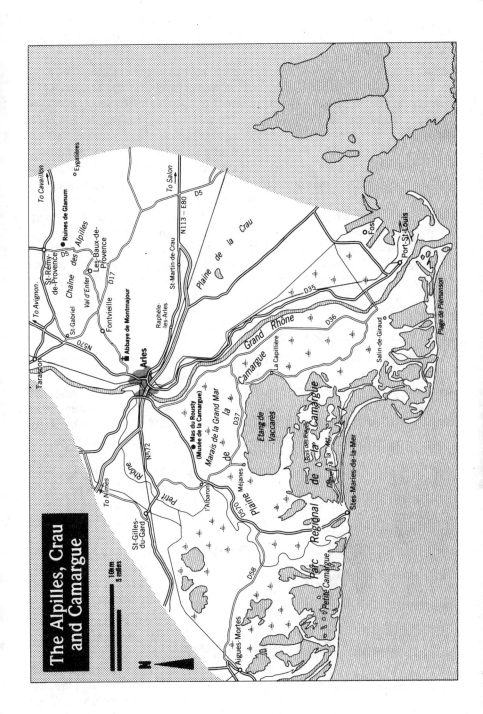

The Alpilles, Crau and Camargue

To Cavaillon

Eygalières

Ruines de Glanum

To Salon

D5

Chaîne des Alpilles

St-Rémy-de-Provence

Les-Baux-de-Provence

Plaine de la Crau

N113 – E80

Fos

Port-St-Louis

To Avignon

Val d'Enfer

D17

St-Gabriel

Fontvieille

St-Martin-de-Crau

D35

Abbaye de Montmajour

Raphèle-les-Arles

Grand Rhône

D36

N570

Arles

La Capilière

Salin-de-Giraud

Plage de Piémanson

Tarascon

Mas du Rousty
(Musée de la Camargue)

Marais de la Grand Mar

Camargue

Etang de Vacarès

de

D37

la

To Nîmes

Petit Rhône

N572

l'Albaron

Méjanes

Plaine

de

Bois des Rièges

Phare de la Mer

la

Camargue

St-Gilles-du-Gard

D570

Parc

Régional

Stes-Maries-de-la-Mer

D58

Aigues-Mortes

Petite Camargue

10 km
5 miles

N

family). Vincent Van Gogh spent his tragic last year in the asylum, which during the First World War was commandeered to hold interned Germans—the one who got Van Gogh's room was Albert Schweitzer.

Nowadays St-Rémy is home to a good many artists, and there are always exhibitions going on. The newest attraction is the bizarre-looking organ in the church of **St-Martin** on Blvd Marceau. Built only in 1983, it is said to be one of the finest in the world; the Organ Festival in August pulls out all the stops, as do the Saturday afternoon concerts in summer and autumn. The old attractions are two fine Renaissance palaces, both around Place Flavier, behind the church, one street to the north: the **Hôtel Mistral de Mondragon** (1550), containing a museum of local folk life and arts, with a special section on Nostradamus; and the **Hôtel de Sade**, with a small but interesting **Archaeological Museum** (*open daily 10–12 and 2–7, guided tours every hour; adm; ✆ 90 92 13 07; a ticket from Glanum will also admit you to both museums*). St-Rémy is the medieval successor to the abandoned Roman town of Glanum (*see* below); finds from Glanum on display here include architectural fragments, statues and reliefs of deities from Hermes to the Phrygian god Attis, and Roman glass and jewellery. You could visit the **Parfumerie Artisanale** on Blvd Mirabeau, but don't miss the **market** for every sort of fish, cheese and meat, seasonable fruits, herbs, fabrics, shoes, leather goods and coats, sad puppies for sale, and crafted objects from the mundane to the meticulous.

Les Antiques, and Van Gogh's Asylum

The Romans had a habit of building monuments and impressive mausolea on the outskirts of their towns, along the main roads. Just a 15-minute walk from the centre of St-Rémy, south on the D 5, stand two of the most remarkable Roman relics in France. They were here long before the D 5 of course; originally they decorated the end of the Roman road from Arles to Glanum, the ruins of which lie just across the D 5. The **Triumphal Arch**, built probably in the reign of Augustus, was one of the first to be erected in Provence. Its elegant form and marble columns show the Greek sensibility of the artists, far different from the strange Celtic-influenced arches of Orange and Carpentras. In the Middle Ages it inspired the creators of St-Trophime in Arles. Evidently, someone long ago carted off the top for building stone; the slanted tile roof is an 18th-century addition to protect what was left.

Next to it, the so-called **Mausoleum** was really a memorial to Caesar and Augustus, erected by their descendants in the early 1st century AD. There is nothing else quite like this anywhere, and it is one of the best-preserved Roman monuments. The form is certainly original: a narrow four-faced arch on a solid plinth, surmounted by a cylinder of columns and a pointed roof, 17m above the ground; inside this are statues of Caesar and Augustus. The **reliefs** on the base are excellent work: mythological scenes including a *battle with Amazons*, a *battle of Greeks and Trojans* and a *boar hunt*. At the top of the arch, you can make out a pair of winged spirits holding a civic crown of laurel—Augustus' symbol for his new political order.

Just across the road from Les Antiques, a shady path leads to the monastery of **St-Paul-de-Mausole**, in a beautiful setting with gardens all around. Founded in the 900s, the complex includes a simple Romanesque church and a cloister with some interesting carved capitals. In 1810, the monastery buildings were purchased for use as a private hospital (it still is; no visits). This is the place Vincent Van Gogh chose as a refuge from the troubles of life in the outside world, in May 1890, not long after he chopped off the ear. He spent a year here, the most intense and original period of his career, painting as if possessed—150 canvases and over 100 drawings, including many of his most famous works, such as the *Nuit Etoilée* ('Starry Night') and *Les Blés Jaunes* ('Cornfield and Cypress Trees'). The blueish mountains in the background of this work and many others are the Alpilles.

Glanum

Glanum began as a Celtic settlement—a proper town, really, under a heavy cultural influence from the Greeks at nearby Marseille. The Romans snatched it around 100 BC, under Marius, but not until the great prosperity of the Augustan empire did the city begin to bloom. Almost all of the ruins visible today (as well as Les Antiques) date from this period. In a prelude to the fall of the Empire, the Franks and Alemanni ranged throughout Gaul in the 250s and '60s. In one of their last hurrahs before the recovering Roman legions drove them out, they sacked Glanum in 270. After that, the townspeople relocated to a healthier and safer site, today's St-Rémy; silt washed down from the Alpilles gradually covered the city, and it passed out of memory until the 19th century, when some accidental finds alerted archaeologists to its presence. Excavations began in 1921, and have since uncovered a fascinating cross-section of Glanum, including its Forum.

More than Vaison-la-Romaine or anywhere else in France, this is the place to really feel at home in the Roman world. But you'll have to work for it; only the foundations remain, and recreating Glanum will require a bit of imagination (see the museum in the Hôtel de Sade first). From the entrance, to the left are the **Maison des Antes** and the **Maison d'Atys**, two typical wealthy homes built around peristyle courtyards. The latter had apparently been transformed into a sanctuary of Cybele and Attis; this cult was one of the most popular of the mystery religions imported from the east in imperial times.

Across the street are remains of a fountain and the **thermae** (baths), with mosaics, a *palestra* (exercise yard) and a *piscina* (pool). Next door is a building with an exedra that was probably a temple; altars to Silenus were found inside. In this part of the street the **sewers** have been uncovered. The **Forum** wasn't very impressive, by the standards of most Roman towns, and it is hard to make anything out today from the confusion of buildings from various ages that have been excavated. Beyond it, to the right, are foundations of temples; to the left are bases of another fountain and a monument. The street closes at a **gate** from Hellenistic times that was retained as the city expanded outside the original walls. Also retained was the **nymphaeum** beyond it, to the left; these decorated fountains were a common feature of Greek cities, built to allow travellers to refresh and clean up before entering the town.

St-Rémy ✉ 13210   *Where to Stay and Eating Out*

St-Rémy gets heaps of tourists, and consequently has a wide choice of places to stay; even for visiting the Alpilles, it will probably prove the most convenient base. Some of the hotels are exceptional: the **Château de Roussan**, 3km west of town on the Rte de Tarascon, off the D 99, ✆ 90 92 11 63, 📠 90 92 37 32, with lovely rooms in an 18th-century mansion, is set in the middle of an extravagant park full of fountains and tree-lined avenues; some rooms are inexpensive, others up to 1000F, but book far ahead. Second choice is the ★★★★**Château des Alpilles**, Route dép. 31, ✆ 90 92 03 33, 📠 90 92 45 17. Outside the busy one-way rush of traffic round the centre, yet just a few steps out of town, this 19th-century château has its own park of trees, some rare, and a tennis court and pool. It's all mirrors, period furniture and the expected comforts, but not pompous.

Near the ruins, the ★★**Villa Glanum**, 46 Ave Van Gogh, ✆ 90 92 03 59, 📠 90 92 00 08; is family-run and has some surprising amenities for an inexpensive hotel: a pool and garden, also a restaurant; a pleasant stay (*closed Nov–beginning Mar*). On Blvd Victor Hugo, ★★**Des Arts**, ✆ 90 92 08 50, 📠 90 92 55 09, has comfortable rooms, as well as being the oldest and most popular restaurant in town (menus 95F, 125–160F). On Tuesdays, when Des Arts is closed, brave the **Bar Tabac des Alpilles**, ✆ 90 92 02 17, opposite. Fight the flies for Toulouse sausage and *frites*, and polish off with the finest crème caramel you're ever likely to encounter, made by the proprietor's wife. Be warned, the centre of town is noisy, but if you want to look out onto the town square as you wake, try ★★**Le Cheval Blanc**, ✆ 90 92 09 28, 6 Ave Fauconnet; the owners are cheerful, and it's adequate. For an inexpensive lunch, you won't do better than **Le Bistrot des Alpilles** on Blvd Mirabeau, ✆ 90 92 09 17; you'll get generous fresh pasta, great desserts and a pleasant terrace.

Les Baux-de-Provence and the Chaîne des Alpilles

The ruins were nice, but there is an even greater treat ahead. The five twisting kilometres of the D 5 that take you from Les Antiques into the heart of the Alpilles are, in fact, one of the greatest sensual experiences Provence can offer. Van Gogh and cypresses, lushness and flowers are left behind; in a matter of minutes the road has brought you to another world. This world, incredibly, is at most 16km across, and a stone's throw from the swamps of the Camargue and the sea. It is made of thin, cool breezes and brilliant light; its colours are white and deep green—almost exclusively—in an astringent landscape of limestone crags and patches of scrubby *maquis.*

From as early as 3000 BC, this exotic massif attracted residents. The Alpilles are full of caves, many of which were once inhabited. The Ligurians took advantage of its natural defences to found an important *oppidum* at **Les Baux**, a steep barren plateau in the centre of the massif, 11km from St-Rémy. In the Middle Ages, this made the perfect setting for the most feared and celebrated of Provence's noble clans. The Seigneurs des Baux are first heard of in the 900s. 'A race of eaglets, vassals never', as their slogan went, they never acknowledged the authority of the French king, the emperors, or anyone else, and their impregnable crag in the Alpilles allowed them to get away with it. They claimed to be descended from Balthazar, one of the magi at Bethlehem, and put the Christmas star on their feudal escutcheon.

The symbol was never a harbinger of glad tidings to their neighbours, however; for the next two centuries the lords of Baux waged incessant warfare on all comers, and occasionally on each other, gradually becoming a real power in Provence. They did it with flair, and the chronicles are full of good stories about them: one seigneur once besieged the castle of his pregnant niece, and sent sappers to undermine her bedchamber. And they met memorable ends; one was stabbed to death by his wife, another flayed alive when he fell into the hands of his enemies. All the while, the family headquarters at Les Baux maintained a polished court where troubadours were always welcome. It ended with a bang in 1372, when an even nastier fellow took over the clan: Raymond de Turenne, a distant relation who was also a nephew of Pope Gregory IX. Taking advantage of confused times, in the reign of Queen Jeanne, this ambitious and bloodthirsty intriguer found enough support, and enough foreign mercenaries, to bring full-scale civil war to Provence, bringing it the same kind of misery to which the rest of France had become accustomed in the Hundred Years War.

When the last heir of Les Baux died in 1426, the possessions of the house were incorporated into the County of Provence. That isn't quite the end of the story; in the 1500s Les Baux began to thrive once more, first under Anne of Montmorency, who rebuilt the seigneurs' castle in the best Renaissance taste, and later under the Manvilles, who inherited it from him and made it a Protestant stronghold in the Wars of Religion. Cardinal Richelieu finally put this eternal trouble-spot to rest in 1632, demolishing the castle and sending the owners the bill for the job. Until the Revolution, the remains of Les Baux were, like St-Rémy, in the hands of the Grimaldis of Monaco.

Les Baux

After the demolition, the village that surrounded the castle of Les Baux almost disappeared; Prosper Mérimée, in the 1830s, reported only a few beggars living among its ruins. But Provençal writers kept the place from being forgotten, men such as Mistral (born at Maillane, near St-Rémy) and Alphonse Daudet, whose famous windmill is just over the Alpilles (*see* below). In the last 50 years, Les Baux has become the second-biggest tourist attraction in

France after the Mont St-Michel. The village below the castle has been rebuilt and repopulated in the worst way, and whatever spark of glamour survives in this tremendous ruin, you will have to run the gauntlet of shops peddling trinkets, knick-knackery, scowling dolls, herbs, santons and soaps to reach it.

The first sight to greet you as you trudge up from the car park is an elegant carved Renaissance fireplace, open to the sky and standing next to a souvenir shop. Trudge a bit further, bearing right, and you will come to the **Musée des Santons** on Place Louis Jou, which you could give a miss. Up the street, past the ramparts, is the **Porte d'Eyguères**, which until the 18th century was the only entrance to the city.

Up the Rue de la Calade you will come to the Place de l'Eglise, where the 16th-century **Hôtel des Porcelets** has now become the **Musée Yves Brayer**, ✆ 90 54 36 99. Brayer's major works are here; pictures of Spain and Italy as well as Provence (*adm*). Even if 20th-century figurative art isn't quite your thing, peek into the 17th-century **Chapelle des Pénitents Blancs** opposite, to see what he made of its interior (*open Apr–Sept 10–12 and 2–6.30, Oct–Mar 10–12 and 2–5, closed Jan–mid-Feb*). Lastly on the Place de l'Eglise stands the **Eglise St-Vincent**, dating from the 12th and 16th centuries. This is probably the coolest and least crowded place to be in Les Baux, and there's a Cistercian nave and stained glass by Ingrand to peer at.

Otherwise in the village are the **Hôtel Jean de Brion** and the **Hôtel de Manville**, on the Grand' rue. The first houses the **Fondation Louis Jou**, ✆ 90 54 34 17, containing Jou's engravings, as well as pre-20th-century ones, prints by Dürer, and early books. In the second is the **Musée d'Art Contemporain**, ✆ 90 54 34 03, and the **Hôtel de Ville**. Both these and the Hôtel des Porcelets date from the architectural development of the 16th century, before the castle was destroyed.

Next, to the **Citadel** (*adm*), and a new museum to keep the tramping tourists from the thing itself. The **Musée d'Histoire des Baux** is perfectly nice, with illustrations and archeological finds as well as models in glass cases, to give you an overview, or to save you the walk over the site outside if the mistral's blowing. When you see Les Baux itself the ambience changes abruptly—a rocky chaos surrealistically decorated with fragments of once-imposing buildings. The path leads through this '**Ville Morte**' (on the left are remains of the hospital and its chapel, and in the chapel a **diaporama**: a slide show in celebration of the olive tree) to the tip of the plateau, where there is a monument to a Provençal poet named Charlon Rieu, and a grand view over the Alpilles.

Turning back, the path climbs up to the château itself, with bits of towers and walls everywhere, including the apse of a Gothic chapel cut out of the rock, and the long eastern wall that survived Richelieu's explosives, dotted with finely carved windows. What looks like a monolithic honeycomb is really a 13th-century pigeonry. Recent excavations have uncovered medieval tombs and foundations. The only intact part is the **donjon**, a rather treacherous climb to the top for a bird's-eye view over the site. Locals say the best time to see it is with a blanket, under a starry night.

An Infernal Valley and a Blonde Sorceress

Beneath Les Baux, on the western side, the **Pavillon de la Reine Jeanne** has nothing to do with the famous queen, but is a pretty Renaissance garden folly of 1581. The road that passes it will take you in another 3km to the **Val d'Enfer**, the wildest corner of the Alpilles, a weird landscape of eroded limestone, caves and quarries. One thing the Alpilles has a lot of is aluminium ore—*bauxite*, a useless mineral until the process for smelting it was discovered in the last century. Now there are bauxite mines all over southern Provence; those to be seen here are exhausted, but Jean Cocteau took advantage of the landscape to shoot part of his *Orphée* here in 1950. Today the quarries host one of Les Baux's big attractions: the **Cathédrale des Images**, ✆ 90 54 38 65, a slick show where thirty projectors bounce giant pictures over the walls; the theme of the show changes annually.

PAVILLON DE LA REINE JEANNE

Off the D 27A, near the crossroads for Les Baux, the **Col de la Vayède** holds scanty remains of the pre-Roman *oppidum*; the lines of the walls can be traced in some places, and there are bits of wall and no fewer than three necropolises, with small niches carved into the rock to hold the ashes of the deceased. On the side of the hill facing the D 27A, you can climb up a dirt path to see the mysterious relief called the **Trémaïé**. Neatly carved on a smoothed rock face are three figures and an effaced Latin inscription. It seems to be a Roman funeral monument, but local legend has it that the figures represent Marius, his wife, and a blonde Celtic sorceress named Marthe who helped Marius in his campaigns against the Teutones. Another relief, less well preserved, can be seen a few hundred metres to the south. Finally, for hikers, there is the GR 6 trail, which traverses the best parts of the Alpilles from east to west. It passes right through Les Baux.

Les Baux ✉ *13520*   ***Where to Stay and Eating Out***

Les Baux, with its tourist hordes, isn't the most desirable place to stop over—and you'll have to pay a lot for the privilege. For a memorable splurge, if you can bear the disdainful hauteur, there's ★★★★**l'Oustau de Baumanière**, ✆ 90 54 33 07, 🖷 90 54 40 46. In magical surroundings in the Val d'Enfer, it's a restored farmhouse with all the amenities, and has a highly rated restaurant (two Michelin stars) and a spectacular terrace view. Seafood is the star: salmon, *langoustines* and such, and there are sumptuous desserts and a formidable wine list of Provençal treasures; menus 450F, but here you're just as well off choosing *à la carte* (*closed Jan and Feb*).

You can do as well for half the price at the ★★★**Mas d'Aigret**, just below Les Baux (east of the village on the D 27A), ✆ 90 54 33 54, ✉ 90 54 41 37. Some rooms have great views, others open onto the gardens; there is a pool, and a restaurant just as good as the Baumanière's (home-produced *foie gras,* breads, own-smoked salmon, and fresh local produce whenever possible). Menus are 90 to 350F, and a tremendous bargain for lunch: 130F. You will receive hospitality—*par excellence*—from an Englishman, who is courteously attentive not just to every detail, but also to the well-being of each of his guests. This is definitely the place to dine in Les Baux (*closed Jan–Mar*); the village itself has only a few tourist-oriented places. The ★★**Hostellerie de la Reine Jeanne**, ✆ 90 54 32 06, ✉ 90 54 32 33, is relatively cheap and is in the village, with a bird's eye view (*closed Nov–Mar*).

Coteaux des Baux-en-Provence

The AOC wine of the Alpilles is rosé, like most of Provence's vintages, but in recent years the reds of Les Baux have made a quantum jump in quality and attracted the most attention. This relatively new *appellation* comes under the heading of Coteaux d'Aix-en-Provence, and a majority of its growers are good environmentalists dedicated to growing grapes free from artificial fertilizers, pesticides and herbicides; the grapes that go into it include grenache, cabernet-sauvignon, syrah, cinsault, carignan and counoise. A good source is the charming **Domaine de La Vallongue** in Eygalières, ✆ 90 95 91 70, ✉ 90 95 97 76, which uses traditional methods to create organic wines: fresh, fruity, fragrant rosés and intense reds, hinting at vanilla and spice; every year between '85 and '90 was a happy success, as were '93 and '94. **Mas Cellier** in St-Rémy, ✆ 90 92 03 90, is a tiny estate, but one of the few vineyards in the region both owned and run by a woman, Dominique Hauvette, whose wines (also organic) have a warm, velvety quality, especially the '90. In Les Baux itself, at the foot of the cliffs, visitors can take a didactic nature walk through the vines of **Mas Ste-Berthe** (✆ 90 54 39 01, ✉ 90 54 46 17) and learn all about the grapes. Some (ugni blanc, sauvignon, and grenache blanc) go into the white wine, while the sombre red, especially the '90, is excellent and still reasonably priced.

St-Gabriel and Fontvieille

The eastern half of the Alpilles is the more scenic, and if you're heading in that direction, lonely roads like the D 78 and D 24 make worthwhile detours that won't take you more than a few kilometres out of the way; **Eygalières**, on the D 24B, is a lovely village with a ruined castle.

Along the western fringes of the Alpilles, on the D 33, you will pass the canal port of *Ernaginum*, later called St-Gabriel, which flourished from Roman times until the Middle Ages. You won't see anything; the drying-up of the old canal doomed the city to a slow death, and Ernaginum has disappeared more completely than any ancient city of Provence, leaving only the impressive 12th-century church of **St-Gabriel** standing alone in open fields. There is little to see inside—and it's never open anyhow; the real interest is one of the finest Romanesque façades in the Midi. Very consciously imitating Roman architecture, it shows a stately portal with a triangular pediment, flanked by Corinthian columns. There are excellent sculpted reliefs on and above the tympanum: an *Annunciation, Daniel in the Lions' Den* and *Adam and Eve*, apparently just realizing they have no clothes on. Above it, a small Italianate rose window is surrounded by figures of the four Evangelists.

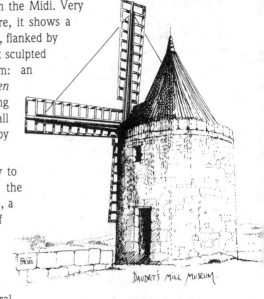

DAUDET'S MILL MUSEUM.

From here, the only village on the way to Arles is **Fontvieille**, best known for the **Moulin de Daudet**, south on the D 33, a rare survivor among the hundreds of windmills that once embellished every hilltop of southern Provence. Alphonse Daudet never really lived here, but his *Lettres de Mon Moulin*, a collection of sentimental tales of the dying life of rural Provence in the late 1800s, is still popular across France today. The windmill has become a museum of Daudet, with photographs and documents. It's very much visited, with a huge car park where coaches like fridges on wheels disgorge cooled tourists, and local driving instructors take their pupils to practice. Two kilometres further south, there are sections of two Roman **aqueducts** that served Arles, along with vestiges of a **Roman mill**, unique in Europe. This huge installation was a serious precursor to the Industrial Revolution, using the flow of the water to power 16 separate mills, along a stretch of canal over a kilometre long; nothing like it has been found anywhere else. It's really something to see; no tourist tic tac, not even a railing. Give Daudet a miss for this.

The Hypogeum of Castellet

On the D 17, at the crossroads with the D 82, you will find a very ruined castle that once belonged to the Counts of Provence. The surrounding area, a low, flat-topped hill called Castellet, contains one of the most unusual and least-known Neolithic monuments in France. The **Hypogeum** consists of four covered avenues, carefully carved out of the rock or earth, under tumuli that have long since disappeared. They were made as collective tombs about 3500 BC or later, by the Ligurians or their predecessors, and probably also served as a kind of temple. Many have carvings, cup-marks and sun-symbols, inside or near their openings. The sites are not marked, and you'll be lucky to find their narrow, trapezoidal entrances in the undergrowth. All are within 200m of the D 17, three south of the road and one north.

From Castellet, you'll see another hill, the **Montagne de Cordes** about a half-kilometre to the south. Like Castellet, this was an island in Neolithic times. Nearby Montmajour (*see* below) was a third. The Cordes is private property, and you'll need permission from the owner (in the farmhouse on the slopes) to see another remarkable tomb-temple. The **Grotte des Fées** is also known as the 'Epée de Roland'; the tapering, 70m tunnel has two small side chambers that give it the shape of a sword.

Fontvieille ✉ 13990

Fontvieille has a surprising number of hotels and is only 11km away from Les Baux. In the luxury class, there is the Relais et Châteaux' ★★★★**Auberge de la Régalido**, Rue Mistral, ✆ 90 54 60 22, ✆ 90 54 64 29, in a restored mill with lovely gardens, including a restaurant that is a little temple of *haute cuisine* with prices to match; menus from 280F for excellent fresh seafood or roast pigeon with *morilles* (*closed Jan*). Less expensively, the ★★★**Le Val Majour**, 22 Route d'Arles, ✆ 90 54 62 33, ✆ 90 54 61 67, with a pool and tennis, has well-furnished quiet rooms, and a restaurant with menus at 110 and 190F. Fontvieille also has the only budget rooms around the Alpilles, at the admirable ★★**Hostellerie de la Tour**, 3 Rue des Plumelets, ✆ 90 54 72 21, and the more down-to-earth ★**Bernard**, 6 Cours M. Bellon, ✆ 90 54 70 35, ✆ 90 54 68 59.

For appetizing home cooking, **Le Homard**, 29 Route du Nord, ✆ 90 54 75 34, is hard to better, although you won't find the eponymous lobster. This is the sort of restaurant people who come to Provence hope to find; *terrine de poisson, filet de rascasse* and *cassoulet* feature on the 115F and 165F menus, washed down with local Coteaux de Baux wines. Be sure to reserve; it's full of locals who know what's best (*closed mid-Nov–mid-Feb*). More cheaply, sit next to an ancient bread oven at **Le Grasilo**, 56 Cours Hyacinthe Bellon, ✆ 90 54 62 08, and tuck into rabbit, lamb, or truffles (in season), again with copious amounts of the local pink and red stuff.

Abbaye de Montmajour

Just before Arles, the D 17 passes one of the most important monasteries of medieval Provence. Founded in the 10th century, on what was then almost an island amidst the swamps, this Benedictine abbey was devoted to reclaiming the land, a monumental labour that would take centuries to complete. By the 1300s, the monastery had grown exceedingly wealthy, a real prize for the Avignon popes, who gained control of it and farmed it out, along with its revenues, to friends and relations. Under such absentee abbots, it languished thereafter, and its great church was never completed. To give some idea of its later decadence, an attempt to reform it in 1639 included importing new monks; the old crew refused to go, and sacked the abbey before they were chased out by royal troops. Montmajour became a national property not in the Revolution, but five years earlier. The 1786 'Affair of the Diamond Necklace' was a famous swindle that involved both Marie Antoinette and the great charlatan Cagliostro. One of the principal players was Montmajour's abbot, the Cardinal de Rohan; he got caught, and all his property, including the abbey, was confiscated. The abbey did service as a farmhouse, and its church as a barn, before restorations began in 1907.

Consequently, there isn't much to see. At the church entrance you'll notice the piers, built into the adjacent wall of the cloister, that would have supported the nave had it been completed. The interior is austere and empty, but gives a good idea of the state of Provençal architecture *c.* 1200, in transition from Romanesque to Gothic. The most interesting part is the **lower church**, a crypt with an unusual plan, including a long, narrow nave and a circular enclosure under the high altar, with radiating chapels behind it; its purpose has not been explained. The **cloister** has some fanciful sculptural decoration; see if you can find the camel. Around the back of the church, you'll see a number of tombs cut out of the rock; these are a mystery too, and may predate the abbey. The mighty 26m **donjon** was built in the 1360s for defence, in that terrible age when the lords of Les Baux and a dozen other hoodlums were tearing up the neighbourhood; next to it, the tiny chapel of **St-Pierre** (usually closed) was the original abbey church, built on the spot where St-Trophime of Arles (*see* below) had his hermitage.

Ste-Croix

A few hundred yards behind the apse of the church, in the middle of a farm, stands what was the abbey's funeral chapel, **Ste-Croix**. Don't miss it, even though you'll have to walk through the farmyard muck (it's visible from the road, near a barn). Few buildings show so convincingly the architectural sophistication of the Romanesque as this small work of the late 11th century, a central-plan chapel with apses along three sides and an elegant lantern on top. Some complex geometry and a mastery of proportions are built into this simple but perfect form, based on the Golden Section. Too much decoration would be superfluous, and there is only a discreet carved floral frieze along the cornice, along with Moorish-style interlocking arches.

Arles

Like Nîmes, Arles has enough intact antiquities to call itself the 'Rome of France'; unlike Nîmes it lingered in the limelight for another 1000 years, producing enough saints for every month on the calendar—Trophimus, Hilarius, Césaire and Genès are some of the more famous. Pilgrims flocked here for a whiff of their odour of sanctity, and asked on their deathbeds to be buried in the holy ground of the Alyscamps. Nowadays Arles holds the distinction of being the largest commune in France, ten times larger than Paris, embracing 750 square km of the Camargue and Crau plains; it has given the world the rhythms of the Gypsy Kings, and the pungent joys of *saucisse d'Arles*, France's finest donkey-meat sausage.

Henry James wrote, 'As a city Arles quite misses its effect in every way: and if it is a charming place, as I think it is, I can hardly tell the reason why.' Modern Arles, sitting amidst its ruins, is still ineffably charming, in spite of the hectic blooms of the 1990s. London, Paris and Brussels boutiques attract and reflect wealthy, shiny young people here, who co-exist amicably with the large numbers of tourists. Arles' new icons are erected in its main square: a life-size model of an American hamburger clown and, outside the tourist office, a red British phone box.

History

In 1975, the remains of a Celto-Ligurian settlement were uncovered near the Boulevard des Lices. It's hard to imagine what its builders thought in the 6th century BC, when Greek traders from Marseille arrived and began to dicker over prices. We know at least that the Greeks were pleased, and over the years they established the site as their principal 'counter' for dealings with the Ligurians, calling it *Arelate* ('near sleeping waters' or less poetically, 'bog town'). Business picked up considerably after Marius' legionnaires made Arelate a seaport by digging a canal to Fos (104 BC). In 49 BC, the populace, tired of getting bum deals from the wily Greeks, readily gave Caesar the boats he needed to punish and conquer Marseille for siding with Pompey. In return Arles was rewarded the spoils and received a population boost with a colony of veterans from the Sixth Legion. Most important of all, it got all of Rome's business that had previously gone through Greek Marseille. A bridge of boats was built over the Rhône, and the Colonia Julia Paterna Arelate Sextanorum was known far and wide for its powerful maritime corporations, called *utriculares* from their rafts that floated on inflated bladders.

At the crossroads of Rome's trading route between Italy and Spain and the Rhône, Arles grew rapidly, each century adding more splendid monuments—a theatre, temples, a circus, an amphitheatre, at least two triumphal arches, and a basilica. Constantine built himself a grand palace and baths as big as Caracalla's in Rome. In 395 Emperor Honorius made it the capital of the 'Three Gauls'—France, Britain, and Spain—and as late as 418 it was recorded that 'Arles is so fortunately placed, its commerce is so active and merchants come in such numbers that all the products of the universe are channelled there: the riches of the Orient, perfumes of Arabia, delicacies of Assyria . . .'

Arles was one of the last cities to fall to the Visigoths, only to become their capital in 476. The Franks inherited it in 536, and Saracen raids were frequent. But on the whole, the Dark Ages were not so dark in Arles; from 879 to 1036 it served as the capital of Provence-Burgundy (the so-called 'Kingdom of Arles'), a vast territory that stretched all the way to Lorraine. Most importantly, Arles was a centre of power for the new Christian religion. Several major Church councils convened here, including one back in 314 that condemned the heresy of Donatism (the quite reasonable belief that sacraments administered by bad priests had no value). Arles' cathedral of St-Trophime became the most important church in Provence; in 597 its bishop, St Virgil, consecrated St Augustine as the first Bishop of Canterbury and as late as 1178, Emperor Frederick Barbarossa was crowned King of Arles at its altar. After a busy career in the 11th and 12th centuries as a crusader port and pilgrimage destination, the city's special history ended in 1239 when Raymond Berenger, Count of Provence, evicted Arles' imperial viceroy. As the city declined even the sea abandoned it, leaving the former port stranded between marshes and the rocky plain of the Crau, compressed in a time capsule of Roman monuments and ancient customs.

With the improved communications of the 19th century, Arles slowly resurfaced. The Roman amphitheatre was restored. The city's women, celebrated for their beautiful Attic features, inspired Daudet's story *L'Arlésienne* (1866) and Bizet's opera (1872). Its furniture makers invented what has become the traditional south Provençal style, more elegantly rococo than the heavy pieces of northern Provence. The Félibres made much of the city for the striking costumes the women continued to wear, for its bullfights and its *farandole*, a dance in 6/4 time dating back at least to the Middle Ages.

The Arles of Van Gogh

Vincent Van Gogh was a fervent admirer of Daudet, and it may well have been his stories that first brought him to Arles in February 1888. To his surprise, the city was blanketed with snow—a very rare occurrence and, in a way, an omen. When the snow melted it revealed an Arles made mean and ugly by new embankments along the Rhône, cutting the city off from its life-blood (previously the flooding of the river had fertilized the countryside, like the Nile in Egypt). At the same time one of France's biggest railway lines was being installed by workers brought in from Belgium, housed in cheap ticky-tacky buildings. Arles had never looked shabbier. But Van Gogh stayed, found a room to rent in a poor neighbourhood by the station, and painted the shabby Arles around him: the *Café de Nuit* with its hallucinogenic lightbulb, *La Maison Jaune*, and *Le Pont de Langlois* (part of a ghastly irrigation project) with colours so intense in their chromatic contrasts they seem to come from somewhere over the rainbow.

Van Gogh's dream was to found an art colony at Arles, similar to the one at Pont Aven in Brittany. He begged his overbearing friend Gauguin to join him, but when Gauguin finally arrived in October he found little to like in Arles, dashing Van Gogh's hopes. The tension between the two men reached such a pitch in December that the overwrought Van Gogh went over the edge and confronted Gauguin in the street with a razor. Gauguin stared him down and Van Gogh, despising himself, went back to his room, cut off his own ear, and gave it to a prostitute. Arles was scandalized, and breathed a sigh of relief when Van Gogh voluntarily committed himself to the local hospital, or Hôtel Dieu. In May 1889 he left for the hospital in St-Rémy.

Van Gogh's output in Arles was prodigious (from February 1888 to May 1889 he painted 300 canvases) but not a single one remains in the city today. His admirers, looking for the places he painted, have just as little to see: the famous bridge, yellow house, and café were destroyed in the Second World War or afterwards; only the clock in the Bar Alcazar in Place Lamartine remains as Van Gogh painted it in *Café de Nuit*. To make up for its belated appreciation of the mad, lonely genius who sojourned here, Arles has converted the Hôtel Dieu into a multi-media gallery, the **Espace Van Gogh**, displaying the works of others.

Getting Around
by train

Arles' train station is in the northern part of town, on Avenue Paulin Talabot, Ⓒ 90 82 50 50. Arles has frequent connections to Paris, Marseille, Montpellier, Nîmes, Aix-en-Provence, and to all the towns along the main line to Spain; there are frequent services to Avignon and Tarascon and a less frequent service to Orange.

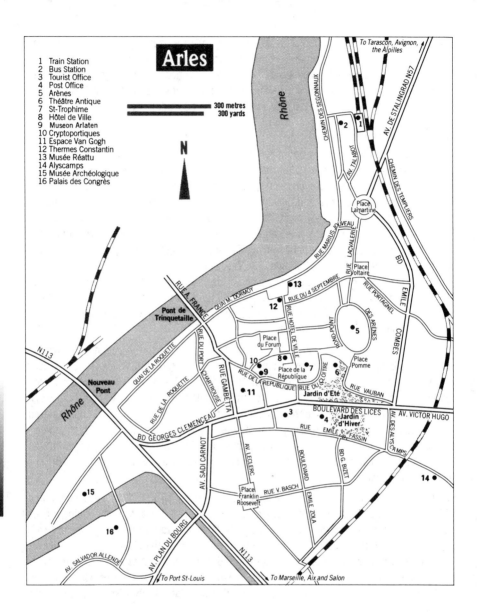

Arles

1 Train Station
2 Bus Station
3 Tourist Office
4 Post Office
5 Arènes
6 Théâtre Antique
7 St-Trophime
8 Hôtel de Ville
9 Museon Arlaten
10 Cryptoportiques
11 Espace Van Gogh
12 Thermes Constantin
13 Musée Réattu
14 Alyscamps
15 Musée Archéologique
16 Palais des Congrès

300 metres
300 yards

N

To Tarascon, Avignon,
the Alpilles

Rhône

CHEMIN DES SEGONNAUX

AV. DE STALINGRAD N57

AV. TALABOT

CHEMIN DES TEMPLIERS

Place
Lamartine

RUE MARIUS JOUVEAU

RUE LACVALERIE

BD EMILE COMBES

Place
Voltaire

RUE PORTAGNEL

DES ARÈNES

ROND-POINT

RUE A. FRANCE

QUAI M. DORMOY

RUE DU 4 SEPTEMBRE

Pont de
Trinquetaille

RUE DU PORT

RUE HOTEL DE VILLE

Place
du Forum

5

Place
Pomme

N113

QUAI DE LA ROQUETTE

RUE DE LA. ROQUETTE

RUE DU PORT

CHARTROUSE

RUE GAMBETTA

RUE DE LA REPUBLIQUE

10

9

8

Place de la
République

7

6

RUE DU CLOITRE

RUE VAUBAN

Nouveau
Pont

Rhône

11

Jardin d'Eté

3

4

BOULEVARD DES LICES

Jardin
d'Hiver

AV. VICTOR HUGO

AV. DES ALYSCAMPS

BD GEORGES CLEMENCEAU

AV. SADI CARNOT

AV. LECLERC

RUE EMILE FASSIN

BOULEVARD EMILE ZOLA

BD G. BIZET

14

Place
Franklin
Roosevelt

RUE V. BASCH

15

16

AV. PLAN DU BOURG

AV. SALVADOR ALLENDE

N113

To Port St-Louis

To Marseille, Aix and Salon

114

The bus station serving nearby towns is just across the street, ✆ 90 49 38 01. **Cars de Camargue**, from Rue J. M. Artaud, ✆ 90 96 36 25, ✉ 90 96 01 90, have coaches to Salon, Aix, Marseille, Nîmes, Stes-Maries-de-la-Mer, Port-St-Louis, St-Gilles and Lunel, and in July and August, to Aigues-Mortes. (Before you hurry into Arles from here, step over the road to the bank of the Rhône and admire the city on the bend of the river; an unlikely spot for an unparalleled view.)

by taxi

For a taxi day or night, call ✆ 90 96 90 03, Jardin d'Eté, Blvd des Lices.

car and bike hire

Europcar, ✆ 90 93 23 24, ✉ 90 96 18 99, or **Hertz**, ✆ 90 96 75 23, ✉ 90 93 21 95, both in Blvd Victor Hugo. Hire a bike at the train station, or at **Dall'Oppio**, Rue Portagnel, ✆ 90 96 46 83 (Mar–Oct), or **Peugot**, 15 Rue du Pont, ✆ 90 96 03 77.

Tourist Information

35 Place de la République, next to Hôtel Jules César, ✆ 90 18 41 21, ✉ 90 93 17 17, and in the station, ✆ 90 49 36 90. If you intend to see most of Arles' monuments and museums, stop here to purchase the 60F **global ticket** to save money. Two-hour **Van Gogh tours** depart every Tues and Fri at 5pm, 15 June–15 September.

The **post office**, ✆ 90 18 41 00, is at 5 Blvd des Lices.

market days

Saturday, Blvd des Lices and Bvld Clémenceau. Wednesday, Blvd Émile Combes. On the first Wednesday of every month there is a *foire à la brocante* on Blvd des Lices.

The Arènes and Théâtre Antique

Despite the pictures in children's history books, Rome was ruined not so much by tribes of horrid Vandals, but by the latter-day Romans themselves, who regarded the baths, theatres and temples they inherited as their private stone quarries. The same holds true of Arles' great monuments, except for the amphitheatre or **Arènes**, ✆ 90 96 03 70 (*open Apr–Sept 9–7, Oct–Mar 10–4.30*), all of 3m wider than its rival at Nîmes. As enormous as it is, it originally stood another arcade higher, and was clad in marble; as in most public buildings in the Roman empire no expense was spared on its comforts. An enormous awning operated by sailors protected the audience from the sun and rain, and fountains scented with lavender and burning saffron helped cover up the stink of blood spilled by the gladiators and wild animals below. This temple of death survived in good repair because it came in handy. Its walls were tricked out with towers by Saracen occupiers and used as a fortress (like the theatres of Rome), and from the Middle Ages on it sheltered a poor, crime-ridden neighbourhood with two churches and 200 houses, built from stones prised off the amphitheatre's third storey. These were cleared away in 1825, leaving the amphitheatre free for bullfights, and able to pack in 12,000 spectators.

But a different fate was in store for the **Théâtre Antique** (*same hours as Arènes*), just south of the Arènes: in the 5th century, in a fury usually reserved for pagan temples, Christian fanatics pulled it apart stone by stone. A shame, because the fragments of fine sculpture they left in the rubble suggest that the theatre, once capable of seating 12,000, was much more lavish than the one in Orange. Of the stage, only two tall Corinthian columns survived; they were nicknamed 'the two widows', after being pressed into service as gibbets in the 17th and 18th centuries. The most famous statue of Roman Provence, the *Venus of Arles*, lay buried at their feet until she was dug up in 1651 and presented to Louis XIV to adorn the gardens of Versailles. Tiers of seats have been rebuilt for modern performances and costume pageants, most of which take place in July.

South of the theatre runs the **Boulevard des Lices** ('of the lists'), where large cafés under the plane trees provide ringside seats for the rollicking Saturday and monthly Wednesday morning markets. Since the 17th century the Boulevard has been the favourite promenade of the Arlésiens, where visitors like Van Gogh would go on Sunday to see the women dressed in their best costumes. On either side of the street are the **Jardin d'Eté** (with a bust of Van Gogh) and **Jardin d'Hiver** (where the 5th-century BC *oppidum* was uncovered).

Place de la République: St-Trophime

From Boulevard des Lices, Rue Jean Jaurès (the Roman *cardo*) leads to the harmonious **Place de la République**, an attractive square on the Roman model, with a fountain built around a granite **obelisk** that once stood in the *spina* (or barrier) of the circus. Overlooking this pagan sun needle is one of the chief glories of Provençal Romanesque, the cathedral of **St-Trophime**.

The original church, built by St Hilaire in the 5th century and dedicated to St Stephen, was rebuilt at the end of the 11th century, and the great **Portal** added in the next. Inspired by the triumphal arches of Glanum and Orange, its reliefs describe the *Last Judgement*, mixing the versions of the Apocalypse and Gospel of Matthew. As angels blast away on their trumpets, the triumphant Christ sits in majesty in the tympanum, accompanied by the symbols of the four Evangelists, the 12 Apostles, and a gospel choir of 18 pairs of angels. Below, St Michael weighs each soul, separating the good from evil for their just desserts in the after-life—the fortunate in their long robes are delivered into the bosoms of Abraham, Isaac and Jacob, while the damned, naked and bound like a chain gang, are led off in a conga-line to hell: as in all great Romanesque art, the figures on this portal seem to dance to an inner, cosmic rhythm. The large saints set back in the columned recesses below are, from left to right: Bartholomew, James the Minor, Trophime as bishop, John the Evangelist, Peter (over the man-eating lions), Paul, Andrew, Stephen (being stoned), James the Major and Philip. Van Gogh found it admirable but 'so cruel, so monstrous, like a Chinese nightmare, that even this beautiful example of so good a style seems to me to belong to another world and I am glad not to belong to it...'

Saint-Trophime, Arles.

After the sumptuous portal, the spartan nudity of the long, narrow nave is as striking as its unusual height (60m). Aubusson tapestries from the 17th century hang across the top, and there are several Palaeochristian sarcophagi along the sides. The best decoration, however, is by a Dutchman named Finsonius, who came down to Arles in 1610. Like Van Gogh, he stayed, mesmerized by the light and colour, and met a bad end, drowning in the icy Rhône in 1642. St-Trophime has three of his paintings: in the crossing, a beautiful *Annunciation* (1610), the *Stoning of St Stephen* over the triumphal arch in the nave, and on the right, a singular *Adoration of the Magi*, with nightmare architecture and animals in attendance.

The Cloister

Same opening hours as the Arènes.

Around the corner in Rue du Cloître is the entrance to St-Trophime's cloister. No other in Provence is as richly and harmoniously sculpted as this, carved in the 12th and 14th centuries by the masters of St-Gilles. Because Arles was as anti-Revolutionary as a town could be, this masterpiece was spared the wanton vandalism that destroyed so much elsewhere.

The north gallery is the oldest, supported by two monumental pillars adorned with statues; those of *St Peter* and *St Trophime* on the northwest are masterpieces of the classically influenced Arles school—even the foliage in the borders has a certain Corinthian air. The capitals in the Romanesque north and east galleries are carved with scenes from the New Testament, their figures moving to the same rhythms as those on the portal. The capitals of the more severe Gothic gallery to the south are carved with the *Life of St Trophime*, while on the west the capitals closely resemble the south gallery of Montmajour's cloister: note the *Magdalene* kissing Christ's feet, and *St Martha* with her Tarasque.

Hôtel de Ville and les Cryptoportiques.

Sharing Place de la République with the church of St-Trophime is Arles' palatial **Hôtel de Ville**, built in 1675 after plans by Hardouin-Mansart, architect of the Hall of Mirrors at Versailles; here, his virtuoso signature is in the remarkable flat vaulting of the vestibule. Facing the inner courtyard are remnants of older civic buildings: sections of the 12th–15th-century palace of the *podestats* (or prefects of the Holy Roman Emperor), and the town hall of 1500, with a Roman tympanum and bell tower modelled after the mausoleum of Glanum.

Just around the corner on Rue Balze is the cryptoporticus of the forum, or **les crypto-portiques** (*open Apr–Sept 9–7, Oct–Mar 10–4.30*). With the ramparts, they were the first large Roman constructions of the colony. Forming three sides of a rectangle measuring 89 by 59 metres, these subterrean barrel-vaulted double galleries of the 1st century BC were built as foundations for the monumental structures of the Forum above. No one knows for sure what other purpose a cryptoporticus may have served—for storage, or perhaps, as on Rome's Palatine Hill, for cool promenades. During the last war the galleries came in handy as an air-raid shelter.

The Museon Arlaten

> Open Nov–Mar 9–12 and 2–5, Apr, May, Sept and Oct 9–12 and 2–6, June and July 9–12 and 2–7.30.

The indefatigable Frédéric Mistral began his collection of ethnographic items from Provence in 1896, and in 1904, when he won the Nobel Prize, he used the money to purchase the 16th-century Hôtel de Castellane-Laval to house his **Museon Arlaten**, 29 Rue de la Republique, ✆ 90 96 08 23. Mistral's aim was to record the details of everyday life in Provence for future generations. The evolution of the traditional Arlésienne costume, one of Mistral's obsessions, is thoroughly documented, with the adjustments made to match fashion changes in Paris. The wearing of it declined along with the use of the Provençal language, in spite of the poet's folklore parades (the 'Festivals of Virgins') in Arles' theatre and his pronouncements that the costume 'in the shadowy transition of the centuries, lets us see a lightning flash of beauty!'

Most memorable and strange are the two life-size dioramas: a Christmas dinner at a *mas*, with a table groaning with wax food, and a visit to a new mother and her infant. The curious gifts of salt, a match, an egg and bread brought by the visitors symbolize the hope that the baby may grow to be (in the same order) wise, straight, full and good. The gallery of rituals has a prickly Tarasque retired from the procession at Tarascon, and a lock of golden hair discovered in a medieval tomb at Les Baux. One room is dedicated to the Félibrige, and another to Mistral himself, with the great man's cradle and cane. In the courtyard, a paved 'little forum' was uncovered, complete with an **exedra** cut with ten niches for statues.

To the north of the Museon Arlaten, the café-filled **Place du Forum** is the centre of modern life in Arles, watched over helplessly by a **statue of Frédéric Mistral,** moustachioed and goateed like his near-double, Buffalo Bill. Mistral himself attended its unveiling in 1909, thanking his admirers, but regretting that they made him look as if he were waiting for a train.

Constantine's Baths and the Réattu Museum

From the Place de la République, Rue Hôtel de Ville leads north to the ruins of Constantine's palace, of which only part of the baths, or **Les Thermes de Constantin**, remain (*open Apr–Sept 9–12 and 2–7, Oct–Mar 10–12 and 2–4.30*).

Across the street on the banks of the Rhône stood the Priory of the Knights of Malta, built in the 14th century. The knights, who came from all over Europe, were divided into eight *langues* or tongues, and this was the local headquarters of the *Langue de Provence*; the façade with gargoyles facing the river gives the best idea of its original appearance. After the Revolution a local academic painter named Jacques Réattu purchased the priory, and his daughter made it into the **Musée Réattu**, Rue du Grand Prieuré, ✆ 90 49 38 34 (*same hours as the Thermes*), the contents of which are so boring you may well wonder how Réattu and his mates stayed awake to paint them. In 1972, the museum was jolted awake with a donation of 57 drawings from Picasso, in gratitude for the many bullfights he enjoyed in Arles. Nearly all date from January 1971 and constitute a running dialogue the artist held with himself on some of his favourite subjects—harlequins, men, women, the artist and his model—and, more unusually, a Tarasque. Other Picassos in the museum include a beautiful portrait of his mother Maria from the 1920s, donated by his widow Jacqueline, and a sculpture of a woman with a violin. There are more recent works by César and Pol Bury, and upstairs, an exhibition gallery devoted to photography.

The Alyscamps

Same opening hours as the Arènes.

One of the most prestigious necropolises of the Middle Ages, the Alyscamps owed its fame to the legend of St Trophime, a cousin of the proto-martyr St Stephen who became a disciple of St Paul. Paul sent Trophime to convert Gaul, where medieval hagiographers later confused him with a 2nd- or 3rd-century Bishop of Arles of the same name. The story has it that Trophime arrived in Arles in the year 46, and held secret meetings with his new converts in the lonesome Roman cemetery of Alyscamps (believed to be a corruption of *Elisii Campi*, or Elysian Fields), which according to Roman custom was built outside the city walls, along the Via Aurelia. Trophime eventually attracted quite a following, and before he died he gave a special blessing to the Alyscamps; Christ himself attended the ceremony, and left behind a stone imprint of his knee.

Burial in such holy ground was so desirable that bodies sealed in barrels with their burial fee attached were floated down the Rhône to Arles. Some rascals in Beaucaire took to robbing the dead of their coins as they floated downstream, but they were found out when the barrels miraculously returned upstream to the scene of the crime. At its greatest extent the necropolis stretched 2.5km and contained 19 chapels and several thousand tombs, many of them packed five bodies deep. Dante mentions it in the *Inferno* (IX, 112) and it makes an appearance in numerous *Chansons de Geste*. Ariosto wrote how Charlemagne's peers, cut down in Roncevalles, were flown here and buried by angels.

The Alyscamps' mystique began to decline in 1152, when the relics of St Trophime were transferred to the cathedral. Grave-robbers pillaged the tombs, and the most beautiful sarcophagi were given away as presents to Renaissance potentates. Under Louis Napoleon the Alyscamps itself was dismembered by a railroad, a canal, factories, and a housing estate, leaving only one romantic, melancholy lane lined with empty, mostly plain sarcophagi. Little holes of mysterious purpose are carved into the stone of many of them, similar to holes in other tombs from the megalithic era; they may have held tiny oil lamps. Of the 19 chapels, only the recently restored **St-Honorat** with its two-storey octagonal tower still stands, rebuilt in the 12th century by the monks of St-Victor in Marseille; in the apse are three Carolingian sarcophagi.

The Archaeological Museum

Open daily Apr–Sept 9–8, Oct–Mar 10–6, closed Mon, adm; © 90 18 88 88, ✆ 90 93 69 59.

Arles' newest museum, the **Musée Archéologique**, Presqu'île du Cirque Romain, Avenue de la 1ère D.F.L., is slightly out of town, opposite the Palais des Congrès. It's a shiny piled and bolted building housing the collected contents of several of Arles' old museums and claims to be one of the best collections of archaeology in the world.

Amongst the exhibits are the pagan statues and sarcophagi of the former Musée d'Art Païen. Nearly everything here was made in the Arles region, with the exception of the beautiful white marble *Hippolytus and Phaedra sarcophagus* (2nd or 3rd century AD), with its hunting scenes. Two exceptional mosaics brought in from nearby Roman villas show the *Rape of Europa* and *Orpheus* enchanting the wild beasts; there's a graceful but damaged dancing girl, a headless statue of Mithras, the god of the legionnaires, his torso decorated with signs of the Zodiac entwined by a serpent. The large statue of Augustus was found in the theatre, as was the **Venus of Arles**, represented here by a copy made before Louis XIV had it 'restored'. Although a fairly chaste specimen as marble love goddesses go, she earned from Théodore Aubanel the most ham-handedly erotic of all Félibre poems:

> *Laisso ti pèd toumba la raubo qu'à tis anco*
> *S'envertouio, mudant tout ço qu'as de plus bèu:*
> *Abandouno toun ventre i pountoun dóu soulèu!*
> *Coume l'èurre s'aganto à la rusco d'un aubre,*
> *Laisso din mi brassado estregne en plen toun maubre:*
> *Laisso ma bouco ardènto e mi det tremoulant*
> *Courre amouros pertout sus toun cadabre blanc!*

> *(Throw to your feet the robe that around your hips*
> *hangs, hiding all that is most beautiful about you:*

Abandon your stomach to the kisses of the sun!
As ivy entwines the bark of a tree,
Let me in my embraces clasp all of your marble;
Let my ardent mouth and burning fingers
run lovingly over your body so white!)

Mothers in Arles use this armless Venus for their own ends. They bring their children to see her and warn: 'The same thing will happen to you if you keep biting your nails!'

Also in the museum are the contents of the former Musée d'Art Chrétien, the best collection of 4th-century Christian sarcophagi of any museum. Carved by Arlésien sculptors between the years 330 and 395, these remarkably preserved tombs make a fascinating documentary of the newly victorious faith; as their pagan ancestors carved scenes from mythology, so these early Christians spared no expense to decorate their last resting places on earth with scenes from the Old and New Testaments. Nearly every figure of importance wears a Roman toga; in the **sarcophage de Trinquetaille**, discovered in 1974, the Three Magi sport Phrygian bonnets.

Festivals and Annual Events

Arles does its best to keep its visitors entertained. The free broadsheet *Farandole* gives details of everything from theatre, concerts, fairs and exhibitions to local basketball results. Easter is celebrated by a **Feria Pascale** with four days of bullfights, most of them Spanish *corridas* (for ticket reservations for Arènes events, call ✆ 90 96 03 70). On 24 June, St John's Day, there are typical Arlésien dances in costume around bonfires, and the distribution of blessed bread. July is the busiest month, with a festival of music, dance and drama, the **Cocarde d'Or** bullfights, and most importantly, photography in the **Rencontres Internationales de la Photographie**, with over a dozen shows and workshops, held in the Théâtre Antique. At the end of August there's the **Festival du Film Peplum**. The last bullfights of the year, on the second Sunday in September, coincide with the **Prémices du Riz**, or rice harvest. There are so many different spectacles and events that there's a permanent fête committee, **Festiv' Arles**, ✆ 90 96 47 00.

Shopping

Besides the Wednesday and Saturday **markets** (*see* p.115), you can find authentic *gardian* costumes at **Camille**, Esplanade des Lices, ✆ 90 96 04 94. For colourful Provençal fabrics, try **Les Olivades**, 2 Rue Jean Jaurès, ✆ 90 96 22 17. **Cabane Soleil**, 15 Rue du 4 Septembre, ✆ 90 96 07 34, has enchanting locally made puppets, as well as other modern curiosities in metal and wood. Buy your *calissons d'Aix* from **Puyricard**, 5 Rue Dulau, ✆ 90 93 46 91, or go just to see the crystallized fruits, marzipan models, chocolates and other bright goodies stacked like small sugared mountains. Any good butcher will sell you spicy donkey-filled **saucisson d'Arles**.

Arles offers relief for the budget-bruised traveller, and charges less for more than you'll get in cities like Avignon or Aix. If you arrive without a reservation, the tourist office has a room-finding service for a small fee.

expensive

The luxurious grand-daddy of hotels in Arles is ★★★★**Jules César** (locally known as *Chez Jules*), Blvd des Lices, ✆ 90 93 43 20, ✉ 90 93 33 47, occupying a former Dominican monastery with a Caesar-ish temple porch tacked on. The rooms are vast, air-conditioned and furnished with Provençal pieces; the pool is heated and the gardens beautiful (*closed Nov–23 Dec*). Its chief competitor, ★★★★**Nord Pinus**, Place du Forum, ✆ 90 93 44 44, ✉ 90 93 34 00, has some columns from a Roman temple embedded in its façade. Once the favourite of the Félibres, poets, and literati like Stendhal, Mérimée, and Henry James, it now draws the top mata- dors and wealthy aficionados; the premises are comfortable and full of heavy dark furniture, bullfighting posters, trophies, and the mounted heads of famous bulls; weekend hunts in the Camargue and private boat excursions to the beach are some of its offerings (*closed Jan–Mar*).

Near the lively Place du Forum, the 12th to 18th-century home of the Comtes d'Arlatan has been converted into the magnificent ★★★**D'Arlatan**, 26 Rue du Sauvage, ✆ 90 93 56 66, ✉ 90 49 68 45. After a warm welcome, wait for the lift standing on glass over Roman excavations; the house was built over part of the Constantine basilica, and in 1988 a Roman drain and a statue plinth from the 1st century BC were uncovered. If you're alone, ask for room 38; a single bed for half the price, if you can do without a TV and your own bathroom, located in a converted chapel overlooking the courtyard where a fountain splatters; a cherub flies at the head of your bed. ★★★**Forum**, at 10 Place du Forum, ✆ 90 93 48 95, ✉ 90 93 90 00, in another old house, doesn't have as much charm but it does have a swimming-pool (*closed for Christmas*). Just north of Arles, a traditional farmhouse and 16th-century chapel are at the core of the ★★★**Mas de la Chapelle**, Petite Rte de Tarascon, ✆ 90 93 23 15, ✉ 90 96 53 74; excellent service, a pool and tennis courts are some of the extras.

moderate

Among the less expensive choices are ★★**St-Trophime**, 16 Rue de la Calade, ✆ 90 96 88 38, ✉ 90 96 92 19, in an old house with a central court (*closed mid-Nov–Feb*). ★★**Diderot**, in the centre of old Arles, 5 Rue Diderot, ✆ 90 96 10 30, has no-nonsense comfortable rooms; at the ★★**Calendal**, 22 Place Pomme, ✆ 90 96 11 89, ✉ 90 96 05 84, rooms overlook a garden with palm trees (*closed Oct–Apr*). To be first at the Musée Réattu in the morning, spend the night at ★★**Hôtel du Musée**, 11 Rue du Grand-Prieuré, ✆ 90 93 88 88, ✉ 90 49 98 15: an attractive converted 17th-century residence opposite the museum. Quiet, subtly chic, and above all friendly, the hotel epitomizes all Arles has to offer (*closed Jan–mid-Feb*).

inexpensive

The **★★Gauguin**, at 5 Place Voltaire, ✆ 90 96 14 35, just south of Place Lamartine, has simple but tidy rooms, some with balconies, and is cheaper than its two–star competitors (*closed Nov*). Arles also has an **Auberge de Jeunesse** at 20 Ave Maréchal Foch, ✆ 90 96 18 25. Bus from Place Lamartine (*open year round*).

Eating Out

Lou Marquès (in the Jules César hotel) is Arles' elegant citadel of traditional *haute cuisine*, featuring dishes such as *croustillant de Saint-Pierre* and *carré d'agneau* with artichokes, and an excellent wine cellar (menus 195–380F). In Place du Forum, **Le Vaccarès**, ✆ 90 96 06 17, ✆ 90 96 24 52, serves delicious renderings of Provence's finest dishes, using the freshest market ingredients (steamed *loup* with a citrus *compote*, *noisettes d'agneau*), washed down with the best wines from the Rhône valley (menus 90–235F). Set in a beautiful vaulted room from the 17th century, **Le Tourne Broche**, 6 Rue Balze, ✆ 90 96 16 03, serves a selection of affordable menus from 80F, including items like salmon terrine and *suprême de volaille* (*closed Mon*). **L'Escaladou**, 23 Rue Porte de Laure, ✆ 90 96 70 43, is open on a Monday, and does a passable *l'aïoli*. It's very popular so you will need to book in summer. For vegetarians, **Vitamine**, 16 Rue du Docteur Fanton, ✆ 90 93 77 36, offers a welcome injection of greenery: 50 different salads for under 50F (*closed Sun, but not in July*).

Entertainment and Nightlife

The most sociable bars in Arles are in Place du Forum; for lazy watching-the-world-go-by, plump for a chair in Place Voltaire or Boulevard des Lices. After dark, the liveliest place in Arles is **Le Méjean**, at Quai M-Dormoy, ✆ 90 93 33 56, a complex that includes a book and record shop, art gallery, concerts, three cinemas and films in their original language, also a bar and restaurant where you can eat for as little as 55F a head. There's a piano bar, **37.2**, at 10 Place Honoré Clair, ✆ 90 96 11 44, and two more cinemas: **Le Capitole**, Rue Laurent Bonnement, ✆ 90 96 05 81, and **Le Femina**, same number, at Rue Emile Zola. If you want to strut your stuff, head for **Le Krystal**, at Moules (✉ 13280), ✆ 90 98 32 40, but most locals head out of town to Avignon for nightlife at the weekend.

Plaine de la Crau

Hercules, after completing his Tenth Labour, the theft of the cattle of Geryon, passed through Provence with the booty on his way back to Greece. He had some trouble with the native Ligurians, who apparently tried to pinch the cows. One thing led to another, and before long Hercules found himself in single-handed battle with the entire nation. As they advanced across the marshy plain, Hercules, armed only with his club, got down on his knees in despair at having nothing to throw at them. Zeus took pity on him, and sent down a shower of stones, with which the hero soon put the Ligurians to flight. This was an unaccountably important story in the mythology of the Greeks. They and the Romans put the Hercules of this battle in the sky; the northern constellation we know as Hercules they called *Engonasis*, the 'kneeler'.

The carpet of stones Zeus sent are still there for all to see, on the weird wasteland called the **Crau**, stretching from Arles to the Etang de Berre, between the Camargue and the Alpilles. The ancients found it fascinating, and many Greek and Roman writers attempted to explain it; Aristotle, a hopeless bird-brain at anything involving natural science, said the stones were formed by volcanoes, and 'rolled down naturally' to the low plain. In fact the rounded stones are alluvial deposits from the Durance, from long ago when the river followed this path into the Rhône delta.

The empty, wind-blown Crau is a major element of the Provençal mystique; Mistral, for example, dragged his poor Mireille across it before she met her sad end. Today it does its best to keep up a romantic appearance. Over 100,000 sheep make their winter home here, nibbling the tufts of grass between the stones before migrating in the old-fashioned way up to the Provençal Alps in May or June; the stone shepherd huts are still one of the few features of the Crau. The French, unfortunately, have been trying to make it disappear. Most of the northern part has been reclaimed for farmland. The rest is criss-crossed with railways, canals and roads, decorated with army firing ranges and the gigantic Istres military airport; there's even a dynamite plant.

There are no good roads over the unspoiled parts of the Crau, and the only village, **St-Martin-de-Crau**, is a dismal spot, but you can still see something of the original effect along the N 568 (for Fos and Marseille) and the N 113 (for Salon), both east of Arles.

Where to Stay and Eating Out

In **St-Martin** (✉ 13310), set in a 35-hectare estate of meadows and century-old forests, you can indulge in the luxurious ★★★★**Château de Vergières**, ✆ 90 47 17 16, a neoclassical manor with six bedrooms, all handsomely furnished with antiques; the *table d'hôte* meal, including aperitifs, wine and liqueurs, is 250F—reservations mandatory (*open Mar–Nov*).

On the edge of the Crau, and also convenient for a visit to Arles, the ★★★**Auberge La Fenière** in **Raphèle-les-Arles** (✉ 13280; on the N 453, 6km from Arles; ✆ 90 98 47 44, 🖷 90 98 48 39) is an attractive, ivy-covered inn; nice rooms, some with air conditioning, and a restaurant with an outdoor terrace which offers Camarguaise beef, duck with olives or salmon roulades on menus from 100 to 250F.

Into the Camargue

To its handful of inhabitants, the Camargue was the *isclo*, the 'island' between the two branches of the Rhône. The river's course has taken many different forms over the millennia, and the present one, with its two arms, has created a vast marshland, France's salt cellar, its greatest treasure-house of water-fowl and home of some of its most exotic landscapes. The two branches, the *Grand* and *Petit* Rhônes, really build separate deltas, leaving the space in between a soupy battleground where land and sea slowly struggle for mastery.

With its unique coastline and wild expanses, the Camargue provides a soothing antithesis to the more crowded areas of the region. It is also ideal for outdoor activities: hiking, climbing, diving, surfing or horse-riding (*see* 'Getting Around' sections below for details).

Getting Around

Due to its proximity, Arles is the traditional jumping-off point for the Camargue.

by train and bus

The only public transport to the centre of the Camargue begins at the Gare Routière in Arles: one or two buses a day each to Stes-Maries-de-la-Mer (via Albaron) and Salin-de-Giraud. There are also one or two SNCF trains to St-Gilles from Arles. St-Gilles has regular bus connections to Nîmes (five a day), a few to Arles and one to Lunel.

on foot, horseback and by bike and jeep

Remember that the Camargue is really quite small—it's never more than 40km from Arles to the coast. A serious hiker could see the whole thing in three days. It is perfect country for bicycling, and there are a few places in Stes-Maries-de-la-Mer to rent some wheels. Horses are even more popular; there are many places to hire one in Stes-Maries-de-la-Mer, or in Aigues-Mortes, the **Ranch del Sol** (© 66 53 99 83) and at l'Etang de l'Estagel, **L'Etrier** (© 66 01 36 76). **Destination Camargue**, © 90 96 70 39 (Sat & Sun © 90 93 42 48) organizes day and half-day trips into the Camargue by jeep.

by boat

This is another possibility: **Blue-Line** (© 66 87 22 66) and other firms in St-Gilles rent boats fit for a few days' trip through the Petite Camargue; at Stes-Maries-de-la-Mer and St-Gilles excursion boats make short cruises around the Camargue.

History

Ancient writers recorded the people of the Camargue hunting boar in the swamp forests and actually raking fish out of the mud; besides remarking on its curiosities, the Greeks and Romans left it entirely alone. In the early Middle Ages, however, at least four monastic colonies were founded on the edges of the Camargue, not only to reclaim land but to collect that most precious of medieval commodities, salt. In this inhospitable country, all of them disappeared long ago; the most important was the Abbey of Psalmody, which became quite a power in Provence. Today only scant ruins can be seen, on a farm still called Psalmody north of Aigues-Mortes, in the region called the 'Petite Camargue' west of the Petit Rhône.

By the 1600s, the monks gave way to cowboys (*gardians*), who created large ranches to exploit the two totem animals of the Camargue: the native black, longhorn cattle that thrive on salt grass, and who have always been the preferred stock for Provençal bullfights; and the beautiful white horse, believed to have been introduced by the Arabs back in the Dark Ages. A true cowboy culture grew up, a romantic image dear to the Provençaux, and especially to Provençal writers like Mistral.

CAMARGUE
gardian branding iron

There are still a few score *gardians* in the Camargue today, keeping up the old traditions. Big changes have come to the swampland in the last century. For a while, the French threatened to dispose rationally of this land altogether, with dikes and drainage schemes turning large areas into salt-pans and rice fields. Fortunately, nature societies secured the creation of a wildlife preserve around the heart of the Camargue in 1928, and the government made a Regional Park of the area in 1970.

Flora and Fauna

First and most spectacularly, there are the flamingos (*flamants roses*), a symbol of the Camargue; several thousand of them nest around the southern lagoons. Probably no place in the Mediterranean has a wider variety of aquatic birds: lots of ducks, grebes, cormorants, curlews and ibis. The little egret is a common sight, though they spend the winter in Africa, as does the avocet, which looks like an aquatic magpie. There are also many purple herons, conspicuously striped on the head and breast. Not all are water birds; you may see an eagle or a majestic red kite (*milan royal*).

Deforestation in favour of ranches destroyed most of the natural habitat for land animals, but there are still boars, beavers, and blue frogs. Trees are rare, although there are umbrella pines and scrubby, pink-flowered tamarisks. Common plants include the purple-flowered *saladelle*, and the *salicorne*, which grows in tough clumps. Among the fauna, we nearly forgot the most important—the hard-drilling, inescapable Camargue mosquito; make her the prime consideration when you visit.

PURPLE HERON

The Musée de la Camargue

Open daily exc Tues, 10–4.15; Apr–Sept daily 9.15–6.45; adm.

It was an inspiration on the part of the Regional Park management, creating this museum in what not long ago was a working Camargue cattle and sheep ranch, the **Mas du Pont de Rousty**, 9km southwest of Arles on the D 570, © 90 97 10 82. The buildings are well-restored and documented, giving a feeling of what life was like on the *mas* a century ago. There are special exhibits on the *gardians*, on the fickle Rhône (you'll learn that 400,000 years ago it flowed past Nîmes), on Mistral's *Miréio*, and other subjects. Outside, there are marked nature trails leading deep into the surrounding swampy plain, the **Marais de la Grande Mar**. About 4km beyond the museum on the D 570, little **Albaron** was one of the first inhabited centres of the Camargue; a stout medieval tower survives, built to guard Arles from any attack or pirate raid up the Petit Rhône.

The Etang de Vaccarès

For all of us lazy motor tourists, the way to see the best of the Camargue is to take the D 37, a left turn 4km south of the museum. After another 4km, a side road leads to the **Domaine de Méjanes**, with horse riding and canoes; on summer weekends the *gardians* put on shows of cowboy know-how, and occasionally bullfights. Call ahead, © 90 97 10 62, for information. Further on, the D 37 skirts the edges of the **Etang de Vaccarès**, the biggest of the lagoons and centre of the Camargue wildlife preserve. In some places you can see flocks of nesting flamingos year-round. A side road, the D 36B, leads down to Salin-de-Giraud, passing the **Centre d'Information la Capillière** (*open daily 9–12 and 2–7; © 90 97 00 97*), with exhibits on flora and fauna and fascinating guided nature walks around the lagoon. On the D 36D, almost at the mouth of the Grand Rhône, is another Regional Park nature centre: **La Palissade**, in a park with white horses and bulls, audio-visual shows, a small aquarium, exhibits on flora and fauna, and guided walks through the area (*open weekdays 9–5; June–Sept daily; adm; © 42 86 81 28*).

If you really want to get away from it all, this part of the Camargue might be the place; the *salins* are barred from the Mediterranean by one of the longest and emptiest beaches in France, the **Plage de Piémanson** at the mouth of the Grand Rhône; the current is a bit treacherous for swimming.

With good local maps, determined swamp fans can hike the 40km or so to Stes-Maries-de-la-Mer in summer, through the most unspoiled parts of the Camargue; a sea-wall, the **Digue de la Mer**, provides a crossing around the lagoons, and the only hazards are secluded beaches that have been taken over by bands of *naturistes*. You might even make it over to the Camargue's forest, **Bois des Rièges**, on a large island at the southern end of the Etang de Vaccarès. Though officially off limits, as part of the nature preserve, it can sometimes be reached on foot in summer. Be careful though; this is the home of the Camargue's Abominable Snowman, the *Bête de Vaccarès*, a mysterious part-human creature first sighted in the 15th century.

Where to Stay and Eating Out

 Almost all of the accommodation in the area is in Stes-Maries-de-la-Mer (*see* below). But if you want to stay in the eastern or central parts of the Camargue, away from the tourists, there are some possibilities. One of these isolated spots, and also a good bet for lunch after visiting the Camargue museum, is ★**Le Flamant Rose** in **Albaron** (✉ 13123), ✆ 90 97 10 18, ✉ 90 97 12 47; simple rooms and 80–160F menus including a *salade fruits de mer* and stewed beef cowboy style—*boeuf à la gardienne*.

Salin-de-Giraud (✉ 13129), amidst its vast salt pans, doesn't even dream of attracting tourists. The family favourite restaurant is **Les Saladelles** at 4 Ave des Arènes in the centre, ✆ 42 86 83 87: a wide choice on 60/120F menus, including more spicy *boeuf à la gardienne*, chops and fish, and seafood lasagne. And of course shakers of the local speciality on every table—all you can eat. There's only one place to stay in the town, the simple and basic ★**La Camargue** on Blvd de la Camargue, ✆ 42 86 82 82.

Les Saintes-Maries-de-la-Mer

Tourist Information

5 Avenue Van Gogh (✉ 13732), ✆ 90 97 82 55, ✉ 90 97 71 15

market days

Monday and Friday mornings

Set among the low sand-dunes, jovial and lively Saintes-Maries-de-la-Mer has an open-armed approach to visitors that long predates any interest in the Camargue and its ecological balance. For this is one of Provence's holy of holies, and if you come out of season you become aware of the dream-like, insular remoteness that made it the stuff of legend.

The pious story behind it all was promoted to the hilt by the medieval Church: after Christ was crucified, his Jewish detractors took a boat without sails or oars and loaded it with three Marys—Mary Salome (mother of the apostles James and John), Mary Jacobe, the Virgin's sister, and Mary Magdalene, along with the Magdalene's sister Martha and their resurrected brother Lazarus, St Maximin and St Sidonius. As this so-called Boat of Bethany drifted off shore, Sarah, the black Egyptian servant of Mary Salome and Mary Jacobe, wept so grievously that Mary Salome tossed her cloak on the water, so that Sarah was able to walk across on it and join the saints. The boat took them to the Camargue, to this spot where the elderly Mary Salome, Mary Jacobe, and Sarah built an oratory, while their younger companions went to spread the Gospel, live in caves, and tame Tarasques. In 1448, during the reign of Good King René (who was always pinched for money) the supposed relics of the two Marys were discovered, greatly boosting the local pilgrim trade. Les Saintes-Maries became, as Mistral called it, the 'Mecca of Provence'.

A few facts blazed the trail for the legend's ready acceptance. In the 4th century, a Roman writer described a settlement on this site called *Oppidum priscum Ra*. This lent its name

128 *Down the Rhône: Alpilles, Crau and Camargue*

to the first Christian church, Notre-Dame-de-Ratis, built over the site of a spring of fresh water—where a Gallo-Roman temple had been dedicated to three sea goddesses. *Ratis* was taken to mean raft (*radeau*), hence the connection not only with the Boat of Bethany but to ancient Egypt, where in the Book of the Dead the deceased sails in a boat without oar or sail, but with the image of Ra. Even the name Mary had a familiar ring to Provence's early Christians; not only for its resemblance to the word for mother (*Matre*) but to Marius, a local cult figure after his defeat of the Teutones, and who was advised by the blonde sibyl Marthe (as pictured at Les Baux; *see* above).

Today Saintes-Maries-de-la-Mer is best known for the pilgrimage of Mary Jacobe on 24 and 25 May. This attracts gypsies from all over the world, who have canonized her servant Sarah as their patron saint. The reason seems to owe something to yet another coincidence—the discovery of the relics coincided with a great convergence of gypsies in Provence in the 1440s, some of whom wandered up from North Africa and Spain, and others who crossed into Europe by way of Greece and the Balkans. The gypsies, however, claim that Sarah was not Egyptian at all, but one of their own, Sarah-la-Kâli ('the black' but also recalling the Hindu goddess Kali), who met the Boat of Bethany here and was the first of their tribe to be converted to Christianity. The Church obliged by 'discovering' the bones of Sarah in 1496.

Getting Around

by bus

There are at least two buses daily from Arles (55 mins), and many more options for exploring the Camargue itself.

by boat

There's an hour-long cruise in the Petit Rhône from the end of March to the beginning of September on the paddle steamer *Tiki III*, © 90 97 81 22.

on horseback

Go for a ride—the best way of exploring the trails (the tourist office has a list of stables, some offering tours for beginners).

by jeep and bike

Camargue Safaris offers jeep tours, © 90 97 86 93; or you can pedal. Hire a bike from **La Vélociste**, in Place des Remparts, © 90 97 83 26 (open Sept–June); **Delta Vélos**, Rue Paul Peyron, © 90 97 84 99 (open all year); and **Camargue Vélo**, 27 Rue F.-Mistral, © 90 97 94 55 (open Feb–Nov).

The Church

In 869, during the construction of a new church to replace the 6th-century oratory 'built' by the two Marys, the Saracens swooped down in a surprise raid and carried off the Archbishop of Arles, who just happened to be down to inspect the work. The pirates demanded a high ransom in silver, swords, and slaves for their hostage, and were dismayed when the bishop died on them—dismayed, but not so put out as to risk losing the ransom. The pirates tied his corpse in all its vestments to a throne and made off with the loot before the Christians realized the hostage was dead.

Faced with the threat of similar shenanigans, stones were shipped down from Arles at great expense to rebuild the church in 1130. The result is, along with St-Victor in Marseille, the most impressive fortified church in Provence: a crenellated ship with loopholes for windows in a small pond of white villas with orange roofs. Inside, along the gloomy nave, are wells that supplied the church-fortress in times of siege; pilgrims still bottle the water to ensure their protection by St Sarah. In the second chapel on the left, near the model of the Boat of Bethany that is carried in the procession to the sea, is the polished rock 'pillow' of the saints, discovered with their bones in 1448. The capitals supporting the blind arches of the raised choir are finely sculpted in the style of St-Trophime. Under the choir is the **crypt**, where the relics and statue of St Sarah in her seven robes are kept; the statue has been kissed so often that the black paint has come off in patches. Here, too, is a *taurobolium*, or relief of a bull-slaying from an ancient Mithraeum, the bits scratched away long ago by women who used the dust to concoct fertility potions, along with photos and ex votos left by the gypsies. From April to mid-November, you can take a stroll below the bell tower, with views stretching across the Camargue that take on a magic glow at sunset (*open 10–12.30 and 2.30–7*).

This roof walk circles the lavish **upper chapel** (*usually closed*), dedicated to St Michael, which in times of need served as a *donjon*. The coffer holding the relics of the Marys is kept here, except during the arcane *deus ex machina* rites unique to this church: during feast days the coffer is slowly lowered through a door over the altar after the singing of a special hymn, *Les Saintes de Provence*; the pilgrimage ends to the tune of *Adieu aux Saintes*, as the relics are slowly raised back into the chapel. In the 18th century this hocus-pocus had a reputation for curing madness, combined with the shock therapy of stripping the afflicted naked and throwing them in the sea. When Mistral attended the pilgrimage as a young man, a beautiful girl from Beaucaire abandoned by her fiancé dramatically flung herself across the altar just as the relics were being lowered, praying for the return of her lover. The girl made a considerable impression on Mistral and became the basis for his heroine Mireille, who arrives in Saintes-Maries-de-la-Mer to make a similar prayer and dies of too much sun and love in the upper chapel of this church, while the congregation in the

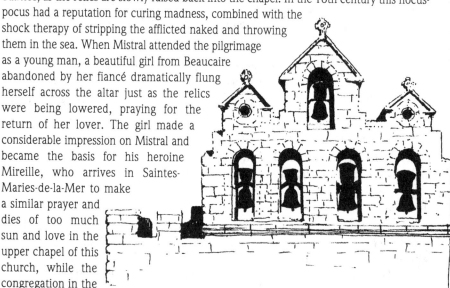

lower church, like the chorus in a Greek tragedy, accuses the holy Marys: *Reino de Paradis, mestresso / De la Planuro d'amaresso* ('Queens of Paradise, mistresses / of the plain of bitterness').

Around Les Saintes-Maries-de-la-Mer, and Pont de Gau

Mireille, in statue form at least, lives on in the main square north of the church, while to the south in Rue Victor-Hugo the **Musée Baroncelli** is devoted to zoology, archaeology and folklore. It is named after the Camargue's secular saint, the Félibre Marquis Folco de Baroncelli-Javon (1869–1943), a descendant of a Florentine merchant family in Avignon, who abandoned all at age 21 to live the life of a *gardian*. Baroncelli spent the next 60 years herding bulls, writing poetry, and doing all he could to maintain the Camargue and its customs intact. Although by trade a cowboy, his heart was with the American Indians and other oppressed minorities; Chief Sitting Bull, in France with Buffalo Bill and his Wild West Show, smoked the peace pipe with the Marquis and named him 'Faithful Bird'.

Festivals

The *Pélérinage des Gitanes* is held on 24–25 May. The gypsies began making the pilgrimage in numbers in the mid-19th century. In 1935, thanks to the intervention of the Marquis de Baroncelli, 24 May was especially set aside as St Sarah's day. Although the famous all-night candle vigil by her statue has been abolished by killjoys, her statue is still symbolically carried to the sea by a procession of gypsies, *gardians* and costumed Arlésiennes, where in imitation of ancient rainmaking ceremonies the statue is sprinkled with sea water while all are blessed by the bishop. Afterwards, the beaches and streets are alive with music and flamenco, *farandoles*, horse races and bullfights, attended by as many tourists as gypsies. The whole ceremony happens again, with considerably fewer gypsies and tourists, on the Sunday nearest 22 October for the other Mary, Mary Salome.

Les Saintes-Maries-de-la-Mer ✉ 13460   **Where to Stay**

There are a lot of choices in Les Saintes, but if you don't book during the summer or pilgrimages, you'll have to join the crowd on the beach. The really luxurious choices are all outside the centre, like the ★★★★**Mas de la Fouque**, 4km on the Rte d'Aigues Mortes, ✆ 90 97 81 02, ☎ 90 97 96 84, set in the midst of the Camargue with all possible comforts, its perfect serenity complemented by a garden, heated pool, golf, and tennis (*closed Jan and Feb*). The little pink ★★★**Mas du Clarousset**, 7km north on D 85A, the Route de Cacharel, ✆ 90 97 81 66, offers a fresh and simple decor. Each room has a private terrace, and there are extras—horses to ride, a pool, jeep excursions and gypsy music evenings in the excellent restaurants (menus from 250F). ★**Le Delta** offers good value for price, and is situated in the centre at Place Mireille, ✆ 90 97 81 12, ☎ 90 97 72 85.

Eating Out

This is the place to try *boeuf gardian*, or bull stewed in red wine with lots of garlic; *bouriroun*, an omelette with elvers from the Vaccarès; *salade de télines*, made of tiny shellfish with garlic mayonnaise; or *poutargue*, Camargue caviar made from red mullet eggs. One of the best places to try the local products of land and sea is **Lou Mas du Juge**, over the Petit Rhône on D 85, *©* 66 73 51 45, a friendly, family-run restaurant, specializing in fresh seafood (menus from 300F). Elegant **Le Brûleur de Loups**, Ave Gilbert-Leroy, *©* 90 97 83 31, *✆* 90 97 73 17, has a terrace overlooking the beach and more delights from the sea, like a seafood mix in white Châteauneuf-du-Pape; menus from 150F, cheaper for lunch (*closed mid-Nov–Mar*). If you have a car, try the **Hostellerie du Pont de Gau**, on the Rte d'Arles, *©* 90 97 81 53, *✆* 90 97 98 54, which offers jolly Provençal decor and a delicious *pot-au-feu de la mer*; menus from 90F (*closed Jan–mid-Feb*).

Entertainment

There are other entertainments in Les Saintes: in the summer, nightly *Courses Camargues* in the bullring, guitars and buskers in the streets and miles of white sand beaches, including a *plage naturiste* 6km to the east. At Pont de Gau, 4km north, there's a **Centre d'Information du Parc de la Camargue** (*open summer 9–6, winter 9.30–5, closed Fri Oct–Mar; © 90 97 86 32, ✆ 90 97 70 82*), and a **Parc Ornithologique** (*open 9–sunset, Feb–Nov 9.30–sunset; © 90 97 82 62*) with walks through the marshlands and aviaries containing some of the rarer birds.

St-Gilles-du-Gard

West of Arles, the N 572 takes you through the drier parts of the Camargue. After crossing the Petit Rhône, you're in the **Petite Camargue**, in the *département* of the Gard, approaching **St-Gilles**, the only town for miles in any direction.

Tourist Information

Maison Romane, Place Frédéric Mistral, *©* 66 87 33 75

market days

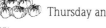 Thursday and Sunday

History

In medieval times and earlier, St-Gilles was a flourishing port, much nearer the sea than it is now. Remains have been found of a Phoenician merchant colony, and the Greek-Celtic *oppidum* that replaced it, but the place did not really blossom until the 11th century. The popes and the monks of Cluny, who owned it, conspired to make the resting place of Gilles, an obscure 8th-century martyr, a major stop along the great pilgrim road to Compostela. The powerful counts of Toulouse helped too—the family originally came from St-Gilles. Soon pilgrims were pouring in from as far away as Germany and Poland;

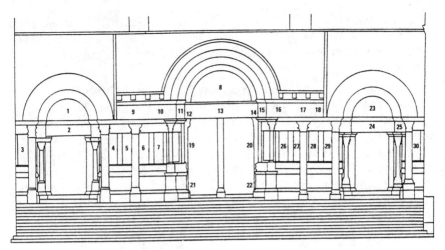

Façade of St-Gilles-du-Gard

the port boomed with the onset of the Crusades, and both the Templars and Knights Hospitallers (who owned large tracts in the Camargue) built important commanderies. In 1116 the **Abbey Church of St-Gilles** was begun, one of the most ambitious projects ever undertaken in medieval Provence.

Destiny, however, soon began making it clear that this was not the place. As the delta gradually expanded, the canals silted up and St-Gilles could no longer function as a port (a major reason for the building of Aigues-Mortes; *see* below). The real disaster came with the Wars of Religion, when the town became a Protestant stronghold; the leaders of the Protestant army thought the church, that obsolete relic from the Age of Faith that took 200 years to build, would look much better as a fortress, and they demolished nearly all of it to that end. It was rebuilt, in a much smaller version, after 1650. What was left suffered more indignities during the Revolution, and it is a miracle that one of the greatest ensembles of medieval sculpture has survived more or less intact.

The Church Façade

This is the masterpiece of the Provençal school of 12th-century sculptors, the famous work that was copied, life-size, in the Cloisters Museum in New York. Created roughly at the same time as the façade of St-Trophime in Arles, it is likewise inspired by the ancient Roman triumphal arches. Instead of Roman worthies and battle scenes, the twelve Apostles hold place of honour between the Corinthian columns. This is a bold, confident sculpture, taking delight in naturalistic detail and elaborately folded draperies, with little of the conscious stylization that characterizes contemporary work in other parts of France. In this too, the Romans were their masters. The scheme is complex, and worth describing in detail (*see* overleaf).

Left portal: tympanum of the Adoration of the Magi (1); beneath it, Jesus' entry into Jerusalem (2). Flanking the door, a beautiful St Michael slaying the dragon (3); and on the right the first four Apostles, SS Matthew and Bartholomew, Thomas and James the Lesser (4–7).

Central portal: tympanum of Christ in Majesty (8), with symbols of the Evangelists; underneath, a long frieze that runs from one side portal across to the other: from left to right, Judas with his silver (9); Jesus expelling the money-changers from the temple (10); the resurrection of Lazarus (11); Jesus prophesying the denial of Peter and the washing of the Apostles' feet (12); Last Supper (13); Kiss of Judas (14); Arrest of Christ (15); Christ before Pilate (16); Flagellation (17); Carrying the Cross (18). Left of the door, SS John and Peter (19); right of the door, SS James the Greater and Paul, with a soul-devouring Tarasque under his feet (20). Beneath these, at ground level, are small panels, representing the sacrifices of Cain and Abel and the murder of Abel (21); a deer hunt and Balaam and his ass, and Samson and the Lion (22).

Right portal: tympanum of the Crucifixion (23); beneath it, two unusual scenes: the three Marys purchasing spices to anoint the body of Jesus, and the three Marys at the tomb. To the left of this, the Magdalene and Jesus (24); to the right, Jesus appearing to his disciples (25). Left of the door, four more unidentifiable Apostles (26–29; note how the 12 represented here are not the canonical list; better-known figures like John the Evangelist and Paul were commonly substituted for the more obscure of the original Apostles). To the right of the door, Archangels combat Satan (30).

The Vis de St-Gilles

The 17th-century interior of the rebuilt church holds little interest, but underneath it the original **crypt** or lower church survives (so many pilgrims came to St-Gilles that upper and lower churches were built to hold them). Behind the church, you can see the ruins of the **choir and apse** of the original, which was much longer than the present structure. Near it, the 'screw' of St-Gilles is a spiral staircase of 50 steps that once led up one of the church's bell towers. Built about 1142, it is a tremendous *tour de force*; the stones are cut with amazing precision to make a self-supporting spiral vault; medieval masons always tried to make the St-Gilles pilgrimage just to see it. Its author, Master Mateo of Cluny, also worked on the great church of Santiago de Compostela, where he is buried.

The Maison Romane

The rest of the town shows few traces of its former greatness. The medieval centre is unusually large, if a bit forlorn. Near the façade of the church, on Place de la République, is a fine 13th-century mansion, claimed to be the house of Guy Folques, who became Pope Clement IV. Today this 'Maison Romane' houses St-Gilles' **Musée Lapidaire**, with a number of sculptures and architectural fragments from the church, and collections of folk life and nature of the Camargue (*open daily 9–12 and 3–7 in summer, 9–12 and 2–5 in winter, closed Jan and Sun, adm; © 66 87 40 42*).

In the Middle Ages scores of pilgrims, sometimes thousands, would stay over at St-Gilles every night; try it now and the innkeepers themselves will wonder why. Best choices are the **★★Heraclée** at 30 Quai du Canal, ✆ 66 87 44 10, 🖷 66 87 13 65, not exciting but well-run; and the venerable, determinedly old-fashioned **★Le Globe**, on Place Gambetta, ✆ 66 87 30 41, with a restaurant to match: *boeuf à la gardienne* and other local favourites in a sweet provincial atmosphere; menus 50F lunch, 90–130F dinner (*closed mid-Nov–mid-Dec*).

Aigues-Mortes

Every French history or geography schoolbook has a photo of Aigues-Mortes in it, and every Frenchman, most likely, carries in his mind the haunting picture—the great walls of the port where St Louis sailed off to the Crusades, now marooned in the muck of the advancing Rhône delta. It is as compelling a symbol of time and fate as any Roman ruin, and as magically evocative of medieval France as any Gothic cathedral.

Tourist Information

Place St-Louis, ✆ 66 53 73 00, 🖷 66 53 65 94; they offer historical tours of the town, year round, beginning at the office at Porte de la Gardette.

Parking: there are signs around all the entrances to the town forbidding cars; these you may ignore, just as everyone else does. There will be no problem driving around Aigues or finding parking, except perhaps in July and August.

market days

Wednesday and Sunday

History

In 1241, the Camargue was the only stretch of Mediterranean coast held by France. To solidify this precarious strip, Louis IX (St Louis) began construction of a new port. In 1248, it was complete enough to hold the 1500 ships that carried Louis and his knights to the Holy Land, on the Seventh Crusade which was to bring Louis disasters both home and abroad (the town was the last he saw of France—he died in Tunis of the plague in 1270). His successor, Philip III, finished Aigues-Mortes and built its great walls. Being the only French port, by the late 13th century it was booming, with perhaps four times as many inhabitants as its present 4800, its harbour filled with ships from as far away as Constantinople and Antioch.

Aigues-Mortes means 'dead waters', and it proved to be a prophetic name. The sea deserted Aigues, and despite efforts to keep the harbour dredged, the port went into decline after 1350. Attempts to revive it in the 1830s failed, ensuring Aigues' demise, but allowing the works of Louis and Philip to survive undisturbed. Forgotten and nearly empty a century ago, Aigues now makes its living from tourists, and from salt; half of France's supply is collected here, at the enormous Salins-du-Midi pans south of town.

Aigues-Mortes **walls** are over a mile in length, streamlined and almost perfectly rectangular. The impressive **Tour de Constance** is a huge cylindrical defence tower that guarded the northeastern land approach to the town (*entry inside the walls on Rue Zola; © 66 53 61 55; open daily 9.30–12 and 2–4.30 in winter, 9–7 in summer; adm—pick up a joint ticket for Carcassonne and Salses if you are going castle-touring further west*). After the Crusades, the tower became a prison to Templars and later to Protestants. One of them, Marie Durand, spent 38 years here in unspeakable conditions. On her release in 1768, she left her credo, *register* ('resist', in Provençal), chiselled into the wall where it can still be seen.

Aigues-Mortes ✉ *30220*　　　　　　　　　　**Where to Stay and Eating Out**

 Aigues-Mortes is well-served with accommodation, and top of the list is the gracious and welcoming **★★★St-Louis**, in a distinguished and beautifully furnished 18th-century building on 10 Rue Amiral Courbet, just off Place St-Louis, © 66 53 72 68, ✆ 66 53 75 92 (*closed Jan–15 Mar*). This establishment also includes a popular restaurant, **L'Archère**, the best in town for steaks and seafood, with good homemade desserts: menus 98F (lunch only), 195F. On Boulevard Gambetta, **★★Les Arcades**, © 66 53 81 13, ✆ 66 53 75 46, offers attractive rooms, some with television, and a good inexpensive restaurant: *taureau à la gardienne* and other local favourites on menus 120–250F. The budget-priced **★La Tour de Constance**, is on Blvd Diderot, outside the northern wall, © 66 53 83 50 (*closed Nov–Feb*). It is rumoured the Gypsy Kings frequent **La Camargue**, 19 Rue de La République, © 66 53 86 88, but even in their absence this is the liveliest place in town, with flamenco guitars strumming in the background: try to eat in the garden in summer (fish, seafood and grilled meat, 100–160F).

Aix — The Cloister of St. Sauveur Cathedral

Metropolitan Provence

Although this is the business end of Provence, the most densely populated, hurly-burly, industrial and everything-else-you've-come-to-get-away-from part of Provence, the region holds several trump cards: the aristocratic city of Aix-en-Provence with its incredible markets and countryside synonymous with Cézanne; a tumultuous coastline ripped into the bones of the earth between La Ciotat and Marseille; and Marseille itself, every bit as good as its magnificent setting, as bad as any big port city, and as ugly as the fish in its heavenly *bouillabaisse*.

Note that on 18 October 1996 France is changing its telephone numbers from 8 digits to 10 digits. All phone numbers in Provence should be preceded by 04 from this date.

Beaches

The beach at Cassis is pretty, with a dramatic backdrop of cliffs, but it gets crowded in summer. Marseille possesses an artificial town beach, lively at all times of the year, but for more adventurous sand, head into the Calanques. Boats run from Cassis and Marseille.

West of Marseille, La Côte Bleue is the playground of the Marseillais and gets crowded at weekends in summer. The beaches are mediocre; the best is at Carro. For real sand head west to the Camargue.

best beaches

Cassis: sand and cliffs.

Calanques: walk the cliff-top path and descend at will (*see* p.142).

Marseille (Plage du David): soccer, kites, skateboards and windsurfers; an action beach, artificial pebbles.

Sausset-les-Pins: sand and caravans.

Carro: the furthest from Marseille, hence the quietest.

La Ciotat, Cassis and the *Calanques*

Before settling down and creating the broad, smooth bay that permits the existence of Marseille, the Provençal coast bucks and rears with the fury of wild horses. La Ciotat, halfway between Toulon and Marseille, is a shipbuilding, hard-nosed and gritty town, while well-heeled Cassis is endowed with a dramatic setting, a bijou harbour and delicate wine.

Getting Around

La Ciotat is a main stop for **trains** between Marseille and Toulon (La Ciotat © 42 83 08 63, Marseille © 91 08 50 50); regular **buses** (© 42 08 90 90) cover the 3km from the station to the Vieux Port. Cassis' train station is just as far from the centre but has less frequent services; if you're coming from Marseille, take one of the frequent coaches that drop you off at Blvd Anatole

France, near the tourist office. For **bike hire** the best is **Lleba Cycles,** 1 Ave Frédéric Mistral, ℰ 42 83 60 30, in La Ciotat.

La Ciotat (✉ 13600): Blvd Anatole France, ℰ 42 08 61 32, 🖂 42 08 17 88
Cassis (✉ 13260): Place Baragnon, ℰ 42 01 71 17

market days

La Ciotat: Tuesday and Sunday morning
Cassis: Wednesday morning

La Ciotat

A safe anchorage with fresh water and beaches, protected from the winds by a queerly eroded rock formation known as the Bec de l'Aigle (the 'eagle's beak'), La Ciotat has seen ancient Greeks, pirates, fishermen and, since the time of François I, shipbuilders—though instead of galleys to battle the Empire, the yards now produce vessels to transport liquefied gas. La Ciotat has also given the world two momentous pastimes: first, motion pictures, pioneered here in 1895, when Auguste and Louis Lumière filmed a train pulling into La Ciotat station (*L'Entrée d'un train en gare de La Ciotat*), a clip that made history's first film spectators jump out of their seats as the locomotive seemed to bear down upon them. And second, *pétanque*, that most Provençal of sports, which came into being here in 1907 when one old-timer's legs became paralysed and he could no longer take the regulation steps before a throw, as laid down in the laws of *boules*. The rules were changed for him and, as everyone enjoyed working up less of a sweat, they stuck.

Most visitors to La Ciotat keep to the beaches and pleasure port around **La Ciotat-Plage** (with a monument to the Lumière brothers), but it's the business side of things, around the **Vieux Port**, that affords the best loafing; in the evening the shipyard cranes resemble luminous mutant insects from Mars. The **Musée Ciotaden,** 51 Rue des Poilus, ℰ 42 71 40 99, 🖂 42 08 25 96 (*open 4–7, Sun 10–12, closed Tues and Thurs*), is dedicated to the history of La Ciotat and its shipyards. Beyond the latter, amid the wind-sculpted rocks and dishevelled Mediterranean flora of the Bec de l'Aigle is the cliff-top **Parc du Mugel** (Bus 3 from the Vieux Port). Ave de Figuerolles continues from here to the red pudding-stone walls and pebble beach of the **Calanque de Figuerolles**, with its hunchback rock formation, known as 'le Capuchin'. The wee islet floating off shore, the **Ile Verte**, can be reached by boat from Quai Ganteaume; it has a simple restaurant and views back to the mainland that explain how the Bec de l'Aigle got its name.

Where to Stay and Eating Out

The nicest hotels are at **La Ciotat-Plage** (✉ 13600), beginning with the ★★★**Miramar,** 3 Blvd Beaurivage, ℰ 42 83 09 54, 🖂 42 83 33 79; a classy, updated old hotel amid pine groves, by the beach; half-board is

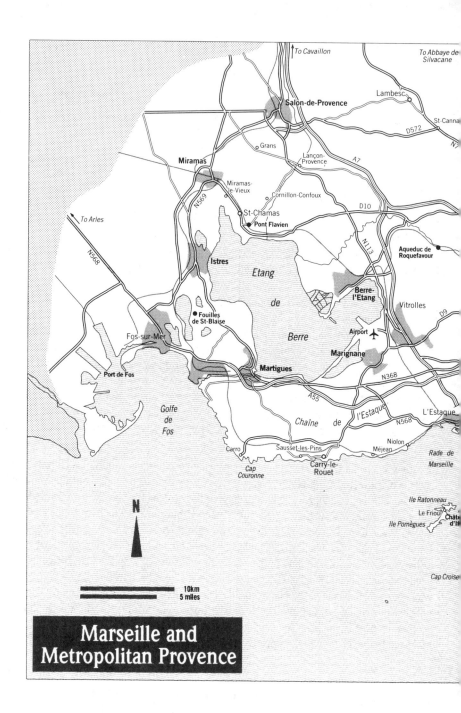

Marseille and
Metropolitan Provence

140

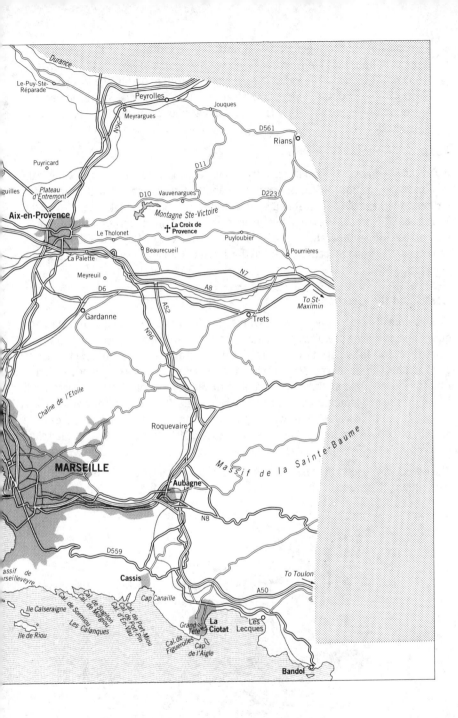

mandatory in the summer, but its restaurant, **L'Orchidée**, is the best in town (menus from 125F). A good budget choice is the **✶Beaurivage**, 1 Ave Beaurivage, ✆ 42 83 09 68, while in La Ciotat town **✶✶Rotonde**, 44 Blvd de la République, ✆ 42 08 67 50, is the best choice near the Vieux Port. Quai Stalingrad near the shipyards has the widest choice of restaurants with cheap menus, most featuring seafood.

Route des Crêtes

If you can sneer at vertigo and laugh in the face of tenuous hairpin turns, ignore the main road between La Ciotat and Cassis and twist and turn along the 17km **Corniche des Crêtes**. Alternatively, a footpath cuts through the road loops and takes about 4 hours. Your pains will be amply rewarded with plunging views from the highest cliffs in France: the **Falaises de Soubeyran**, or 'Big Head' (399m), and craggy **Cap Canaille**. From Pas de la Colle the road and path descend to the ancient Gallo-Roman *Portus Carcisis*, now known as Cassis.

Cassis and the *Calanques*

The old coral-fishing village of Cassis, with its fish-hook port, white cliffs, beaches, and quaint houses spilling down steep alleyways was a natural favourite of the Fauve painters. Since their day, the village has made the inevitable progression from fishing to artsy to chic, and beyond the purse of most fishermen and artists. The swanky modern Casino Municipal does a roaring trade thanks to its proximity to the gambling-mad Marseillais. When they're not counting wads of banknotes, the Cassidans bestir themselves to make one of the most delicious white wines of Provence and export their crystalline white stone. The latter is quarried in the sheer limestone cliffs between Cassis and Marseille, pierced by tongues of lapis lazuli called *calanques*.

The easiest way to visit the ***calanques*** is by motor boat from Cassis port, although these tours don't allow you to disembark. More

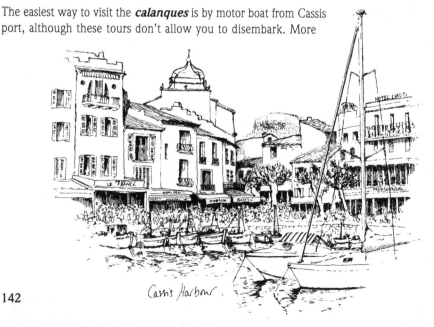

Cassis Harbour.

strenuous but more rewarding is the walk along the path that first leads to **Port-Miou**, where the hard, white stone was hewn for the Suez Canal; another mile's hike will take you to **Port-Pin**, with a pretty beach, and **En-Vau**, its sheer cliffs a favourite challenge for daring human flies. Take a picnic, and spend a day skinny dipping in the exhilarating crystal water. Serious walkers can continue along GR 98 all the way to Marseille.

Cassis AOC

 In Cassis, they say their white wine obtained its divine quality when God came down the road from heaven and shed a tear at the plight of a family trying to scratch a living from the rocky amphitheatre overlooking the village. The divine tear fell on a vine and *voilà*, it gave birth to a dry wine of a pale green tint, with a bouquet of heather and rosemary.

The Cassis district is minute, but was one of the first to be granted AOC status (1936). Ugni blanc, marsanne, clairette and bourboulenc are the dominant grapes of this pale cocktail, popularized abroad by the late James Beard and considered by the Marseillais to be the only liquid worthy of washing down a *bouillabaisse*, a grilled red mullet, or lobster. Try some in the vast, ancient *caves* of **Clos Sainte-Magdeleine**, ✆ 42 01 70 28, and **Château de Fontcreuse**, Route de La Ciotat, ✆ 42 01 71 09, ✉ 42 01 32 64, the district's only real château, which between the wars was the property of a retired English colonel, who improved the stock and carved out new vineyards in the steep limestone hills.

Cassis ✉ *13260*   ***Where to Stay and Eating Out***

Don't expect any bargains in Cassis. Most spectacular, perched on the promontory overlooking Cassis bay, is ★★★★**Les Roches Blanches**, Route des Calanques, ✆ 42 01 09 30, ✉ 42 01 94 23. Rooms are a tad small, but very comfortable; there's a private beach and sun terraces, and as usual half-board is mandatory in season. Set amid lemon groves and bougainvillea, ★★★**Les Jardins du Campanile**, Rue Favier, ✆ 42 01 84 85, ✉ 42 01 32 38, is a lovely Provençal-style oasis, with a pool (*closed Nov–Apr*). Book months in advance for the more reasonable (and restaurant-less) ★★**Grand Jardin**, 2 Rue Pierre Eydin, ✆ 42 01 70 10, ✉ 42 01 33 75. Otherwise try ★★**Hôtel Laurence**, at 8 Rue de l'Arène, ✆ 42 01 88 78, with a view up to the château (*closed mid-Nov–1 Mar*). To the west of Cassis, overlooking the *calanques*, France's most remote youth hostel, **La Fontasse**, ✆ 42 01 02 72, is an hour's walk from town or from the Marseille–Cassis bus stop *Les Calanques*. This hostel has a magnificent setting, but is not for sissies—beds, lights, and cold water are the only creature comforts (*closed Jan and Feb*).

The local, rosy-pink sea-urchins, *oursins*, often crop up on the menu in the company of other tasty sea creatures at the excellent **La Presqu'île**, in Quartier de Port-Miou, ✆ 42 01 03 77, ✉ 42 01 94 49. There's a menu at 300F, *tout compris*, or ask what's best and eat *à la carte* (*closed Dec to Feb and Sun eve*).

Among the many places on the waterfront, **El Sol**, 23 Quai des Baux, © 42 01 76 10, has reasonably priced food (*closed Wed*). For *bouillabaisse,* neighbouring **Chez Gilbert**, 19 Quai des Baux, © 42 01 71 36, is esteemed; menus 115 and 160F (*closed Tues eve, Wed in winter*).

Marseille

> *Marseille is tired of being Marseille.*
>
> A current saying

Amid Provence's carefully-nurtured image of lavender fields, rosé wine and *pétanque,* Marseille is the great anomaly, the second city of France and the world's eighth-largest port. Like New York, it has been the gateway port to a new world for hundreds of thousands of new arrivals—especially Corsicans, Armenians, Jews, Greeks, Turks, Italians, Spaniards and Algerians. Many immigrants have gone no further, creating in Marseille perhaps the most varied mix of cultures and religions in Europe, 'the meeting place of the entire world' as Alexandre Dumas called it. The grateful Armenian community even talks about funding a Statue of Liberty for the harbour.

Unfortunately, Marseille also shares many of New York's less savoury traits: racial hostility towards whoever was the last off the boat, the petty crooks and hardened gangsters of the French mafia, or *milieu,* heroin and prostitution rings, political and financial scandals, and an international reputation put about by films like *The French Connection.* It is the great anti-Paris, ever defiant of central authority and big-wigs be they Julius Caesar, Louis XIV, Napoleon, Hitler, or De Gaulle.

These days Marseille suffers from the rapid growth of air transport over sea transport, de-industrialization, and the effects of decolonization. Unemployment is disproportionately high and xenophobia thrives: three recent municipal elections have been won by the National Front, and in the spring of 1995 a young immigrant was shot dead after a struggle with National Front bill posters.

'These Marseillais make Marseilles hymns, and Marseilles vests, and Marseilles soap for all the world; but they never sing their hymns, or wear their vests, or wash with their soap themselves,' wrote Mark Twain. So what *do* they do? Marseille (pop. 850,000) is a metropolis that in its 2600 years has contributed precious little to Western civilization; it is the eternal capital of great expectations, 'a city that's been waiting for Godot', according to an editor in one of Marseille's young publishing houses. There are hints (in theatre, the plastic arts, and research) that its long bottled-up juices are ripe and ready to flow; if nothing else it comes as an unclogging shot of *pastis* to your blood after the mental cholesterol of the Côte d'Azur.

History

The story goes that in 600 BC Greek colonists from the Ionian city of Phocaea, having obtained the approval of the gods, loaded their ship with olive saplings and sailed towards

Gaul. They found a perfect bay, and their handsome leader Protis went to the local king to obtain permission to found a city. That very day the king was hosting a banquet for the young men of his land, after which, according to tradition, his daughter Gyptis would select her husband. Protis was invited to join, and, thanks to his great beauty, was chosen by the princess. For his new wife's dowry, Protis asked for the land the Greeks coveted near the mouth of the Rhône, including the Lacydon (the *Vieux Port*). He named the new city Massalia.

Massalia boomed from the start; by 530 BC it had its own treasury at Delphi, and its own colonies, from Málaga to Nice; it traded for tin with Cornwall and its great astronomer Pytheas explored the Baltic and in 350 BC became the first scientist to accurately calculate latitudes. Rivalling Carthage, it allied itself with Rome, and profited from the latter's conquests in Spain and Gaul. By the 2nd century BC, Massalia had a population of 50,000, and was ruled by a merchant oligarchy whose political astuteness was admiringly described by Aristotle and Cicero. This astuteness failed them when they sided with Pompey, calling down the vengeance of Caesar, who conquered their city after a long siege and seized all of Massalia's colonies, with the exception of Nice and Hyères. Yet even after the 2nd century AD, when Massalia adopted Roman law, it remained a city apart, the westernmost enclave of Hellenism, with famous schools of Greek rhetoric and medicine.

As the Pax Romana crumbled, Marseille nearly went out of business, taking hard knocks from Goths, Franks, Saracens and then more Franks again in the 700s under Charles Martel. Plagued by pirates, business stayed bad until the 11th century, when the Crusaders showed up looking for transport to the Holy Land. This was the best get-rich-quick opportunity of the Middle Ages, and although Genoa and Venice grabbed the biggest trading concessions in the Levant, Marseille too grew fat on the proceeds. Briefly a republic, the city's real power soon passed to a merchant oligarchy; between 1178 and 1192 the big boss was the cultivated En Barral, patron of two of Provence's greatest troubadours, the mad Peire Vidal and Folquet of Marseille (*see* p.59).

Trumped by Kings: Charles d'Anjou to Louis XIV

When Charles d'Anjou acquired Provence in 1252, he confiscated Marseille's entire fleet to achieve his conquest of Sicily. Thanks to the monumental arrogance of the Angevins, the ships were annihilated in the revolt of the Sicilian Vespers (1282). With her legitimate commerce undermined by her own rulers, Marseille became a den for pirates and went into such a decline that it became an easy target for the Angevins' rival, Alfonso V of Aragon, who destroyed as much of it as he could in 1423.

Coming under French rule in 1481 meant, for Marseille, tumbling headlong into the power-grasping scrum known as the Wars of Italy (1494–1559). The city's galleys went to war again, and attracted the fury of Emperor Charles V, who sent his henchman, the rebel Constable of Bourbon, to besiege the city. Marseille resisted heroically, and François I showed his gratitude by giving the city the freedom to trade at will in the eastern Mediterranean. Once again the money rolled in, to be pumped into new industries, especially soap and sugar.

Marseille's longing to be left alone to mind her own affairs put her squarely at odds with Louis XIV; for 40 years the city thumbed her nose at his Royal Sunniness while scrambling to retain her autonomy. By 1660, the King had had enough, and opened up a great breach in Marseille's walls, humiliating the city by turning its own cannons back on itself. The central authority installed by Louis was much more lax than the city had previously been about issues crucial to the running of a good port—like quarantine. The result, in 1720, was a devastating plague that spread throughout Provence.

Tunes, Booms and Busts

Marseille sprang back quickly. Trade with the Levant, North Africa, and the new markets in America made it Europe's greatest port. Its industries (soap, woollens, porcelain, tarot cards) blossomed, only to wither in the Revolution, which for ten years divided the proletariat and the oligarchs. Volunteers from Marseille contributed much to the upholding of the Revolution, however; as 500 of them set off for Paris in July 1792, someone suggested singing the new battle song of the Army of the Rhine, recently composed by Rouget de l'Isle. It caught on, and as the volunteers marched, they improved the rhythm and harmonies so that by the time they reached Paris, the 'song of the Marseillais' was perfected and became the hit tune of the Revolution, and subsequently, the most blood-curdling of national anthems.

But as the Revolution evolved into the Terror, Marseille was found so wanting in proper politics that it was known as the *ville sans nom*, and any building that had sheltered an anti-Revolutionary was demolished, including the ancient monastery of St-Victor. The misery continued under Napoleon, another bugbear in Marseille's books for provoking the blockade by the British and ruining trade. Recovery came with the Second Empire, the conquest of Algeria in 1830, and the construction of the Suez Canal. Soon Marseille was more prosperous than ever before, and more populous, with some 60,000 new immigrants every decade between 1850 and 1930—Greeks and Armenians fleeing the Turks, Italians fleeing Fascism, and later, Spaniards fleeing Franco.

After becoming one of the first French cities to vote socialist (1890), Marseille's reputation took a nosedive. Corruption, rigged elections and an open link between the Hôtel de Ville and the bosses of the *milieu* were so rampant that in 1938 Paris dissolved the municipal government and ran the city at a distance. Yet the '30s also saw the release of Marcel Pagnol's classic Marseillais film trilogy *Marius*, *Fanny* and *César*, which helped create throughout France an insatiable appetite for *operette marseillaise*; even Josephine Baker sang the tunes of Marseille's great songwriter, Vincent Scotto.

In 1953, Marseille elected a socialist mayor—Gaston Deferre, the antagonist of De Gaulle, who reigned until his death in 1986. Deferre oversaw rapid changes: the decline of Marseille's trade as France lost its colonies, and a population that exploded from 660,000 in 1955 to 960,000 in 1975. To accommodate the new arrivals (mostly North Africans and French refugees from Algeria) the city infested itself with the shoddy high-rise housing that still scars most quarters; unemployment rose as the traditional soap and fat industries plummeted, and new projects such as the steel-mills and port at Fos failed to provide as many jobs as expected—fuelling the racial tensions and organized crime that still give the city a rough reputation. Even when the city, or at least its revered soccer team, L'Olympique de Marseille, won the European championship in 1993, the team got itself banned from 1994 European competition on charges of match fixing and bribery. The team's flamboyant ex-owner, maverick politician, businessman and Euro-deputy Bernard Tapie futilely denied everything; since then he has been constantly on trial for one thing or another—many Marseillais think he's been framed by the *classe politique* in hated Paris. Only his immunity as a Euro-deputy has kept him out of the calaboose.

Less well known than all the scandals is Marseille's reorientation, for the first time in its history, away from the Mediterranean and towards Europe. New high-speed rail links are being built, and a canal will link the Rhône with the Rhine by 2010. Marseille is now the most important research centre in France after Paris, home of a major science university, inventor of a new fifth-generation computer language, and site of COMEX, the world's leading developer of underwater technologies.

Getting There
by air

Marseille's airport is to the west at Marignane; ✆ 42 89 09 74 for flight information. (Air France, ✆ 91 39 39 39; Air Inter, ✆ 91 39 36 36.) A bus every 20 minutes (✆ 91 50 59 34) links the airport with the train station, Gare St-Charles, and takes 25 minutes.

by train

Gare St-Charles is the main train station, and the only one in France that could star in a Busby Berkeley musical, with its big stagey staircase, draped with buxom statues representing Asia and Africa. There are connections to nearly every town in the south, and the TGV that will get you to Paris in 4 hours and 40 minutes. For train information, call ✆ 91 08 50 50; reservations ✆ 91 08 84 12.

by boat

Ferries sail to Algeria, Corsica, Sardinia and Tunisia; contact SNCM, 61 Blvd des Dames, ✆ 91 56 30 10.

by metro and bus

Marseille runs an efficient bus network and two metro lines: the metro is safe, quick and highly efficient, but the buses are quite an experience. Pick up the useful *plan du réseau* at the tourist office or at the RTM (Réseau de Transport Marseillais) information desk by the Bourse, 6–8 Rue des Fabres, ✆ 91 91 92 10. Tickets are transferable between the bus and metro. The coach station, ✆ 91 08 16 40, is behind the train station at 3 Place Victor Hugo, with connections to Cassis, Nice, Arles, Avignon, Toulon and Cannes. RTM also has guided tour buses: the *Bus Pagnol*, for sites associated with Pagnol's childhood, and a *Histobus*, a tour of historic Marseille.

by taxi

If you need a taxi, call ✆ 91 03 60 03 or 91 05 80 80, and make sure the meter is switched on at the start of your journey.

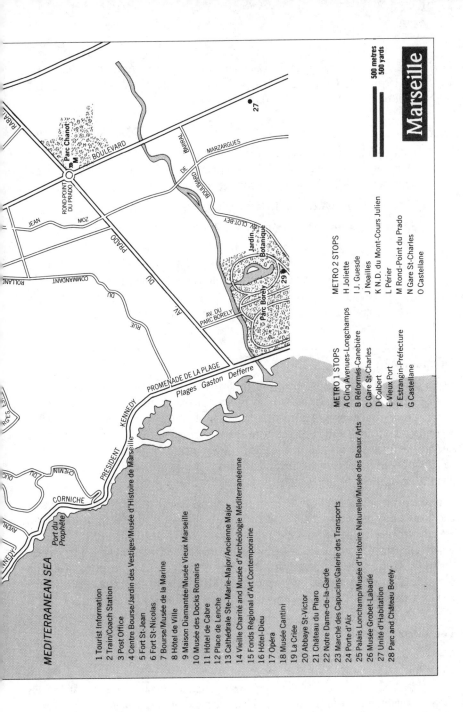

Marseille

MEDITERRANEAN SEA

1 Tourist Information
2 Train/Coach Station
3 Post Office
4 Centre Bourse/Jardin des Vestiges/Musée d'Histoire de Marseille
5 Fort St-Jean
6 Fort St-Nicolas
7 Bourse/Musée de la Marine
8 Hôtel de Ville
9 Maison Diamantée/Musée Vieux Marseille
10 Musée des Docks Romains
11 Hôtel de Cabre
12 Place de Lenche
13 Cathédrale Ste-Marie-Major/Ancienne Major
14 Vieille Charité and Musée d'Archéologie Méditerranéenne
15 Fonds Régional d'Art Contemporaine
16 Hôtel-Dieu
17 Opéra
18 Musée Cantini
19 La Criée
20 Abbaye St-Victor
21 Château du Pharo
22 Notre Dame-de-la-Garde
23 Marché des Capucins/Galerie des Transports
24 Porte d'Aix
25 Palais Lonchamp/Musée d'Histoire Naturelle/Musée des Beaux Arts
26 Musée Grobet-Labadié
27 Unité d'Habitation
28 Parc and Château Borély

METRO 1 STOPS
A Cinq Avenues-Longchamps
B Réformés-Canebière
C Gare St-Charles
D Colbert
E Vieux Port
F Estrangin-Préfecture
G Castellane

METRO 2 STOPS
H Joliette
I J. Guesde
J Noailles
K N.D. du Mont-Cours Julien
L Périer
M Rond-Point du Prado
N Gare St-Charles
O Castellane

500 metres
500 yards

Some car hire firms are in the Gare St-Charles, including **Avis**, ✆ 91 08 41 80. Others include **Hertz**, at 16 Blvd Charles Nédelec (1er), ✆ 91 14 04 24, and **Thrifty**, 8 Blvd Voltaire, ✆ 91 05 92 18.

Tourist Information

By the Vieux Port, at 4 La Canebière, ✆ 91 13 89 00, ✉ 91 13 89 20. Open Mon–Sat 9–7 in winter, 8.30–8 in summer, Sun 10–5. Or try the office in the train station, ✆ 91 50 59 18, but don't expect any politeness.

The central **post office** is at 1 Place de l'Hôtel des Postes (1er), ✆ 91 15 47 31.

Emergencies: Police ✆ 17; Ambulance ✆ 18; Hospital, 264 Rue St Pierre, ✆ 91 38 60 00.

Special Information Centres exist for **young people**, at the very helpful CIJ, 4 Rue de la Visitation, ✆ 91 49 91 55; **disabled visitors**, at the Office Municipal pour Handicapés et Inadaptés, 128 Ave du Prado (8e), ✆ 91 81 58 80; and **crime victims**, at AVAD, 56 Rue Montgrand (6e), ✆ 91 54 81 00, which will help out if you're robbed.

Orientation

Marseille, with 110 neighbourhoods and 16 *arrondissements*, is one of Europe's largest cities, sprawling over twice as many acres as Paris. The northern neighbourhoods are the poorest, the first addresses of many new immigrants; the Panier (*see* below) and neighbourhoods around the station constitute the North African quarters, lively during the day but uncomfortable to wander in after dark. The southern neighbourhoods, with their parks and access to the beaches, are distinctly more monied and sanitized. A circle of hills divides the city from the mainland, physically and psychologically.

The Vieux Port, the heart of the city since its founding, is now used only for pleasure craft and boats out to the islets of Frioul and the Château d'If, while commercial port activities are concentrated to the north in the *Rade de Marseille*. To the south of the Vieux Port, where the golden Virgin of Notre-Dame de la Garde is the chief landmark, the Parc du Pharo marks the start of a *corniche* road along the coast to Cap Croisette, lined with coves, beaches and restaurants, with a mountain, Marseilleveyre, that you can climb at the end for a view of all the above.

The Vieux Port

Marseille the urban mangrove entwines its aquatic roots around the neat, rectangular Vieux Port, where people have lived continuously for the past 2600 years. Now a pleasure port, its cafés have fine views of the sunset, though in the morning the action and smells centre around the Quai des Belges and its boat-side **fish market**, where the key ingredients of *bouillabaisse* are touted in a racy *patois* as thick as the soup itself. From the Quai des Belges *vedettes* sail to the Château d'If and Frioul islands (*see* below), past the two bristling fortresses that still defend the harbour: to the north, **St-Jean**, first built in the 12th century by the Knights of St John, and to the south **St-Nicolas**, built by Louis XIV to keep a close eye on Marseille rather than the sea.

A bronze marker in the Quai des Belges pinpoints the spot where the Greeks first set foot in Gaul. And yet Marseille concealed its age until this century, when excavations for the glitzy new shopping mall, the Centre Bourse, revealed the eastern ramparts and gate of Massalia, dating back to the 3rd century BC, now enclosed in the **Jardin des Vestiges**. On the ground floor of the Centre Bourse, the **Musée d'Histoire de Marseille**, ✆ 91 90 42 22 (*open Mon–Sat 12–7*), displays models, everyday items, mosaics, and a 3rd-century BC wreck of a Roman ship, discovered in 1974. Built of 15 different kinds of pine, it had become so fragile that it had to be freeze-dried like instant coffee to prevent further deterioration.

Elaborate antique models of later ships that sailed into the Vieux Port and items related to Marseille's trading history are the main focus of the **Musée de la Marine et de l'Economie de Marseille**, ✆ 91 39 33 33 (*open 10–12 and 2–6, closed Tues*). It's housed in the 1860 **Palais de la Bourse**, France's oldest stock exchange, built under Napoleon III to obliterate an unrepentant democratic quarter that spilled much blood in the Revolution of 1848. But this corner, stock exchange or not, remained a vortex for violence: a plaque on the Canebière side of the Bourse recalls that King Alexander of Yugoslavia was assassinated here in 1934.

Le Panier

North of the Vieux Port, the Panier ('the Basket', named after a 17th-century cabaret) is Marseille's oldest quarter—an irregular weave of winding narrow streets and stairs dating from the ancient Greeks, many in the perpetual shadow of steep houses and flapping laundry. When the well-to-do moved out in the 18th century, the Panier was given over to fishermen and a romanticized underworld; guides were published to its 'private' hotels and the hourly rates of their residents.

Before the war it was a lively Corsican and Italian neighbourhood, and later its warren of secret ways absorbed hundreds of Jews and other refugees from the Nazis, hoping to escape to America. In January 1943, Hitler cottoned on and, in collusion with local property speculators, ordered the dynamiting of everything between the Vieux Port and halfway up the hill, to the Grand'Rue/Rue Caisserie. Given one day to evacuate, the 20,000 departing residents were screened by French and German police, who selected 3500 for the concentration camps, sent out of the city in a long line of tram cars. A monument in the quarter commemorates the destruction and deportees who never returned.

Two buildings were protected from the dynamite: the 17th-century **Hôtel de Ville** on the quay, and behind it, in Rue de la Prison, the **Maison Diamantée**, Marseille's 16th-century Mannerist masterpiece, named after the pyramidical points of its façade. It holds the **Musée du Vieux Marseille**, ✆ 91 90 80 28 (*open daily 10–5 winter, 11–6* *summer*), a delightful attic where the city stashes its odds and ends—Provençal furniture; an extraordinary relief diorama made in 1850 by an iron merchant, depicting the uprising of 1848; 18th-century Neapolitan Christmas crib figures and *santons* made in Marseille; playing and tarot cards, long an important local industry; and poignant photos of the Panier before it was blown to smithereens.

The dynamite was responsible for revealing the contents of the **Musée des Docks Romains**, 2 Place Vivaux, © 91 91 24 62 (*open daily 10–5 winter, 11–6 summer; adm*), built over a stretch of the vast 1st-century AD Roman quay, where wine and grains were stored in *dolia* or massive jars. Exhibits describe seafaring in the ancient Mediterranean. One last survivor of the pre-war Panier is the oldest house in Marseille, the **Hôtel de Cabre** (1535), a Gothic-Renaissance confection on Grand'Rue. The rest of the lower Panier was rebuilt on the cheap after the war, and still fulfils its traditional role as the first address of Marseille's most recent arrivals, now largely Arab.

Once you walk north of Rue Caisserie, the Panier retains some of its old character in the web of lanes atop the steps of **Montée des Accoules**, and around **Place de Lenche**, the former *agora* of the Greeks. Just to the north, looming over the tankers and cargo ships drowsing in Marseille's outer harbour basin, are the two 'majors'. The striped neo-Byzantine **Cathédrale de la Major** (*closed Mon and 12–2*) was built in 1853 with the new money coming in from the conquest of Algeria—enough to make it the largest church built in France since the Middle Ages, held up by 444 marble columns; adjacent, with less bombast and more charm, stands its Romanesque predecessor, the **Ancienne-Major**. Although the transept was brutally amputated for the new cathedral, note the Ancienne-Major's crossing, a fantasy in brick that sets an octagonal dome on four stepped conical squinches, a typically Provençal conceit. One chapel has a *Descent from the Cross* (early 1500s), a late work from the Della Robbias' Florentine workshop, and the altar of *SS. Lazarus, Martha, and Mary Magdalene* by Francesco Laurana (1475–81), considered by Anthony Blunt to be 'the earliest purely Italian work on French soil'. What you don't get to see is the Ancienne-Major's old curiosity shop of locked-away relics, but it is said to include part of Jesus' cradle and one of His tears, St Peter's tooth, and best of all, the fish-bones left over from the feast at the Sermon on the Mount.

Near the cathedral at the top of Rue du Petit-Puits is a gem of a different cut, the Baroque **Vieille-Charité**, designed by Pierre Puget, a student of Bernini and court architect to Louis XIV—and a native of the Panier. Built by the city fathers between 1671 and 1745 to take in homeless migrants from the countryside, this is one of the world's most palatial workhouses: three storeys of arcaded ambulatories in pale pink stone, overlooking a court with a sumptuous elliptical chapel crowned by an oval dome—a curvaceous Baroque work forced into a straitlaced neo-Corinthian façade in 1863. Although the complex became a barracks after the Revolution, it returned to its original purpose in 1860, housing families displaced first by the construction of the Bourse and later by the Nazis' destruction of the Panier. By 1962, the Charité was in so precarious a state that everyone was evacuated, and in 1985 it reopened, all restored—no longer a shelter for the homeless but for art, photography, and video exhibitions as well as the **Musée d'Archéologie**

Méditerranéenne, © 91 56 28 38 (*open daily except Mon, 10–5 winter, 11–6 summer*), featuring Egyptian art and mummies, finds from Cyprus, Susa, Mesopotamia and the reconstructed **Sanctuary of Roquepertuse** from Velaux, near Aix. Built by a headhunting Celto-Ligurian tribe called the Salians, the sanctuary has pillars pierced with holes to hold skulls, a lintel incised with the outline of four horse heads (who symbolically transported the dead soul), and Buddha-like figures sitting in the lotus position. Similar temples found in Entremont (*see* p.176) and Mouriès prove a common religion, perhaps a chthonic cult in which warriors went to commune with the spirits of their dead heroes. Living artists from Provence have a showcase in a former convent around the corner at the **Fonds Régional d'Art Contemporain**, 2 Place F. Chirat, © 91 91 27 55.

South of the Vieux Port: St-Victor and Notre-Dame de la Garde

The *filles*, they say, are more discreet on this side, especially around the **Opéra**, two blocks south of the Quai des Belges in Place Reyer. Built in 1924, it is graced with a pure Art Deco interior and a fine reputation for Italian opera. Two streets back, in the **Musée Cantini**, 19 Rue Grignan, © 91 54 77 75 (*open daily 11–6; adm*), there are even more square yards of 20th-century art—by Picabia, Max Ernst, André Masson, Francis Bacon, Balthus, César, Niki de Saint-Phalle, Arman, Ben, and so many more that only a fraction can be displayed at a time. It also displays an exceptional collection of faïence made in Marseille and Moustiers, dating back to the 17th century.

Quai de Rive Neuve is lined with ship chandlers' shops and the new national theatre, **La Criée**, installed in a former fish auction house (*see* below). Among the salty Rive Neuve bars, the **Bar de la Marine** was the set for the famous card-playing scene in Marcel Pagnol's *Marius*, and has a mural of the same. Further along the *quai*, castle walls good enough for Hollywood hide one of the most intriguing Christian sites in Provence, the **Abbaye St-Victor**, © 91 33 25 86. St-Victor was founded *c.* AD 416 by Jean Cassien, formerly an anchorite in the Egyptian Thebaid. One account has it that he brought with him from Egypt the mummy of St Victor, though the more popular version says Victor was a Roman legionary who converted to Christianity, and slew at least one sea serpent before being ground to a pulp between a pair of millstones.

The first chapels of the fortified abbey were built into the flank of an ancient stone quarry, and near a Hellenistic necropolis, expanded for Christian use as a *martyrium* (rock-cut burials surrounding the tomb of a martyr). In the 11th and 12th centuries, when the monks adopted the Rule of St Benedict, they added the church on top, turning the old chapels into **crypts and catacombs** (*small adm fee*). These are strange and clammy with ancient mystery—the primitive bas-reliefs and sarcophagi date from the 3rd century AD, and some of the latter were found to contain seven or eight dead monks crowded like sardines, proof of the popularity of an abbey that founded 300 other monastic houses in Provence and even Sardinia. Then there's the 5th-century **Chapel of Notre-Dame-de-Confession** (*open 8–6.30 all year*), enshrining one of Marseille's three Black Virgins (according to some students, they are Christian versions of Artemis, the patroness of Massalia). A primordial Candlemas rite takes place here every 2 February: the archbishop comes to bless green candles before the black statue, and in the abbey's ancient bakery, small loaves are made in the shape of boats, or *navettes*—a similar custom, in the temple of Isis, used to herald the beginning of the navigation season. The faithful then take the green candles home to light at wakes as a symbol of rebirth.

Below St-Victor is Louis XIV's inaccessible Fort St-Nicolas, and beyond that, the **Château du Pharo** (bus 83 from the Vieux Port), built by Napoleon III as a gift for his wife, the Empress Eugénie, who never got around to seeing it. The gardens, with striking views over the port, are used for concerts and summer theatre under the stars; beyond are the *calanques* (*see* p.157). The prize 360° view, however, is from Marseille's watchtower hill—an isolated limestone outcrop towering 162m above the city, crowned by **Notre-Dame de la Garde**, a neo-Byzantine/Romanesque pile with an unfortunate resemblance to a locomotive (a killer walk, and even fairly hair-raising to drive; let bus 60 do the work, from Place aux Huiles on Quai de Rive Neuve). This landmark supports France's largest golden mega-Madonna, 10m high and shining like a beacon out to sea. In 1214 a monk of St-Victor built the first chapel here, and over the decades it gained a reputation for the miracles performed by a statue of the Virgin, Marseille's 'Bonne Mère'. The chapel's florid Second Empire architecture attracted some real bombs when the Nazis made it their headquarters and last stand, and you can still see some of the dents. But besides the view, the main attraction is the basilica's great **collection of ex-votos**, painted by fishermen and sailors.

La Canebière

Before La Canebière itself was laid out in Louis XIV's expansion scheme of 1666, this area was the ropemakers' quarter. The hemp they used has given its name to Marseille's most famous boulevard—*chanvre* in French, but in Provençal more like the Latin *cannabis*—a not entirely inappropriate allusion, for this was the high street of French *dolce far niente*, an essential ingredient of music-hall Marseille, which could swagger and boast that 'the Champs-Elysées is the Canebière of Paris'. In its day La Canebière sported grand cafés, fancy shops and hotels where travellers of yore had their first thrills before sailing off to exotic lands, but these days La Canebière—or 'Can o' beer' as English sailors know it—has suffered the same fate as the Champs-Elysées: banks, airline offices and heavy traffic have chased out all but the seediest nightclubs and tourist traps. Some of the old flavour lingers in the lively streets to the south around 'Marseille's stomach', the **Marché des Capucins**. Here, too, is Noailles station, the last resting-place for the city's retired omnibuses and tramways (**Galérie des Transports**, *©* 91 54 15 15, *open 11–6 summer, 10–5 winter, closed Sun and Mon*) although Marseille's last working tram still has its terminus here. Behind this hurly-burly stretches the **Cours Julien**, a favourite promenade and *pétanque* court, lined with antique shops, galleries and restaurants.

North, and perpendicular to La Canebière, extends another tarnished grand boulevard, **Cours Belsunce**. Until 1964 No. 54 was the site of the famous neo-Moorish/Art Nouveau music-hall where Maurice Chevalier and Fernandel once starred, and where Tino Rossi and Yves Montand had their stage débuts. Now the Cours leads only to the **Porte d'Aix**, a fuzzy-minded Roman triumphal arch, vintage 1823, erected to Louis XVI or Liberty or both, adorned with statues of virtues such as Resignation and Prudence, whose heads (much like Louis XVI's) suddenly fell off in 1937 and rolled down the street. This quarter, like the Panier, is now mostly Arab: Marseille's mosque is just on the other side of the arch.

Palais Longchamp and Environs

In 1834 Marseille suffered a drought so severe that it dug a canal to bring in water from the Durance. This 80km feat of aquatic engineering ends with a heroic splash at the **Palais Longchamp**, a delightfully overblown nymphaeum and cascade, populated with stone felines, bulls, and a buxom allegory of the Durance (Ⓜ Longchamp-Cinq-Avenues; bus 80 from La Canebière). Behind the palace stretch the public gardens, an observatory (one of four in this city, which has been the home of many famous astronomers) and a little zoo; in the right wing of the palace itself, some of the same creatures are embalmed in the **Musée d'Histoire Naturelle**, sharing space with their fossilized ancestors (*open 10–12 and 2–6, closed Tues and Wed am*).

The left wing of the Palais Longchamp houses the **Musée des Beaux Arts**, ℂ 91 62 21 17 (*open daily 10–5 in winter, 11–6 summer; adm*). Formed around art 'conquered' by Napoleon's army, it has some second-rate canvases by Italian masters such as Perugino, and stagey burlesques like Rubens' violent *Boar Hunt* (in which ladies daintily watch the spurting blood) or Louis Finson's *Samson and Delilah* (1600), with a nasty Delilah tugging the ear of a very dirty-footed Samson. The mood changes with Michel Serre's scrupulously dire *Scenes of the Marseille Plague of 1720*, where a large percentage of the plague's 40,000 victims are shown dropping like flies while healthy rich men in suits prance by on horseback, looking politely sympathetic.

These same gentlemen never dismounted to assist Marseille's native artists, either—even an establishment figure like Baroque sculptor, architect, and painter Pierre Puget (1671–1745); the rooms devoted to him feature models for buildings and a lovely square that Marseille regretfully never built. Then there's Françoise Duparc, a follower of Chardin (1726–76), who worked most of her life in England; and the satirist Honoré Daumier (1808–97), who went to prison for his biting caricatures of Louis-Philippe's toadies, here represented by Spitting Image-style satirical busts modelled after his drawings. Here, too, is Van Gogh's roving, bohemian precursor, Adolphe Monticelli

(1824–86), who sold his paint-encrusted canvases of fragmented colour for a day's food and drink in the cafés along La Canebière. Also of note are paintings by Provençal pre-impressionists, especially 18th-century scenes of Marseille's port by Joseph Vernet and sun-drenched landscapes by Paul Guigou.

Just across Boulevard Longchamp at 140, the **Musée Grobet-Labadié**, © 91 62 21 82 (*open daily 10–5 winter, 11–6 summer, closed Mon; adm*), contains a private collection as interesting for its eclecticism as for any individual painting, table, plate, musical instrument, tapestry, or iron lock.

Heading South: Le Corbusier and Mazargues

> *The building that achieves speed will achieve success.*
>
> Le Corbusier

To pay your respects to Modular Man, take bus 21 from the Bourse down dreary Boulevard Michelet to the *Corbusier* stop. In 1945, at the height of Marseille's housing crisis, the French government commissioned Le Corbusier to build an experimental **Unité d'Habitation**, derived from his 1935 theory of 'La Cité Radieuse'. Le Corbusier thought the solution to urban *anomie*, transport, and housing problems was to put living-space, schools, shops, and recreational facilities all under one roof, in a building designed according to the human proportions of Leonardo da Vinci's Renaissance man-in-a-circle, reborn as Le Corbusier's wiggly Modular Man symbol. You can see the Man in relief on the huge rough concrete *pilotis*, or stilts, the most revolutionary aspect of the building, which lift it quite literally above the ground level of everyday human affairs.

For a city like Marseille, where people enjoy getting out and about at ground level, the building was a ghastly aberration, and they nicknamed it the *casa de fada* or 'house of the mentally deranged'. Plans for other *unités* were stifled and in 1952 the state sold the flats off as co-ops. But architects were entranced; for the next 30 years thousands of buildings in every city in the world went up on *pilotis*, before everyone realized that the Marseillais were right all along: it was madness to deprive a building of its most important asset, a ground floor. The Unité's good points, however, had few imitators—each of its 337 flats is built on two levels and designed for maximum privacy, with views over the mountains or sea. Of the original extras, only the school, the top-floor gym, and the communal hotel for residents' guests (*see* 'Where to Stay', below) have survived.

Bus 21 continues towards **Mazargues**, a once-fashionable *banlieue* under the Massif de Marseilleveyre, famous in the 19th century for its climate. And when its residents died, at a ripe old age, they often chose to be remembered in the local **cemetery** by a mini-monument to their life's work—there are stone hedge-clippers, fishing boats, hoes, and on the tomb of an omnibus driver, a tramway.

Marseille's Corniche and Parc Borély

Why go to the Riviera when Marseille has one of its very own? From the Vieux Port, you can catch bus 83, and pass the Parc du Pharo, to Corniche Kennedy, a dramatic road overlooking a dramatic coast that must have reminded the ancient Greek colonists of home—now improved with artificial beaches, bars, restaurants, villas, and nightclubs.

Amazingly, until the road was built in the 1850s, the first cove, the **Anse des Catalans**, was so isolated that the Catalan fisherfolk who lived there as squatters in the ruins of the old Lazaretto (or quarantine station) could hardly speak French. This now has the most popular (and the only real) sandy beach. From the bus stop *Vallon des Auffes* you can walk down to the fishing village of **Anse des Auffes** ('of the ropemakers'), isolated from the corniche until after the Second World War and still determinedly intact. Other typical quarters with still more piquant names lie further on: **Anse de Maldormé** and **Anse de la Fausse Monnaie**.

The *corniche* then descends to the artificial **Plages Gaston Deferre**, where a copy of Michelangelo's *David* holds court at the corner of Ave du Prado, looking even more smugly ridiculous than he does in Florence. Beyond the big fellow opens the cool green expanses of **Parc Borély**, with a botanical garden, duck ponds, and the **Château Borély**, an 18th-century palace built according to the strictest classical proportions for a wealthy merchant, unique for its surviving interior decoration.

The *Calanques* and Grotte Cosquer

To continue along the coast from Parc Borély, you'll need to change to bus 19, which poops out just after **Calanque du Mont Rose**, Marseille's nudist beach. Bus 20 from here continues to **Cap Croisette**, a miniature end-of-the-world at the base of the Massif de Marseilleveyre—forming a backdrop to the fishing hamlet in the **Calanque des Goudes**—and the pebble beach at **Calanque de Samena**, facing the islets of Maïre and Tiboulen. The road gives out at the narrow **Calanque de Callelongue**, where the GR 98 coastal path to Cassis begins. Another path from here leads in two hours to the summit of Marseilleveyre (432m), with grand views over Marseille, its industrial *rade*, and islands.

In 1991, the next *calanque*, chalky jagged **Calanque de Sormiou**, made national headlines when local diver Henri Cosquer discovered a hollow 40m under the sea that hid the entrance to a tunnel. Cosquer swam up the tunnel, and after 200m found himself in a subterranean cave above sea level, to his astonishment covered with paintings of running bison, horses, deer and the ancestors of the modern penguin. Along with the art, Cosquer found 'negative' handprints, made by blowing colour around a hand to create its outline on the wall. Similar 'artists' signatures' mark the famous painted caves in the Dordogne.

Although first dismissed as a forgery, mainly because no similar works have ever been found in Provence, the **Grotte Cosquer** (named in honour of its discoverer) is now recognized by prehistorians as a contemporary of Lascaux (*c.* 17,000 BC). At the time, when much of the northern hemisphere's water was concentrated in Ice Age glaciers, the level of the Mediterranean was much lower, so that the entrance of the cave was on dry land. The climate of Provence was also considerably colder—hence the bison and penguins. A thorough study of the cave, begun in September 1993, is expected to take several years. But the chances of the Grotte Cosquer ever opening up to the public is doubtful, not only because of the technical difficulties of access (a shaft would have to be bored through the roof) but because of the inevitable deterioration caused by human breath on works of art vacuum-packed for millennia. A more immediate threat to the cave is the plan of the Marseille municipal government to develop the *calanques* into a vast pleasure port to generate some hard cash for the city's empty coffers. Fortunately the *calanques* between Marseille and Cassis have been listed as a protected site since 1975, and to spoil this striking stretch of coast, one of the last wild segments left in France, will pit the city against environmentalists as well as archaeologists.

Sormiou and the more distant *calanques* can be most painlessly reached from Marseille by boat, operating mid-June to mid-September from the Quai des Belges (Groupement des Armateurs Côtiers Marseille, © 91 55 50 09). Alternatively, take bus 21 from La Canebière to the end of the line (Luminy) and walk 40 minutes to **Calanque de Morgiou**, dotted with seaside *cabanons*, or to the wilder **Calanque de Sugiton**.

The Château d'If and Frioul Islands

If in French means yew, a tree associated with death, and an appropriately sinister name for this gloomy precursor of Alcatraz built by François I in 1524 (*boats from the Quai des Belges, as above, departures hourly 9–7 in the summer, in winter 9, 11, 2, 3.30 and 5*). Even when Alexandre Dumas was still alive, visitors came to see the cell of the Count of Monte-Cristo, and a cell, complete with escape hole, was obligingly made to show to visitors. Real-life inmates included Mirabeau, imprisoned by his father-in-law for running up debts in Aix (*see* p.170); a Monsieur de Niozelles, condemned to six years in solitary for not taking his hat off in front of Louis XIV; and after the revocation of the Edict of Nantes, thousands of Protestants who either died here or went on to die as galley slaves elsewhere.

The two other islands in the Archipel du Frioul, **Pomègues** and **Ratonneau**, were originally hunting and fishing reserves that witnessed, in 1516, one of the first rhinoceroses in Europe, who rambled here en route to Pope Leo X's menagerie in Rome. Later used as quarantine islands, they are now linked by a causeway at Port du Frioul, a pleasure port designed by Le Corbusier's pupil, José-Luis Sert; scores of swimming coves can be easily reached by foot, along paths lined with aromatic herbs that the Marseillais pick for their *bouquets garnis.* A 20-minute path leads to the **Hôpital Caroline**, built in the 1820s on Ratonneau, where the winds blow the strongest, on the theory that they would help 'purify' infectious diseases. Now used for a summer festival, the hospital has excellent views of Marseille—as Marseille was meant to be seen, from the sea—that must have been heartbreaking to the imprisoned patients.

Shopping

Marseille holds a remarkable market of clay Christmas crib figures, the *Foire aux Santons*, from the end of November to January; at other times, you can find *santons* at **Marcel Carbonel**, near St-Victor at 47 Rue Neuve Ste Catherine (7e), © 91 54 26 58, and see them being made (*open 9–1 and 2–7, closed Sun and Aug*). Year-round markets include the daily old book, postcard, and record market in Place A. et F. Carli, near the Noailles métro, or the Sunday morning flea-market in Rue Frédéric-Sauvage (14e) (Bougainville, then bus 30). For the best in Provençal food and wine, try **Georges Bataille**, 18 Rue Fontange, ✆ 91 47 06 23.

Sport and Activities

France's champion **football** squad, **L'Olympique de Marseille** (OM), is also the most enthusiastically supported and tickets often sell out (Stade Vélodrome Municipal, Blvd Michelet (8e), ✆ 91 77 07 28). **Windsurf boards** can be hired at **Pacific Palissades**, Port de la Pointe Rouge, ✆ 91 73 54 37, or neighbouring **Sideral's Time Club**, ✆ 91 25 00 90. On rainy days you can roll the rock or shoot some pool until 2am at **Le Bowling Notre-Dame**, 107 Blvd Notre-Dame (6e), ✆ 91 37 15 05.

Marseille ✉ *13000*   **Where to Stay**

Marseille's top-notch hotels are the bastion of expense-account businessmen and women, while its downmarket numbers attract working girls of a different kind. In between, you can sleep where Chopin and George Sand canoodled—at the central, wood-panelled ★★★**Hôtel Pullman Beauvau**, 4 Rue Beauvau (1er), ✆ 91 54 91 00, ✆ 91 54 15 76, overlooking the Vieux Port and comfortable with air-conditioned, sound-proofed rooms (no restaurant). Up in the hills south of the Vieux Port, the modern ★★★**New Hotel Bompard**, 2 Rue des Flots Bleus (7e), ✆ 91 52 10 93, ✆ 91 31 02 14, (bus 61 from ✆ Joliette or St-Victor), seems remote from the city, set in its own peaceful grounds, with rooms overlooking a garden; those in bungalows have their own kitchenette. A special treat for students of architecture is the hotel incorporated into the Unité d'Habitation, ★★**Le Corbusier**, 280 Blvd Michelet (8e), ✆ 91 77 18 15, ✆ 91 16 78 28; reserve one of its 23 rooms as early as possible. Near La Canebière, the ★★**Moderne**, 30 Rue Breteuil (6e), ✆ 91 53 29 93, has nice rooms, most with shower. Other very palatable budget choices include ★**Montgrand**, 50 Rue Montgrand (6e) (off Rue Paradis, behind the Opéra), ✆ 91 33 33 81, and ★★**Azur**, 24 Cours Roosevelt (1er), ✆ 91 42 74 38, ✆ 91 47 27 91, with frills such as colour TV and garden views (✆ Réformés). Near the Gare St-Charles the most benign choice is the ★**Little Palace**, 39 Blvd d'Athènes (1er), ✆ 91 90 12 93, at the foot of the grand stair. The best of Marseille's two youth hostels is in a château overlooking the city at 76 Ave de Bois-Luzy: **Auberge de Jeunesse de Bois-Luzy**, ✆ 91 49 06 18 (bus 6 or 8 from La Canebière, or bus K after dark; ✆ direction La Rose).

There's a fair smattering of choices overlooking the sea: Marseille's most refined, exclusive hotel, ★★★★**Le Petit Nice**, off Corniche Kennedy, at Anse de Maldormé (7e), ✆ 91 59 25 92, ✆ 91 59 28 08, is a former villa overlooking the Anse de Maldormé, with a fine restaurant, Le Passédat (*see* below). ★★**Péron**, 119 Corniche Kennedy (7e), ✆ 91 31 01 41, ✆ 91 59 42 01, near the Plage des

Catalans, has an unusual cast-iron façade and good rooms. Or try the inexpensive **Le Richelieu**, 52 Corniche Kennedy (7e), ✆ 91 31 01 92, @ 91 59 38 09; best rooms here are nos. 28, 29 and 30.

Eating Out

The Marseillais claim an ancient Greek—even divine—origin for their bally-hooed *bouillabaisse*; one story claims that Aphrodite invented it to beguile her husband Hephastios to sleep so that she could dally with her lover Ares—seafood with saffron being a legendary soporific. Good chefs prepare it just as seriously, and display like a doctor's diploma their *Charte de la Bouillabaisse* guaranteeing that their formula more or less subscribes to tradition: a saffron and garlic-flavoured soup cooked on a low boil (hence its name), based on *rascasse* (otherwise notorious as the ugliest fish in the Mediterranean, and always cooked with its leering head attached), which lives under the cliffs and has a bland taste that enhances the flavour of the other fish, especially conger eel, *grondin* and perhaps lobster. When served, the fish is presented on a side dish with *rouille*, a paste of Spanish peppers. The real McCoy does not come cheap; anything less than 200F will probably be skimpy and disappointing. The best, if the swankiest, *bouillabaisse* may be had at **Michel-Brasserie des Catalans**, 6 Rue des Catalans (7e), ✆ 91 52 30 63: you'll be mixing with politicians and showbiz people (250F and up, open every day, all year). Or there's the reliable, traditional stuff at **Miramar**, by the Vieux Port at 12 Quai du Port (2e), ✆ 91 91 10 40; 250F (*closed Sun and Aug*). **Chez Fonfon**, at 140 Rue du Vallon des Auffes (7e), ✆ 91 52 14 38, prides itself on the freshness of its fish; 250F and up (*closed Sun, Mon midday, and Feb*). **Le Chaudron Provençal**, 48 Rue Caisserie (2e), ✆ 91 91 02 37, presents an acceptable version (200F for *bouillabaisse*, or a seafood menu starting at 160F, *closed Sun and Aug*). At the friendly **Le Faucigny**, near Ste-Marie-Major at 56 Rue de Mazenod (2e), ✆ 91 90 95 21, the dish is just as delicious and much more reasonable, though you must order 3 days ahead for a minimum party of 4 (*bouillabaisse* 200F, 220–275F for a full meal; *closed Sun*).

But there's more than *bouillabaisse* in Marseille. For a genuine Provençal spread try **Maurice Brun: Aux Mets de Provence**, 18 Quai Rive-Neuve (7e), ✆ 91 33 35 38, a 50-year-old restaurant with an overwhelming menu that starts with eight different hors-d'oeuvres. The haughty gourmet **Passédat**, Anse de Maldormé (7e), ✆ 91 59 25 92, offers ravishing food in its exotic garden (weekday lunch menu 300F; otherwise 590F plus). The fare is much simpler (*daube*, etc.) but a delight at **Chez Madie**, 138 Quai du Port (2e), ✆ 91 90 40 87 (menu 145F with wine; *closed Sun*). For perfect oysters, go to **Dégustation Toinou**, 3 Cours Saint Louis (1e), ✆ 91 33 14 94; 240F (*closed Sun and Mon*).

Marseille's unique ethnic mix produces an unrivalled selection of inexpensive cuisines from around the world: try **Ashoka** for Indian, 7 Rue Fortia, ✆ 91 33 18

80; **L'Adagio** for Italian, 41 Rue Thiers, ✆ 91 42 47 33; **Le Roi du Couscous**, 63 Rue de la République, ✆ 91 91 45 46, for the best couscous in town; **Erevan**, 10 Rue Fort Notre Dame, at the Old Port (7e) ✆ 91 33 70 29, for Armenian (*closed Sun*); or **Shabu Shabu**, 30 Rue de la Paix (1e), ✆ 91 54 15 00, for Japanese (*closed Aug*). Fine chocolates, pastries, and *plats du jour* are the fare at **Chocolat Théatre**, 59 Cours Julien (6e), ✆ 91 42 19 29; 192F (*closed Sun*). Night owls can assuage their hunger pangs at **Le Mas**, by the Opéra at 4 Rue Lulli (1er), ✆ 91 33 25 90, open daily until 6am offering good pasta dishes and grills for around 120F (*closed Aug*). Then there's the even cheaper 24-hour **O'Stop**, 1 Place de l'Opéra, ✆ 91 33 85 34, with similar fill-ups whenever you need them. If you're sick of meat there's **Country Life**, at 14 Rue Venture (1e), ✆ 91 54 16 44 (lunchtimes, weekdays only), or **La Gentiane**, 9 Rue des Trois Rois (6e), ✆ 91 42 88 80; 110F (*closed Sun and Mon*).

Entertainment and Nightlife

Marseille may be going on 3000 years, but the old girl's still kicking—sometimes in the wrong places, especially after 10 in the back-streets between the station and the Vieux Port, where British lorry drivers say you can get stabbed in the back and no-one would notice. But you don't have to be a brawny sailor to have a good time: Marseille has lively after-dark pockets, especially around Place Thiers, Cours d'Estienne d'Orves and Cours Julien. You can find out what's happening in *Taktik*, distributed free by the tourist office, or in the pages of *La Marseillaise*, *Le Provençal* or the Wednesday edition of *Le Méridional*. Or try the book and record chain **FNAC**, in the Centre Bourse, ✆ 91 39 94 00, which not only has information on events, but sells tickets as well.

In the last decade, most of the cultural excitement in Marseille has been generated in its theatres. Since 1981, **Théâtre National de la Criée**, 30 Quai de Rive Neuve (7e), ✆ 91 54 70 54, directed by Marcel Maréchal, has put on performances to wide critical acclaim. **Théâtre des Bernadines**, 15 Blvd Garibaldi (1er), ✆ 91 24 30 40, puts on experimental dance and theatre. There's more of the same at **Théâtre du Merlan**, Ave Raimu (14e), ✆ 91 11 19 21. **Système Friche Théâtre**, La Friche de la Belle de Mai, 41 Rue Jobin (33e), ✆ 91 11 42 13, is more modern theatre and dance, where you will also find the **Massalia Théâtre de Marrionettes**, ✆ 91 11 45 65, France's first all-puppet theatre.

Old and avant-garde films in their original language (*v.o.* for *version originale*) are shown in the **Institut National de l'Audiovisuel**, in the Vieille Charité. The three **Breteuil** cinemas also run *v.o.* films at 120 Blvd de Notre-Dame (6e), ✆ 91 37 88 18, as does the **Nouveau Paris**, 31 Rue Pavillon (1er), ✆ 91 33 15 59.

The city has always had a special affinity for music: Berlioz claimed that Marseille understood Beethoven five years before Paris. At the **Opéra Municipal** in Place Reyer (1er), ✆ 91 54 70 54, the bill includes Italian opera and occasional ballets from the **Ballet National de Marseille** (Roland Petit), 20 Blvd Gabès (8e), ✆ 91

71 03 03. Music from around the world is performed at **La Maison de l'Etranger**, 12 Rue Antoine Zattara (3e), ✆ 91 28 24 01. Another concert venue, the **Abbaye de St-Victoire**, 3 Rue de l'Abbaye (7e), ✆ 91 33 25 86, hosts a chamber music festival in Oct–Dec. Jazz, rock, and reggae are all on offer at **Espace Julien**, 39 Cours Julien (6e), ✆ 91 47 09 64, where there's also a music café (Café Espace Julien); nearby at the **Maison Hantée**, 10 Rue Vian, off Rue des Trois Mages, ✆ 91 92 09 40, there's a wide variety of rock and R&B. More R&B happens on weekends at **May Be Blues**, 2 Rue Poggioli (6e), ✆ 91 42 41 00. Marseille's clubs are not great ('Marseille's nightlife is in Aix'), but during university term-time there are some interesting nights to be had. In Place Thiers (1e) watch the Harley Davidsons pull up to the fountain opposite the subterranean **L'Ascenseur**, 22 Place Thiers, ✆ 91 33 13 27, with a cramped dancefloor for a sweaty bop. Off Quai de Rive Neuve, **Le 116**, 5 Rue du Chantier, ✆ 91 33 77 22, is a rowdy student hang-out. **Le Perroquet Bleu**, 72 Blvd des Dames (2e), ✆ 91 91 11 18, has acid jazz and funk. If you're tired of everyone else's efforts, sing it yourself—a little way out (8e)—at the karaoke **Café de la Plage**, 148 Ave Mendes France, ✆ 91 71 21 76, Escale Borély.

West of Marseille: Chaîne de l'Estaque and the Etang de Berre

Whatever personality of its own this region once had has been thoroughly chewed and swallowed by the metropolis next door. Once sheltering attractive, out-of-the-way retreats, the Estaque coast and the broad lagoon of Berre behind it have in the last three decades totally succumbed to creeping suburbia; isolated corners that once knew only hamlets of poor fishermen now suffer some of the biggest industrial complexes in France. Still, the 'Côte Bleue', as the tourist offices call the Estaque coast, is a very attractive piece of coastline. Especially in the east, the mountains plunge straight into the sea, with sheltered *calanques* between them; there is no road along the coast until Carry-le-Rouet.

Tourist Information

Salon: (✉ 13300): 56 Cours Gimon, ✆ 90 56 27 60, ✆ 90 56 77 09

Martigues (✉ 13500): 2 Quai Paul Doumer, ✆ 42 80 30 72, ✆ 42 80 00 97

market days

Martigues: Thursday and Sunday

Salon: Wednesday

Leaving Marseille on the N 568, you'll pass the industrial suburb, docks and marinas of **L'Estaque**—a favourite subject of Cézanne, whose vision of a new, classical Provence transformed the town's smokestacks into Doric columns. The road then crosses over the **Souterrain du Rove**, the world's longest ship tunnel. A partial collapse closed it in the 1960s, and no one has found it worth repairing since. Tortuous side-roads from the N 568 will take you down to two pleasant enclaves harbouring old fishing villages, **Niolon** and **Méjean**.

The reputation of **Carry-le-Rouet**, the biggest town on the coast, is based on the two very odd-looking gifts it has bestowed on the world: the horse-faced actor Fernandel and prickly-stickly sea-urchins; it celebrates the latter with a festival each February. There is a beach, often oversubscribed; Carry is fast being surrounded by the weekend villas of the Marseillais. **Sausset-les-Pins**, the next town, is much the same; however, if you press on further there are popular but not too crowded beaches around **Carro** and **Cap Couronne**.

Martigues

On the lagoon side of the Chaîne de l'Estaque, facing inland across the Etang de Berre, the distinguished old city of **Marignane** has been completely engulfed by Marseille's sprawl and airport. In the centre of the old town, you can visit its 14th-century **château** (now the *mairie*), an eccentric work with mythological frescoes. From here, making a clockwise tour around the Etang de Berre, the next stop is **Martigues**, a sweet little city full of salt air and sailboats, not a compelling place to visit but probably a wonderful place to live. If Carry-le-Rouet serves up sea-urchins to visitors in February, Martigues can answer with its own speciality—fresh sardines—during its Sardine Festival in July and August.

Martigues sits astride the Canal de Caronte, linking the lagoon and the sea, lending it a slight but much-trumpeted resemblance to Venice. According to legend the city was founded by and named after the Roman General Marius; the oldest part of town is the Ile Brescon, at the head of the channel, with the Baroque church of the Madeleine and a number of 17th- and 18th-century buildings. One of its prettiest corners is a quay called the **Miroir des Oiseaux**, the 'mirror of birds'. On the mainland, the **Musée Ziem**, Blvd du 14 Juillet, *©* 42 80 66 06 (*open 10–12 and 2.30–6.30, afternoons only in winter, closed Mon and Tues*), has paintings left to Martigues by landscape artist Félix Ziem, and works by Provençal painters Guigou, Monticelli, and Loubon, as well as archaeology exhibits.

Fos

The French, fascinated with technology, actually come to visit this gigantic industrial complex. Fos has an information centre on Ave Jean Jaurès, *©* 42 47 71 96, and there are guided tours. You too might consider a drive through; in its way Fos is the most astounding, unsettling sight in Provence. Before 1965, when France's Mephistophelean economic planners commandeered it to replace the overcrowded port of Marseille, this corner of the Camargue was pristine marshland. Today it is the biggest oil port, and the biggest industrial complex, on the entire Mediterranean. In area, it is considerably larger than Marseille.

To a degree, it makes sense to concentrate unpleasant industry all in one place. But driving past its 19km of chemical plants, steel-mills and power-lines, rising out of the void like a mirage, the senses rebel. Economically, the 'ZIP' (*zone industriel-portuaire*) is a failure; as planning, it is stupidly primitive, ecologically disastrous, and demeaning to the people who live and work in it, the perfect marriage of corporate gigantism and bureaucratic simple-mindedness.

West and North of the Etang de Berre

Along the west shore there is more of the same, engulfing ancient villages like **St-Blaise**, with a Romanesque church and a wealth of ruins currently being excavated, including a rare stretch of Greek wall. Of the two large towns, **Istres** has a Provençal Romanesque fortified church, Notre Dame de Beauvoir, but **Miramas** is more attractive, with ruins of its medieval predecessor nearby at **Miramas-le-Vieux**. There's also a railway museum, © 90 56 31 38. **St-Chamas**, to the southeast, has an impressive Baroque church. The Via Domitia passed this way, and over a small stream south of the village stands one of the finest and best-preserved Roman bridges anywhere, the **Pont Flavien**. Built in the 1st century AD, the single-arched span features a pair of very elegant triumphal arches at the approaches, decorated with Corinthian capitals, floral reliefs and stone lions. But life went on here even earlier than that, and there are troglodyte dwellings to prove it.

North of the Etang, towards Salon, lie three attractive villages: **Cornillon-Confoux**, on a steep hill with a wide view, **Grans** and **Lançon-Provence**, the latter being home of some of the most exquisite AOC Coteaux-d'Aix-en-Provence wines (*see* p.177).

Salon-de-Provence

The home of Nostradamus should be a more interesting place. Aix-en-Provence's disagreeable little sister, Salon is quite well-off from processing olive oil and from being home to the French air force training school. The town seems aptly named: a little bourgeois parlour, smug and stuffy and neat as a pin. Its spirit is captured perfectly in the antiseptic, gentrified *vieille ville*, ruined by a hideous and insensitive restoration programme in the last few years. Even the antiseptic has its surprises, however: surely the snazziest tiled loos in France (underneath Place du Général de Gaulle) and the **L'Ecole de Bergers,** France's national school for shepherds.

The old quarter, surrounded by a ring of boulevards, is entered by the 18th-century **Porte de l'Horloge**, with an iron-work clock tower. In the centre, at the highest point of Salon, is the **Château de l'Empéri,** © 90 56 22 36, parts of which go back to the 10th century. Long a possession of the Archbishops of Arles, it now houses the **Musée de l'Empéri** (*open daily exc Tues, 10–12 and 2.30–6.30; adm*) and contains a substantial hoard of weapons, bric-a-brac and epauletted mannequins on horseback, covering France's army from Louis XIV to 1918, with an emphasis on Napoleon.

Nostradamus

Salon's most famous citizen was born in St-Rémy in 1503, to a family of converted Jews. Trained as a doctor in Montpellier, young Michel de Nostredame made a name for himself by successfully treating plague victims in Lyon and Aix. In 1547, he married a girl from Salon and settled down here, practising medicine and pursuing a score of other interests besides—studying astrology, publishing almanacs and inventing new recipes for cosmetics and hair dyes. The first of his *Centuries*, ambiguous quatrains written in the future tense, were published in 1555, achieving celebrity for their author almost immediately.

Nostradamus himself said that his works came from 'natural instinct and poetic passion'; in form they are similar to some other poetry of the day, such as the *Visions* of du Bellay. It may be that he had never really intended to become an occult superstar—but when the peasants start bringing you two-headed sheep, asking for an explanation, and when the Queen Regent of France sends an invitation to court, what's a man to do? Nostradamus went to Paris, and later Charles IX and Catherine de' Medici came to visit him in Salon. The Salonnais didn't appreciate such notoriety; if it had not been for Nostradamus's royal favour, they might well have put him to the torch. Now they've made up, and you can visit **Nostradamus's House**, Rue de Nostradamus, © 90 56 27 98, just inside the Porte de l'Horloge (*open 2–6, excluding Tues; adm*). On his death in 1566, Nostradamus was oddly buried inside the wall of the Cordeliers' church; tales spread that he was still alive in there, writing his final book of prophecies. After his tomb was desecrated in the Revolution, he was moved to the 14th-century Dominican church of **St-Laurent**, on Rue Maréchal Joffre, where he rests today.

The **Musée Grévin de Provence**, © 90 56 36 30 (*open daily 10–12 and 2–6 winter, 6.30 summer*), is run by the Parisian waxwork family Grévin, which displays the history of Provence in 54 waxwork figures, from Marius' battle with the Barbarians, through a lifeless Napoleon, to Pagnol's *Manon des Sources*. If you can face yet another museum there's **Le Musée de Salon et Le Crau**, Ave de Pisavi, © 90 56 28 37 (*open 10–12 and 2–6, closed Tues, Sat and Sun mornings*), with a dry, old-fashioned exhibition of costumes, furniture and paintings.

Where to Stay and Eating Out

Carry-le-Rouet (✉ 13620)

In Carry-le-Rouet, there's plenty of seafood along the Promenade du Port; try the roast lobster or sea bass grilled with spices on the attractive seaside terraces of **L'Escale**, © 42 45 00 47; menus approx 300F. If it's full there are the moderately priced and no more than ordinary **Le Calypso** on Quai Vayssiere, © 42 45 10 64 and **Le Madrigal** on Ave G. Montus, © 42 44 58 63. Since most people here have villas or are on a day-trip from the city, accommodation is scarce and functional, as at ★★**La Tuilière** on 53 Ave Draïo-de-la-Mer, © 42 44 79 79, @ 42 44 74 40.

Martigues (✉ 13500)

In the centre, there's ★★**Le Provençal**, 35 Blvd 14 Juillet, © 42 80 49 16, @ 42 49 26 71, or on the outskirts, the fancier ★★★**Eden**, Blvd Emile Zola, © 42 07 36 37.

Salon (✉ 13300)

Spending a night in Salon should be contemplated only if neccessity demands it. At the luxury end of the scale is the ★★★★**Abbaye de Ste-Croix**, 5km out of town on Route du Val de Cuech (the D 17), © 90 56 24 55, @ 90 56 31 12, with expensive and lovely rooms overlooking a medieval cloister. There's a swimming pool and horse-riding, an ultra-posh restaurant with shrimps flambéed in *pastis* and lamb in truffle sauce, and a big wine list. Rooms start at 600F (*closed Nov to Mar*). At the opposite end of the scale, try the gracefully mouldering ***Hôtel Wilson**, 159 Rue Kennedy, © 90 56 46 20. For dinner, there's **Le Mas du Soleil**, Chemin Saint Côme, © 90 56 06 53, traditional but not predictable, with beautifully presented dishes; try the pigeon, if you can resist the tender *agneau* (menus 170–450F).

Aix-en-Provence

Elegant and honey-hued, the old capital of Provence is splashed by a score of fountains, a charming reminder that its very name comes from its waters, *Aquae Sextiae*—sweet water, mind you, with none of the saltiness of Marseille. For if tumultuous Marseille is the great anti-Paris, Aix-en-Provence is the stalwart anti-Marseille—bourgeois and homogeneous, reactionary and haughtily proud of its aristocratic grandeur and good taste. Since 1948 Aix has hosted France's most elite festival of music and opera, while its 580-year-old university not only teaches the arts and humanities to the French but instructs foreign students in the fine arts of French civilization (the more 'practical' science departments are in Marseille); if a fifth of Aix's 150,000 souls are students, another large percentage are doctors, lawyers, and professors, not to mention financial and underworld nabobs who commute to Marseille; and you can be sure that the National Front posters on reactionary Aix's walls remain unsullied by graffiti. But as much as Aix tries to out-poodle Paris, it can never quite live down having mocked and laughed at Cézanne, the one real genius it ever produced.

History

The first version of Aix, the *oppidum* of Entremont, was the capital of the Celto-Ligurian tribe, the Salyens, who liked to decapitate their enemies and tie their heads to the tails of their horses. By 123 BC they had pulled this trick once too often on the Greeks of Massalia, who called in their Roman allies to clobber them. Under Sextius Calvinus, the Romans did just that, and founded a camp at a nearby thermal spring which they named *Aquae Sextiae Salluviorum*. Only 20 years later, in 102 BC, these Latin frontiersmen woke up one day to find 200,000 ferocious Teutones with covered wagons full of wives and children at their door, on route to Italy—looking not for a place to camp but for *Lebensraum*. The strategies of the great Roman general Marius caught them unawares, and in the battle that raged around Aix, so many Teutones were killed or committed suicide that for decades Aix enjoyed bumper crops thanks to soil enriched with blood and corpses; the mountain where Marius's final triumph took place was renamed Montagne Sainte-Victoire.

Although by the next century Aquae Sextiae was a bustling town on the Aurelian Way, invaders in the Dark Ages destroyed it so thoroughly that next to nothing of this settlement remains. Only in the 11th century did Aix begin to revive: the Bourg St-Sauveur grew up around the cathedral with such vigour that in the early 13th century the counts of Provence chose it as their capital. In 1409 Louis II d'Anjou endowed the university; and in the 1450s Aix was the setting for the refined court of Good King René, fondly remembered, not for the way he squeezed every possible *sou* from his subjects, but for the artists he patronized such as Francesco Laurana, Nicolas Froment and the Maître de l'Annonciation d'Aix, and his initiating of popular celebrations, especially the masquerades of the Fête-Dieu (*see* below).

After René died at Aix, in 1486, France absorbed his realm and kept the city as the capital of Provence, the home of the provincial Estates, the governor, and the king-appointed Parlement—the latter institution so unpopular that it was counted as one of the traditional three 'plagues' of Provence, along with the mistral and the Durance. In the 17th and 18th centuries, the aristocratic magistrates who came to reside in the capital built themselves refined *hôtels particuliers*, bequeathing Aix a rare, stylistically harmonious ensemble inspired by northern Italian Baroque architecture. Even the real plague of cholera in 1720 contributed to Aix's unique embellishment, when it contaminated the water; once new sources had been piped in, the city built its charming fountains to receive them.

In 1789, the tumultuous Count Mirabeau became a popular hero in Aix by eloquently championing the people and condemning Provence's Parlement as unrepresentative; in 1800, the whole regional government was unceremoniously packed off to Marseille. Aix settled down to a venerable retirement, tending its university, its thermal spa, its almond confectioneries, and its reputation as the 'Athens of the Midi'.

Getting Around

by train

The station is on Rue G. Desplaces, at the end of Ave Victor-Hugo, ✆ 36 35 35 35; there are hourly connections to Marseille, where you'll have to change to get anywhere else.

by bus

The tumultuous coach station is in Rue Lapierre, ✆ 42 27 17 91, with buses every 20/30 mins to Marseille and others to Avignon, Cannes, Nice, Arles and more.

by taxi

Cours Mirabeau, ✆ 42 21 61 61, or at night, call ✆ 42 26 29 30.

bike and car hire

Bike hire is available at **Cycles Naddéo**, Ave de Lattre-de-Tassigny, ✆ 42 21 06 93, and **Troc-Vélo**, 62 Rue Boulegon, ✆ 42 21 37 40.

You can rent a car at **Rent A Car**, 35 Rue de la Molle, ✆ 42 38 58 29, and **ADA Discount**, 114 Cours Sextius, ✆ 42 96 20 14, as well as the big multinational companies. Drivers should try to avoid playing chicken with the locals' Mercs in the narrow alleys of Vieil Aix, and park in the Place des Cardeurs, Place Carnot, or by the bus station.

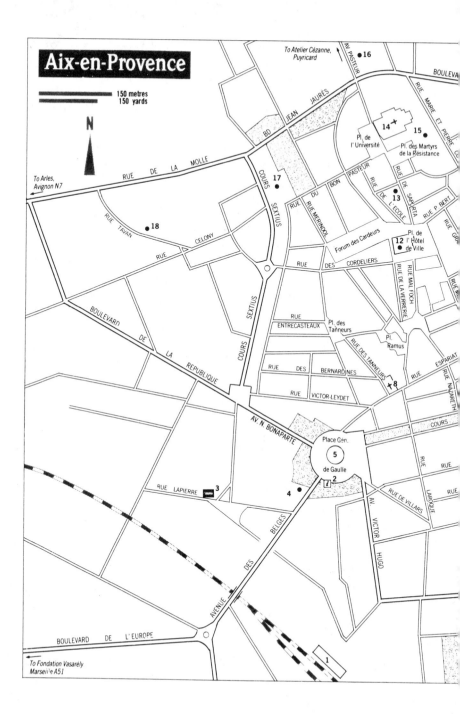

Aix-en-Provence

150 metres
150 yards

N

To Arles,
Avignon N7

To Atelier Cézanne,
Puyricard

● 16

BOULEVA

RUE MARIE ET PIERRE

JEAN   JAURÈS

BD

COURS   SEXTIUS

RUE DE LA MOLLE

14 ✚

15 ●

Pl. de
l' Université

Pl. des Martyrs
de la Résistance

RUE

PASTEUR

RUE DE SAPORTA

RUE DE L' ECOLE

RUE P. BERT

RUE GAR

17 ●

RUE DU

RUE MERINDOL

BON

13 ●

RUE TAVAN

18 ●

RUE

CELONY

Forum des Cardeurs

RUE   DES   CORDELIERS

12
Pl. de
l' Hôtel
de Ville ●

RUE MAL FOCH

RUE DE LA VERRERIE

RUE

SEXTIUS

COURS

BOULEVARD   DE   LA   REPUBLIQUE

RUE
ENTRECASTEAUX

Pl. des
Tanneurs

RUE DES TANNEURS

Pl.
Ramus

ESPARIAT

RUE NAZARETH

RUE   DES   BERNARDINES

RUE

✚ 8

RUE   VICTOR-LEYDET

AV. N. BONAPARTE

COURS

RUE LAPIERRE   ▦ 3

4 ●

Place Gén.
5
de Gaulle

ℹ 2

RUE

RUE

RUE DE VILLARS

LAROQUE

RUE

BELGES

AV. VICTOR HUGO

DES

AVENUE

BOULEVARD   DE   L'EUROPE

To Fondation Vasarely
Marseille A51

1

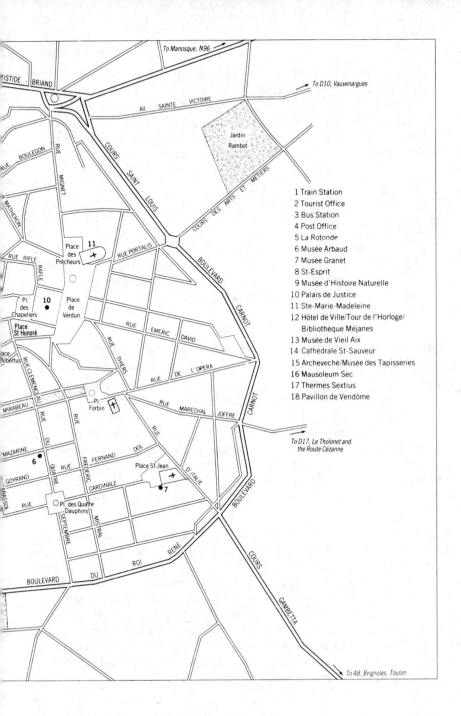

1 Train Station
2 Tourist Office
3 Bus Station
4 Post Office
5 La Rotonde
6 Musée Arbaud
7 Musée Granet
8 St-Esprit
9 Musée d'Histoire Naturelle
10 Palais de Justice
11 Ste-Marie-Madeleine
12 Hôtel de Ville/Tour de l'Horloge/
   Bibliothèque Méjanes
13 Musée de Vieil Aix
14 Cathédrale St-Sauveur
15 Archeveché/Musée des Tapisseries
16 Mausoleum Sec
17 Thermes Sextius
18 Pavillon de Vendôme

Place du Général de Gaulle, © 42 16 11 61, @ 42 16 11 62: without doubt one of the most pleasant tourist offices in the south of France. Aix is one of the rare places that actually seems to welcome tourists. There are a host of circuits to navigate and explore, either by yourself with a map or in guided groups by foot, bus or car—in town or around the countryside, and whether your interest is painting, architecture, history or just a good walk. Contact this office or the bus station (*see* above).

market days

Food, fruit, and local produce every morning in Place Richelme; Tues, Thurs, Sat in Place des Prêcheurs and Place de la Madeleine. Flowers in Place de la Mairie on Tues, Thurs and Sat; in Place des Prêcheurs on Mon, Wed, Fri and Sun. Fleamarket (bits, bobs, odds and ends) in Place de Verdun on Tues, Thurs and Sat. The Marché au Déballage is on Cours Mirabeau every Tues, Thurs and Sat and is not to be missed; on Saturday night it's bustling and brightly lit, and the birds squawk indignantly in the trees above. You might well pick up some unusual pottery or jewellery.

Cours Mirabeau

Canopied by its soaring plane trees, decked with fountains and flanked by cafés, banks, pâtisseries, and *hôtels particuliers* of the 17th and 18th centuries, **Cours Mirabeau**, 'the most satisfying street in France', is the centre stage for Aixois society. Laid out in 1649 to replace the south walls, it begins in Place du Général de Gaulle, which takes the old roads from Marseille and Avignon and spins them around the pompous Second Empire fountain **La Rotonde**. Other fountains punctuate the Cours itself, like the lumpy, mossy **Fontaine d'Eau Chaude**, oozing up its much esteemed 34°C water, and at the far end, the **Fontaine du Roi René**, with a fairy-tale statue of the good monarch holding up a bunch of the muscat grapes he introduced to Provence (along with the turkey and silkworm, which the sculptor left out).

Of the fine mansions on the Cours, No. 12 is where Mirabeau wed the aristocratic Emilie de Covet-Marignane in 1772, after playing her a dastardly trick. When the young lady refused his marriage proposal, Mirabeau sneaked into her house and appeared in the morning on her balcony, clad only in his nightshirt and socks, publicly compromising her virtue. In revenge, his new father-in-law refused the couple any money, and when Mirabeau ran up huge debts, he signed the order to have him imprisoned in the Château d'If. Mirabeau returned to Aix to plead in the subsequent divorce case, and despite his unparalleled eloquence he lost the appeal. Thus rebuked by his noble peers, he returned to Aix in 1789 as a member of the Third Estate and proceeded to attack their privileges—a trial run for his major role in igniting the Revolution in Paris.

Cézanne grew up at 55 Cours Mirabeau, the son of a hatter who later turned banker (on the façade you can still make out the sign of the *chapelier*). Nearby, at No. 53, the elegant mirrored café **Les Deux Garçons** ('Les Deux G') has been Aix's smartest place to see and be seen since the Second World War, with a reputation and price list similar to Paris's famous café-citadels of artsy existentialist mumbo-jumbo; until recently North Africans were not admitted to enjoy its rarefied air. It looks across towards the weighty façade of the 1647 **Hôtel Maurel de Pontevès** (No. 38), the building that was the inspiration for Aix's secular Baroque—still supported after all these years by two musclebound stone giants, 'the only ones who do any work at all on the Cours' as the saying went in the days of Aix's parliament.

South of Cours Mirabeau lies the **Quartier Mazarin**, its straight lanes laid out according to the rules of Renaissance urban design by the archbishop brother of the famous cardinal. At 2a Rue du Quatre Septembre, the **Musée Paul Arbaud** (*open daily 2–5, closed Sun; adm*) is the city's overflow tank for odds and ends, especially Provençal ceramics and a few hundred portraits of Mirabeau's overlarge pockmarked head.

Musée Granet

Place St-Jean, ℰ 42 38 14 70; open daily 10–12 and 2–6, closed Tues Sept–May only; adm.

Two streets south of the Musée Arnaud, and left at the Fountain of the Four Dolphins (unusually equipped with teeth and scales) are the meatier archaeology and art collections of the **Musée Granet** in the former 1675 Priory of the Knights of Malta. In the basement and ground floor sections there's a superb **statue of a Persian Warrior** (200 BC) of the Pergamon school, finds from Roman Aquae Sextiae, and unique **sculptures from the Salian sanctuary at Entremont**, believed to be the oldest in Gaul. Appropriately enough for residents of the land that would invent the guillotine, the overall theme is cult decapitation. The remains of 15 embalmed heads were found in the sanctuary, and the sculptures on display here, like death masks, may have been carved to replace real heads that mouldered away; according to Tertullian, the Celts would spend nights with their dead ancestors, seeking oracular advice. One head, with a hand on top, has the same face as the famous gold mask of Agamemnon from Mycenae (thanks to the proximity of Marseille, Greek stylistic influences are strong); another head resembles not a dead man, but a resurrected youth.

A far more insidious worship of death waits upstairs. The Aixois François Granet (1775–1849), after whom the museum is named, was a minor neoclassical artist and a crony of Ingres, enabling him to secure for Aix the latter's enormous *Jupiter and Thetis* (1811), arguably Ingres' most objectionable canvas. But the real culprit behind this smirking art is Napoleon, whose totalitarian approach to statecraft opened a Pandora's box of kitsch: art like this is born when cloying sentiment and a cynical manipulation of the classical past are evoked to serve political ends. The expression on Jupiter's magnificently stupid face not only sums up a whole era, but looks ahead to the even more cynical kitsch-mongers of the 20th century, who make Napoleon look like Little Red Riding Hood.

The museum also has Ingres' far more palatable and subtle *Portrait of Granet*, painted while the two artists sojourned at Rome's Villa Medici, and canvases by other neoclassical painters including David, Gros, and Granet himself. There is an extensive collection of Dutch and Italian Baroque paintings; flattering 17th-century aristocratic portraits of Aixois nobility by Largillière and Rigaud; and works by Provençal painters such as Guigou, Loubon, and Monticelli. But what of Cézanne, who took his first drawing-classes in this very building? For years he was represented by only three measly watercolours (no one in Aix would buy his works), until 1984 when the French government rectified the omission by depositing eight small canvases here that touch on the major themes of his work.

Vieil Aix

Shops, cafés, and sumptuous, overflowing outdoor markets of every kind fill the narrow lanes and squares of Vieil Aix, north of Cours Mirabeau. Enter by way of Rue Espariat from Place Général de Gaulle, and you'll come to a cast-iron Baroque campanile and the church of **St-Esprit**, where a 16th-century retable has portraits of 12 members of the first Provençal Parlement cast in the roles of the apostles. Further up, just beyond Aix's most elegant little square, the cobbled, fountained **Place d'Albertas**, you can pop into the lavish, Puget-inspired Hôtel Boyer d'Eguilles of 1675, now the **Musée d'Histoire Naturelle** at 6 Rue Espariat, ✆ 42 26 23 67 (*open 10–12 and 2–6, closed Sun am*)— well worth it for an impressive 17th-century interior, a grand stair, and a notable clutch of petrified dinosaur eggs.

The street ends at the neoclassical **Palais de Justice**, a dull building of the 1760s that hardly merited the demolition of a well-preserved Roman mausoleum and the medieval palace of the counts of Provence. Aix's flea-market occupies the adjacent Place de Verdun; opposite, the **Place des Prêcheurs** was laid out in 1450 by King René for popular entertainments and all kinds of executions. In 1772 the Marquis de Sade and his valet were burned in effigy here after sodomizing some prostitutes in Marseille. Facing the square, the church of **Ste Marie-Madeleine** has paintings by Rubens and Van Loo, though the showstopper is the central panel of the *Triptych of the Annunciation*, a luminous work of the 1440s painted for a local draper. The panel has provoked endless controversy over its attribution (it is perhaps by the same painter who illuminated King René's courtly allegories in the famous *Livre du Coeur d'Amour Epris* in Vienna's National Library), and over its singular iconography that would seem to detract from the pious message: the angel Gabriel with wings of owl feathers (a bird of evil omen) kneels in the porch of a Gothic church, decorated with a bat and a dragon. From on high, an unconventionally gesturing God the Father sends down a bizarre foetus in a golden ray, just missing a monkey's head; a vase of flowers holds poisonous belladonna.

The more orthodox blooms of Aix's flower market lend an intoxicating perfume to the square in the very heart of Vieil Aix, in front of the stately **Hôtel de Ville** (1671), a perfectly proportioned building decorated with stone flowers and fruits and intricate iron grilles. Next to the town hall, the flamboyant **Tour de l'Horloge** (1510) has clocks telling the hour and the phase of the moon, as well as wooden statues that change with the season. From here, Rue de Saporta leads to the **Musée du Vieil Aix**, © 42 21 43 55, at No. 17 (*open 10–12 and 2–5 winter, 2.30–6 summer, closed Mon, Nov; adm*), housed in another grand 17th-century *hôtel* with another magnificent staircase. It stores some quaint paintings on velvet, a bevy of *santons*, and marionettes made in the 19th century to represent the biblical, pagan, and local personages who figured in King René's Fête-Dieu processions, beginning with a figure representing Moses and someone tossing a cat up and down, and ending with Death swinging his scythe.

Cathédrale de St-Sauveur, the Tapestry Museum and Joseph Sec

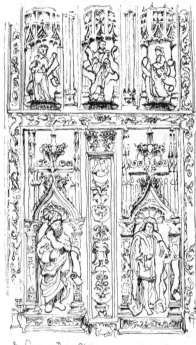

St. Sauveur Door, Aix

Rue de Saporta continues north to the **Cathédrale de St-Sauveur**, a curious patchwork of periods and styles that houses a treasure trove of art. The statues that adorned the central flamboyant portal of 1340 were destroyed in the Revolution, except for the Virgin, who was spared when someone popped a red cap of Liberty on her head and made Mary a Marianne. The interior has a central Gothic nave, a Baroque aisle on the left and a Romanesque aisle on the right; on the walls are 26 tapestries on the lives of Christ and the Virgin made in Brussels in 1510. These originally hung in Canterbury Cathedral, but were sold by the Commonwealth, and purchased by a cathedral canon in Paris for next to nothing in 1656.

The cathedral's most famous treasure, Nicolas Froment's Flemish-inspired **Triptyque du Buisson Ardent** (1476), is on the right wall of the Gothic nave, and opened only on request, by the eloquent sacristan (though usually not on Tues and Sun). On the two folding panels are portraits of King René, who commissioned the work, and his second wife, kneeling amongst saints, while the central scene depicts the vision of a monk of St-Victor of Marseille, who saw the Virgin and Child appear amidst the miraculous burning bush vouchsafed to Moses. The flames in the green bush symbolize her virginity, as does the unicorn; the mirror held by the Child symbolizes his incarnation. The meticulously detailed castles in the background may have been inspired by the towers of Tarascon and Beaucaire. The sacristan will also unlock the covers over the fine walnut panels of the west door, carved in 1504 by Jean Guiramand of Toulon with figures of four Old Testament prophets and the twelve sibyls who were said to have predicted the coming of Christ to the pagans.

Another curious painting of the same period, the *Martyrdom of St Mitre* is behind the high altar, an illustration that Aix's ancient interest in decapitation still lingered into the 1400s. Mitre, a Christian accused of sorcery, had his head chopped off by Roman soldiers. His trunk then picked up the head (already adorned with a halo) and carried it into the cathedral. The sight scared the children but made the Romans, who had a modern sense of humour, laugh until they cried.

The Romanesque aisle on the right harbours the oldest section of St-Sauveur, the 5th-century octagonal **baptistry**, its pool encircled by recycled columns from the temple of Apollo that once stood on this site. Nearby, the 5th-century sarcophagus of St Mitre has a hole that emits an ooze collected by the faithful to heal eye diseases. In the Baroque aisle, the Chapelle de Ste-Anne has the Renaissance **altar des Aygosi** (1470), attributed to Francesco Laurana. The *Crucifixion* shows the skull of Adam at the base of the Cross, while above Christ's head is a pelican, who according to medieval legend, feeds her nestlings with her own blood. Below stand SS. Anne, Marcel, and Marguerite, the latter piously emerging from the shoulders of the dragon that swallowed her whole. Last, but not least, don't miss the light, airy, twin-columned, 12th-century **cloister**, with capitals daintily carved, though in an awful state of repair.

To the right of the cathedral, the grand 17th–18th-century residence of Aix's archbishops, **L'Archevêché** is the setting for the festival's operas. It also houses the **Musée des Tapisseries,** Place de l'Ancien Archevêché, ✆ 42 23 09 91 (*open 10–12 and 2–5.45, closed Tues; adm*), containing three sets of lighthearted Beauvais tapestries, which were hidden under the roof during the Revolution and rediscovered only in the 1840s. The set known as the *Grotesques* (1689) features arabesques, animals, dancers, and musicians; there are nine rococo scenes from the story of *Don Quixote* (1740s), and four on the subject of *Jeux Russiens* (1769–93), inspired by the rustic frolics that the court of Louis XVI got up to in the backwoods of Versailles.

Just north of the cathedral on Ave Pasteur stands an eccentric relic, the 1792 **Mausoleum Sec**, believed to be a symbolic discourse on the Revolution that spoiled those pampered bucolic daydreams. Joseph Sec, the builder, was a Jacobin who made his fortune floating timber down the Durance, and no one has ever satisfactorily explained the meaning behind the reliefs and statues of biblical characters, allegories, and masonic symbols he chose for his mausoleum.

Cézanne, Vasarély, the Pavillon de Vendôme and L'Espace Méjanes

Paul Cézanne spent an idyllic childhood roaming Aix's countryside with his best friend, Emile Zola, and as an adult painted those same landscapes in a way landscapes had never been painted before. The **Atelier Cézanne**, 9 Ave Paul Cézanne, ✆ 42 21 06 53 (*open 10–12 and 2–5, summer 2.30–6, closed Tues; adm*), the studio he built in 1897, a half-kilometre north of the cathedral, has been grudgingly maintained as it was when the master died in 1906, with a few drawings, unfinished canvases, his smock, palette, pipe and some of the bottles and skulls used in his still-lifes. But for a better understanding of

Cézanne's art, pick up the free *Circuit Cézanne* from the Tourist Office, a guide to his favourite landscapes around Aix.

Cézanne's family home at Jas de Bouffan is now dominated by the irritating black and white cubic forms of the **Fondation Vasarély**, 1 Ave Marcel Pagnol, ✆ 42 20 01 09 (a 25min walk southwest of town, or bus 12 from La Rotonde; *open daily, closed Tues in winter; adm*). Inaugurated in 1976 by the same op/geometric/ kinetic artist who created Gordes' 'didactic' museum, it is just as pretentious, claiming as its goal the desire to promote 'more human' buildings, especially low-income housing estates. A laudable goal surely, which Vasarély could have served better by spending his money on houses poor people could actually live in, instead of on cute capers like the *trompe-l'oeil* 'mural integrations' displayed here in hexagonally shaped rooms. The foundation offers endless images to look at, and lots of words; pack an aspirin.

Along the boulevards west of Aix visit the lavish 1665 summer house and gardens built for a cardinal, the **Pavillon de Vendôme**, 32 Rue Célony, ✆ 42 21 05 78 (*open 10–12 and 2–5 winter, 2–6 in summer*). It has yet another impressive grand stair and patrician furnishings, and on the façade, a pair of Atlantes, who by their expressions have just been staring into one of Vasarély's more fiendish optical illusions.

Just to the south of the bus station, the modern Espace Méjanes contains the **Bibliothèque Méjanes**, ✆ 42 25 98 88 (*open Tues, Thurs, Fri, 12–6, Wed and Sat 10–6*), with its rich collection of incunabula and illuminated manuscripts, some of which are usually on display; as well as the **Fondation St-John Perse**, ✆ 42 25 98 85 (*open Tues, Wed, Fri, Sat 2–6*), a museum and study centre bequeathed to Aix by the French poet who won the Nobel Prize in 1960.

Aix-urbia: Montagne Ste-Victoire, Puyricard and the Arc Valley

The serene, gently rolling countryside around Aix is the quintessence of Provence for those who love Cézanne: the ochre soil, the dusty green cypresses—as still and classical as Van Gogh's are possessed and writhing—the simple geometric forms of its houses and the pyramidal prow of the bluish-limestone **Montagne Ste-Victoire**. These landscapes east of Aix along the D 17 (the **Route Cézanne**) are so inextricably a part of Cézanne's art that one can only wonder who created what. What if this grouchy, lonely genius had been born in Birmingham or New Jersey?

The Route Cézanne leads to the wooded park and Italianate château of **Le Tholonet**, where Cézanne often painted the view towards the Ste-Victoire, a mountain that appears in at least 60 of his canvases ('I am trying to get it right,' he explained). The château belongs to the local canal authority, while the park is used as a venue for Aix's music festival (bus from La Rotonde). The entire 60km route around the mountain by way of Beaurecueil, Puyloubier and **Pourrières** is especially lovely, decked with the vineyards that produce Coteaux d'Aix-en-Provence. Pourrières is said to be named after *Campi putridi*, the field of putrefaction, where the unburied corpses of the Teutones rotted after Marius's victory; local farmers made vine trellises from their bones. A trophy was erected to Marius here, showing the victorious general carried shoulder-high on his shield by his soldiers. When it eroded away, parts of it were salvaged and reconstructed as a fountain.

The two-hour path (GR 9) to the top of the Ste-Victoire requires only a pair of sturdy shoes, water and stamina, and begins on the north side from Les Cabassols, near **Vauvenargues** in the Vallée de l'Infernet. At the summit, there's a 17th-century stone *refuge* with water and a fireplace if you want to spend a night, and the 17m **Croix de Provence**, which Cézanne never painted, but has been here, in one form or another, since the 16th century. Legend has it that Marius stood on this precipice, watching his troops annihilate the Teutones, then, at the urging of his sibyl Martha, had 300 defeated chieftains brought up and tossed into the celebrated chasm called the **Garagaï**.

One legend claims the floor of the Garagaï is occupied by an enchanted lake and meadows, abode of the legendary Golden Goat of Provence; shepherds would lower their sick sheep and cows down on ropes to graze the therapeutic grass. Others speculated that it was the entrance to hell, or linked to the Fountain of Vaucluse (and indeed, fluoride released here surfaced there three months later). In the 17th century, curiosity reached such a pitch that the Parlement in Aix offered a condemned man his freedom if he would agree to be lowered into the Garagaï and tell what he found. Carefully trussed, the man went down, but was strangled in the ropes before he reached the bottom.

Vauvenargues' 14th-century château was the home of Luc de Clapiers (1715–47), Marquis de Vauvenargues and author of the *Introduction à la connaissance de l'esprit humain*, in which he wrote that 'the highest perfection of the human soul is to make it capable of pleasure'. In 1958, the château was purchased by Picasso, who probably would have agreed with him. Although the building is closed to the public you might catch a glimpse through the gate of Picasso's grave and a few of his sculptures in the garden. One of the most idyllic roads in the area, the D 11 (parallel to GR 9) descends north of Vauvenargues for 13km to **Jouques**, sheltered in a cool, green valley.

Four km to the north, overlooking modern Aix, is the plateau where the city's story began, the Celto-Ligurian **Oppidum of Entremont**. Similar to the prehistoric Nages in Languedoc, its primitive stone houses were built in clusters along parallel streets, and you can trace the foundations of the large public building that produced the Granet museum's sculptures (*open 9–12 and 2–6 exc Tues*; bus 20 from the BNP on Cours Sextius every half-hour). The same bus continues north to Puyricard, and the **Chocolaterie Puyricard**, 420 Route du Puy Ste Réparade, ✆ 42 96 11 21, ✉ 42 21 47 10, where some of the most delectable (and expensive) fresh chocolates you'll ever taste are made in the traditional pre-Willy Wonka manner; try the *clous de Cézanne*.

To the west of Aix, the D 64 continues for 10km from the Fondation Vasarély to the impressive three-tiered **Aqueduc de Roquefavour** (1847), twice as high as the Pont du Gard and built across the valley of the River Arc to bring the waters of the Durance to Marseille. The wooded setting is delightful—the Arc is the river where Cézanne painted his famous proto-Cubist scenes of bathers. The edge of the Arc valley is dotted with old farms and *villages perchés*: **Eguilles**, north on the D 543, with fine views from its William Morris-style medieval château (now the *mairie*); and south, off the busy Aix–Marseille routes, lofty **Cabriès** and **Mimet**. **Gardanne**, an old village often painted by Cézanne, has remained unchanged, defended by an ugly ring of industry.

Coteaux-d'Aix-en-Provence and La Palette

One of the hottest political potatoes in Provence is the route of the *TGV Provençal* planned for 1997, which would cut out the heart of this relatively recent AOC district just as it has begun to make a name for its red, rosé and white wines. Coteaux-d'Aix-en-Provence originates in 50 *communes* in the highlands stretching from the Durance to Marignane, and west to Salon and east to the flanks of Montagne Ste-Victoire, and consists of the region's traditional syrah, grenache, cinsault, mourvèdre, and carignan grapes, enhanced in the past 20 years with the addition of cabernet-sauvignon, a stock that has improved the wine's ageing ability. Coteaux-d'Aix's sunny whites are made from sauvignon, grenache blanc and ugni—but never from René's sweet muscat grapes, although these now grow merrily in Roussillon.

Many growers welcome visitors, such as Puyricard's **Château du Seuil**, a handsomely restored 13th-century bastide, where the '90 reds and whites are an excellent buy (℡ 42 92 15 99, ℠ 42 92 18 77). Or head further north, 20km from Aix, to Le Puy Ste-Réparade and the lush estate of **Château de Fonscolombe** on the banks of the Durance, where the Marquis de Saporta raises swans and produces classic, fragrant red, rosé, and white wines (℡ 42 61 89 62, ℠ 42 61 93 95). Further afield, another estate that welcomes visitors also supplies some of France's best restaurants: Denis Langue's 120-hectare **Château de Calissanne**, overlooking the Etang de Berre on the site of an ancient Celtic *oppidum* (on the D 10, near Lançon-Provence, ℡ 90 42 63 03, ℠ 90 42 40 00). On the south bank of the lagoon, one of the sunniest corners of France, **Château St-Jean** produces prize-winning rosés (dominated by counoise, an old-fashioned stock, mixed with grenache and carignan) and reds full of old-fashioned finesse (at Port de Buc near Fos, ℡ 42 21 01 02, ℠ 42 23 97 87).

La Palette is a venerable microscopic AOC region on a north-facing limestone scree east of Aix, on the left bank of the Arc; although fairly sheltered from the mistral, it has cooler summer and winter temperatures than its environs. La Palette's red, white, and rosé nectar has been served for the royal fêtes of such diverse monarchs as King René and Edward VII, but only two estates still produce this rare fine wine of the south, aged in small casks: the celebrated 150-year-old **Château Simone,** at Meyreuil (off the pretty D 58H, ✆ 42 66 92 58) where dark, violet-scented reds are kept for three years in caves carved out by 16th-century Carmelites, and **Château Crémade,** a 17th-century bastide in Le Tholonet, which bottles magnificent, well-structured red wines and a fruity blanc de blancs (✆ 42 66 92 66, ✉ 42 66 81 99).

Festivals

Aix publishes a free monthly guide to events, *Le Mois à Aix,* which comes in especially handy during Aix's summer festivals. Headquarters and general booking office for these is the **Comité Officiel des Fêtes,** Complexe Forbin, Cours Gambetta, ✆ 42 63 06 75. The most famous is the **International Music Festival,** featuring celebrity opera and classical music during the last three weeks of July. This highbrow (and *very* expensive) affair is supplemented with lively alternative performances in the streets and smaller theatres. It is preceded by a less formal **Rock Festival,** an umbrella title that includes jazz, big band music, and chamber music during the second and third weeks of June. This is followed, in the first part of July, by the **International Dance Festival,** ranging from classical ballet to jazz and contemporary dance.

Shopping

The traditional souvenirs of Aix are its almond and melon confits, *calissons,* which have been made here since the 1470s; buy them at **Bechard,** 12 Cours Mirabeau, ✆ 42 26 06 78, or **Confiserie Brémond,** 2 Rue Cardinale, ✆ 42 38 01 70, or best of all **Chez Mestre Micoulin,** in les Tours-Venelles, ✆ 42 54 13 11, a veritable citadel of sweet wizardry. If you can't make it up to the chocolate factory at **Puyricard,** they have a shop at 7 Rue Rifle-Rafle, off Place des Prêcheurs, ✆ 42 21 13 26. There's **L'Italie des Gourmets,** at 10 Rue de la Couronne, ✆ 42 26 26 52, for all that's best in charcuterie; after all, Italy's not that far away. **Terre du Soleil,** at 6 Rue Aude, ✆ 42 93 04 54, has local, world-renowned pottery. Don't miss the local wines, Les Coteaux d'Aix-en-Provence, nor the *huile d'olive du pays d'Aix:* Aix calls itself 'the capital of the olive tree since the eighteenth century'.

Aix-en-Provence ✉ *13100*   ## Where to Stay

If you want to come in the summer during the festivals, you can't book early enough; Aix's few cheap hotels fill up especially fast. In the luxury category, there's the romantic ★★★★**Le Pigonnet,** on the outskirts at 5 Ave du Pigonnet, ✆ 42 59 02 90, ✉ 42 59 47 77, with rose arbours, lovely rooms furnished with antiques, and views out over the Aix countryside. Or stay in the centre, at the ★★★★**Villa Gallici,** Ave de la Violette, ✆ 42

23 29 23, ✆ 42 96 30 45, with all the warm atmosphere of an old Provençal bastide, with garden, parking and pool. The renovated, elegant 18th-century ★★★Grand Hôtel Nègre-Coste, 33 Cours Mirabeau, ✆ 42 27 74 22, ✆ 42 26 80 93, still hoists guests in its original elevator (no restaurant), or try the ★★★Mercure Paul Cézanne, 40 Ave Victor Hugo (near the train station), ✆ 42 26 34 73, ✆ 42 27 20 95, an exceptional little hotel, furnished with antiques and serving delicious breakfasts. Two of Aix's medieval religious buildings have been converted into hotels: the 12th-century convent of ★★★Des Augustins, 3 Rue de la Masse, ✆ 42 27 28 59, ✆ 42 26 74 87, just off Cours Mirabeau, which has soundproofed rooms and a breakfast garden (prices start at 600F), and ★★★Le Manoir, 8 Rue d'Entrecasteaux, ✆ 42 26 27 20, ✆ 42 27 17 97, built around a 12th-century cloister. The home of composer Darius Milhaud (who grew up in Aix) has been restored as a hotel, ★★La Renaissance, 4 Blvd de la République, ✆ 42 26 04 22, ✆ 42 27 28 76. Outside the centre, the most charming choice is the 17th-century ★★Le Prieuré, Rte de Sisteron, ✆ 42 21 05 23. Cheaper choices in town include ★★Du Casino, off Rue Espariat at 38 Rue Victor-Leydet, ✆ 42 26 06 88, ✆ 42 27 76 58, and ★Paul, 10 Ave Pasteur, ✆ 42 23 23 89, ✆ 42 63 17 80. The modern Auberge de Jeunesse is by the Fondation Vasarély, at 3 Ave Marcel Pagnol (bus 12), ✆ 42 20 15 99.

Beaurecueil (✉ 13100)

For a spectacular setting it is difficult to beat the ★★★Mas de la Bertrande, off the Route de Cézanne in Beaurecueil, ✆ 42 66 90 09, ✆ 42 66 82 01. There's a salt water pool and shaded terraces, and a restaurant and grill with many a plaque to commend it. But beyond the surface plaques beware the room over the noisy restaurant, the chalet thrumming to the boilers like cars coming and going all night, and the derisory hauteur you incur, as a mere guest. The pylons that walk their way over the valley to Fos make the radio scream, and your hair stand on end as you pass beneath them; best stay nearer Cézanne's mountain at the ★★★Relais Ste-Victoire, ✆ 42 66 94 98, ✆ 42 66 85 96 (closed Jan and Feb) which is air-conditioned, has a pool, a good restaurant, and above all, tranquillity. Both have rooms starting at 350F; book early.

Eating Out

Unlike Marseille's, Aix's 400 restaurants aren't famous for their food, and the food they serve is not a bargain, though always remember a lunch menu costs a lot less than dinner. This is especially true at places like Le Bistro Latin, 18 Rue de la Couronne (just north of Place Général de Gaulle, ✆ 42 38 22 88), featuring imaginative variations on local themes such as leg of lamb with herbs, at refreshingly reasonable prices: lunch menu 87F; dinner 110F and up. Le Clos de la Violette, 10 Ave de la Violette, ✆ 42 23 30 71, has long been considered the best in Aix, and does wonderful things with crab and rabbit (lunch menu 185F, dinner menus from 300F). Being mentioned in Peter Mayle's *A Year in Provence* seems to have gone to the head of **Chez Gu et Fils**, 3 Rue F. Mistral, ℂ 42 26 75 12, and prices have risen accordingly, although the bistro still has tasty Provençal dishes and fresh pasta (from 100F).

Most of the cheaper choices have an ethnic twist. Especially good is the Egyptian, **Kéops**, 28 Rue de la Verrerie, ℂ 42 96 59 05 (menus 60F and 90F); the Tunisian **Djerba**, 8 bis Rue Rifle-Rafle, ℂ 42 21 52 41, with couscous and a lot more for around 100F; the Iranian **Le Jasmin**, 6 Rue de la Fonderie, ℂ 42 38 05 89 (menus 85 and 105F); and Italian **Al Dente**, 14 Rue Constantin, ℂ 42 96 41 03, with great pasta including *tagliatelle au saumon fumé et à l'aneth.* Least expensive of all is the eternally popular **L'Hacienda**, 7 Rue Mérindol (near Place des Cardeurs), ℂ 42 27 00 35, which has a 58F menu including wine. More serious drinkers should head to **Le Petit Verdot**, 7 Rue d'Entrecasteaux, ℂ 42 27 30 12, an authentic bistro where musty red wines are accompanied by ancient jazz records (*plat du jour* 65F).

Entertainment and Nightlife

Outside the festival season, the large student population of 'Sex-en-Provence', as they call it, keeps a number of jazz clubs in business, such as **Hot Brass**, west of the centre on Chemin de la Plaine-des-Verguetiers, ℂ 42 21 05 57, or **Le Scat**, 11 Rue de la Verrerie, ℂ 42 23 00 23. For a good stomp and a beery crowd, head to **L'IPN**, downstairs at 23 Cours Sextius, ℂ 42 26 25 17, or **Le Richèlme**, at 24 Rue Verrerie, ℂ 42 23 49 29. Clubs outside town include **Club 88**, at La Petite Calade north on the RN 7, ℂ 42 23 26 88, and **Retro 25,** south on the RN 8 at Pont-de-Luynes, ℂ 42 24 01 00. **La Chimère**, outside of town at Route d'Avignon, ℂ 42 23 36 28, is Aix's main gay bar and disco.

Films in their original language are shown at **Le Mazarin**, 6 Rue Laroque, ℂ 42 26 99 85.

WINE CHATEAU - GIGONDAS

Northern Provence: the Vaucluse

The 'Three Plagues of Provence', according to tradition, were the mistral, the Durance and the *Parlement* at Aix. The *Parlement* is ancient history, but the other two still serve to define the troublesome boundaries of this region: the long curve of the wicked, boat-sinking, valley-flooding River Durance to the south, and a line of long, ridge-like mountains, Mont Ventoux and the Montagne de Lure, to the north—folk wisdom has always credited these northern boundary-stones of Provence as the source of the terrible mistral. But the lands in between these natural prodigies are the eye of the hurricane, some of the most civilized countryside and loveliest villages to be found in the Midi. These have not passed without notice, of course, and the rural Vaucluse is now what the Côte d'Azur was forty years ago: the in-place for both the French and foreigners to find a bit of sun-splashed holiday paradise amongst the vineyards.

Not everything included in this section is actually in the *département* of Vaucluse (Manosque and Forcalquier are in Alpes-de-Haute-Provence); and the Vaucluse's two cities, Orange and Avignon, will be found in **Down the Rhône: Orange to Tarascon**, pp.65–98. The remainder divides neatly into three areas: the mountainous Lubéron, cradled in the Durance's arc, a *pays* of especially pretty villages; the old papal Comtat, nearer the Rhône, rich agricultural lands rightfully called the 'Garden of France'; and Provence's definitive northern wall, including the dramatic Mont Ventoux and the Dentelles de Montmirail, along with the Roman city of Vaison.

Note that on 18 October 1996 France is changing its telephone numbers from 8 digits to 10 digits. All phone numbers in Provence should be preceded by 04 from this date.

Down the Durance

Getting Around

The valley of the Durance is the main corridor for public transport. A **rail-line** passes Manosque and continues along the bottom edge of the Lubéron, serving Pertuis on its way to Aix and Marseille (five or six daily). Manosque is also the hub for **buses**, with several daily to Aix and Marseille, also one or two a day to Forcalquier and to Digne, stopping in Les Mées.

Tourist Information

Forcalquier (✉ 04300): Place du Bourget (*mairie*), ✆ 92 75 10 02
Manosque (✉ 04100): Place Dr Joubert, ✆ 92 72 16 00, ✆ 92 72 58 98

market days

Manosque: Saturday
Forcalquier: Monday
Banon: Tuesday

St-Donat and Ganagobie

Coming down from Digne and the Provençal Alps, a startling landmark punctuates your entry into the Durance valley: Les **Mées** (a Provençal word for milestones), 2km of needle-like rock formations, eroded into weird shapes overlooking the D 4. There is a bridge at the village of Les Mées, crossing over to **Peyruis** and its ruined castle. Up in the hills, 5km above Peyruis, is the church of **St-Donat**, in a wonderful setting on a little wooded plateau. This graceful building, one of the earliest Romanesque monuments in Provence (11th-century), was built for pilgrims visiting the relics of St Donat, a 5th-century holy man from Orléans who ended his life as a hermit here.

The Durance was a major trade route in the Middle Ages, following the Roman Via Domitia, and religious centres grew up along it from the earliest times. The one most worth visiting is just down the N 96, south of Peyruis. The **Priory of Ganagobie**, in a setting as lovely as that of St-Donat, was founded in the 9th century as a dependency of Cluny. The remarkable church was built some 200 years later. Its portal, though rebuilt in the 1600s, still has its original tympanum relief: a **Christ in Majesty** with the four Evangelists, one of the finest such works in Provence. Inside is another rare decoration, **mosaics** with geometric designs and peculiarly styled animals done in red, black and white; discovered and restored in the 1960s, they were part of the church's original pavement.

Ganagobie used to have the relics of a certain St Transit; he is not found in any hagiography, and it seems that in the Middle Ages the habit of carrying holy relics in procession on a holiday (a *transit*) led to the invention of a new saint. Such things happened all the time in the Midi. (And there must have been some Provençaux colonists involved in a similar occurrence very much later, in New Orleans. The faithful in one parish there still beseech favours at the altar of Ste Expédite. A statue of a female saint had arrived during the building of the church; no one knew who she was—but they found her name on the packing crate.) Ganagobie is still a monastery, but you can visit (*open daily 3–5, closed Mon*); don't be confused by the roads—coming from the north, the village of Ganagobie is up a separate side road; you'll want the D 30, about 3km further south. The lovely area around the Priory is a great place for a picnic, or for some unambitious hiking along the old trails, with a few *bories* (*see* p.200), medieval quarries and views over the valley.

Forcalquier

Nowadays a rather dull village that only comes to life for the Monday market, Forcalquier was once a miniature capital—in the 11th and 12th centuries, when its independent counts carved out a little mountain state for themselves, and often made life difficult for the counts of Provence. Alphonse II managed to swallow it up in 1209, by marriage, but later Provençal rulers like Raymond Berenger V made Forcalquier a favoured residence throughout the 1300s. They left few traces: Europe's only listed cemetery, a tower and other scanty remains of Forcalquier's **citadel**, overlooking the town; and the well-restored 13th-century **Couvent des Cordeliers**, parts of which were originally the counts' palace,

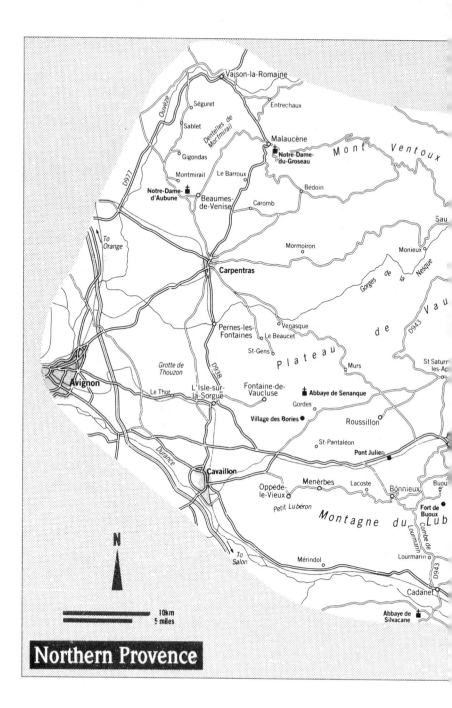

Northern Provence

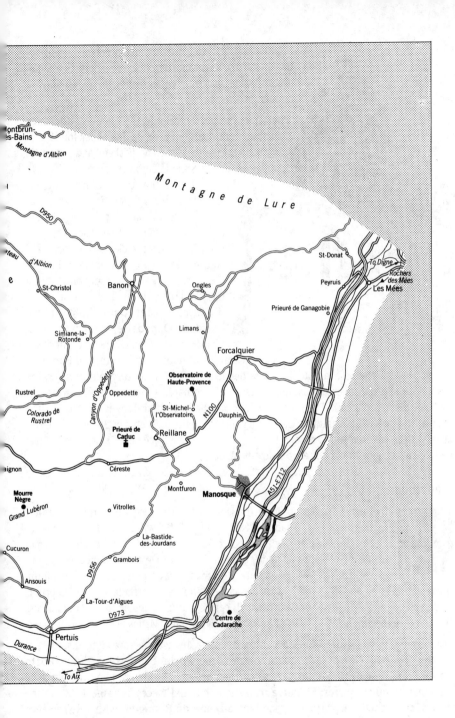

given to the Franciscans (called *cordeliers* in France because of their rope belts) by Raymond Berenger V. There is a small museum inside, and frequent concerts and exhibitions in summer.

The lands around Forcalquier are some of the most beautiful in this part of Provence, full of oak forests and sheep meadows, rustic and peaceful and not yet as touristy as the Lubéron to the south. Twelve km south of the town, **Saint-Michel-l'Observatoire**, ✆ 92 76 60 04, was attracted to the area by a study in the 1930s that found that the *pays de Forcalquier* had the cleanest, clearest air, and the least fog of anywhere in France; there are guided tours, sadly only during the day (*Wed, 3pm*). This is a region of *villages perchés*: **Dauphin**, just to the south; **Oppedette**, to the west, over-looking the scenic canyon of the River Calavon; **Limans** to the north, and **Banon** to

FORCALQUIER CHAPEL

the northwest, the first famous for its rather luxurious 16th-century *pigeonniers*, the second for sheep's cheese. Most impressive of all, perhaps, is **Simiane-la-Rotonde**, set high on a small plateau. The *'rotonde'* is a peculiarly shaped donjon dominating the village, all that's left of a feudal castle. Simiane is by far the most chic of the villages in this area, with plenty of restored second homes; it's a charming place nevertheless, with a late Gothic church and an old **covered market-place**.

Manosque

By far the biggest town in this part of the Durance valley (pop. 20,000), Manosque is unavoidable. It isn't, however, a town to spend much time in. Once a drowsy place, with no other distinction than being the home town of Jean Giono, Manosque today presents the spectacle of a Provençal village out of control. Acres of concrete suburban sprawl press against the hilltop medieval centre, and the traffic can be as ferocious as Marseille's. The culprit is Cadarache, France's national nuclear research centre, a huge complex to the south across the Durance, begun in 1959; most of its workers live around Manosque.

Manosque's tidy, teardrop-shaped centre, an oasis amidst the sprawling disorder, is entered by two elegant 14th-century gates, the **Porte Saunerie** and the **Porte Soubeyran**, designed more for decoration than defence. Inside are two unremarkable churches on quiet squares: **St-Sauveur**, made in bits and pieces from the 1200s to the 1700s, but attractive nevertheless, and **Notre-Dame-de-Romigier**, with a Renaissance façade; the altar here is an early Christian sarcophagus with reliefs of the Apostles.

Forcalquier (✉ 04300)

Lodgings can be hard to find in the thinly settled region around Forcalquier. The village itself is the best bet; the ★★★**Hostellerie des Deux Lions**, 11 Place du Bourguet, ✆ 92 75 25 30, 🖷 92 75 06 41, stands out, with lovely rooms (280–400F) and a justifiedly popular restaurant, with menus that change daily and the best local cheeses and wines. Less expensively, there is the not-so-grand but perfectly acceptable ★★**Grand Hôtel** at 10 Blvd Latourette, ✆ 92 75 00 35; also a bed-and-breakfast *ferme-auberge*, the **Ferme de Bas-Chalus**, 2km from the village, ✆ 92 75 05 67, 🖷 92 75 67 57.

Manosque (✉ 04100)

Manosque has a good selection of hotels, though nothing really special, from the modern but pleasant ★★**Le Provence** on the outskirts, Route de la Durance, ✆ 92 72 39 38, 🖷 92 87 55 13, to the unstarred but passable **Mont d'Or**, in the centre at 8 Place de l'Hôtel de Ville, ✆ 92 72 13 94, 🖷 92 87 41 65. The only luxury hotel-restaurant in this area is outside Manosque, the ★★★★**Hostellerie de la Fuste** (Valensole ✉ 04210), ✆ 92 72 05 95, 🖷 92 72 92 93, across the Durance on the D 4, just north of the D 907 near Oraison. The rooms are fine, in a restored *bastide* with a covered pool, but the real attraction is an elegant, highly rated restaurant: game dishes and truffles in season, marinated trout; menus go from 250F up to a spectacular *menu dégustation* with a little bit of everything for 450F.

Manosque really comes into its own at lunch-time; at number 7 Promenade Aubert-Millot, near the Porte Saunerie by the statue of a dog, look for a crowded hole-in-the-wall with no sign: **Le Petit Pascal**, ✆ 92 87 62 01, a one-woman operation with delicious, filling home-cooking (menus 50F, 75F, lunch only); second choice is **Chez André**, 21 Place du Terreau, ✆ 92 72 03 09, with menus at 75F and 87F. Or if you've had enough French, try Indonesian at **Chez Dadang**, 62 Ave J. Giono, ✆ 92 72 57 18 (*closed Wed*).

The Lubéron

As is the case with many a fair maiden, the Lubéron's charms are proving to be her undoing. This is Peter Mayle country, the stage set for his surprise bestseller, *A Year in Provence*. Yes, this is that magical place where the natives are endlessly warm and human, the vineyards ever-so-lovely in autumn, and the lunch in the little bistro worth writing about for pages and pages. All true, in fact—but everybody knows it, and the trickle of outsiders who began settling here in the 1950s, permanently or in holiday homes, has now become a flood.

How you experience the Lubéron will also depend on what time of year you come. Most of the year it's as quiet as a graveyard; in summer it can seem like St-Tropez-under-the-

Poplars, with vast crowds of Brits, Yanks and Parisians milling about, waiting for lunchtime. It's hard to imagine why anyone would want to come here in August, but if you insist, make sure you have your hotel reservations months in advance.

The Regional Park

Like many parts of rural Provence, the Lubéron presents a puzzling contrast—how these villages became such eminently civilized places, set amidst a landscape (and a population) that is more than a little rough around the edges. The real Lubéron is a land of hunters stalking wild boar over Appalachian-like ridges, and weatherbeaten farmers in ancient Renaults full of rabbit cages and power tools. There are other regions of Provence, equally scenic and rustic, that merit being frozen into a nature preserve, but the Lubéron was the one most in danger of being destroyed by a rash of outsiders and unplanned holiday villas. The **Parc Régional du Lubéron** was founded in 1977, a cooperative arrangement between the towns and villages that covers most of the territory between Manosque and Cavaillon; quite a few (often where the mayor is an estate agent or a notary) have decided not to participate at all. The Lubéron is not an exceptional nature area like the Mercantour. Still, the Park is doing God's work, protecting rare species like the long-legged Bonelli's eagle, a symbol of the Midi that needs plenty of room to roam and is nearing extinction; most of all, it is a reasonably effective legal barrier to keep the Lubéron from being totally overwhelmed by the kind of building madness that wrecked the Côte d'Azur.

Park Information: the **Maison du Pays du Lubéron**, 1 Place Jean Jaurès in Apt, with exhibits, slide shows and a gift shop; ✆ 90 04 42 00, 📠 90 04 81 15.

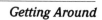

Getting Around

Public transport is woefully inconvenient in the Lubéron; it's possible to get around the villages, but just barely. Apt is on an SNCF branch line, with a few **trains** daily to Cavaillon and Avignon. **Buses** from Apt leave from the Place de la Bouquerie by the river; there are one or two daily to Roussillon, to Avignon, to Aix, stopping at Bonnieux, Lourmarin, Cadenet and Pertuis; also one to Digne, stoping at Céreste. Cavaillon is on the main Avignon–Marseille rail line, and there are also buses to L'Isle-sur-la-Sorgue, Pernes-les-Fontaines and Carpentras (several daily), to Apt and Avignon, and very occasionally to Bonnieux and other western Lubéron villages.

Finding a **horse** is no problem in most areas; in Cucuron, try the Gîte Equestre La Rasparine, ✆ 90 77 21 46; and in St-Martin (north of Pertuis), phone ✆ 90 68 38 59.

La Tour d'Aigues (✉ 84240): in the château, ✆ 90 07 50 29, 🖷 90 07 35 91

Cadenet (✉ 84160): Place du Tambour ✆ 90 68 38 21; includes a shop for Cadenet's basket-weavers, the village's old craft speciality

Lourmarin (✉ 84160): Ave Philippe de Girard, ✆ 90 68 10 77; summer only

Bonnieux (✉ 84480): Place Carnot, ✆ 90 75 91 90, 🖷 90 75 92 94

Cavaillon (✉ 84300): Place F. Tourel, ✆ 90 71 32 01, 🖷 90 71 42 99

market days

Cadenet: Monday morning, Saturday morning in summer

Pertuis: Friday morning

The Pays d'Aigues

The southern end of the Park is the sleepier corner of the Lubéron, a rolling stretch of good farmland sheltered by the Grand Lubéron mountain to the north. **Pertuis**, along the D 973, is its modest capital, with a bit of an aristocratic air; prosperity in the 1600s has left it a number of fine buildings. Of the smaller villages, a few stand out: **Grambois** to the northeast, is a neatly rounded hilltop hamlet; the church of Notre-Dame-et-St-Christophe has both its patrons represented in art inside: a good Renaissance altarpiece of the Virgin, and an original 14th-century fresco of St Christopher. **Ansouis** (✉ 84240), north of Pertuis on the D 56, is a *village perché* built around the sumptuously furnished **Château de Sabran**, ✆ 90 09 82 70 (*open daily, exc Tues in winter, 2.30–6*), still in the hands of the original family: a Henry IV monumental stair leads to Flemish tapestries, Italian Renaissance furniture, portraits and later Bourbon bric-a-brac. The atmosphere is wonderfully snooty, but they let us in to visit just the same.

For an airier, pleasanter castle without the bric-a-brac, try **La Tour d'Aigues**, just to the east. The **Château** here, in fact, doesn't even have a roof. The Baron of Cental was still making repairs to damage caused by a fire in 1782 when the Revolution came, and the local peasantry torched the place for good and all. What's left is a thoroughly elegant Renaissance shell, begun in 1555 by an Italian architect, Ercole Nigra, imitating the styles then fashionable in Paris. The entrance is a massive triumphal arch, carved with trophies, inspired by the Roman arch at Orange. One of the château's side towers has been rebuilt, and the Conseil de Vaucluse, which now owns it, plans to restore the rest a little at a time as funds are available. There is a small **museum**, ✆ 90 07 50 29, down in the cellar, exhibiting both pottery and the history of regional Aigues (*open daily exc Tues, Sat, and Sun morning ; summer 10–12 and 1.30–7, winter 9.30–11.30 and 2–3; adm*). La Tour also has an unusual Romanesque church, **Notre-Dame-de-Romegas**, with an apse at either end—originally built facing the east, it was turned around in the 1600s when some clerical stickler for the rules had a second apse built.

Lourmarin and Cadenet

Further west, into the heart of the Lubéron, **Lourmarin** was the last home of Albert Camus. This is an unusual village, densely packed almost to the point of claustrophobia; many of its houses have tiny courtyards facing the street—too cute for its own good, as few villages even in the Lubéron are so beset by tourists. Its only attraction is another 16th-century **château**, ☎ 90 68 15 23, 🖷 90 09 97 78 (*open for guided tours except Tues, closed Nov–Mar; adm*). Well restored, it's now the property of the Académie of Aix, who use it for cultural programmes, concerts and exhibitions. If you are looking for the co-founder of existentialism, Albert Camus is buried on the left-hand side of the pretty cemetery, next to his wife.

Château de Lourmarin

Cadenet, a big village overlooking the rocky bed of the Durance, is only 5km away, but the difference is like day and night. An ancient place, Cadenet began as a pre-Celtic *oppidum*; even older are some of the cave dwellings that can be seen in the cliffs behind the village (others were refuges for persecuted Waldensian Protestants in the 1500s). It's also a very attractive village. On the Place du Tambour, one of the focal points of the Monday market, is the bronze statue of Cadenet's favourite son, André Estienne, a 15-year-old drummer boy who once managed a difficult river crossing for Napoleon's troops—wading right in and beating the charge under direct Austrian fire. The embarrassed soldiers could only follow. Have a peek inside the parish church, **St-Etienne**, on the northern edge of town. The baptismal font has well-preserved reliefs of a Bacchic orgy; scholars call it 3rd-century, but disagree over whether it was originally a sarcophagus or a bathtub.

West of Cadenet, **Mérindol** isn't much to look at, but worth a mention as a symbol of a very dark page of the Lubéron's history. When plagues and war depopulated the region in the 1300s, immigrants from the Alps and from Italy came to work the land. Many were peaceful, hard-working Waldensian dissenters; when the Reformation began, the authorities could no longer tolerate them. In 1540, the Parlement of Aix oversaw the burning of 19 Waldensian villages in the Lubéron, including Mérindol, and Lourmarin as well. Over 3000 innocents were butchered, and hundreds more were sent off to the King's galleys.

Abbaye de Silvacane

Open daily exc Tues, 9–12 and 2–5; adm; © 42 50 41 69.

Life as a medieval Cistercian was no picnic. Besides the strict discipline and a curious prejudice against heating, there was always the chance the Order might send you to somewhere in the middle of a swamp. They built this, the first of the 'Three Sisters of Provence', in just such a location because they meant to reclaim it—the 'forest of rushes' (*silva cana*), south of the Durance, 7km from Cadenet. It took a century or two, but they did the job, as you can see today from the fertile farmlands around Silvacane. A Benedictine community had already been established here when the Cistercians arrived in 1147. Work began on the present buildings soon after, partially financed by the barons of Les Baux, and Silvacane became quite prosperous. Bad frosts in the 1300s killed all the olives and vines, starting Silvacane on its long decline. When the government bought the complex to restore it in 1949, it was being used as a barn.

The church is as chastely fair as its younger sisters at Sénanque and Thoronet, perhaps more austere and uncompromising still; even the apse is a plain rectangle. Of sculptural decoration there is hardly any (though scores of masons' marks on the columns and vaulting). The adjacent **cloister** now contains a herb garden, around a lovely broken fountain. Note the capitals on the arcades, carved, oddly, with maple leaves.

Where to Stay and Eating Out

La Bastide-des-Jourdans (✉ 84240)

Coming down from Manosque, there is a pleasant hotel on the D 27/ D 956 to La Tour-d'Aigues: the picture postcard ★**Auberge du Cheval Blanc**, © 90 77 81 08, with a restaurant that specializes in game dishes and trout on an outdoor terrace. Rooms are 200–320F.

La Tour-d'Aigues (✉ 84240)

The best bet for lunch is ★★**Les Fenouillets**, just outside the village on the D 956, © 90 07 48 22, ◉ 90 07 34 26. Rooms are simple, but there's a swimming-pool, and an inexpensive restaurant with outdoor tables.

Lourmarin (✉ 84160)

Lourmarin, small as it is, has become the chic rendezvous in the southern Lubéron. One of the classiest establishments to open here in recent years is the newly refurbished ★★★★**Le Moulin de Lourmarin**, © 90 68 06 69, ◉ 90 68 31 76, on the western perimeter of the village on Rue du Temple. A one-time olive mill with views over the château and nearby hills, now Provençal meets Art-Nouveau in its tasteful decoration, whilst the restaurant serves attractive and delicious Provençal dishes (rooms 500–1200F). Just east of the village on the Route de Vaugines is a similarly immaculately restored farmhouse, the ★★★**Hôtel de Guilles**, © 90 68 30 55, ◉ 90 68 37 41, beautifully decorated, with lots of antiques and all the amenities: tennis court, pool and gardens. For something less expensive, there's **Le Paradou,** Route d'Apt, ✆ 90 68 04 05, in a dreamy setting north of Lourmarin on the D 943, at the entrance to the Combe de Lourmarin, rooms 190–230F. Or, for even less, **La Villa St Louis,** 35 Rue Henri de Savournin, ✆ 90 68 39 18, ✉ 90 68 10 07, on the edge of the village, a charming *chambres d'hôte* in a 19th-century house run by the warm and affable Mme Lassallette. Lourmarin can also offer some of the best restaurants in the Lubéron. **La Fenière**, on Rue du Grand Pré in the centre, ✆ 90 68 11 79, combines innovative cooking with old Provençal favourites: a menu might include Vietnamese spring rolls, batter-fried courgette flowers and a hearty *daube*. Menus 180F–450F (*closed Sun eve and Mon*). For lunch, try **La Récréation**, 15 Rue Philippe de Girand, ✆ 90 68 23 73, ✉ 90 68 01 60, with a terrace facing the castle—fresh Provençal fare for 95 or 125F.

Cadenet (✉ 84160)

Cadenet, less expensive and touristy than Lourmarin, is a good alternative for a stay in this region. The ****Hôtel Aux Ombrelles**, Avenue de la Gare south of the village on the D 943, ✆ 90 68 02 40, ✉ 90 68 06 82, combines nice inexpensive rooms with a fine restaurant.The truffle omelettes are very popular, but there's a wide choice of menus from 100F to 150F (*closed Dec–Jan*). Even cheaper, but acceptable, is the old hotel-restaurant ***Le Commerce**, 2 Ave Gambetta, ✆ 90 68 02 35.

Northern Lubéron: Along the N 100

Tourist Information

Apt (✉ 84400): 28 Ave Philippe de Girard, ✆ 90 74 03 18, ✉ 90 04 64 30

Roussillon (✉ 84220): Place de la Poste, ✆ 90 05 60 25

Gordes (✉ 84220): Le Château, ✆ 90 72 02 75, ✉ 90 72 04 39

Fontaine-de-Vaucluse (✉ 84800): Chemin de la Fontaine, ✆ 90 20 32 22, ✉ 90 20 21 37

market days

Apt: Saturday morning

Cavaillon: Monday

Under the Grand Lubéron

Coming from Forcalquier, this route follows the northern slopes of the mountains, generally much more scenic country than the other side, with pretty villages like **Reillane**, almost deserted a century ago, but now making a comeback, even attracting a few artists; and **Céreste**. Between the two, you can make a excursion to the **Prieuré de Carluc,** with a Romanesque chapel and unique ruins of the original early Christian priory, partly carved out of a rocky outcrop; like Notre-Dame du Groseau on Mont Ventoux (*see* p.210), this was an ancient religious site, built around a sacred spring; the ruins around the rock include a Gallo-Roman cemetery.

The narrow roads south of the N 100 are some of the most beautiful in the Lubéron, passing through **Vitrolles** or through **Montfuron**, with its lofty ruined castle, on their way to the Pays d'Aigues. There are also several hiking trails, from Vitrolles or from **Saignon** near Apt, leading up to the summit of the Grand Lubéron, the **Mourre Nègre**, with views that take in all of the Vaucluse and beyond. Saignon itself is a beautiful village between two crags, with a well-preserved 12th-century church.

Apt

The capital of the Lubéron (pop. 15,000 and growing) also claims to be the 'World Capital of Candied Fruits', with one big factory and plenty of smaller concerns that make these and every other sort of sweets. There is a certain stickiness about Apt; everyone in the Lubéron comes here for the huge, animated Saturday market, but no one has ever admitted to liking the place, at least not in print. Roman *Colonia Apta Julia*, a colony refounded over a Celtic village, was the capital of the area even then. Despite languishing for a few dark centuries, before being rebuilt in the 1100s, the streets still bear traces of a rectangular Roman plan, bent into kinks and curves through the ages.

The Cathedral, and More Dubious Provençal Saints

We can guess that the **Rue des Marchands**, the main shopping street, roughly follows the course of its Roman predecessor. It leads to the **Tour de l'Horloge** (1567), the bell tower of Apt's old cathedral of **Ste-Anne**. Begun in the late 12th century and tinkered with incessantly until the 18th, the ungainly exterior conceals a wealth of curiosities within. There is fine 14th-century stained glass in the apse, and an early Christian sarcophagus and an odd golden painting of John the Baptist in two chapels on the north side; also an interesting **trésor** with books of hours, reliquaries and some Islamic ivories. Another trophy from the east is a linen banner, brought back from the Crusades by a lord of Simiane; as its origin was forgotten, it came to be revered in Apt as the **Veil of St Anne**.

Few regions of Europe had such a longing for relics as Provence in the Dark Ages. Other peoples, the Germans and Venetians, had a kleptomanic urge to steal holy bones when no one was looking; the Provençaux, showing less initiative but greater imagination, simply invented them. We met St Transit at Ganagobie (*see* above), and the **crypt** here has two more. According to legend the bones of St Anne, the mother of Mary, were miraculously discovered in this crypt in the 700s, occasioning the building of the first cathedral. In those days, any early Christian burial dug up was likely to be elevated to saint status; beyond that, scholars guess the Anne invented for the occasion was less the biblical figure than a dim memory of the primeval pan-European mother goddess, who was known as Ana, or Dana, to the Celts, the Romans (*Anna Perenna*), and nearly everyone else. Next to her are the bones of 'St Auspice', claimed to be Apt's first bishop—really the sacred auspices of pagan times (divination from bird flight or from the organs of sacrificed animals), another verbal confusion like St Transit.

Fruits and Fossils

Apt also has a good, well-laid-out **Museum** on Rue de l'Amphithéâtre, ✆ 90 74 00 34 (*open daily exc Tues, Sun in winter; in winter 2–5, Sat mornings 10–12; in summer 10–12 and 2.30–5.30; adm*), with archaeological finds going back to the Palaeolithic period, late Roman sarcophagi, painted ex votos and a display of Apt's once flourishing craft of faïence, which had its heyday in the 18th century. The town's other attraction is the **Maison du Pays du Lubéron**, 1 Place Jean Jaurès, ✆ 90 04 42 00, ✆ 90 04 81 15, the headquarters and information centre of the Regional Park; it has exhibits on the region's natural life, including a push-button Palaeontology Museum for the children, an interesting gift shop, and all the information you'll ever need on the wild areas of the Lubéron. Finally, you can take a tour of the **Apt-Union Factory**, west of town on the N 100, ✆ 90 74 65 64, where they make most of those crystallized fruits. It's an interesting process; they suck the water out of the fruit and replace it with a sugar solution—a bit like embalming.

Where to Stay and Eating Out

Apt (✉ 84400)

As rooms in the smaller villages are hard to come by, you'll probably find yourself staying in Apt. Nothing special here; the most pleasant is outside town, the **★★Relais de Roquefure**, on the N 100, 4km west, ✆ 90 04 88 88, an old stone-built inn with an inexpensive restaurant; rooms 200–350F (*closed Jan–mid-Feb*). In the town centre is the **★★★Auberge du Lubéron** on the river at 17 Quai Léon Sagy, ✆ 90 74 12 50, ✆ 90 74 11 86; menus 167F to 345F; the speciality is rabbit with figs, and other dishes with *confit d'Apt*. Also in the centre is **★★Du Palais** at 19 Place Gabriel Péri, ✆ 90 04 89 32, which includes a pizzeria with an 85F lunch menu and other dishes apart from pizza, particularly a good *ratatouille* (*closed Nov–1 Apr*).

Saignon (✉ 84400)

Nearby in Saignon, to the southeast, **Auberge du Presbytère**, ✆ 90 74 11 50, ✆ 90 04 68 51, is worth the detour: at the centre of the village on Place de la Fontaine, it has a magnificent view over the Lubéron and a respectable restaurant with menus from 135F (*closed mid-Nov–mid-Jan*).

Red Villages North of Apt

Technically this isn't part of the Lubéron, though it is within the boundaries of the Regional Park. Above Apt, on the southern slopes of the Plateau de Vaucluse, the geology changes abruptly. The plateau is mostly limestone, which erodes away to make caves and

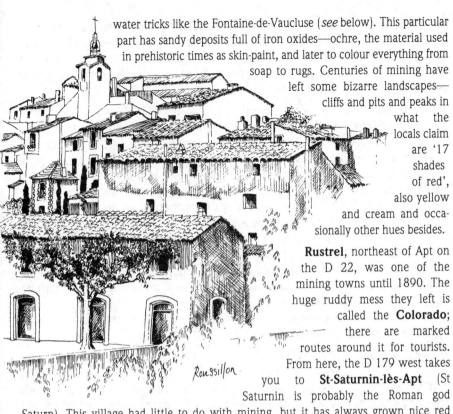
Roussillon

water tricks like the Fontaine-de-Vaucluse (*see* below). This particular part has sandy deposits full of iron oxides—ochre, the material used in prehistoric times as skin-paint, and later to colour everything from soap to rugs. Centuries of mining have left some bizarre landscapes—cliffs and pits and peaks in what the locals claim are '17 shades of red', also yellow and cream and occasionally other hues besides.

Rustrel, northeast of Apt on the D 22, was one of the mining towns until 1890. The huge ruddy mess they left is called the **Colorado**; there are marked routes around it for tourists. From here, the D 179 west takes you to **St-Saturnin-lès-Apt** (St Saturnin is probably the Roman god Saturn). This village had little to do with mining, but it has always grown nice red cherries; there are plenty of ruins, including a castle and bits of three different sets of walls (13th- to 16th-century), also a simple Romanesque chapel from the 1050s. **Roussillon**, to the southwest, occupies a spectacular hilltop site, and well it should, for centuries of mining have removed nearly everything for miles around. The *Association Terre d'Ochres*, an organization that wants to get the business going again, has an information centre in the village, and can direct you on a tour through the old quarries, known locally as the *Sables de Roussillon*. Samuel Beckett spent the war years exiled in Roussillon; rural peace and quiet gave him a nervous breakdown.

South of Roussillon, near the meeting of the N 100 and D 149 (south of the N100), is a well-preserved Roman bridge, the **Pont Julien**.

Villages of the Petit Lubéron

West of Apt, and south of the N 100, is a string of truly beautiful villages that have become the high-rent district of the Lubéron, one of the poshest rural areas in France. Don't come here looking for that little place in the country to fix up; it's all been done, as long as 40 years ago. The first to arrive were the Parisians, including many artists, intellectuals and eccentrics, giving the place a reputation as 'St-Germain-in-the Lubéron'. Since the '60s, a wave of outsiders looking for Provençal paradise, including many Americans, have transformed the place. None of this is readily apparent, apart from the infestations of swank villas on many hillsides outside the Regional Park boundaries. The villagers, a bit richer now, take it in their stride and carry on as they always have—separate worlds, existing side by side.

Biggest and busiest of the villages, **Bonnieux** is also one of the loveliest, a belvedere overlooking all the Petit Lubéron. The ungainly modern church at the bottom of the village contains four colourful 16th-century wood paintings of the *Passion of Christ*; the other attraction, so to speak, is the **Musée de la Boulangerie**, on Rue de la République, © 90 75 88 34 (*open 10–12 and 3–6.30, closed Tues in Jan and Feb*), which as the name suggests will tell you everything you wanted to know about Provençal bread. There are some wonderfully scenic excursions from here: take the D 36/D 943 south to Lourmarin; this is the only good road across the spine of the Lubéron, and passes through a long and beautiful gorge called the **Combe de Lourmarin**. East of Bonnieux off the D 943 a side road, the D 113, takes you up into the mountains, passing the slender, elegant Romanesque bell tower of the **Prieuré de St Symphorien**, and up to the hamlet of **Buoux**; above it, the ruined medieval **Fort de Buoux** offers tremendous views over the heart of the Lubéron. Nearby is the beginning of a **nature trail** marked out by the Regional Park, with informative placards on the Lubéron's flora and fauna all along the way.

Lacoste, west of Bonnieux on D 109, is a trendy *village perché*, home to an American school run by the Cleveland Institute of Art. Overlooking the village is a gloomy ruined **castle**, the home of no less a personage than the Marquis de Sade (d. 1814). The French are a bit embarrassed by the author of *120 Journées de Sodome*, but he certainly wasn't insane, and he is a literary figure of some note, taking to extremes the urge for self-expression that came with the dawn of the Romantic movement. He did have his little weaknesses, which kept him in and out of the calaboose for decades, on charges such as pushing 'aphrodisiac bonbons' on servant girls, and worse. Scion of an old respectable Provençal family, he spent a lot of time here when Paris grew too hot for him. Oddly enough, the Marquis seems to have been a descendant of Petrarch's Laura—Laura de Sade (*see* 'Avignon', p.74). The thought of it obsessed him for life, and he saw her in visions in the castle here. The castle, burned in the Revolution, is currently undergoing a slow restoration by the local *commune* (open to group visits if you reserve two weeks ahead; © 90 75 80 39).

Continuing along the D 109, you come to **Ménerbes**, honey-coloured, artsy and cuter than cute (with an attitude to match). Ménerbes is so narrow, from some angles it looks like a ship, cruising out of the Lubéron toward Avignon; at the top is a small square, about 6m across, with balconies on either side. The D 188 from here takes you amongst waves of vines which lap the road. Fittingly here is the world's first and only corkscrew museum, **Le Musée du Tire-Bouchon** at Domaine de la Citadelle, © 90 72 41 58, ✇ 90 72 41 59 (*open 10–12 and 2–6 daily*), just to the west of Ménerbes. Created by a French film producer, the museum houses a collection of weird and wonderful corkscrews, from 17th-century attempts, to a bejewelled Cartier deluxe model. Lovers of lasciviousness will enjoy the extensive display of pornographic corkscrews. From here the road continues almost to the top of the Petit Lubéron, and **Oppède-le-Vieux**, with its even gloomier ruined castle, one that can be explored. Perhaps it has a curse on it; this was the home of the bloodthirsty Baron d'Oppède, leader of the genocide against the Waldensians in the 1540s.

MÉNERBES — LUBÉRON

Where to Stay and Eating Out

Roussillon (✉ 84220)

If you book ahead, you can find something in the villages. One of the few real luxury places is in Roussillon. **★★★Mas de Garrigon**, ✆ 90 05 63 22, 🖷 90 05 70 01, is a well-restored farmhouse with all the amenities, lovely rooms and a good restaurant; but both, unfortunately, are woefully overpriced; 720F for a room, menus 225–330F (*restaurant closed Dec*). **Le Bistrot de Roussillon** on Place de la Mairie, ✆ 90 05 74 45, attempts to combine Parisian bar food with Provençal atmosphere and for the most part succeeds. Try the *pieds et paquets*. Otherwise there is the popular **La Gourmandine**, Place de l'Abbé-Avon, ✆ 90 05 68 86; menus from 60F (*closed Nov–Mar*).

St-Saturnin (✉ 84490)

St-Saturnin is a friendly village and though a bit out of the way it is a good choice for a base; stay at the delightfully old-fashioned **★Hotel des Voyageurs** on Place Gambetta, ✆ 90 75 42 08 (*closed Jan*), or at the **Saint Hubert** on Place de la Fraternité, ✆ 90 75 42 02, 🖷 90 75 49 90, which has a slightly better restaurant; menus 120F, 180F (*open all year*).

Bonnieux (✉ 84480)

Bonnieux has a real find, the **★★★Hostellerie du Prieuré**, ✆ 90 75 96 00, a 17th-century priory in the village centre; rooms with a view and a garden (*closed Nov–Mar*). Inexpensively, there is the **★Hotel César** on Place de la Liberté, ✆ 90 75 80 18. Neighbouring **Le Pistou** serves local produce on its imaginative menu (100–200F).

To really get away, there is an isolated hotel above **Buoux** (✉ 84480), near the Fort, the **Auberge des Seguins**, ✆ and ✉ 90 74 16 37, Les Seguins (off the D 113); simple rooms and home-cooking in a memorable setting, half-board obligatory. In **Oppède-le-Vieux**, eat beneath ruined medieval walls at **L'Oppidum**, Place de la Croix, ✆ 90 76 84 15, which serves good-value local produce alongside local works of art (menus 68F to 158F).

Côtes-du-Lubéron

Between the mountains of the lower Durance and the Calavon Valley around Apt are the vineyards that produce AOC Côtes-du-Lubéron— mostly young ruby wines made from grenache, syrah, cinsault, mourvèdre and carignan; the whites come from bourboulenc and clairette. This is produced in an extraordinary, high-tech works at the **Château Val-Joanis**, in Pertuis (✆ 90 79 20 77, ✉ 90 09 69 52), where the red, with a high percentage of syrah (60 per cent) is both good and a good buy.

On the other hand, **Château de l'Isolette**, on the main road between Bonnieux and Apt, ✆ 90 74 16 70, is run by the Pinatels, a family that has been making wine since the 1500s. Over the past decade the estate has won scores of medals, especially for its red wines aged in oak barrels, like the '82 *Grande Sélection*; they also do a fine blanc de blancs and rosé.

In Bonnieux itself, look for **Château La Canorgue** (Rte du Pont-Julien, ✆ 90 75 81 01), a beautiful 16th-century château which won a gold medal at Blaye for its '88 red, which has a bouquet of violets.

Cavaillon

Lacking anything more compelling, Cavaillon is famous for its melons. As one of the biggest agricultural market towns in France, it ships a million tons or so of these and all the other rich produce of the surrounding plains to Paris every year. It also has a local market (on Mondays) that competes with Apt's as the most important in the Vaucluse. The town is built under a steep hill overlooking the Durance, the **Colline St-Jacques**, where a Neolithic settlement has been uncovered; it is a short climb from the centre of town, with a medieval chapel and great views over the river valley.

Roman-era Cavaillon has left behind only a 1st-century AD **arch**, at the foot of the hill. Unlike the arches of Carpentras and Orange, this one probably doesn't mark any particular triumph; it is four-sided, a *quadroporticus*, and like the only similar construction, the Arch of Janus in Rome, it probably was a simple decoration for—appropriately enough—a market-place; its decorative reliefs, mostly fruits and flowers, are now too eroded to be seen very clearly.

Cavaillon's other attractions include a small **Archaeological Museum**, ✆ 90 76 00 34, in the chapel of the Ancien Hôtel-Dieu on Cours Gambetta (*closed Tues*); the Romanesque cathedral of **Notre-Dame et St-Véran**, with a tatterdemalion 17th-century interior; and an ornate 18th-century **synagogue**, similar to the one in Carpentras, with a small museum, on Place Castil-Blaze. Before the Revolution, Cavaillon had the biggest Jewish population in the papal enclave; among them were the ancestors of the composer Darius Milhaud. Segregated in a tiny ghetto around the synagogue, the community prospered despite occasional gusts of papal persecution; after the Revolution, most of Cavaillon's Jews moved to the larger cities of Provence, and there are hardly any living in the town today.

Cavaillon ✉ *84300*   ***Where to Stay and Eating Out***

In Cavaillon, even though the *parc* has become a car park, the old ★★**Hôtel du Parc**, Place F. Tourel, ✆ 90 71 57 78, ✆ 90 76 10 35, is still a pleasant place to stay. Slightly more expensive, there's the equally venerable and well-kept ★★**Toppin**, 70 Cours Gambetta, ✆ 90 71 30 42, ✆ 90 71 91 94.

For lunch, the **Fin de Siècle**, 46 Place du Clos, ✆ 90 71 12 27, by the Roman Arch, is a good bet, a café-restaurant that takes its name from its old-fashioned decor; menus 65–120F, with treats like stuffed chicken breast and salmon cakes on even the cheaper menus (*closed Sun*). At 5 Place Philippe de Cabassole, in the centre, the eccentric **Le Pantagruel**, ✆ 90 76 11 30, lives up to its name with a Rabelaisian 118F '*menu des ogres*', more than you can eat, including a slab of ham with *cèpes*, or a *coquelet*. There is also a slimmer 69F menu, an even fatter 146F one, and a pretty terrace.

Gordes

The first thing you'll notice about this striking *village perché* is that it has a rock problem. They have it under control; the vast surplus has been put to use in houses and sheds, and also for the hundreds of thick stone walls that make Gordes seem more like a south Italian village than one in Provence. The stones made agriculture a bad bet here, so the Gordiens planted olives instead, and became famous for them—at least until the terrible frost of 1976 killed off most of the trees. But without ever asking for it, Gordes has found something easier and more profitable: art tourism, with exhibits and concerts in the summer, and two of the slickest artistic roadside attractions in Provence.

Gordes was a fierce resistance stronghold in the war and suffered for it, with wholesale massacres of citizens and the destruction of much of the village; after the war the village was awarded the Croix de Guerre. All the damage the Nazis did has been redeemed; the village centre, all steep, cobbled streets and arches, is extremely attractive. At the centre, you may see flocks of well-scrubbed art students lounging on the steps of the imposing **château** built by the lords of Simiane in the 1520s. They are making their pilgrimage to an avant-garde that no longer exists.

The Vasarély Didactic Museum

Open daily exc Tues, 10–12 and 2–6; © 90 72 02 89.

Hungarians are renowned for their cleverness; they say a man from Budapest can enter a revolving door behind you and come out in front. Victor Vasarély, a poster artist, arrived in France from Budapest in 1929; he always had his mind set on something a little more serious, and the abstract madness of the post-war era finally gave him a chance. With a modicum of talent and a tidal wave of verbal mystification about the 'plastic alphabet' and 'escaping the ephemerality' of figurative art, Vasarély became an op-art celebrity in the '60s, planting his little bulging circles and cubes in museums and corporate offices around the world. Few artists have ever managed to commandeer a castle as a personal monument; he convinced the village to allow it by paying for the restorations. Unlike Vasarély's other self-celebration, at Aix, this one is meant to ensure we understand the various stages of his career. Early attempts at actually drawing are mostly self-portraits; the later works that made him famous are all very tidy and colourful; some have been turned into Aubusson tapestries, flanking a fine Renaissance fireplace, one of the few decorations that survives from the pre-Vasarély château.

To see what real art's all about, walk over to Gordes' parish church of **St-Fermin**, with a memorable 18th-century interior of purple, pink and gilded jiggumabobs, a lodge brother's fantasy seraglio. A statue of the Magdalen on the right looks down on it with a jaundiced eye.

Around Gordes: Les Bories, and Another Bore

Across the Midi they are called *bories*, or *garriotes*, or *capitelles*, or a dozen other local names. In Provence there are some 3000 of them, but the largest collection in one place is the **Village des Bories** south of Gordes, off the D 2. A *borie* is a small dry-stone hut, usually with a well-made corbelled dome or vault for a ceiling. From their resemblance to Neolithic works (like the *nuraghi* of Sardinia) they have always intrigued scholars. Recently it has been established, however, that though the method of building goes way back, none of the *bories* you see today is older than the 1600s. Elsewhere they are usually shepherds' huts, but these are believed to have been a refuge for the villagers in times of plague. This group of 12 *bories* has been restored as a rural museum (*open daily 9–8 summer, 9–5.30 winter; adm*). You'll see other *bories* all around Gordes; some have been restored as holiday homes, and one has even become an expensive restaurant. Determined *borie*-hunters should also tour the large concentrations in the countryside around Bonnieux, Apt, Buoux, St-Saturnin, and Saumane, north of Fontaine de Vaucluse.

South of Gordes, there is a beautiful, simple Romanesque church at the hamlet of **St-Pantaléon**. West of that, watch out for the well-publicized **Museum of Stained Glass**, © 90 72 22 11 (*closed Tues*), where another little Vasarély has set up shop. There are indeed exhibits on the history of stained glass, but their only purpose is to suck you into the adjacent gallery to look at the high-priced and gruesome work of Duran and others. Further south still, at **Coustellet**, the **Musée de la Lavande**, © 90 76 91 23, ✆ 90 76 85 52, reveals all you have ever wanted to know about lavender and more (*open 10–12 and 2–6, closed Mon*).

Abbaye de Sénanque

The loveliest of the Cistercian Three Sisters lies 4km north of Gordes on the D 177. The church may be almost a double of the one at Thoronet (*see* p.247), but built in the warm golden stone of the Vaucluse and set among lavender fields and oak groves, it makes quite an impression. Now it is in the hands of the same cultural association that controls the abbey at St-Maximin-la-Ste-Baume; oddly enough they use the place for studies of Saharan nomads, and there is a room of exhibits on the subject. The Benedictine monks of Ile St-Honorat, who hold the title, seem interested in occupying it again, so Sénanque's status is uncertain. Meanwhile, it is a favourite venue for summer concerts, often of medieval music.

The **church** (*open daily 10–12 and 2–6; adm*), begun about 1160, shows the same early Cistercian seriousness as Thoronet and Silvacane, and has been changed little over the centuries; even the original altar is present. Most of the monastic buildings have also survived, including a lovely **cloister**, the *chauffoir*, the only heated room, where the monks transcribed books, and a refectory with displays giving a fascinating introduction to Sénanque and the Cistercians.

Fontaine-de-Vaucluse

Over a century ago, explorers found the source of the Nile. They're still looking for the source of the little Vaucluse river called the Sorgue. It's underground; the best spelunkers in France have been combing the region's caves for decades without success, and in 1983 a tiny, specially made submarine probe (the *Sorguonaute*) sent back data from some 250m below the surface of the **Fontaine-de-Vaucluse**, where the Sorgue makes its daylight debut, through a dramatic gaping hole in a cliff in the beautiful narrow valley the Romans called *Vallis Clausa*—the origin of *Vaucluse*. A second probe, *Sorguonaute II*, was sent down in 1984, and imploded soon after immersion; finally, in 1985, a sophisticated device usually used in oil exploration—the *Modexa 350*—plunged to a sandy bed 312m below the surface, though the passages that carry the stream into this remain unexplored.

Medieval legends record St Véran, patron of Cavaillon, dispatching a big snake near the source—a sure sign this was an ancient holy place, given the close connection between underground water and mythological serpents everywhere in Europe. The more prosaic Romans channelled the water into an aqueduct, remains of which can still be seen along the D 24 towards Cavaillon. In later times, among those attracted by Provence's greatest natural wonder was Petrarch, who spent many seasons in a villa by the river bank from 1327 to 1353, the year a band of brigands sacked the village and frightened him back to Italy.

The Fontaine is still an exquisite place, but the 540 or so residents of the town of Fontaine-de-Vaucluse have not been able to keep the place from being transformed into one of Provence's more garish tourist traps. To reach it, from the car park next to the church, you'll have to walk a noisy 2km gauntlet of commerciality, everything from *frites* stands to a museum of authentic Provençal *santons*, and a museum of medieval torture instruments. Incredibly, many of the attractions are worthwhile. There is **Norbert Castaret's Subterranean World**, a museum of underground rarities and informational exhibits overseen by France's best-known cave explorer (*open 10–12 and 2–6; closed Tues, Jan and Feb*) and **Vallis Clausa**, a paper-mill powered by old wooden wheels in the river that keeps up an old craft tradition on the Sorgue, making paper the 15th-century way for art books and stationery (*open 10–8, closed Tues: guided tours and sales*). Most surprising of all, in a sharp modern building, is the **Musée de la Résistance**, ✆ 90 20 24 00, ✆ 90 20 22 44 (*open 10–8 summer, 10–12 and 2–6 winter, closed Tues and Jan–Mar*), a government-sponsored institution that recaptures the wartime years vividly with two floors of explanatory displays, vignettes of daily life under the Nazis, newsreels and magazines, weapons and other relics. As at Gordes, Resistance life around Fontaine-de-Vaucluse was no joke; among the exhibits is a tribute to Fontaine's own mayor, Robert Garcin, whose aid to the *maquis* earned him a one-way ticket to Buchenwald in 1944.

Finally, there is the source itself, well worth the trouble even in its off-season. In the spring, and occasionally in winter, it pours out at a rate of as much as 200 cubic metres per second, forming a small, intensely green lake under the cliff. From the late spring until autumn it is greatly diminished, and often stops overflowing altogether (the water appears slightly further down the cliff); its unpredictability is as much a mystery as its source. It is a beautiful spot; if you're ambitious, it is also the beginning of two excellent hiking trails (GR 6 and 97), leading up into some of the most scenic parts of the Plateau de Vaucluse. More easily, you can climb up to the romantically ruined 13th-century **château** overlooking the spring.

Before you leave, have a look at the village church, **Ste-Marie-et-St-Véran**. Begun in 1134, this lovely Romanesque building incorporates Roman and Carolingian fragments, including some bits of floral arabesques and the columns and capitals around the altar. The cornice outside is decorated with winsome rows of human and animal faces. Inside, there is the 6th-century Merovingian tomb of St Véran, and a good painted altarpiece of the *Crucifixion*, donated in 1654 by the village's *confrérie* of papermakers. Also on the way out, peek in at the **Musée Pétrarque**, ✆ 90 20 37 20 (*open 10–12 and 2–6.30 summer, 6 winter, closed Tues and Jan*), a subdued look at the life and times of the poet during his stay in the town.

Gordes (✉ 84220)

Gordes is big business; several fancy villa-hotels have sprung up on the outskirts, but the whole Gordes scene is expensive, over the top, and a bit exploitative of the credulous, who want it and deserve it. If you must, there's **★★★La Mayanelle**, Rue de la Combe, ✆ 90 72 00 28, ✎ 90 72 06 99, just below the centre on the Cavaillon road; unpretentious, comfortable, and a good bargain, with an authentic Provençal kitchen to help you forget Vasarélian didacticism, and an outdoor terrace. Some rooms have a grand view. Another honest establishment, outside the village, the **★★Auberge de Carcarille**, southwest of town on the D 2, ✆ 90 72 02 63, is a carefully restored *mas*, with pretty rooms, some with balconies, and a reasonable restaurant specializing in fish and game (menus 98, 140 and 180F).

Fontaine-de-Vaucluse (✉ 84800)

Fontaine-de-Vaucluse, in spite of its touristic vocation, is a quite pleasant place in which to stay or dine. The **Hostellerie Le Château**, ✆ 90 20 31 54, ✎ 90 20 28 02, in Fontaine's old *mairie*, overlooking the Sorgue, has an outdoor terrace (behind glass, so you won't get splashed by the water-wheel in front). Excellent cooking on menus from 85 to 145F includes delicate sautéed frogs' legs and *truite en papillotte*; also five nice inexpensive rooms. **★★Du Parc**, near the river and centre at Les Bourgades, ✆ 90 20 31 57, ✎ 90 20 27 03, is a simple but pretty hotel wrapped in roses; its restaurant serves some of the best Italian food in Provence (150F). The closest restaurant to the spring isn't a bad one: **Restaurant Philip**, Chemin de la Fontaine, ✆ 90 20 31 81; mostly seafood, on 105F and 155F menus, with an outside terrace by the river (*closed Nov–Easter*).

From Cavaillon to Carpentras

Until the Revolution, the western Vaucluse plains from Cavaillon north to Vaison-la-Romaine were known as the *Comtat Venaissin*, a county that was a part of the papal dominions in France, though legally separate from Avignon. St Louis had stolen the territory from the Counts of Toulouse in 1229, part of the French kings' share of the booty after the Albigensian crusade, and Philip III passed it along to the popes in 1274 to settle an old dispute. It was a worthy prize—medieval irrigation schemes had already made the rich lands of the Comtat the 'Garden of France', an honorific it holds today as the most productive agricultural region in the country. Besides Cavaillon's famous melons, this small area has 5 per cent of all France's vineyards, including its best table grapes, and still finds room to grow tons of cherries, asparagus, apples and everything else a Frenchman could desire. All this intensive agriculture doesn't do the scenery any harm, and passing through it you'll find some fat, contented villages that make the trip worthwhile.

L'Isle-sur-la-Sorgue

The Sorgue, that singular river that jumps out of the ground at Fontaine-de-Vaucluse and makes fly fishermen happy all the way to the suburbs of Avignon (it's one of France's best trout streams), has one more trick to play before it reaches the Rhône. At L'Isle-sur-la-Sorgue, it briefly splits into two channels to make this Provençal Venice, a charming town of 17,000 souls, an island indeed. In the Middle Ages, as a scrappy semi-independent commune, L'Isle-sur-la-Sorgue dug two more channels, and put the water to work running mills and textile factories; when trouble came, as during the Wars of Religion, the town knew how to keep out invaders by flooding the surrounding plains and making itself even more of an island.

Today, L'Isle-sur-la-Sorgue still makes fabrics and carpets, but it is best known as the antiques centre of Provence, with a number of permanent shops on the southern edge of town, around Avenue des Quatre Otages, and a big 'Antiques Village' by the train station, open on Sundays (some booths open Sat and Mon also). Circumnavigating the town is a pleasant diversion, passing a number of old canals and wooden **mills**, some still in use. There are two along Rue Jean Théophile, a street that will also take you to the 18th-century **Hôtel-Dieu**, with a sumptuous chapel and a perfectly preserved pharmacy of that era that can be visited, an ensemble of Moustiers faïence and ornate carved wood. There are frequent art exhibitions in an 18th-century palace, the **Hôtel Donadel Campredon** at 2 Rue Dr Tallet, ✆ 90 38 17 41 (*open 10–1 and 2.30–6.30 summer; 9.30–12.30 and 2.30–5.30 winter, closed Tues*). And finally, right in the centre, is the town's beached whale of a church, 17th-century **Notre-Dame-des-Anges**, sprawling across Place de l'Eglise. Even in a region full of marvellously awful churches, this one is a jewel, a mouldering imitation of Roman Baroque outside and gilt everything within. Opposite the façade, note the old firm of Fauques-Beyret, the prettiest drapery shop in Provence, with a fine Art Nouveau front; inside and out, nothing seems to have changed since the turn of the century.

West of L'Isle-sur-la-Sorgue, the N 100 leads to Le Thor, with one of the best Romanesque churches in Provence, carrying the intriguing name of **Notre-Dame-du-Lac**. Begun about 1200, it is a work of transition, the Provençal Romanesque giving way to Gothic influences, as seen in the pointed vaulting of the nave. The sculptural decoration is spare but elegant, emphasizing the perfect symmetry of one of the last great medieval buildings in this region.

Some 3km north of Le Thor on the D 16 is the **Grotte de Thouzon** (*open daily in July and Aug, 9.30–7; rest of year 10–12 and 2–6; adm*). Of all the caves in Provence, this may be the one most worth seeing—weird and colourful, with rare needle-slender stalactites hanging down as much as 3m.

Pernes-les-Fontaines

L'Isle-sur-la-Sorgue's tiny neighbour to the north, Pernes-les-Fontaines has only a single drowsy stream passing through it, the Nesque. In the 18th century, perhaps out of jealousy, the Pernois took it into their heads to build decorative fountains instead. They got a bit carried away, and now there are 37 of them, or one for every 190 inhabitants. The fountains contribute a lot to making Pernes one of the most thoroughly delightful towns in the Vaucluse. It is an introspective place, still turning its back on the world, sheltering inside a circuit of walls that was demolished a hundred years ago, to be replaced by a ring of boulevards. Pernes is for walking; the Pernois have used the centuries to make their town an integrated work of art, looking exactly the way they want it to look; there's a surprise around every corner—or at least, a fountain.

Starting from the centre, the old **bridge** over the Nesque is embellished at both ends, with the 16th-century **Porte de Notre-Dame**, the **Cormorant Fountain** and the small chapel of **Notre-Dame-des-Graces**, from the same era. Behind it, the 12th-century church of **Notre-Dame-de-Nazareth** includes some Gothic chapels and reliefs of Old Testament scenes. The relative simplicity of its interior, in contrast to so many other Provençal churches, is a reminder of Pernes' earnest Catholicism through the centuries (one of its current economic mainstays, incidentally, is making the communion hosts for all the churches of France). Ask at the Tourist Office for a guide to take you around to the **Tour Ferrande**, on Rue Gambetta. This unassuming medieval tower, next to a fountain with carved grotesques, contains some of the oldest frescoes in France (*c.* 1275): vigorous, primitive scriptural scenes, Charles of Anjou in Sicily, St Sebastian and St Christopher, and a certain Count William of Orange battling against a giant.

East of Pernes-les-Fontaines is a very odd place, **Le Beaucet** (on the D 39 south of St-Didier), where the people used to live in cave houses, some of which can still be seen, along with a ruined castle; above it, in the mountains, a source similar to Fontaine-de-Vaucluse has given rise to one of the biggest pilgrimage sites in Provence, a well-decorated chapel dedicated to the 12th-century **St-Gens**, a rain-maker and tamer of wolves. **Venasque**, further east, was the old capital of the Comtat Venaissin, and gave the county its name. Though a pretty village, and lately fashionable, nothing is left of its former distinction but the usual ruined fortifications and a venerable **baptistry**, really a 6th-century Merovingian funeral chapel reworked in the 1100s. The twisting D 4, connecting Carpentras and Apt, was the main road of the Vaucluse in medieval times; it is still an exceptionally lovely route, passing eastwards from Venasque through the **Forêt de Venasque** and some rocky gorges on the edge of the Plateau de Vaucluse.

L'Isle-sur-la-Sorgue (✉ 84800)

L'Isle-sur-la-Sorgue can be a delightful place for a stay, when not being ravaged by summer tour buses, and its accommodation is fine. Outside the town there is a restored inn from the 1700s, the ★★★**Mas de Cure Bourse** (at Velorgues, 2km south of town on the D 938, Route de Caumont, ✆ 90 38 16 58, ✆ 90 38 52 31), with a pool and extensive gardens, thirteen rooms, and a restaurant where the Lubéron lamb in garlic sauce is a treat; menus from 175F. In town, ★★**La Gueulardière** on Route d'Apt, right in the centre, ✆ 90 38 10 52, ✆ 90 20 83 70, has cosy rooms and a garden terrace for dining; specialities of the house include salmon terrine and duck with olives. The best budget hotel is ★**Le Bassin** on Ave du Général de Gaulle, ✆ 90 38 03 16, by the river, with a simple restaurant. For lunch, the **Saigon**, ✆ 90 20 83 18, a Vietnamese place on Route d'Apt, offers 75–145F menus. **La Basilic**, on Place Gambetta, ✆ 90 38 39 84, offers a somewhat eccentric menu with things you won't often see in the Vaucluse—from chili to *carpaccio*, 50–150F.

Pernes-les-Fontaines (✉ 84210)

Pernes-les-Fontaines offers two two-star hotels: the ★★**L'Hermitage**, on Route de Carpentras, ✆ 90 66 51 41, ✆ 90 61 36 41; and the ★★**Prato Plage**, ✆ 90 61 35 33, ✆ 90 61 33 34, with 20 rooms from 280 to 400F, slightly less expensive than its competitor. Both are open all year round. The ★★**Mas de la Bonoty**, off the D28 to Saint Didier, on the Chemin de Bonoty outside the village, ✆ 90 61 61 09, ✆ 90 61 35 14, also has a restaurant with creditable 145–195F menus and stunning views up to Mt Ventoux (*closed Jan–mid-Mar*).

Carpentras

The average French town of 30,000 or so, unless it has some great historical importance or major monument, is likely to be a rather anonymous place. Carpentras isn't. Perhaps because of its long isolation from the rest of France, under papal rule but really run by its own bishops, Carpentras has character and a subtle but distinct sense of place. A bit unkempt, and unconcerned about it, immune to progress and to any sudden urges for urban renewal, it is nevertheless an interesting place to visit. There are some cockeyed monuments, and some surprises. The rest of Provence pays Carpentras little mind; ask anyone, and they'll probably remember only that the town is famous for caramels, mint-flavoured ones called *berlingots*.

Getting Around

Carpentras is the node for what little there is of **coach transport** in the northern Vaucluse, with good connections to Avignon (some going by way of Pernes-les-Fontaines and L'Isle-sur-la-Sorgue) and Orange, one to Marseille; also one or two a day to Vaison-la-Romaine and some villages of the Dentelles de Montmirail, including Beaumes-de-Venise and Gigondas. Almost all of these stop at Place Aristide-Briand, on the ring boulevard. There are also several daily SNCF **trains** to Orange and Avignon.

Tourist Information

170 Allée Jean-Jaurès, ✆ 90 63 57 88, ✉ 90 60 41 02

market day

Friday morning (truffles from Dec until Feb)

As in so many other French towns, you'll have to cross a sort of motorway to get into the centre: a ring road of boulevards that was created when the town walls were knocked down in the last century (it's one-way and very fast; miss a turn and you'll have to go all the way around again; the French find these very entertaining). One part of the fortifications remains, the towering 14th-century **Porte d'Orange**, built in the 1360s under Pope Innocent IV.

If you can get in, you'll find an amiable and lively town, especially when the gorgeous produce of the Comtat farmers rolls in for Friday market. The stands fill half the town, but the centre is Rue des Halles, with the **Passage Boyer**, an imposing glass-roofed arcade, built by Carpentras' unemployed in the national public works programme started after the 1848 revolution.

Cathédrale St-Siffrein

Undoubtedly this is one of the most absurd cathedrals in Christendom. So many architects, in so many periods, and no one has ever been able to get it finished and get it right. Worst of all is the mongrel façade—Baroque on the bottom, a bit of Gothic and who knows what else above—like a mutt with a spot around its eye, likeable somehow, the kind that follows you home and you end up keeping him. Begun in the 1400s, remodellings and restorations proceeded in fits and starts until 1902. Some of the original intentions can be seen in the fine flamboyant Gothic portal on the southern side, called the **Porte Juive** because Jewish converts were taken through it, in suitably humiliating ceremonies, to be baptized. Just above the centre of the arch is Carpentras' famous curio, the small sculpted *Boule aux Rats*—a globe covered with rats. The usual explanation is that this has something to do with the Jews, or heretics. But bigotry was never really fashionable among 15th-century artists, and more likely this is a joke on an old fanciful etymology of the town's name: *carpet ras*, or 'the rat nibbles'.

The interior, richly decorated in dubious taste, includes some stained glass of the 1500s (much restored) and an early 15th-century altarpiece (left of the high altar) by Enguerrand Quarton of the Avignon school. The sacred treasures are in a chapel on the left: the relics of St Siffrein, one of the most obscure of all saints, not even mentioned in any early hagiographies; and the *Saint-Mors*, the 'holy bridle bit', said to have been made by

St Helen out of two nails of the Cross as a present for her son, Emperor Constantine (*closed Sat and Sun*). Next to the cathedral, the **Palais de Justice** (1640) is the former Archbishop's Palace, occupying the site of an earlier palace that, for the brief periods that popes like Innocent IV chose to stay in Carpentras, was the centre of the Christian world. The present building, modelled after the Farnese Palace in Rome, contains some interesting frescoes from the 17th and 18th centuries: mythological scenes, and also views of Comtat villages and towns (ask the concierge to be shown round).

The Triumphal Arch and the Secret Cathedral

Everyone knows that if you walk around a church widdershins (against the sun: counterclockwise), you'll end up in fairyland, like Childe Harolde. Try it in Carpentras, and you'll find some strange business. The 9m Roman **Triumphal Arch**, tucked in a corner between the Cathedral and the Palais de Justice, was built about the same time as that of Orange, in the early 1st century AD. Anyone who hasn't yet seen Orange's would hardly guess this one was Roman at all. Of all the ancient Provençal monuments, this shows the bizarre Celtic quality of Gallo-Roman art at its most stylized extreme, with its reliefs of enchained captives and trophies. In the 1300s, the arch was incorporated into the now-lost Episcopal Palace. By 1640, when it was cleared, it was serving an inglorious role separating the archbishop's kitchens from his prisons. Originally, it must have connected the palace with the Romanesque cathedral.

Now, look at the clumsily built exterior wall of the present cathedral, opposite the arch. There are two large gaps, through which you can have a peek at something that few books mention, and that even the Carpentrassiens themselves seem to have forgotten: the **crossing and cupola** of the 12th-century cathedral, used in the rebuilt church to support a bell tower (later demolished) and neglected for centuries. In its time this must have been one of the greatest buildings of Provence, done in an ambitious, classicizing style— perhaps too ambitious, since its partial collapse in 1399 necessitated the rebuilding. The sculpted decoration, vine and acanthus-leaf patterns, along with winged creatures and scriptural scenes, is excellent work; some of it has been moved to the town museum.

The Synagogue and Museums

Behind the cathedral and palace, two streets north up Rue Barret, is the broad Place de l'Hôtel de Ville, marking the site of Carpentras' Jewish Ghetto. Before the Revolution, over 2000 Jews were forced to live here in unspeakable conditions, walled in and forced to pay a fee any time they wanted to leave. All that is left today is the **Synagogue** at the end of the square. Built in 1741, it has a glorious decorated interior in the best 18th-century secular taste (*open Mon–Fri, 10–12 and 3–5, Fri 4*). Other attractions in town include the **Hôtel-Dieu** on Place Aristide Briand, an 18th-century hospital with another well-preserved pharmacy and an attractive chapel, containing the tomb of Carpentras' famous bishop (1735–73) and civic benefactor, the Monseigneur d'Inguimbert. This hospital is his monument, along with the important library he left to the town and the beginning of the collections in the **Musée Comtadin-Duplessis** on Blvd Albin-Durand (the ring road),

℗ 90 63 04 92. Here are displayed artefacts and clutter from Carpentras' history, old views of the town, as well as 16th- and 17th-century paintings, many by local artists (*open daily exc Tues; adm*). And there's a **Poetry Museum** on Route de Pernes, ℗ 90 63 19 49 (*open daily 2–6*).

Carpentras ✉ *84200*   ***Where to Stay and Eating Out***

Carpentras somehow manages to be left out of the annual tourist visitations, and accommodation here is limited. For something cosy in the centre, there is the elegant old **★★Le Fiacre**, ℗ 90 63 03 15, ✉ 90 60 51 21, in an 18th-century building at 153 Rue Vigne, near the Syndicat d'Initiative. The budget choice is the **★Hôtel du Théâtre**, 7 Ave Albin Durand, ℗ 90 63 02 90, on the ring boulevard, where the friendly proprietor may try to corner you into a game of chess.

You'll do well at dinner-time, even if there aren't a large number of choices. For original cooking, try **Le Galant Vert** on Rue des Clapiès, ℗ 90 67 15 50; 150–220F for strictly fresh seafood. If the day's catch is unspectacular, you won't go wrong with their *suprême de pigeon* or grilled lamb either (also 80F lunch menu). **L'Orangerie** at 26 Rue Duplessis, ℗ 90 60 11 61, ✉ 90 60 58 76, is a similar place both in price and in its innovative tinkering with old local favourites: the lamb flavoured with mint (unheard of!), also a memorable seafood platter, *délices aux fruits de mer*; menu 88F (lunch only), otherwise up to 200F. For less than a 100F note, you won't do better than the popular and friendly **Le Marijo** on Rue Raspail, ℗ 90 60 42 65, sometimes serving genuine fresh seafood, or at least a well-cooked trout, 55–105F.

East of Carpentras

If you plan to head north, for Mont Ventoux and Vaison-la-Romaine, you might consider a slight detour to the east, along the D 974; towards the village of **Bédoin**, a small resort below Mont Ventoux, you will pass Carpentras' **aqueduct**—not Roman but a 17th-century work, and impressive nevertheless. **Caromb**, west of the D 974 on the D 55, is an attractive village that has kept parts of its medieval fortifications, as well as a surprisingly grand church, **Notre-Dame-et-St-Maurice**, with a wealth of Renaissance decoration inside. From here the skyline is dominated by **Le Barroux**, a dramatically perched village built around a 13th-century castle that belonged to the Seigneurs of Baux.

Or take a tour through the centre of the Plateau de Vaucluse, on the D 942 almost as far as Sault, then return on the D1. Few ever take it, though they miss the most spectacular scenery the Vaucluse has to offer: the dry, rugged **Gorges de la Nesque**, leading to Sault and the Plateau d'Albion (*see* below). **Monieux**, at the eastern end of the Gorges, is a strange and isolated village that seems to have grown out of the rocky cliffs. There are caves and underground streams in the neighbourhood; experiments with dyeing the water have suggested that one of the sources of the Fontaine-de-Vaucluse may be here.

Mont Ventoux

You can pick it out from almost anywhere on the plains around Carpentras, a commanding presence on the northern horizon. **Mont Ventoux**, a bald, massive humpbacked massif over 20km across, is the northern boundary stone of Provence, and it has always loomed large in the Provençal consciousness. For the Celts, as for the peoples who came before them, it was a holy place, the Home of the Winds; excavations early this century at its summit brought to light hundreds of small terracotta trumpets, a sort of ex voto that has never been completely explained. Winds, in Provence, inevitably suggest the mistral, and as the source of that chilling blast Mont Ventoux has always had a somewhat evil reputation among the people; medieval Christians sought to exorcize it, perhaps, with the string of simple chapels that mark its slopes.

Mountain climbers will find a special interest in Mont Ventoux, if only because the sport was invented here. Petrarch, that admirably modern soul, went up with his brother in 1336—this, according to historian Jacob Burckhardt, was the first recorded instance of anyone doing such an odd thing simply for pleasure. The experience had an unexpected effect on the poet. Reading a passage from his *Confessions of St Augustine* at the summit, he was seized with a vision of the folly of his past life, and resolved to return to Italy: ' . . . and men go forth, and admire lofty mountains and broad seas, and roaring torrents, and the course of the stars, and forget their own selves in doing so.' For us the trip will be easier, if perhaps less profound; Edouard Daladier, the Carpentrassien who became French Prime Minister in the 1930s, had a road built to the top (the D 974).

Tourist Information

Malaucène (✉ 84340): Place de la Mairie, ✆ 90 65 22 59

Bédoin (✉ 84410): Espace Marie-Louis Gravier ✆ 90 65 63 95

market day

Malaucène: Wednesday

Malaucène and the Fountain of Groseau

The base for visiting the mountain is **Malaucène**, an open, friendly village on the road from Carpentras to Vaison; its landmark is the impressive church of **St-Michel-et-St-Pierre**, built in 1309 by Pope Clement V. From here, the D 153 was the ancient route around Mont Ventoux, passing a pair of medieval chapels and a ruined defence tower around the village of Beaumont-du-Ventoux (it now peters out into a hiking trail, the GR 4). The D 974, into the heart of the massif, passes a pre-Celtic site dedicated not to wind, but water. **Notre-Dame-du-Groseau** marks the spot today, an unusual 11th-century octagonal chapel. Originally this was part of a large monastery, now completely disappeared. Pope Clement V used it as his summer home, and his escutcheon can be seen painted inside (the *curé* at Malaucène has the key). But this was also a holy spot in remotest antiquity; the iron cross outside the chapel is planted on a stone believed to have been a Celtic altar. *Groseau* comes from *Groselos*, a Celtic god of springs; the object of veneration is a short distance up the road, the *Source du Groseau*, pouring out of a cliff face. The Romans, as they did at Fontaine-de-Vaucluse, channelled the spring into an aqueduct for the city of Vaison; fragments of this can still be seen.

Further up the mountain, the almost permanent winds make themselves known and vegetation becomes more scarce (despite big reforestation programmes in this century). The D 974's big day comes, almost every summer, when the Tour de France puffs over it, probably the most tortuous part of the race; it was here that the English World Champion Tommy Simpson collapsed and died in 1967. The top of Ventoux (1890m) is a gravelly wasteland, embellished with communications towers and a meteorological observatory. Coming down the eastern side of the mountain takes you into one of the least-visited backwaters of Provence, a land of shepherds, boar and *cèpes*. There are a few attractive villages: **Sault**, with a quirky **museum** of fossils, village curios and archaeology, even a mummy (*open Mon, Wed and Sat mid-June–mid-July, rest of year by appointment*); and further north, two medieval *villages perchés*, **Aurel** and **Montbrun-les-Bains**. South of Sault, the lonely **Plateau d'Albion** takes its name (like the English Albion, the Alps and the Provençal village of Aups) from an ancient Indo-European root meaning white—from the odd limestone mountains around it, that seem to be covered in snow. The landscape can be a bit eerie, even more so when you consider that much of this territory, around the village of St-Christol, has been taken over for a complex of bases where France keeps most of its nuclear missiles.

Côtes-du-Ventoux

The vineyards of this little known AOC region are situated on the lower slopes of Mont Ventoux. The area is known principally for its reds, which are similar in style to those Côtes-du-Rhone AOC. The best estates, such as that of Englishman Malcolm Swan at **Domaine des Anges**, make wines with a high proportion of syrah in the blend giving them depth and structure.

A 15th-century glassworks, **Domaine La Verrière** at Goult, ℭ 90 72 20 88, ℮ 90 72 40 33, has been transformed into another of the area's best sources of wine. M. Maubert produces a wine of unusual concentration, full of broad, spicy flavours which complement the local dishes perfectly. The Perrin brothers, famous for producing one of the finest and most sought-after Châteauneuf-du-Pape at Château de Beaucastel, also make a very fine Côtes-du-Ventoux at their purpose-built winery on the outskirts of Orange, **La Vieille Ferme**, ℭ 90 34 64 25.

Les Dentelles de Montmirail

Montmirail's 'lace' is a small crown of dolomitic limestone mountains, opposite Mont Ventoux on the other side of Malaucène. Eroded by the wind into a lace-like fantasy of columns and arches, they form an ever-changing pattern as you circle around them. You can do this easily from Malaucène, beginning with the D 938 north to Vaison, then down the D 977 south, following an anti-clockwise tour that ends up back in Malaucène.

Gigondas (✉ 84190): Place du Portail, ✆ 90 65 85 46, 📠 90 65 88 42

Beaumes-de-Venise (✉ 84190): Cours Jean-Jaurès, ✆ 90 62 94 39

Wine and Antiques

The western slopes of the Dentelles are Côtes-du-Rhône country (*see* below); the D 88 south towards **Séguret** is the beginning of a great wine road, passing miles of immaculately tended vineyards. Séguret is the prettiest of the Montmirail villages, and it has attracted a few artists and antique dealers. It is a good base for hiking; there are two trails (GR 4 and 7) and one village track that passes through a gap in the Dentelles to the eastern side.

Further south come the wine villages of **Sablet** and **Gigondas**, little jewels in a setting of high Dentelle walls and cypresses, and **Montmirail**, a thriving thermal spa in the last century, now gone slightly to seed. Along the D 81, there is the Romanesque chapel of **Notre-Dame-d'Aubune**, on a height overlooking the Comtat plains, and **Beaumes-de-Venise**, with a ruined castle to explore, and a small archaeological museum.

Côtes-du-Rhône Sud

Wines called Côtes-du-Rhône originate in 263 communes within the 200km between Vienne and Avignon. Because of the diversity of growing conditions in such a vast area, from hot rocky plains to steep green slopes, the district is a crazy quilt of local varieties, which as a general rule are better than wines merely labelled Côtes-du-Rhône. You may find any mix of 13 varieties of grapes in a bottle of southern Côtes-du-Rhône, but the dominant forces are grenache, which gives it tannin and its famous sturdy quality, while cinsault counterbalances with its delicacy and finesse, and syrah contributes fragrance and ability to age.

The star of the Dentelles is Gigondas, its very name derived from 'joy', or *Jocunditas*, from a holiday camp for Roman soldiers. Part of their delight, according to Pliny, was in the wine, one of the most subtle, noble, dark, and fragrant of all Côtes-du-Rhônes, the perfect match for pheasant, partridge, wild rabbit, or truffles. Two excellent wines to buy and keep around are the *Signature* '90 and *Pavillon de Beaumirail* '88, aged in oak barrels at the **Cave des Vignerons de Gigondas** (✆ 90 65 86 27, 📠 90 65 80 13), responsible for 20 per cent of the total Gigondas production. As usual, for the finest wines, one has to go to the individual estates, where the best winemakers can concentrate on producing small quantities of wine from the very best vineyard sites. Jean-Marc Autran, the young superstar of Gigondas, makes elegant Gigondas and rich Sablet at the **Domaine Piaugier**, Sablet, ✆ 90 46 96 49, 📠 90 46 99 48. The **Domaine les Pallières** in Gigondas, ✆ 90 65 85 07, is currently run by the latest generation of Roux. The label still bears the name of their late father, a former dynamo of the region largely responsible for encouraging his fellow producers to improve quality. The **Domaine Les Goubert** (✆ 90 65 86 38, ✉ 90 65 81 52), also in Gigondas, offers the remarkably dense *Cuvée Florence* '90 and, more unusual for the Dentelles, a *Sablet Blanc*, a fine white wine from ancient clairette vines. Vacqueyras, the minute region just to the south of Gigondas, produces sober and full-bodied wines; some of the finest are made by a Provençal-speaking Pole named Jocelyn Chudzikiewicz at the **Domaine des Amouriers**, Les Garrigues, Sarrians, ✆ 90 65 83 22, ✉ 90 65 84 13 (the '87 has a fine truffle perfume, and the '88 is so dense it's almost black). **Couranconne**, run by the meticulous Gérard Meffre, makes the very finest Seuret, similar to and better value than Gigondas. Try the **Château de Montmirail**, in Vacqueyras, ✆ 90 65 86 72, ✉ 90 65 81 31, a long-established family vineyard which also does a delightfully mellow Gigondas.

The small *appellation* of Beaumes de Venise produces good reds but is rightly famous for its rich sweet white wine made from the muscat grape. The wine is made by partially fermenting very ripe grapes and arresting the fermentation by the addition of alcohol which kills off the yeasts, leaving much of the sugar and giving the wine an extra potency. The locals find the rather eccentric English habit of treating the wine as a dessert wine highly amusing as they drink it as an aperitif! The local cooperative makes a very good example. The two leading estates are **Domaine Durban** which is owned by M. Leydier, 84190 Beaumes de Venise, ✆ 90 62 94 26, ✉ 90 65 01 85, and the Perrin brothers of **La Vieille Ferme**, ✆ 90 34 64 25, on the outskirts of Orange.

Where to Stay and Eating Out

Crillon le Brave (✉ 84410)

South of Mont Ventoux, between Carpentras and Bédoin, the ★★★★**Hostellerie de Crillon le Brave**, ✆ 90 65 61 61, ✉ 90 65 62 86, is a sunny, sumptuous hotel in an old manor house, run by Peter Chittick, a Canadian infatuated with Provence. Glorious views of Mont Ventoux are supplemented with the hotel's helpful guide to walks in the area.

Malaucène (✉ 84340)

Malaucène, the best base for tackling Mont Ventoux, is well equipped to make your stay a comfortable one. Among the hotels, the clean and shipshape ★★**L'Origan**, in the centre on Cours des Isards, ✆ 90 65 27 08, ✉ 90 65 13 51, stands out; the restaurant offers some hearty cooking—dishes such as guinea-fowl with *morilles*, on menus of 80F, 100F and 120F (*closed Nov–Mar*). If you make it to the other side of Ventoux, stop at **Aurel** (✉ 84390) and the ★**Relais du Ventoux**, ✆ 90 64 00 62; plain but comfortable rooms and a restaurant with no surprises on the 85F menu, but it's the best you'll do in this little-visited region (*closed mid-Nov–mid-Mar*). East of the summit of Ventoux, at the corner of the

D 164 and D 974, the **Chalet-Reynard**, ✆ 90 61 84 50, is the only restaurant for miles, a cosy, wood-lined bar where the local lumberjacks tuck into boar and a *pichet de rouge* at lunch-time; menus from 98F.

Séguret (✉ 84110)

In the **Dentelles de Montmirail**, the one special place to stay is in Séguret, the ★★★**Auberge de Cabasse**, ✆ 90 46 91 12, 🖂 90 46 94 01, part of a Côtes-du-Rhône estate on the D 23 towards Sablet; a few comfortable rooms with terraces at 200–650F, a pool, and an excellent restaurant that has truffles in season and other rather extravagant dishes year-round; menus 140–170F, more at weekends; (*closed Jan, Feb and Mar*). To dine well in Séguret, head for **Le Mesclun** in the village, ✆ 90 46 93 43, 🖂 90 48 93 48, and its à la carte selection of local delights for around 150F (*closed Mon*).

The only inexpensive place is in **Beaumes-de-Venise** (✉ 84190), the **Auberge St-Roch** on Ave Jules Ferry, ✆ 90 62 94 29, 🖂 90 65 05 07, with a modest restaurant that does seafood and local dishes (*closed mid-Nov–Mar*). One of the old spa establishments of **Montmirail** (✉ 84190) has been reopened, without the waters: the ★★★**Hôtel de Montmirail**, ✆ 90 65 84 01, 🖂 90 65 81 50, with a pool, garden, and a restaurant; rooms 255–410F.

Vaison-la-Romaine

Vaison, in all its 2400 years, has never been able to make up its mind which side of the River Ouvèze it wanted to be on. Locals have always been wary of the river's mighty potential for destruction, and the town's peregrinations from bank to bank have left behind a host of monuments, including extensive Roman ruins. Such circumspection was proved justified in 1992 when, on the night of 22 September, the Ouvèze burst its banks and swept away houses, caravans, bridges and roads, drowning 30 people in one of the worst French floods this century. The town's riverside is still being rebuilt, and the scars of the tragedy are yet to heal. Yet, as the tourist office proclaims, the best way to support Vaison is to continue to visit. The Roman ruins were untouched, and life goes on: Vaison is a pleasant and beautiful place (with a good market if you are staying locally), and despite the summer crowds, if you're interested in the Romans or the Middle Ages it will be a mandatory stop on your Provençal agenda. The recently created Vaison Festival draws large crowds from July to September, when theatre groups, choirs and musicians from France and the world gather for performances in venues ranging from the Roman amphitheatre to the town's car parks. For information contact the tourist office, or call the festival organizers, ✆ 90 28 84 49.

Tourist Information

Place du Chanoine Sautel, ✆ 90 36 02 11, 🖂 90 28 76 04. There is a vast car park across the street for visitors.

Vaison-la-Romaine (the lower town): Tuesday

History

Vaison began on the heights south of the Ouvèze as a Celtic *oppidum*. In the late 2nd century BC, the Romans took control and refounded it as *Vasio Vocontiorum*, a typical colony on the gentler slopes to the north of the river. For an out-of-the-way site, Vasio prospered spectacularly for the next five centuries, an *urbs opulentissima* with a large number of wealthy villas and as many inhabitants as it has today (about 6000). Vaison survived the age of invasions better than many of its neighbours; church councils were held here in the 6th century, a time when the city could afford to begin its imposing cathedral.

For the following centuries, bishops ruled in Vaison as the city gradually declined. Perhaps in the 700s, the Counts of Toulouse acquired the site of the old Celtic *oppidum* and built a castle on it. They carried on a chronic quarrel with the bishops; meanwhile most of the people were abandoning the Roman town (and the bishops) for the freedom and safety of the heights, the beginnings of what is now the Haute-Ville. In the 1300s Vaison fell into the hands of the pope, along with the rest of the Comtat Venaissin, and did not become part of France until the Revolution. In the 1900s, on the move once more, the Vaisonnais were abandoning the Haute-Ville for the river bank. In 1840, the first excavations were undertaken in the Roman city. Vaison nevertheless had to wait for a local cleric, the Abbé Sautel, to do the job seriously. He dug from 1907 until 1955, financed mostly by a local businessman.

The Ruins

> *Open daily 10–12 and 2–4.30, closed Tues in winter; 9–12 and 2–6.45 in summer; same adm for both, also includes cathedral cloister.*

The Abbé uncovered almost 11 hectares of Roman Vaison's foundations, while the modern town grew up around the digs. There are two separate areas, the **Quartier de la Villasse** and the **Quartier de Puymin**; their entrances are on either side of the central Place Abbé-Sautel, by the Tourist Information pavilion. Vaison's ruins are an argument for leaving the archaeologists alone; with everything sanitized and tidy, interspersed with gardens and playgrounds, there is the unmistakable air of an archaeological theme park. The Villasse is the smaller of the two areas; from the entrance, a Roman street takes you past the city's **baths** (the best parts are still hidden under Vaison's post office) and the **Maison au Buste d'Argent**, a truly posh villa with two *atria* and some mosaic floors. It has its own baths, as does the adjacent **Maison au Dauphin**; beyond this is a short stretch of a **colonnaded street**, a status embellishment in the most prosperous Roman towns.

The Puymin quarter has more of the same: another villa, the **Maison des Messii**, is near the entrance. Beyond that, however, is an *insula*, or block of flats for the common folk, as well as a large, partially excavated quadrangle called the **Portique de Pompée**, an enclosed public garden with statuary that was probably attached to a temple. On the opposite side of the *insula* is a much-ruined *nymphaeum*, or monumental fountain. From here you can walk uphill to the **theatre**, restored and used for concerts in the summer, and the **museum**, displaying the best of the finds from the excavations. You'll learn more about Roman Vaison here than from the bare foundations around it; there is a model of one of the villas as it may have looked. All the items a Roman museum must have are present: restored mosaics and fragments of wall painting, some lead pipes, inscriptions, hairpins and bracelets, and of course statuary: municipal notables of Vaison, a wonderful monster *acroterion* (roof ornament) from a mausoleum, and a few marble gods and emperors—including a startling family portrait with the Emperor Hadrian completely naked and evidently proud of it, next to his demurely clothed Empress Sabina, smiling wanly.

The Cathedral of Notre-Dame-de-Nazareth

The French, with their incurable adoration of anything Roman, go on forever about the ruins and neglect Vaison's real attraction, one of the most fascinating medieval monuments of the Midi. A treasure-house of oddities, it is a reminder that there is more to the art and religion of the Middle Ages than meets the eye, and much of significance that is lost to us forever. It stands a half-km west of the ruins, on Avenue Jules Ferry.

The church was begun in the 6th century. Its **apse** is the oldest part; looking at it from the outside, you'll see where excavations have uncovered the dressed Roman stones and drums of columns that were recycled to serve as a foundation. The rest of the structure dates from a rebuilding that began in the 1100s, including some handsome sculptural decoration around the portals, cornices and bell tower. The first clues to the mystery of this church can be seen near the top of the façade: a rectangular **maze**, and a triangular figure that may be a mystic representation of the Sun. Even with this, the exterior is subdued, and the muscular perfection of the columns and vaults inside comes as a surprise. The 12th-century nave is Romanesque at its best, but still the eye is drawn down it to the magnificent, arcaded interior of the apse. There is nothing like this apse in France; it is a place to muse on time and fate—the last surviving work of Roman Provence, the wistful farewell of a civilization that can be heard across the centuries. Almost incredibly, the 6th-century marble **altar** is still present, carved in a beautiful wave-like pattern. Also here are the original bishop's throne, and benches set around the semicircle of the apse where the monks would sit: the earliest form of a choir, as in the churches of Ravenna. In the medieval nave, some of the decoration is as provocative as that on the façade. At the rear, near a column that survives from the original basilica, you'll notice the figure of an unidentifiable 'hairy person', extending a hand in a gesture of benediction. Elaborate masons' marks are everywhere. Odd figures of the Evangelists embellish the squinches of the fine octagonal cupola; behind one of them, high up, on the second column on the right side of the nave, is what appears to be a little *devil*. You'll meet his big brother in the cloister.

The Cloister

Look around as you enter. Grinning over the ticket-booth to the cloister is Vaison's most famous citizen—Old Nick himself, with horns and goatee, carved into the stone as big as life. This is not a personage one usually sees portrayed in cathedral cloisters, and no one has ever come up with an explanation for his presence here—one unlikely guess is that it's really Jesus, superimposed over a crescent moon. This is a small but graceful cloister from the 1100s, with a number of finely carved capitals (one with a pair of entwined serpents) and architectural fragments displayed around the walls.

And if you think the Devil and all the other curiosities were simply fanciful decoration, look up from the cloister at the Latin verse inscription, running the entire length of the church's southern cornice:

> *I exhort you, brothers, to triumph over the party of Aquilon* [the north], *faithfully maintaining the rule of the cloister, for thus will you arrive at the south, in order that the divine triple fire shall not neglect to illuminate the quadrangular abode in such a way as to bring to life the arched stones, to the number of two times six. Peace to this house.*

The medieval Latin is in parts obscure enough for other interpretations to be possible, but these tend to be even stranger. The twelve stones seem to be pillars of the cloister, the 'quadrangular abode'. The rest is lost in arcane, erudite medieval mysticism, wrapped up with the architecture and unique embellishments, and undoubtedly with a monastic community that was up to something not entirely orthodox. Like most medieval secrets, this one will never be completely understood.

Chapelle St-Quenin

A bit of a climb to the north, on Avenue de St-Quenin, you can continue in this same vein of medieval peculiarity. **St-Quenin**, a chapel dedicated to a 6th-century bishop who became Vaison's patron saint, fooled people for centuries into thinking it a Roman building. Its apse, unique in France, is triangular instead of the usual semicircle, and crowned with a cornice that includes fragments from Roman buildings as well as primitive reliefs that may date from Merovingian times. It is difficult to ascribe any special significance to this odd form. Probably built in the 11th or 12th century, it may be simply an architectural experiment, typical of the creative freedom of the early Romanesque. On the front of the chapel is a Merovingian-era relief of two vine shoots emerging from a vase, a piece of early Christian symbolism that has become the symbol of Vaison.

The Haute-Ville

From Roman and modern Vaison, the medieval version of the town is a splendid sight atop its cliff, a honey-coloured skyline of stone houses under the castle of the Counts of Toulouse. Almost abandoned at the turn of the century, the Haute-Ville is becoming quite chic now, with restorations everywhere and more than a few artists' studios. You reach it by crossing the Ouvèze on a **Roman bridge**, still in good nick after 18 centuries of service; then climb up to the gate of the 14th-century fortifications, next to the **Tour Beffroi**, the clock-tower which is the most prominent sight of the Haute-Ville's silhouette. The cobbled streets and the shady **Place du Vieux-Marché** with its fountain are lovely; trails lead higher up to the 12th- to 14th-century **castle**, half-ruined but offering a view.

Vaison has plenty of room, and in the crowded summer months you might end up here even if you had preferred to be in one of the villages of the Dentelles—for a compromise, try the **★★Hôtel Les Auric**, ✆ 90 36 03 15, a modernized old farmhouse with a pool, west of Vaison on the D 977 and convenient to both (*closed Dec–Apr*). In town, staying up in the Haute-Ville is not entirely convenient—but it can be very gratifying: **★★★Le Beffroi**, Rue de l'Evêché, ✆ 90 36 04 71, ● 90 36 24 78, is a picturesque 16th-century house, furnished to match, a bargain for its category (*closed Dec–mid-Mar*). The budget choice is the old **★Théâtre Romain**, Rue Abbé Sautel, ✆ 90 36 05 87, in the centre, very accommodating, though some rooms can be a little noisy. The restaurant serves standard 100–160F menus.

Despite the quantities of tourists, exceptional restaurants are few. All the hotel restaurants have rather unexciting offerings, and there are plenty of pizzerias and such. One place that stands out is in the Haute-Ville, **La Fête en Provence** on Place du Vieux Marché, ✆ 90 36 36 43, serving its own *foie gras de canard*, followed by a *magret* or lamb with olives, on a bargain 90–240F menu (*closed mid-Nov–mid-Apr, Wed*). For a change, there are West Indian specialities at **Le Colibri** on Cours Taulignan, ✆ 90 36 09 18; menus 80–135F (*closed Mon*).

MOUSTIERS - SAINTE-MARIE.

The Provençal Alps

The Côte d'Azur has an admirably spacious back garden, rolling over mountains and plateaux from the Italian border to the valley of the Durance, and covering the better part of three *départements*. Yet it has only two towns of any size in it, Digne and Draguignan. Between them are plenty of wide open spaces, landscapes on an Arizonan scale including even a Grand Canyon worthy of the name.

But is there really anything up here to tempt you away from the fleshpots of the Côte d'Azur? The stars of this huge and diverse area are beyond doubt the spectacular mountains, Italianate villages and frescoed churches of the **Alpes-Maritimes**, inland from Monaco and Nice. Everything to the west is limestone, eroded into fantastically shaped mountains and deep gorges, such as the *clues* north of Grasse and the canyons that run almost the entire length of the Verdon—including the Grand one, a sight not to be missed. Further south the landscapes become gentler and greener; you may find the Provence you're looking for in the amiable and relatively unspoiled villages and wine country around Draguignan.

Note that on 18 October 1996 France is changing its telephone numbers from 8 digits to 10 digits. All phone numbers in Provence should be preceded by 04 from this date.

The Alpes-Maritimes

Lacet means a shoelace, or a hairpin turn. It's a word you'll need to know if you try to drive up here, on the worst mountain roads in Europe, designed for mules and never improved. When you see a sign announcing '20 *lacets* ahead', prepare for ten minutes in second gear, close encounters with demented lorry drivers, and a bad case of nerves.

So, what do you get for your trouble, in this corrugated department where the Alps stretch down to the sea? For starters these are *real* Alps—arrogant crystalline giants, which make their contempt felt as we crawl through the valleys beneath. Up in Switzerland, they would have enough altitude to make the geography books. Close to the sea, their numbers aren't overwhelming—but if you think 2803m Mt Bégo is a foothill, try climbing it. Bégo is a holy mountain, an Ararat or a Mount Meru, a prehistoric pilgrimage site for the ancient Ligurians.

The scenery defies any travel writer's verbiage, a jigsaw-puzzle panorama at the turn of every *lacet*. The best parts have been set aside as the **Parc National du Mercantour**. In the valleys of the Roya and the Tinée, there's another attraction—all those *lacets* will also take you to the some of the finest Renaissance painting in the Midi.

The Parc Mercantour

The highest regions of this *département* are contained in the **Parc National du Mercantour**, stretching along the Italian border for over 128km, and joining with the adjacent Argentera National Park in Italy to make a unique preserve of Alpine and

Mediterranean wildlife. Established only in 1979, it consists of a central 'protected zone', a narrow strip of the most inaccessible areas, including the Vallée des Merveilles with its prehistoric rock carvings (*see* below), and a much larger 'peripheral zone' that includes all the villages from Sospel to St-Etienne-de-Tinée and beyond. There are many excellent hiking trails, some of which allow you to cross over into Italy. The park rangers, all local people, have an excellent reputation for helpfulness and knowledge. They enforce some strict rules in the protected zone: no tents, dogs, or fires, no motor vehicles (though all-terrain vehicles have recently been allowed on trails only, as an experiment), and no collecting flowers, insects or anything else.

The most spectacular Alpine fauna, and the sort you're most likely to see, are the birds of prey: golden eagles, falcons and vultures; a recent addition, reintroduced from the Balkans after becoming extinct here, is the mighty *gypaète barbu* (lammergeyer), a 'bearded' vulture with a bizarre face, orange-red feathers, black wings and a reputation for carrying off lambs and children. On the ground, there's the ubiquitous stoat, or ermine, popping out of the snow in his white winter coat and looking entirely too cute to be made into royal coat linings, also his bulkier cousin the marmot, and plenty of boars, foxes, *mouflons* (wild mountain sheep), chamois and, in the more inaccessible places, *bouquetins* (ibex). All of these have been rapidly increasing in number since the establishment of the park.

MERCANTOUR
SEMPER VIRUM

As for wildflowers, the symbol of the park is the spiky *saxifrage multiflora*, one of 25 species found here and nowhere else. Edelweiss exists, but is as elusive as anywhere else. Beyond these exotic blooms, there is a tremendous wealth of everything that grows. Blue gentians and anemones are everywhere, plus hundreds of other species, in micro-climates that range from Mediterranean to Alpine. Half the flowers of the whole of France are represented here.

There are several **Park Information Centres:**

Tende (✉ 06430): Gare de St Dalmas, ✆ 93 04 67 00.

Casterino (Vallée des Merveilles): Maison de la Minière, ✆ 93 04 68 66. Summer only.

St-Martin-Vésubie (✉ 06450): Rue Kellermann Sérurier, Pl. de la Mairie, ✆ 93 03 23 15.

St-Etienne-de-Tinée (✉ 06660): Quartier de l'Ardon, ✆ 93 02 42 27.

St-Sauveur-sur-Tinée (✉ 06420): on the D 2205, ✆ 93 02 01 63.

In Nice, there is a helpful information centre for the Parc National du Mercantour at 23 Rue d'Italie, ✆ 93 87 86 10.

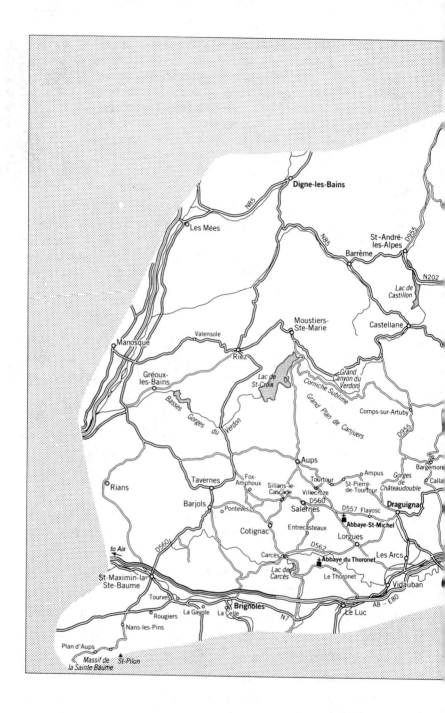

Alpes de Provence

N

20km
10 miles

The Vallée de la Roya

As you climb up into the mountains from the coast, you'll see evidence of the prosperous peasant culture these mountains once supported. Terraced vineyards and fields line the lower slopes, most no longer in use.

Getting Around

In all the hinterlands of Provence, this is the region most difficult to navigate by car, and the most convenient for **public transport**. One of the best ways to see the Vallée de la Roya is from that Alpine rarity—a **train**. The railway line from Nice that runs to Cuneo in Italy offers spectacular scenery and serves all of the local villages: L'Escarène, Sospel, Breil, St-Dalmas and Tende (five each, daily). One train a day goes on to Turin.

Sospel also has four daily **buses** (no. 910) to and from Menton, which take twenty minutes. There is a regular bus service from Nice to L'Escarène and Contes—some five a day, and also five a day from Nice to Lucéram (© 93 85 61 81).

Tourist Information

Sospel (✉ 06380): on the Pont Vieux, © 93 04 15 80.

market days

Sospel: Thursday. *Marché de produits locaux*, Sunday.

Sospel

Travelling along the road from Nice, Sospel greets you with rusty cannons and machine guns, pointing out over the road from **Fort St-Roch** (*open daily May–Oct exc Mon, otherwise Sat and Sun, 2–6*). The fortress, almost entirely underground, shows only a few blockhouses, in a sort of military Art Deco; it dates from a 1930s counterpart of the

Maginot Line. Inside, exhibits show details of its short career. The fort was designed to keep the Italians out, which it did with ease until the French surrender in 1940. Four years later, in September 1944, Sospel found itself on the front line again—the vexing *sitzkrieg* of the Provençal mountains, where the Allies had no effort to spare for a serious advance. The Germans held out in Sospel until almost the end of the war.

Through all that, the town suffered considerable damage, now entirely, and lovingly, restored, including Sospel's landmark, the **Pont Vieux**, the base of which dates back to the 10th century. The tiny tower in the middle of the bridge was the toll on the **salt road**; in the Middle Ages, salt from the flats of Toulon and Hyères was taken by boat to Nice, and from there by convoys of mules to Piedmont and Lombardy. Now the toll bridge houses the tourist information office. The Cathedral of **St-Michel** retains its original 12th-century bell tower, but the rest has been Baroqued with charming tastelessness inside and out, including a wonderful circus-tent baldachin over the altar, dripping with gilt and tassels; a chapel to the left discreetly hides a fine *Annunciation* by Ludovico Brea, as well as another retable of the Virgin in a Gothic frame, possibly also by Brea or one of his followers.

Breil and Saorge

To the north, the D 2204 is the best route into the Vallée de la Roya, with only a few dozen *lacets* and one mountain pass; the other route, following D 93 and the N 204, is slightly shorter, but it passes two border crossings in and out of Italy. **Breil-sur-Roya**, the first town in the French part of the valley, has two peculiar attractions: the unidentifiable black pseudo-turkeys who live in the River Roya under the bridge, and the 18th-century church of **Sancta-Maria-in-Albis**, with large cracks in its ill-formed walls that seem ready to bring the place down around the ears of the faithful. Inside is another retable attributed to Brea, though not a very good one. Further north, the village of **La Giandola** sits among the olive groves that once were the valley's only resource, and beyond that come the **Gorges de Saorge**.

After the gorges, the village of **Saorge** is a magnificent sight—neat rows of Italian slate-roofed, green-shuttered houses, perched on a height like some remote Byzantine monastery, punctuated by church steeples with cupolas of coloured tiles. Saorge guards the Roya valley, and the Piedmontese made it a key border stronghold. You won't see more than ruins of their fort today—it was destroyed after a young commander named Bonaparte took it during the wars of the Revolution. The town suffered during the Second World War, when its inhabitants were evacuated and forced to spend the duration in Antibes.

Saorge is just as attractive from close up, an ancient border village with customs and a dialect all its own, a little bit Occitan and a little bit Ligurian Italian; instead of *rue* or *via* on the street signs, you'll see *caréra* or *chu* or *ciassa*. The streets, stairways more often than not, climb and dive and duck under arches. The sights require a kilometre's hike to the outskirts: the 18th-century **Franciscan Monastery**, in elegant Piedmontese Baroque, and beyond that the 11th-century chapel of the **Madonna del Poggio**, with Renaissance frescoes including a *Marriage of the Virgin*. West of Saorge, you can penetrate into the southernmost corner of the Mercantour National Park, up the narrow D 40 into the **Forêt de Caïros**.

Vallée des Merveilles

Before going further, understand that the Roya is a cul-de-sac; there's no way out besides retracing your steps or continuing through the Tende tunnel to Cuneo, Italy. After Saorge, the mountains close in immediately, with the **Gorges de Bergue et de Paganin**; these end at the village of **St-Dalmas-de-Tende**, once the border post between France and Italy and now the gateway to the Vallée des Merveilles.

From about 1800 BC, the Ligurian natives of these mountains began scratching pictures and symbols on the rocks here. They kept at it for the next 800 years, until over 100,000 inscriptions decorated the valley: human figures, religious symbols (plenty of bulls, horns and serpents), weapons and tools. Most defy any conclusive interpretation—circles, spirals and ladders or chequerboard patterns of the kind found all over the Mediterranean; the Val Camonica in northern Italy has even more carvings, from the same era. Why they were made is an open question; one very appealing hypothesis is that this valley, beneath Mont Bégo, was a holy place and a pilgrimage site, and that the carvings can be taken as ex votos made by the pilgrims.

The presence of these symbols has brought the valley some notoriety—superstition gave the surroundings place names like Cime du Diable ('Devil's Peak') and Valmasque (*masco*, or mask, was an old local word for sorcerer). The first person to study the site systematically was an Englishman, Clarence Bicknell, in the early part of this century. As the prime attraction of the Parc Mercantour, the valley gets its share of visitors these days. Besides the carvings, the landscape itself is worth the hike, including a score of mountain lakes, mostly above the tree line, all in the shadow of the rugged, uncanny **Mont Bégo**, highest of the peaks around the Roya; the mountain's name, as far as anyone can tell, comes from an Etruscan god of storms.

Don't just wander up here like some fool tourist, looking for Neolithic etchings. Plan the trip out beforehand, with advice from the Park information offices. They will probably recommend a guided tour; the symbols are plentiful, but nonetheless inconspicuous and hard to find; apart from the summer months, many will be covered in snow. To tour the valley is *at least* a 20km round-trip trek from the *refuge* at Les Mesches, at the end of the road west from St-Dalmas; there are hotels in nearby Casterino (*see* below) and *refuges* within the park if you want to stay over; make arrangements at the park office. Jeep-taxis can also take you around (expensively) from St-Dalmas.

La Brigue and Notre-Dame-des-Fontaines

Vittorio Emanuele II, the last king of Piedmont-Sardinia and the first of unified Italy, may have been utterly useless at his job, but as a hunter few crowned heads could match him. When he arranged to give away the County of Nice in 1860, he stipulated only that the Upper Roya, above St-Dalmas-de-Tende, be left for him as a hunting reserve (to add to a few others he had, strung out across Italy, including the famous Isle of Montecristo). The few inhabitants had already voted (under French supervision) for union with France; suspiciously, 73 per cent of the electorate abstained. But this had to wait until 1947, when another plebiscite was held and the valley became France's latest territorial acquisition.

Tende, a dour slate-roofed *bourg*, is the only town. No longer a dead end since the road tunnel through to Italy was built, it has become a busy place by local standards. It has the ruined castle of the Lascaris, long-time feudal lords of the Roya, and a late Gothic church, **Ste-Marie-des-Bois**, with a painted façade and ceiling.

East of St-Dalmas-de-Tende, the D 143 takes you into La Brigue, a minute region (partly in Italy) that grows apples and pears and raises trout. **La Brigue**, the tiny capital, has some fine painting in its church of **St-Martin**, another late Gothic work of the 1400s: three altarpieces by Ludovico Brea and his followers, along with Italian paintings from the 17th and 18th centuries. The people who live in La Brigue seem to have an elevated opinion of tourists, since the only ones who pass through have come a long way to see their paintings and, more importantly, those by Giovanni Canavesio at **Notre-Dame-des-Fontaines**, 4km from the village of La Brigue. The name comes from seven intermittent local springs, miniature versions of the Fontaine de Vaucluse, gushing out of the rock or stopping according to pressure and the water-table; these can still be seen, though now they are on the Italian side of the border.

The Upper Roya may not have been much of an economic or strategic gain for France, but artistically it was a real prize—the country's total number of good Renaissance frescoes went up considerably. Giovanni Canavesio, from Piedmont, is not well known outside his own region, but he was a painter in the best north Italian Renaissance tradition: bright colours, exquisite, stylized draughtsmanship and an ability to put genuine religious feeling in his frescoes that recalls Fra Angelico. His works in this rural chapel, done in the 1490s, include 26 large scenes of the *Passion of Christ* in the nave, and on one of the side walls a tremendous **Last Judgement**, a gentle reminder that God wasn't joking. All the tortures of the damned are portrayed in intricate detail, as the devils sweep them into the gaping Mouth of Hell. Around the choir, on the triumphal arch, he painted scenes from the Life of Mary, from the *Birth of Mary* at the upper left to the *Presentation at the Temple* at the bottom right.

The frescoes in the choir itself are by another hand, Giovanni Baleison. Done in the 1470s, in a more old-fashioned style that still shows the influence of Byzantium, these include the *Four Evangelists* on the vaulted ceiling, the four *Doctors of the Church* (Ambrose, Jerome, Gregory and Augustine) under the arch, more scenes from the Life of Mary, including an *Assumption* on the back wall, over the *Reproach of Thomas* and the *Visit to the Tomb*.

Where to Stay and Eating Out

Sospel (✉ 06380)

There's little choice between the five hotels in Sospel: ★★**Des Etrangers**, 7 Ave de Verdun, ✆ 93 04 00 09, ⊜ 93 04 12 31, is marginally the more expensive, and has a pool (*closed Dec–Jan*). ★★**L'Auberge Provençal**, Route du Col de Castillon, ✆ 93 04 00 31, has a *terrasse* with a magnificent view over Sospel. Outside Sospel off the D 2566 towards Moulinet at La Vasta (you will need a car) is a *chambre d'hôte*, **Domaine du Paraïs**, ✆ 93 04 15 78; this villa, taken over by officers during the war, has now been proudly restored by its owners. You must stay a minimum of two nights; book ahead.

L'Escargot d'Or, at 3 Rue de Verdon, ✆ 93 04 00 43, is the best place to eat in Sospel, and menus start at only 115F. Ring to reserve, and to check they're open out of season—they'll close if they anticipate a quiet night (*closed Fridays*). In Place St Michel, you can lunch slapbang opposite the Cathedral at **T+** (Thé Plus), ✆ 93 04 06 28, where you will be welcomed and served bubbling pots by a lady who travelled the world before stopping to settle here.

Breil-sur-Roya (✉ 06540)

Breil-sur-Roya is not the most enchanting place to stay in the Roya, but it has several hotels, including the comfortable modern ****Castel du Roy** near the river on the Route de Tende, ✆ 93 04 43 66, ✆ 93 04 91 83 (*closed Nov–Feb*); and the functional ****Hôtel le Roya** in the village square, ✆ 93 04 48 10, ✆ 93 04 92 70. **L'Etoile**, ✆ 93 04 41 61, offers rabbit and trout, or dine at the well-recommended restaurant of the **Castel du Roy** (*see* above).

Saorge (✉ 06540)

There is only one hotel in Saorge, **Le Bellevue**, ✆ 93 04 51 37, reasonably priced (160–200F) and open all year. On the N 204, 2km to the north at Fontan, there is a simple but adequate inn: ***L'Auberge de la Roya**, ✆ 93 04 50 19, with a popular restaurant serving a 95F menu. For lunch, **Lou Pountin** on Rue Revelli, ✆ 93 04 54 90, makes excellent pizzas (75F menu). The best choice of the three hotels in **La Brigue** (✉ 06430) is ****Le Mirval** on Rue St-Vincent Ferrier at the west end of the village, ✆ 93 04 63 71; some rooms have good views, and the management can arrange a trip (expensive) into the Vallée des Merveilles (*closed Nov–Apr*).

Casterino (✉ 06430)

If you're doing the Merveilles on your own, it's convenient to start from Casterino, a hamlet at the end of the D 91; the nicest of the three hotels here is ***Les Melèzes,** ✆ 93 04 64 95, ✆ 93 04 77 99, with small but comfortable rooms and a good restaurant; rooms from 210 to 255F (*closed mid-Nov–27 Dec*). Also with a restaurant is the ***Marie-Madeleine**, ✆ 93 04 65 93, open all year; try the smoked trout.

West of Sospel: the Paillon Valley

There is some painting here too, in the rugged mountains between Sospel and the valley of the Var. The Italian influence shows itself in another way—the road map looks like a plate of spaghetti, with more twists and bends than anywhere in the *département*. Lacking a mule, you'll need to return to Sospel to get out of the Roya. The D 2204 west will take you to **L'Escarène**, a lovely Italianate village with houses overhanging the river. Here, you can visit the **Chapelle des Pénitents-Blancs**, with spectacular rococo plaster decoration. There are some peculiar landscapes to the south: stone quarries on the road to Nice that have carved out a huge, nearly perfect ziggurat (perhaps the Médecins of Nice could tunnel inside and make it their family tomb); the road is sometimes closed in the mornings for blasting. In the hills above, around Blausasc, 19th-century deforestation has left a lunar wasteland of bare rock; the government is currently building water channels to keep the erosion from spreading.

Lucéram

North of L'Escarène, **Lucéram** is an old shoe of a village, well-worn and a bit out at the toes. Full of arches and tunnels like Saorge, it has some remains of walls and towers on the mountain-side, a steep but pleasant excursion if you want to circumnavigate them. The church of **Ste-Marguerite** is second only to Notre-Dame-des-Fontaines as an artistic attraction. Amidst the gaudy Baroque stucco of the interior, the altarpieces of the Nice school seem uncomfortably out of place. The best, with an innocence and spirituality matched by few other saintly portraits, is the *Retable de Ste-Marguerite* over the main altar, attributed to Ludovico Brea. Marguerite, a martyr of Antioch, is another popular Provençal dragon-slayer, often confused with Ste-Martha (*see* Tarascon, p.396). Brea made her exceedingly lovely; the Tarasque-like demon at her feet obviously never stood a chance. The other retables around the church include *SS Peter and Paul* (with the keys and sword); *St Claude*, *St Lawrence* (with his gridiron, upon which he was barbecued) and *St Bernard*, all by unknown 15th-century artists; Giovanni Baleison contributed a good one of *St Anthony of Padua* (1480) in the Chapelle du Trésor, keeping company with a **Trésor** of awful clutter: reliquaries, monstrances and statuettes including a silver image containing relics of Ste Marguerite.

Outside the church, the **Chapelle St-Jean** was built by the Knights of St John—the Knights of Malta, who had a commandery here. Its beautiful exterior, painted to imitate precious marble, is currently under restoration (though the inside is still full of electricity generators).

If you have the time, there are some worthwhile digressions into the mountains around Lucéram, beginning just outside the village with two more chapels with frescoes by Giovanni Baleison, similar to his work at Notre-Dame-des-Fontaines: **St-Grat** (on the road towards L'Escarène) and **Notre-Dame-de-Bon-Coeur** (on the road for Coaraze; the sacristan in Lucéram has the keys for both). East of Lucéram, a half-hour climb up into the hills, there is a wild spot with a huge circular prehistoric wall, the site of a fortified village from the time of the inscriptions in the Vallée des Merveilles—a logical place for such a settlement, with a fine view of holy Mont Bégo.

North of Lucéram, the D 21 and D 2566 take you past Peïra-Cava, a resort for the French military and their families, to the **Forêt de Turini**, centred around a 1520m mountain pass, the Col de Turini, at the tip of three river valleys. Up above the pass are several old forts, near the summit of Mont L'Authion, an eyrie that commands almost all the Alpes-Maritimes. These were one of the Germans' last redoubts in the war; signs of the battle are still evident, especially around the **Fort des Mille Fourches**, reduced, incredibly, by bombardment from the sea in 1945.

The Devil's Tail, and Other Tales

A long tour on the D 2566/D 15 west from Lucéram (7km for the crow, 19 for you) will take you with some difficulty to **Coaraze**, a village that is a magnet for attracting stories. One is its name, *Caude Rase* in medieval times, or the 'cut tail'—of the Devil. The villagers back then somehow trapped Old Nick, who had to give up his tail like a lizard to get away. Coaraze has also attracted its share of artists lately; one has given the village centre a lizard mosaic to commemorate the event. Other artists, including Cocteau, have contributed a number of colourful ceramic **sundials** around the village. Another legend deals with the abandoned village of **Roccasparvière**, an hour's walk from Coaraze in the mountains. Queen Jeanne of Provence, the story goes, once took refuge from her enemies here. The plot differs in every version, but in most of them someone in the village kills Jeanne's twin sons, and serves them up for dinner. '*Roc, méchant roc*,' Jeanne cursed. '*Un jour viendra où plus ne chantera ni poule ni coq*.' No chickens indeed are singing in Roccasparvière today, but spoilsport historians say it was because the village well dried up.

Another tortuous 10km south of here on the D 15, **Contes** has its stories too. One fine day in 1508, the village was attacked by a horde of caterpillars. Apparently it was not the first time; the area has a colourful species the French call *chenilles processionnaires*, who enjoy a promenade in town every now and then. This time, the Contois had had enough; they called in the Bishop of Nice, who brought inquisitors and exorcists, and made anathemas and proclamations until the caterpillars finally grew uncomfortable and went home. Such affairs were not uncommon, especially in old France. Animals, too, were considered subject to God's law; horses and dogs occasionally went on trial for their indiscretions when times were dull. Contes has another altarpiece in the Brea manner in its church, and down by the river a well-preserved **forge** with a water-powered hammer, near the communal olive oil press. Here, and in many villages in the mountains, the oil presses are still in use. Across the river, and 9km up in the Ferion mountains, there is another abandoned village to explore, outside **Châteauneuf-de-Contes**.

Where to Stay and Eating Out

Chic sophistication goes only as far as the foothills. In these mountains, so close to Nice and Monte Carlo, you'll find both food and accommodation surprisingly basic and humble.

Lucéram (✉ 06440)

In the centre of Lucéram, the former **Hotel-Restaurant de la Mediterranée**, ✆ 93 79 51 54, is now only a restaurant, serving a 70F menu during the week, 80F at the weekend. At the top of Col de Turini, you can stop for the view and lunch at the **★★Trois Vallées** at Moulinet, ✆ 93 91 57 21, 🖅 93 79 53 62, on roast boar and such for 160–250F; rooms at 320F.

Coaraze (✉ 06390)

Coaraze, with its sundials and restored houses, seems to get more visitors than the other villages, and not entirely coincidentally it has the most attractive mountain hideaway in the area. Despite having no star, the **Auberge du Soleil**, ✆ 93 79 08 11, 🖅 93 79 37 79, has a lot going for it: a dreamy location at the top of the village, a pool, and a fine restaurant with a memorable view from the terrace; this end of the village is closed to traffic—call ahead if you need help with your baggage. The restaurant has an excellent menu; hotel prices begin at 320F for a single room.

Contes (✉ 06390)

There is a less expensive alternative in Contes, the **★Auberge le Cellier**, 3 Blvd Charles-Alunni, ✆ 93 79 00 64, with only five rooms and a simple but nourishing restaurant (menu 80F).

The Valleys of the Vésubie and the Tinée

The extensive valley of the River Vésubie is almost completely isolated from the regions to the east; from Lucéram the only ways across are the D 21 / D 2566 / D 70 through the Col de Turini, or the miserable D 2566 / D 73 directly over the mountains. There's an equally tortuous route from Contes—the D 815 / D 19.

Getting Around

There are no trains in either the Vésubie or the Tinée valleys, and the coach service is sketchy. St-Martin-Vésubie can be reached by **coach** from the *gare routière* in Nice (Cars TRAM, ✆ 93 89 47 14); **buses** for St-Sauveur and St-Etienne in the Tinée also leave from here. Roads in this area are as difficult as those to the east; service stations are few so keep your tank full.

Tourist Information

Levens (✉ 06670): 93 79 71 00

St-Martin-Vésubie (✉ 06450): Place Félix Faure, ✆ 93 03 21 28

Levens to Lantosque

The Vésubie flows into the Var near **Levens**, a big walled village on a small plain. Beneath it, the main road up the valley, D 2565, follows the scenic **Gorges de la Vésubie**. From St-Jean-la-Rivière, at the end of the gorge, a winding 15km detour leads to the sanctuary of the **Madone d'Utelle**, one of the most popular pilgrimage sites in Provence, with a chapel full of naïve ex votos to Notre-Dame-des-Miracles, many from sailors, and a spectacular view as far as the sea. **Lantosque**, the next village up the valley from St-Jean, is a humble place, regularly shaken by landslides and earthquakes. Lantosque was occupied by the Austrians in the Revolution. One of them must have been *un bon coq*, as the French say; it's a joke in the other villages that you can always find someone in Lantosque named Otto.

St-Martin-Vésubie

At the top of the valley, St-Martin is the only town for a great distance in any direction, and a base for tackling the upper part of the Mercantour. It's as unaffectedly cute as a town can be, and once it was a spa of some repute. In the delightful and shady town square is an old fountain where the mineral waters used to flow, with inscriptions testifying to their 'organoleptic properties'. The medieval centre is traversed by a lovely street (Rue Dr Cagnoli) with a mountain spring flowing down a narrow channel in the middle, as in a garden of the Alhambra. On this street you'll see an impressive Gothic mansion, the **Maison des Contes de Gubernatis,** and the parish church, housing an altarpiece attributed to Brea and a polychrome wooden statue of the Virgin from the 1300s.

In the vicinity, **Venanson** is a beautiful village up in the mountains above St-Martin, with a small church full of frescoes by Giovanni Baleison. To the east, up into the Parc Mercantour on the D 94, the **Sanctuaire de la Madone de Fenestre** was an ancient holy site near the present Italian border; the name comes from a natural window in a nearby mountain peak. The chapel has burned four times. In the Middle Ages the Templars held the site; they were massacred in the 14th century, and their ghosts were often seen in the neighbourhood. Hiking trails from here can take you on a very scenic route to the Vallée des Merveilles. Another road from St-Martin, the D 89, leads northwest up a valley between the peaks of Mont Archas and Cime du Piagu to the resort village of **Le Boréon**; this is a lovely area, with many hiking trails, a waterfall (near the village) and some mountain lakes near the Italian border.

The Valley of the Tinée

There's nothing splashy or spectacular about the Tinée. People who love the Mercantour follow the slow D 2205 along its length, from the N 202 out of Nice, up to the protected zone of the Parc; skiers flock in winter to the modern resorts of Isola 2000 and Valberg. But outside their punctual visitations, there is a sort of pious hush in this valley, serenely beautiful even by Alpine standards. In the lower part of the valley, the scenery is as much indoors as out; prosperity in the 15th and 16th centuries allowed the villages of the Lower Tinée to decorate their modest churches with fine Renaissance frescoes by artists of the Nice school.

The river flows into the Var with a climax, at the **gorges**, across the mountains from Utelle; to the northeast, **La Tour** has frescoes of 1491 in its **Chapelle des Pénitents-Blancs.** The traditional subjects are represented: the *Passion* and a colourful *Last Judgement*, with Christ sitting on a rainbow and allegorical figures of the Seven Deadly Sins riding on fantastical animals, accompanying the damned to hell.

The next paintings are at **Clans**, in two chapels just outside the village: **St-Antoine** offers more Sins, from an unknown, late-15th-century hand; they accompany some 20 rather peculiar scenes from the *Life of St Anthony*—cooking eggs and exorcizing female demons. **St-Michel** has frescoes by an Italian named Andrea de Cella, *c.* 1515, including St Michael 'fishing for souls', an odd conceit that goes back to Byzantine art. The parish church in the centre of the village has pictures too: surprisingly, a rare late medieval hunting scene. Next up the valley, there is a pleasant detour on the D 2565 through Valdeblore, the only reasonable road through to the Vésubie. It begins at **Rimplas**, and the nearby **Chapelle de la Madeleine**, a conspicuous landmark occupying a gorgeous site overlooking the valley; and continues through **St-Dalmas-Valdeblore**, where there is a large and sophisticated Romanesque church: the **Eglise de l'Invention de la Sainte-Croix**, with fragments of its original frescoes.

Continuing up the Tinée, the next stop is **St-Sauveur-sur-Tinée**, throbbing metropolis of the valley, with its 496 souls. From here the D 130 follows the Vionène valley west, through the rugged and lovely villages of **Roure** and **Roubion**. The former, set amidst the biggest larch forest in Europe, has more painting: a Brea (attributed) altarpiece in the church of **St-Laurent**, and unusual frescoes of the lives of St Sebastian and St Bernard in the chapel outside the village—all these chapels outside villages, incidentally, are a regional peculiarity, set outside the gates as if to avert evil influences, and often dedicated to plague saints like Sebastian. Roubion has a Sebastian chapel too, with another frescoed set of Deadly Sins. Continuing in this direction, the next town is the modern ski resort of **Valberg**. There is Alpine scenery in these parts but little else; the best of it is in the long, lonely canyons stretching south off the D 30/D28: the **Gorges Supérieures du Cians** and the **Gorges de Daluis**.

The uppermost part of the Tinée, following the D 2205, runs through the northern half of the Parc Mercantour, never more than a few kilometres from the Italian border. After St-Sauveur come the **Gorges de Valabres**, decorated with an EDF electric plant that somehow managed to sneak inside the park borders. **Isola**, on the other side of the river, has some more appealing sights, both just off the D 2205: a magnificently tall waterfall, the **Cascade de Louch**, and an impressive Romanesque bell tower, the only survival of an abbey washed away by a flood 300 years ago. A good road takes you up to the Italian border and **Isola 2000**, a British-built, modern, concrete ski resort that does good business due to its proximity to the coast. Everywhere else to the north is at ski level, and almost all the villages have learned to bend their lives and habits to the seasonal invasions of the ski-bunnies. If you haven't yet had enough Renaissance frescoes, you may also want to follow the Tinée to its source. In **Auron**, the 12th-century church of **St-Erige** has a sequence of paintings of that obscure Provençal saint, along with the Parisian St Denis, a stranger in these parts. **St-Etienne-de-Tinée** has two painted rural chapels: **St-Sébastien** with a cycle of works by Canavesio and Baleison, in very bad shape, and the chapel of **Couvent des Trinitaires** where the subject is, of all things, the great naval victory of the Venetians and Spaniards over the Turks at Lepanto in 1571.

Lantosque (✉ 06450)

On the way up to the Parc Mercantour, there's a gracious country hotel in Lantosque: the ★★★**Hostellerie de l'Ancienne Gendarmerie**, ✆ 93 03 00 65, 🖃 93 03 06 31. The 'former police station' occupies a pretty hillside site, with garden-side rooms and a pool. The restaurant specializes in trout and *escargots*; menus 165F and 285F (*closed Nov–Jan*).

St-Martin-Vésubie (✉ 06450)

★★**La Bonne Auberge** in St-Martin-Vésubie, ✆ 93 03 20 49 🖃 93 03 20 69, is as good as its name, a welcoming and pretty place on the main Place Félix Faure, with nice rooms starting at 200F and a cosy cellar restaurant with a boar's head over the chimneypiece—grilled chops, *escargots*, *civet du lapin* and profiteroles, menus at 90F and 140F. Small wonder this is where Nice's soccer team prepares for matches. If the Auberge is full, settle for the modern and plain ★**Des Alpes** across the square, ✆ 93 03 21 06.

In St-Martin, you can step out for some of the best pizza this side of the border—baked in a proper pizza oven—at **La Treille** on Rue Dr Cagnoli, ✆ 93 03 30 85; also pasta and a menu of more ambitious dishes, 90–150F. On the Place du Marché, **La Trappa**, ✆ 93 03 21 50, serves up mountain fare and heady house wine with menus at 90F and 120F.

Le Boréon

Outside the town, **Le Boréon**, ✆ 93 03 20 35, in the village of the same name, is a chalet-style place with a few simple rooms and a good restaurant, serving 80–170F menus including *truite aux amandes*, and homemade desserts. Also in Le Boréon, ★★**La Chaumière du Cavalet**, ✆ 93 03 21 46, 🖃 93 03 34 34, is a simple abode in a dreamy lakeside setting, at the forest edge. The excellent restaurant is open only at lunchtime (menus from 85F), whilst *demi-pension* is required for hotel guests.

The Tinée Valley

Don't expect anything out of the ordinary in the sparsely-populated, little-visited Tinée valley: simple country inns with restaurants are the rule, like the **Auberge St-Jean** in **Clans** (✉ 06420), ✆ 93 02 90 21; or in **St-Etienne** (✉ 06660), ★★**La Pinatelle**, Blvd d'Auron, ✆ 93 02 40 36 🖃 93 02 47 90 (menus from 85F). These two, and most of the others, require half-board in the summer. At **Valdeblore** (✉ 06420) there is a *ferme-auberge* called **Chalet du Val de Blore** on the D 2565 west of St-Dalmas, ✆ 93 02 83 29, 🖃 93 02 83 06: four simple rooms in a modern chalet with Italian-Niçoise home cooking.

When in the mountains, look out for locally made liqueurs, an Alpine speciality: *myrtille* (bilberry), pear, or something called *Genépi Meunier*—made from an Alpine herb that is closely related to absinthe.

The Alpes de Haute-Provence

Getting Around

Buses are so rare they aren't worth the trouble, but it can be fun seeing this region by the scenic rail-line familiarly called the **Train des Pignes**, from Nice to Digne; it follows the Var, and a few trains stop at villages along the way: Villars, Puget-Théniers, Entrevaux and Annot—five a day at the most. This is not the SNCF, but a separate line called *Chemin de Fer de Provence* (in Digne, call ✆ 92 31 01 58 for details). The *Train des Pignes* is currently being modernized—in the future it will be much quicker (2 hours instead of 4), if less fun.

Tourist Information

Puget-Théniers (✉ 06260): ✆ 93 05 05 05, open July and August only

Entrevaux (✉ 04320): at the Porte Royale, ✆ 93 05 46 73, ✉ 93 05 43 91

Castellane (✉ 04120): Rue Nationale, ✆ 92 83 61 14, ✉ 92 83 76 89. Ask about the guided tours organized by the *mairie*.

Riez (✉ 04500): 4 Allée Louis Gardiol, 92 77 82 80, ✉ 92 77 79 67

Digne (✉ 04000): Place Tampinet, ✆ 92 31 42 73, ✉ 92 32 27 24

market days

Moustiers: Friday

Riez: Wednesday and Saturday

Digne: Wednesday and Saturday

Villars to Entrevaux along the N 202

The N 202 is the east–west traffic chute, following the upper Var, and the only convenient way to get through the mountains north of Grasse. It isn't scenic, though the gravelly, impossibly blue Var makes a refreshing sight alongside; it may however be an antidote to claustrophobia after traversing too many gorges. The trip begins with a local novelty— wine—at **Villars-sur-Var**. The centre of the only, tiny AOC wine region in the mountains, Villars was almost abandoned before the awarding of the *dénomination* in the 1970s. Production has vastly increased since then, and you'll occasionally see this variety of Côtes-de-Provence in trendy restaurants on the coast—perhaps more for its curiosity value than for anything else. The village church has a few Renaissance pieces: a retable of *St John the Baptist*, and an Italian fresco of the *Annunciation*, both anonymous works of the early 1500s.

Next comes a postcard shot: **Touët-sur-Var**, seemingly pasted up on the side of a cliff, with much of its medieval defences still intact in case anyone tries to storm the place. **Puget-Théniers**, the biggest village on this stretch of the Var, is more open and welcoming, a shady oasis after the stark mountain landscapes, where you may stop for lunch and look at more pictures—two genuine jewels among a number of altarpieces in the parish church: Antoine Ronzen's *Notre-Dame de Secours* and Mathieu d'Anvers' *Passion*, both done about 1525. A monument by Aristide Maillol in the town square commemorates Puget's pride: a local boy named Auguste Blanqui who became one of the leaders of the Paris Commune in 1870.

Entrevaux is the strategic key to the valley. There has been a fort of some kind here since Roman times, and its present incarnation is particularly impressive—the work of Louis XIV's celebrated engineer Vauban, high up on the cliffs above the village, complete with Second World War additions. At the time it was built the French-Piedmontese border was only a few miles away (it is now the departmental boundary between Var and Alpes-Maritimes). The entrance is a **fortified bridge**, rebuilt by Vauban on medieval foundations. Around the village, vestiges of its old garrison days can be seen: barracks and powderhouses, and an ancient **drawbridge**, still in working order, behind the 17th-century **cathedral**. There's a honeycomb of buildings and narrow alleys where people are living; if you wander through the smelly damp alleys there are flowers high up in the windows, duvets thrown over the sills in the mornings. The serious part of the fort is a hard fifteen-minute climb if you're fit; take iron rations, a sunhat and some historical imagination. A 10-franc piece gets you through the turnstile and after that hard climb you're on your own to explore the deliciously dangerous and derelict tunnels and dungeons. Look down on to a landscape as unlikely as an Alpine train set, and see your train arrive (the *Train des Pignes*). By next year, sadly, it will be more tidied up, with shops up top. But people visit like bees to a honey pot; see it before 9am, before it gets lost underneath them all. By 9.10 the first of the coaches are beginning to fit themselves in below. (Check out the barking dog behind the hotel just across the road from the gate; it's a parrot.)

Entrevaux.

The *Clues* and the Esteron Valley

South of the Var is a grim and lonely region; you can see Nice and Cannes from the summit of the **Montagne du Cheiron** in its centre, but from here the Riviera beaches seem a world away. A *clue*, or more properly *cluse*, is a transverse valley, formed between the limestone folds of the mountains; here the name is given to the many narrow gorges that make life and communications in the area difficult. Local villages are humble and crumbling and few, and the roads across are winding and exasperating. From Puget, the D 2211A/D 17 takes you to **Roquesteron**, a fortified village divided into two parts (before 1860 one was Piedmontese, one French); west of the village, a bad road, the D 10, leads off into the isolated **Clue d'Aiglun**, perhaps the most dramatic of the *clues*, with a big waterfall. On the other side of the mountains, the D 2211A leads to **Briançonnet**, a spectral village with great views and bits of Roman inscriptions built into the old houses; beyond here is the **Clue de St-Auban**.

The more southerly route—with a choice of roads running east–west, some conveniently reached from Vence or Nice—passes some lovely *villages perchés*: **Bézaudun-les-Alpes**, **Coursegoules**, **Gréolières** and **Cipières** (follow D 1/D 8/D 2, from Carros on the Var, north of Nice), all starting to be colonized by people from the Riviera. Gréolières, under the Montagne du Cheiron, has an enormous ruined castle; from here you can follow the D 603 into the **Gorges du Loup** towards Grasse, or take the D 2/D 802 onto the Cheiron and the new ski station of **Gréolières-les-Neiges**.

Where to Stay and Eating Out

Being the only good road across this region, the N 202 has the best selection of places to stay and eat, with a few rather better than the average *routier*.

Touët-sur-Var (✉ 06710)

In Touët-sur-Var, the **★Auberge des Chasseurs**, ✆ 93 05 71 11, has a few rooms, but does most of its business serving fish and game to appreciative locals; ravioli and rabbit stew figure on menus at 110–180F.

Puget-Théniers (✉ 06260)

The local favourite in Puget-Théniers is **La Guignette** on Rue 4 Septembre just off the main square, ✆ 93 05 09 97; 60 and 95F menus with an emphasis on seafood and trout. There are two hotels, both two-star: **★★Alize** on Rue Alexandre Barety, ✆ 93 05 06 20, and **★★Langier** on Place Carnil, ✆ 93 05 01 00, which is picturesque, but has a noisy bar and uncomfortable beds.

Entrevaux (✉ 04320)

Entrevaux, with so many tourists, surprisingly has only one place to stay; the unstarred **Vauban**, ✆ 93 05 42 40. A good stop for lunch, **L'Echauguette** has outside tables on the central Place de la Mairie, ✆ 93 05 46 89, with 75F and 110F menus, including some seafood and, for starters, a salad served with the local speciality, a beef sausage called *secca*. Or try the **Bar/Restaurant du Pont Levis**, Place Louis Moreau, ✆ 93 05 40 12, for good home cooking and a great view of fort, village and valley.

The Grand Canyon of the Verdon

After Entrevaux, the Var turns northwards, while the main road continues west, past the modest mountain resort of **Annot** and the **Gorges du Galange**. Further west the country becomes even stranger and lonelier; long monotonous stretches lull you to sleep until suddenly the road sinks into a wild gorge, or confronts a patch of striated mountains that look like gigantic *millefeuille* pastries tumbled over the landscape. Grey is the predominant colour, making a startling contrast with the opaque blue sheet of the **Lac de Castillon**, backed up behind the Barrage de Castillon, a mighty 89m concrete dam begun in 1942 under the Vichy government, with a distinctly grim, wartime look about it.

The D 955 passes over this on its way to **Castellane**, a village that has become the capital of the Grand Canyon, and the base for visiting one of the greatest natural wonders in Europe. It's centred round a pretty square of plantains (the grilles surrounding the trees are worked in the shapes of plantain leaves) where boules is played, and people amiably hang about. But its edges are deep in up-to-the-minute sports shops supplying slick whizz-gimicry for any sport you could or couldn't conceive (such as bungeejumping), cafés, cameras, and post cards. If you penetrate into the shops themselves you will find nothing you did not expect; lavender, nougat, honey and faïence (the one exception is a toyshop selling irresistible bright wooden toys, just below the tourist office). Castellane's also a stop for those following the **Route Napoléon**, the route taken by the emperor on his return from the island of Elba, now a tourist trail starting from his landing point at Golfe Juan and ending at his destination, Grenoble. There is a pretty *mairie* and a church behind which begins the 182m ascent up the famous rock: pick up the key for the chapel on top from outside the *curé*'s house, or collect it on your way up from the last person coming down.

The most surprising thing about the **Grand Canyon du Verdon** is that it was not 'discovered' until 1905. That the most spectacular canyon on the continent could be so overlooked speaks volumes about the French—their long-held aversion to nature, which they are now working so enthusiastically to correct, and the traditional disdain of Parisian authorities for the Midi. The locals always knew about it, of course; agriculturally useless and almost inaccessible, the 21km canyon had an evil reputation for centuries, as a haunt of devils and 'wild men'. Even after a famous speleologist named Martel brought it to the world's attention at the beginning of the century, many Frenchmen weren't impressed. In the '50s the government decided to flood the whole thing for another dam (the tunnels they dug are still visible in many places at the bottom); when the plan was finally abandoned, it was for reasons of cost, not natural preservation.

The name 'Grand Canyon' was a modern idea; when the French became aware of its existence, comparisons with that grand-daddy of all canyons in Arizona were inevitable. It does put on a grand show: sheer limestone cliffs as much as a half-km apart, snaking back and forth to follow the meandering course of the Verdon; in many places there are vast panoramas down the length of it. There are roads along both sides, though not for the entire distance. Most of the best views are from the so-called **Corniche Sublime** (D 71) on the southern side; if you want to explore the bottom, ask about trails and the best way to approach them (it's a long trek) at the tourist information office in Castellane.

The lands south of the Canyon are some of the most desolate in France; you will find them either romantic or tiresome depending on your mood. But either mood will be definitively broken when columns of tanks and missile-carriers come rattling up the road. The Army has appropriated almost all of this area, the **Grand Plan de Canjuers**, for manoeuvres and target practice; you'll see their base camp on the D 955 towards Draguignan.

Directly west of the Canyon, a less spectacular section of the Verdon has indeed been dammed up, forming the enormous **Lac de Ste-Croix**; there is yet another dam further downstream, and the next 40km of the river valley are under water too: the **Gorges du Verdon**, in parts as good as the Canyon, but sacrificed forever to the beaverish Paris planners. It's wild country on both sides, and access is limited since the roads are few. Beyond the dam on the way to Manosque and the Lubéron, **Gréoux-les-Bains**, with its above-average number of launderettes and poodles, is a favourite with the rheumatic set who treat their aching bones to a jolt of sulphurous, radioactive water at the baths. *Les Bains* is a clinical, eerie, hair-dresser smelling place, with New Age oddities on sale like money-changers at the temple. Gréoux was a fashionable resort in the early 1800s, when Napoleon's tearaway sister Pauline Borghese dropped by, but never since. It's a long street jammed with caravan traffic, and the pedestrianized area has nothing you won't find anywhere else in Provence. The village turns its back on the shabby **castle**, built in the 12th century by the Templars, which occasionally is used as a theatre. Normally you won't be allowed inside the walls.

Riez and Moustiers

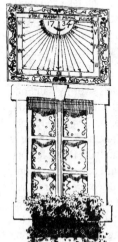

The **Plateau de Valensole**, north of the Verdon and the Lac de Ste-Croix, is a hot, dry plain of olive and almond trees, and one of the big lavender-growing areas of Provence. **Riez**, at its centre, is an old centre for lavender-distilling, now become adapted to tourism. Ruined medieval houses have been restored, and artists and potters have moved in. It's pretty but bustling, a good place to dawdle in. Visit the market which is a flourishing mix of rolled up knickers and army surplus along with beautiful pottery, lavender honey, nougat, every sort of herb, cheese, meat, sweet, and dazzling fish. Try a pizza from the antique pizza-van, and watch it being cooked, or survey all this quaintness from one of the cafés opposite. But get there quick; everyone packs up pronto at twelve o'clock, and at quarter past they're hosing the market-place down. Riez was an important Celtic religious site, though it isn't clear exactly which deity it honoured. Testimonies to later piety can be seen at the western edge of town, thought to have been the centre of Roman-era Riez: four standing columns of a Roman **Temple of Apollo**, and a 6th-century **Baptistry** that is one of the few surviving monuments in France from the

Merovingian era; octagonal, like most early Christian baptistries (after the original, in the Lateran at Rome), it has eight recycled Roman columns and capitals; all the rest was heavily restored in the 1800s. Inside is a small museum of archaeological finds (ask for the key at the tourist information office). Inside the medieval gates are two pretty fountains recycled from Roman remains, and a number of modest palaces and chapels that recall Riez's prosperity in the 16th to 18th centuries. Fourteen km west of Riez, **Valensole** is an ancient village, built over the ruins of its Roman predecessor.

To the east, some 15km on the D 952, **Moustiers-Ste-Marie** sits near the western end of the Grand Canyon du Verdon. Like Castellane on the other side, it is a popular base for visiting the Canyon, and busy in summer. The town will be familiar to any one who haunts the museums of the Midi, as Moustiers in the old days was Provence's famous centre for painted ceramics. The blue and yellow faïences, usually painted with country scenes or floral designs, were often works of art in their own right; first popular in the time of Louis XIV, they were made here as late as the 1870s. Today a large number of potters, some talented and some pretty awful, clutter the village streets, capitalizing on the perfect clay of the region (and on the tourists). You can compare their efforts with the originals at the **Musée de la Faïence**, a small collection on Place du Presbytère, © 92 74 61 64 (*closed Tues*).

In the middle of the village is the deep-set 12th-century **parish church** with a kink in it. Moustiers' other distinction, as everyone in Provence knows, is the **Cadeno de Moustié**, a 225m chain suspended between the tops of two peaks overlooking the village. A knight of the local Blacas family, while a prisoner of the Saracens during the Crusades, made a vow to put it up if he ever saw home again; the star in the middle comes from his coat of arms. The original (thought to be solid silver, but really plated) was stolen in the Wars of Religion, and a replacement didn't appear until 1957. A climb up under the chain will take you to the **chapelle Notre-dame-de-Beauvoir** where a notice piously requests that pilgrims do not write on the walls but inscribe their names on the heart of the virgin saint instead.

Also Worthy of Your Attention . . .

Riez in French is a singular or plural imperative: laugh! **Digne** means 'worthy', and one suspects a degree of deliberate etymological mutation in the gradual name change from the local Gaulish tribe, the *Bodiontici*, whose capital this was, to Roman *Dinia*, and finally to *Digne*. The capital of *département* number 04 (Alpes de Haute-Provence), and the only city in a long stretch of mountains between Orange and Turin, over in Italy, Digne has one thriving boulevard of cafés and touristic knick-knackery mixed with smart shoe-shops, posh chocolates and more than one bookshop. Digne has recently rediscovered its role as a spa, and you will be given a glossy pamphlet in the tourist office consisting entirely of pictures of people smiling in the thermal baths. In the minuscule medieval centre is the crumbling, down-at-heel, 15th-century **Cathédrale de St-Jérome**, and its surrouding brightly painted houses stand shoulder to shoulder with some daring grey municipal buildings. Out of town (27 Avenue du Maréchal Juin) is something entirely unexpected: the **Fondation Alexandra David-Neel**, the former home of a truly remarkable

Frenchwoman who settled here in her 'Himalayas in miniature' after a lifetime exploring in Tibet (© *92 31 32 38, guided tours with her former secretary, daily in summer at 10.30, 2, 3.30 and 5, otherwise at 10.30, 2 and 4*). Ms David-Neel called this house *Samten Dzong*, the 'castle of meditation', and Tibetan Buddhist monks attended her when she died here in 1969, at the age of 101. The Dalai Lama has since come twice to visit; there are exhibits of Tibetan art and culture, photographs, and also Tibetan crafts on sale. In summer there are up to 40 people crammed into this tiny museum, so be prepared to wait in the garden. If you don't speak French, they will be happy to play the commentary in English; don't be afraid to ask.

At Place Paradis in an old bunker in the hillside is the **Museum of the Second World War** (*open Apr–Oct Tues, Wed, Thur 2–6; © 92 31 45 29*). At St Benoit, the **Geology Centre** (*open 9–12 and 2–5.30, 4.30 Fri; closed Sat and Sun Apr–Nov; © 92 31 51 31*) houses the largest geology collection in Europe. And at 64 Blvd Gassendi, the **Musée Municipal**, © 92 31 45 29 (*open daily exc Mon 10.30–12 and 1.30–6, Sun until 5, winter afternoons only; adm*), has a collection of mostly 19th-century Provençal painters, archaeological finds and local curiosities. Follow Blvd Gassendi to the eastern edge of town, passing the peculiar neoclassical **Grande Fontaine** (1829), and you will find Digne's former cathedral, **Notre-Dame-du-Bourg**, a large Lombard-style Romanesque building of the 1100s, complete with a bell tower of that date, a deep-set Romanesque arch below a beautiful rose window, and inside some fragments of frescoes.

Where to Stay and Eating Out

Moustiers-Ste-Marie (✉ 04360)

This region isn't quite so wild as the badlands to the east; after a day's tramping through the Grand Canyon du Verdon you can splurge for a memorable dinner at the newly opened **La Bastide de Moustiers**, © 92 74 62 40, ✉ 92 74 62 41, at the foot of the village. The food is predominantly local, but innovative (herb and vegetable tart, spit-roasted baron of lamb followed by cherries baked in batter). It's a stupendous hotel too, with seven individually fashioned rooms. Prices reflect the quality; a single room begins at 700F, but menus start at a very reasonable 180F. On the road to Riez at Roumoules (✉ 04500) is **Le Vieux Castel**, © 92 77 75 42, restored and run by its owners, the Allègres. It's tranquil, elegantly simple and far less expensive than anywhere else. Try the *table d'hôte*, if you can stand the other guests, and sit at the huge table, medieval-style. The formula of courteous no-nonsense hospitality works; the Allègres are currently restoring a large monastery down the road just outside Moustiers, partially open soon. Up in the village is the affordable **★★Belvédère**, © 92 74 66 04. Highly recommended for a meal is **Les Santons** in the Place de l'Eglise, © 92 74 66 48; menus 160–390F (*closed Tues*). Be sure to reserve. If you're just passing through, there's the **Boucherie/ Charcuterie** at Rue Courtil, where everything is simply delicious (*open 8–12.30 and 3–7.30, closed Sun eve and Mon*).

Castellane (✉ 04120)

Ma Petite Auberge, ✆ 92 83 62 06, is inexpensive and acceptable for a short stay (*closed Nov–Apr*). At the foot of the rock next to the church is **La Forge**, ✆ 92 83 62 61, with a terrace from which to view the village and the walkers going up and down the *roc*. ★★★**Du Commerce**, on the Place de l'Eglise, ✆ 92 83 61 00, ✉ 92 83 72 82, is friendly and comfortable (*closed Nov–Easter*). The best way to see the Canyon is from the glassed-in restaurant terrace of the ★★**Hôtel du Grand Canyon**, looking 300m down onto the Verdon. It is situated 14km east of the village of Aiguines, at the Falaise des Cavaliers, ✆ 94 76 91 31, ✉ 92 76 92 29 (*closed Oct–April*).

Quinson (✉ 04500)

Further south, in the middle of the Gorges du Verdon at Quinson, is the **Hotel Restaurant Relais Notre Dame**, ✆ 92 74 40 01, ✉ 92 74 02 10 (*closed mid-Dec–mid-Mar*) with a garden and swimming pool, but most importantly a real welcome and very good food.

Digne (✉ 04000)

Digne can be an urban oasis in which to relax after too many empty spaces. There's a distinguished hotel in a restored monastery: ★★★**Du Grand Paris**, 19 Blvd Thiers, ✆ 92 31 11 15, ✉ 92 32 32 82, with an excellent restaurant featuring truffles and seafood; rooms 400–460F (*closed Christmas–Mar*). Next door is the family-run ★★★**Mistre**, ✆ 92 31 00 16, less of a grand hotel, but just as comfortable and just about the same price. Central and comfortable is ★**Le Provence**, 17 Blvd Thiers, ✆ 92 31 32 19, ✉ 92 31 48 39, with rooms starting at 170F, and a good restaurant. **Le Petit St-Jean** on Cours des Arès, ✆ 92 31 30 04, might look quaint but your view—if you have one—will be tainted with the whiff of chip oil from the neighbouring restaurant. If you have to stay here, eat elsewhere.

From Grasse to Aix

Getting Around

Driving in this southern half of the Provençal mountains will prove much less trouble than the areas to the north and east; **roads** are better and service facilities more common. You can take the A 8 /E 80 motorway straight across and miss everything—but the villages to the east and west of Draguignan offer some of the most delightful opportunities for casual touring in Provence—good bicycling country too. Two possible itineraries for you: from Fayence (west of Grasse on D 562) to Le Muy, through the lovely villages along the D 19 and D 25 (the latter is the wine route); or from Draguignan, travel west on the D 557, dipping into the mountains on the D 77 for Aups, then the D 22 for Sillans-la-Cascade and Cotignac, and west again (D 32) to Fox-Amphoux or Barjols.

The main Provençal **railway** follows the motorway from Aix and Marseille to Cannes; for Draguignan you'll usually have to change at Les Arcs. Draguignan and Brignoles are well served, unlike almost everywhere else. Draguignan is also the hub for village buses, though as always these are few and generally inconvenient: several daily to Grasse, stopping at Bargemon, Seillans and Fayence along the way, and several daily in the other direction, to Tourtour and Aups, with at best one or two to the other villages.

Tourist Information

Fayence (✉ 83440): Place Léon Roux, ✆ 94 76 20 08

Draguignan (✉ 83300): Blvd Clemenceau, ✆ 94 68 63 30, ✆ 94 47 10 76

Seillans (✉ 83440): ✆ 94 76 85 91

market days

Fayence: Tuesday, Thursday and Saturday

Draguignan: Wednesday and Saturday

Fayence, Mons and Seillans

The first leg of this journey, as far as Draguignan, is close enough to the coast to have become thoroughly colonized by the holiday-home set. **Fayence**, a large village of moderate cuteness, has plenty of Englishmen and estate agents. Built on a steep hillside like Grasse, its road winds back and forth up to the centre, which is pleasant enough: there is a *mairie* perched on an arch over the main street, a forgotten 18th-century church and a view not to be missed from the Tour de l'Horloge at the very top of the village: check the view you see against the ceramic panorama painted and baked into tiles under your hands. North of Fayence, there is some lovely, wild countryside; off the D 37, **Roche Taillée** has a Roman aqueduct still in use—but don't expect the Pont du Gard. This one is entirely carved out of the rock, along a steady descent of some 5km. Also from the D 37, you'll see the towers of an impressive 17th-century castle, the **Château de Beauregard**, a private home. Further north, **Mons** is a beautiful and strange village of narrow streets overhung with arches. The language of its inhabitants still conserves some Ligurian Italian words; the people of Mons were totally wiped out in the Black Death of 1348, and colonists from the area around Genoa and Ventimiglia were brought in to replace them. There are a large numbers of **dolmens** in the area; some are inaccessible on the base of the Canjuers army camp, the borders of which are only 2km away.

West of Fayence, the farmhouses may now all be bijoux holiday-homes, but the scenery is delicious; the main road, the D 562 to Draguignan is fine, but even better is the winding D 19/D 25, passing through three pretty villages. **Seillans** has been occupied since the time of the Ligurians, giving it some two and a half millennia to perfect its charm, with cobbled streets leading up to the restored castle. It's one of the most beautiful villages in France, it's official; and it's got a plaque to prove it. The village lives on flowers, and was the last home of Max Ernst. **Bargemon**, further west, is just as old; behind its medieval gates are several fountains and a 15th-century church. Last before Draguignan is **Callas**, under a ruined castle. The D 25 south of Callas, as far as Le Muy, is a beautiful drive through forests, with the **Gorges de Pennafort** and a waterfall along the way; it is also one of the best wine roads in the region, with a few places to stop and sample Côtes-de-Provence along the way (*see* p.250).

Draguignan

 Draguignan gets a bad press, especially from the timid English: ugly, depraved, full of soldiers; *avoid it if you can*... Under the garish Provençal sunlight, we watched a young fellow on the Boulevard de Maréchal Joffre being run in by a pair of municipal policemen—clean-shaven, brutishly intelligent, all dressed up, military-style, in black and silver like American cops. Beautiful women waltzed by, swinging their handbags and smiling at the unfortunate; flaccid shopkeepers squinted furtively through immaculately clean windows.

After the Casino at Monte Carlo, there's no better free theatre in Provence. Tough, sharp-edged Draguignan is not French so much as French Colonial. The Army owns it—it's the biggest base in France—and its dusty palm-shaded boulevards pass the national schools of artillery and military science. The town's symbol is the *drac*—yet another Provençal dragon, chased out by an early bishop, though its fire-spitting image can still be seen everywhere. Draguignan could be Saigon or Algiers or Dakar, a cinematic fantasy in a wreath of *Gauloise* smoke, waiting for the Warner Bros cameras to capture Bogart, Lorre and Greenstreet conspiring in some tawdry nightclub.

Anyhow, have your papers in order, and try not to exceed the speed limits. Touring in Provence you'll be bound to pass through here once or twice, and it's a pleasant stop, really. The Saturday market is especially good, and there are a few things to see: the 17th-century **Tour de l'Horloge**, Draguignan's architectural pride; a small **Municipal Museum** on Rue de la République, © 94 47 28 80 (*closed Mon am*) with a picture gallery and faïences from Moustiers (also porcelain from China); and the **Musée des Arts et Traditions Populaires**, at 15 Rue de la Motte, © 94 47 05 72 (*open daily exc Sun morning and Mon, 10–12 and 2.30–6; adm*). This is a complete, didactic overview of everything you'll never see in the real Provence any more—from mules to silk culture, along with reconstructions of country life, including kitchens, barns, festivals and, naturally, some antique *boules* and *tambourins*; a pretty old merry-go-round with painted horses steals the show. And just outside town, on the D 955 towards the Verdon Canyon, is one of the biggest dolmens in Provence, the **Pierre de la Fée**.

A metal drac

Fayence (✉ 83440)

In the centre of Fayence, on the Place de la République, two restaurants, much of a muchness, compete. **Le Temps des Cerises**, ✆ 94 76 01 19 (*closed Mon eves and Tues*), serves up an uncomplicated but satisfying lunch or dinner: *canard à la forestière*, steaks and chops on 79F and 119F menus. Or at the neighbouring **Le France**, ✆ 94 76 00 14, try the frogs' legs, or *bouillabaisse marseillaise* if you order 24 hours in advance. **Le Poelon**, Rue Font de Vin, ✆ 94 76 21 64, with menus at 75 and 120F, is small, cheerful and well-recommended (*closed Oct–Easter*). There are inexpensive hotels, including the ★**Auberge de la Fontaine**, Route de Fréjus, ✆ 94 76 07 79; but the only places you're likely to remember are the ★★★**Moulin de la Camandoule**, Chemin Notre-Dame-des-Cyprès, ✆ 94 76 00 84, ✆ 94 76 10 40, a lovely old olive-oil mill, prettily restored (by a British couple) with all the amenities—pool, garden, etc and a restaurant; menus 185F and 285F, rooms from 265F; and the small starless **Sousto**, 4 Rue du Paty in the centre of town, ✆ 94 76 02 16, with its charming rooms overlooking the valley.

Bargemon (✉ 83620)

Bargemon is a good place to rest without breaking the bank. There are simple, inexpensive hotels, like the ★★**Auberge des Arcades** on Ave Pasteur, ✆ 94 76 60 36, ✆ 94 76 68 33, and one fine restaurant with an outside terrace: the **Auberge Pierrot**, Place Chauvier, ✆ 94 76 62 19; menus 86–260F.

Draguignan (✉ 83300)

Don't expect red-carpet treatment in military Draguignan; the only really decent place is outside town, clean, modern and colourless—but with a view: ★★★**Les Etoiles de l'Ange** on the D 557 towards Lorgues, ✆ 94 68 23 01, ✆ 94 68 13 30. In town, you'll do no better or worse than the stolid and plain ★★**Hôtel Dracénois**, 14 Rue du Cros, ✆ 94 68 14 57.

Seillans (✉ 83440)

The ★★★**Deux Rocs**, ✆ 94 76 87 32, ✆ 94 76 88 68, is a much-lauded hotel. If you don't hear the bombs from the army range, the radio blaring from the kitchen, or the lorries that race up and down the hill to the perfumery behind (which you may not visit), you might appreciate the matriarchal welcome. Near perfect food: a favourite with Americans. The alternative is ★★★**De France**, Place du Thouron, ✆ 94 76 96 10, ✆ 94 76 89 20, which is not as quaint, but busy with its swimming pool overlooking the valley (*closed Nov–Jan*). Don't miss **La Chirane**, ✆ 94 76 96 20, for a meal—a converted stable underneath the houses halfway up the hill, painted jolly blue, and with tables outside looking down over the lower village. Run by an Alsatian who came and stayed for 25 years, there's live jazz monthly; reserve on Saturday nights. Specialities include chicken in garlic, ham from the bone, and home-baked bread (*closed Tues and Sat afternoons*).

Villages of the Central Var

Heading west from Draguignan, there are two choices; if aesthetics are a bigger consideration than time, don't bother with the A 8 motorway or the parallel road through Brignoles and St-Maximin (for which, *see* below); instead, take the D 557 or 562 directly west for a leisurely tour through some of Provence's loveliest and most typical landscapes. Though this area gets its share of foreign and Parisian summer folk, it isn't quite chic—compared to similar but totally colonized places like the Lubéron. But there's enough lavender and blowing cypresses, plenty of wine, and a dozen relentlessly charming villages that won't trouble you with any strenuous sightseeing.

Tourist Information

Aups (✉ 83630): Place de la Mairie, ✆ 94 70 00 80

Barjols (✉ 83670): Blvd Grisolle, ✆ 94 77 20 01

market days

Aups: Wednesday and Saturday. Truffle market on Thursdays.

From Lorgues to Aups

Lorgues is the first village, with a complete ensemble of 18th-century municipal decorations, proof that the *ancien régime* wasn't quite so useless after all: a fountain, the dignified church of **St-Martin**, and the inevitable avenue of venerable plane trees, one of the longest and fairest in Provence. To the north, along the D 10, you'll pass the **Monastery of St-Michel**, a recently refounded Russian Orthodox community; its handmade wooden chapel, a replica of a Russian church, may be visited. Further north, there are a number of pretty villages around the valley of the Nartuby: **Ampus**, **Tourtour**, up on a height with views down to the sea, and **Villecroze**. At the edge of the Plan de Canjuers, this last village is built up against a tufa cliff; there is an unusual park at the base of it, with a small waterfall and a cave-house dug into the rock in the 16th century.

Aups was a Ligurian settlement, and a Roman town; its name comes from the same ancient root as *Alps*. It has a reputation for being different; a monument in the town square records Aups' finest hour, when the citizens put up a doomed republican resistance to Louis Napoleon's coup of 1851. The village is known in the region for its Thursday truffle market, held through the winter months. The village church is oddly below surface level; the ground level around it was raised to avoid the frequent flooding of the old days. Aups, like the other villages, has not completely escaped Riviera modernism. The **Musée Simon Segal**, ✆ 94 70 12 98 (*adm*), founded by an eponymous Russian artist, has his and other 20th-century works and is on Ave Albert I. **Salernes**, south of Aups, has been known for over 200 years as a manufacturer of tiles: the small, hexagonal terracotta floor-tiles called *tomettes* that are as much a trademark of Provence as lavender. They still make them, and in a day when French factory-made tiles all come in insipid beige, they are at a premium. Lately Salernes' factories and individual artisans have been expanding into coloured ceramics and pottery; there are a few shops in the village and factory showrooms on the outskirts. With such a workmanlike background, the village itself is rather drab, with a medieval fountain and a simple 13th-century church in the centre.

Further west, **Sillans** has lately been calling itself Sillans-la-Cascade, to draw attention to the 36m waterfall just south of the village (it dries up in summer); beyond that **Fox-Amphoux** is worth a visit just to hear the locals pronounce the name; this minuscule and well-restored village of stepped medieval alleys sits on a defensible height. There is a ruined castle, and on the trail to the hamlet of Amphoux, an odd cave-chapel, **Notre-Dame-de Secours**, hung with ex votos, many from sailors.

Thoronet Abbey

Open Mon–Sat 9–7 summer, 9–12 and 2–5 Sun, 10–12 and 2–5 winter; adm.

South of Salernes, **Entrecasteaux** is dominated by a 17th-century castle, completely restored in the 1970s by a Scotsman named McGarvie-Munn; visitors are admitted, but there's nothing to see and the fee is exorbitant. Further south, the artificial **Lac de Carcès** has been a favourite with fishermen since the dam was built in the 1930s. To the east are the biggest bauxite mines in France, which are playing hell with one of the most impressive medieval abbeys in Provence.

The **Abbaye de Thoronet** was the first Cistercian foundation in Provence, on land donated by Count Raymond Berenger of Toulouse in 1136; the present buildings were begun about 1160. Like most Cistercian houses, it was in utter decay by the 1400s; and like so many other medieval monuments in the Midi, it owes its restoration to Prosper Mérimée, Romantic novelist (*Carmen*, among others) and State Inspector of Historic Monuments under Napoleon III; he chanced upon it in 1873, when most of the roof was gone, the galleries were overgrown with bushes and the only beings dining in the refectory were cows.

It often seems as if the restoration is still under way; you may find it full of props, scaffolding and concrete piers, as its keepers experiment desperately to keep Thoronet from being shaken to pieces by the bauxite lorries rumbling past on the D 79. The mines themselves (nearby, but screened by trees) have caused some subsidence, and cracks are opening in the walls. Nevertheless, this purest and plainest of the Cistercian 'Three Sisters' of Provence (with Silvacane and Sénanque) is worth a detour. Following the stern austerity of Bernard of Clairvaux, it displays sophisticated Romanesque architecture stripped to its bare essentials, with no worldly splendour to distract a monkish mind, only grace of form and proportion. The elegant stone bell tower would have been forbidden in any other Cistercian house (to keep local barons from commandeering them for defence towers), but those in Provence got a special dispensation—thanks to the mistral, which would have blown a wooden one down with ease. There are no such compromises in the blank façade, but behind it is a marvellously elegant interior; note the slight point of the arches, a hint of the dawning Gothic—Thoronet was begun in the same year as France's first Gothic churches, in the north at St-Denis and Sens. The **cloister** with its heavy arcades is equally good, enclosing a delightful stone fountain-house. There's a cellar to visit, too, to see how the monks fared; and a modern chapel where people pray, and visitors gawp and take photographs over the sign clearly requesting that they do not.

Cotignac and Barjols

Its inhabitants might be unaware of it, but **Cotignac** is one of the cutest of the cute, a Sunday supplement-quality Provençal village where everything is just right. There are no sights, but one looming peculiarity: the tufa cliffs that hang dramatically over it. In former times these were hollowed out for wine cellars, stables or even habitations; today there are trails up to them for anyone who wants to explore; at the base of the cliffs there is a meadow where Cotignac holds its summer music festival.

Westwards on the D 13/D 560, the landscapes are delicious and drowsy; **Pontevès** will startle you awake again, a castle with a remarkable setting atop a steep conical hill. Long the stronghold of the Pontevès family, feudal rulers of most of this region, the apparition loses some of its romantic charm after the climb up; there's nothing inside but a few houses, *La Poste* and a food shop. Three km further on, **Barjols** has little cuteness but much more character. This metropolis of 2000 souls owes its existence to leather tanning, an important industry here for the last 300 years. There is still one shoe factory left, but Barjols is now little more than a market town, although it retains an urban and somewhat sombre air: elegant rectangular squares of the 18th century, and moss-covered fountains similar to the ones in Aix. If you stop in at the tourist office you can get a '*circuit des fontaines*' to guide you round all thirty of them.

To see Barjols at its best, you'll have to come on 16–17 January, the feast of St Marcel (Marcellus, the 4th-century pope) whose gaudy relics, stolen in the Middle Ages from a Provençal monastery, can be seen in the 16th-century parish church. There'll be a bit of dancing (*la danse des tripettes*) and, equally unusual for Provence, the essentially pagan slaughter and roasting of an ox, accomplished to the sound of flutes and *tambourins*.

Where to Stay and Eating Out

Lorgues (✉ 83510)

Lorgues, 13km from Draguignan, is a more pleasant place than Draguignan to stop over if you're passing through the area; the venerable, classy hotel in the centre, a bit down on its luck but still comfortable, is the **Hôtel du Parc**, 25 Blvd Clemenceau, ✆ 94 73 70 01, with a restaurant with 60F and 235F menus. Rooms start at 120F. The **Brasserie du Parc** next door does a great *café au lait*. There are several decent restaurants in the centre, but for a better than average meal locals go to **Chez Pierrot**, 18 Cours de la Republique, ✆ 94 67 67 15.

Tourtour (✉ 83690)

Tourtour, easily the poshest of the villages in this region, also has the most luxurious accommodation: the ★★★★**Bastide de Tourtour**, Montée St Denis, ✆ 94 70 57 30, 🖷 94 70 54 90, a modern complex with pool, tennis and all the amenities, including a highly reputed restaurant with a blend of Provençal cooking and *nouvelle cuisine*, menus 180F (lunch)–350F. Three km east of the village at **St-Pierre-de-Tourtour**, the ★★★**Auberge St-Pierre**, ✆ 94 70 57 17, is a find—an up-to-date working farm built around a hotel; exceptional rooms in an 18th-century house and a fine restaurant, with authentic Provençal food (largely the farm's own produce); menus 160F and 200F. It also offers a swimming-pool, horse-riding and other activities.

Salernes (✉ 83690)

In Salernes, the ★**Grand Hôtel Allègre**, 20 Rue Rousseau, ✆ 94 70 60 30, is another old establishment, like the one in Lorgues, with a bit of faded grandeur and some of its 1920s decor intact. The cooking's a bit faded too; you'll do better with a simple *magret* or stewed rabbit at **La Fontaine** on Place 8 Mai 1945 (outside tables, menus at 98 and 150F; ✆ 94 70 64 51). If you're going to **Sillans** (✉ 83690), the first thing you'll see, right on the D 32, is the **Auberge des Pins**, ✆ 94 04 63 26, 🖷 94 04 72 71, a very popular restaurant in an old stone house, serving grilled meats with shrimps for openers on 80–170F menus, also a few rooms at 200F (*closed Jan and Feb*).

Fox-Amphoux (✉ 83670)

One of the most pleasant village inns in Provence is in Fox-Amphoux: the ★★★**Auberge du Vieux Fox**, ✆ 94 80 71 69, 🖷 94 80 78 38, with rooms overlooking the Place de l'Eglise, and a delightful restaurant; try the *carré d'agneau* (loin of lamb); menus 135–270F. Now open all year, ★★★**Lou Calen**, 1 Cours Gambetta, ✆ 94 04 60 40, 🖷 94 04 76 64, is an unexpectedly stylish hotel-restaurant in the centre of **Cotignac** (✉ 83570), with a lovely hidden garden and pool; only eight rooms, and as many (more expensive) suites; also a somewhat unexciting restaurant, menus 125–190F and upwards. Less expensively, the ★**Hotel du Cours**, ✆ 94 04 66 34, across the street is simple and friendly.

Off the Motorway from Draguignan to Aix

With the Var's rocky coast, and the mountains behind it, the only easy route across the *département* is a narrow corridor through Brignoles and St-Maximin-la-Ste-Baume. The French have obligingly plonked down a motorway across it, successor to the Via Aurelia and the old St-Maximin pilgrims' route as the great high road of Provence.

Tourist Information

St-Maximin-la-Ste-Baume (✉ 83470): Place de Ville, ✆ 94 78 00 09

Brignoles (✉ 83170): Parking des Augustins, ✆ 94 69 01 78

Brignoles: Saturday

St-Maximin: Wednesday

Les Arcs

Picking up the D 555 south of Draguignan, you'll pass through **Les Arcs**, a well-exploited village of stepped streets, pink stone and ivy. Next comes **Le Luc**, practically strangled by the motorway and the parallel national routes but a game town nevertheless, with another steep medieval centre, a castle on top, and a restored Romanesque church flanked by an unusual hexagonal tower from the 1500s. To entertain the hordes of coast-bound tourists there's a museum of philately on Place de la Convention (*open all summer and by appointment;* ✆ *94 47 96 16*) and another small museum in a 16th-century church, the **Musée Historique du Centre Var**, 24 Rue Victor Hugo, ✆ 94 60 90 70, with a collection ranging from fossils and Neolithic finds to medieval art.

Côtes-de-Provence: La Vie en Rose

Half of all French rosés originate in the Republic's largest AOC region, the 18,000-hectare Côtes-de-Provence. The growing area stretches from St-Raphaël to Hyères, with separate patches around La Ciotat, Villars-sur-Var, and a wide swathe south and west of Aix. Based on grenache, mourvèdre, cinsault, tibouren, cabernet and syrah grapes, Côtes-de-Provence rosé is a dry, fruity, and elegant summer wine that doesn't have to worry about travelling well: more than enough eager oenophiles travel to it every holiday season. Unfortunately, its price in the past couple of years has travelled too, and there are no prizes for guessing which way. It is however possible to find good inexpensive alternatives since some estates produce a *vin de pays*. This is often as good as wines with full *appellation contrôlée* status. An excellent example is **Château d'Astros** at Vidauban, ✆ 94 73 00 25, 🖷 94 73 00 18, which produces a wonderful range of Vin de Pays des Maures: red, white and rosé. The property is run by the Buisines family for an absentee banker from Marseille. A visit to this grand rambling house and estate in the forest is great fun. One can also buy *en vrac*—either supply your own containers or buy one from M. Buisine.

Côtes-de-Provence reds (20 per cent of the production) are much finer today than the rough plonk Caesar issued to his legions, most notably the special *cuvées* put out by the better estates. The whites, of clairette and ugni blanc grapes, are scarcer still, and account for only 5 per cent of the AOC label.

With 57 cooperatives and 350 private cellars, Côtes-de-Provence wine is easily sampled, especially along the signposted 400km *Route des Vins*, which you can pick up at Le Luc or Le Muy from the A 8 or N 7 or at Fréjus, Les Arcs, and Puget-sur-Argens. Two of the best-known producers are at Trets, on D 56 east of Aix: **Château Ferry-Lacombe**, ✆ 42 29 33 69, where the vines are planted on ancient

Roman terraces (along with the pink stuff, you can find the excellent Cuvée Lou Cascaï); and the 1610 **Château Grand'Boise**, ✆ 42 29 22 95, where the subtle red Cuvée Mazarine and a flowery blanc des blancs are grown amidst a large forest. Near Le Luc, Hervé Goudard's **Domaine de St-Baillon**, on the N 7 at Flassans-sur-Issole, ✆ 94 69 74 60, ✉ 94 69 80 29, mixes syrah and cabernet bordelais to produces its truffle-scented Cuvée du Roudaï. Just under the landmark cliffs of Mont Ste-Victoire, **Domaine Richeaume** at Puyloubier, ✆ 42 66 31 27, is owned by German ex-pat Henning Hoesch, who combines a love of modern abstract art with wine, in Provence's most modern and efficient *cave*, producing along with rosés an interesting selection of red wines, one of pure syrah and another of pure cabernet-sauvignon. At La Londe-les-Maures (west of Bormes-les-Mimosas) **Domaines Ott**, Clos Mireille, Route de Brégançon, ✆ 94 66 80 26, offers one of the appellation's top white wines, of ugni and sémillon grapes aged in wooden barrels.

A much higher percentage of red wine is produced in the cooler, drier **Coteaux Varois**, a region of 28 communes around Brignoles in the central Var, beginning a few miles north of the Bandol district and extending north as far as Tavernes. This old **vin de pays** has recently been elevated to the ranks of VDQS, and all the vintners along the N 7 and the other roads outside Brignoles hang out signs to lure you in. You can try a good (and completely organic) Coteaux Varois at the **Domaine de Bos Deffens**, on the Cotignac road just east of Barjols. Or sample both Côtes-de-Provence and Coteaux Varois (especially the '90 reds) at **Château Thuerry**, set in a magnificent wooded landscape at Villecroze, ✆ 94 70 63 02, ✉ 94 70 67 03.

Brignoles

The biggest date in Brignoles' history, perhaps, is 25 September 1973, when several thousand dead toads rained down from the sky, an event that does not seem to be commemorated in any way. Little else has ever happened here. This gritty but somehow likeable place earns its living mining bauxite. It has an attractive medieval centre, and a museum to remember.

Le Musée du Pays Brignolais (Regional Museum)

Closed Mon and Tues, otherwise 9–12 and 2.30–6; adm; ✆ *94 69 45 18.*

Situated at the top of the old town, on Place du Palais des Comtes de Provence in a palace that was those counts' summer residence, Brignoles' incredible curiosity shop has grown to fill the whole building since a local doctor began the collection in 1947. Amidst two big floors packed full of oil presses, fossils, cannon-balls, reliquaries and roof tiles, you'll see some things you never dreamed existed. In the place of honour, near the entrance, is the original model of a great invention by Brignoles' own Joseph Lambot (1814–87): the **steel-reinforced concrete canoe**. Contemporary accounts on display suggest the thing floated, though the idea somehow never caught on. Lambot probably never collected a *sou* for his revolutionary new construction technique, since found to be better adapted to skyscrapers.

Admittedly, a hard act to follow, but just across the room is a provocative **sarcophagus**, dated *c.* AD 175–225, nothing less than the earliest Christian monument in France. Well sculpted and well preserved, the imagery is a remarkable testament to religious transition. The centre shows a familiar classical scene, a seated god receiving a soul into the under-world—but whether the god is Hades, Jesus, or another remains a mystery. Also present are Jesus as the 'Good Shepherd' (the most common early Christian symbol), a figure that may be St Peter (fishing, figuratively, for souls), another that seems to be a deified Sun, and another early Christian symbol, an anchor. The sarcophagus is believed to be Greek, possibly made in Antioch or Smyrna; how it got here no one knows.

Nearby is a rare but badly worn Merovingian tombstone, and a part of the counts' palace, the **Chapel of St-Louis-d'Anjou**, a Provençal bishop who may be better known in California—the town of San Luis Obispo is named after him. The chapel houses a hoard of gaudy church clutter, with Louis' chasuble and rows of wax saints under glass. After that, you may inspect a **reconstructed Provençal farm kitchen**, and a **reconstructed mine tunnel**. Other prizes await on the second floor: a **plywood model of Milan Cathedral** by a local madman, a **stuffed weasel**, and large collections of **owls** and **moths**. Local painters are exhaustively represented: some of the finest works are 19th-century ex votos in the French tradition, with the Virgin Mary blessing people falling off wagons and out of windows. Even after all this, Gaston Huffman's *Allegory of Voluptuous Folly* takes the cake, a medieval conceit in a modern style, with a delicious lady in a little boat enjoying the caresses of a cigar-smoking pig. Rue des Lanciers, the spine of old Brignoles, begins opposite the museum's front door, passing the 13th-century **Maison des Lanciers**, where the counts' guards stayed when they were visiting.

West of Brignoles, there are two sights of some interest off the main road, both of which you'll need to talk your way in to visit: first the half-ruined **Abbaye de la Celle**, an ancient foundation (started in the 6th century) that made a reputation for itself due to the open licentiousness of its nuns, and which was dissolved in 1770; the buildings are now part of a farm. Second, also on a farm, off the D 205 6km east of Tourves, is the **Chapelle de la Gayole**, an early Romanesque cemetery chapel in the shape of a Greek cross (built in 1029, though parts of it go back to the 700s).

St-Maximin-la-Ste-Baume

For proof that Provençal sunlight softens the Anglo-Saxon brain, consider St-Maximin. 'Considerable charm', gushes one guidebook; 'another pretty Provençal village', yawns another. Prosper Mérimée, back in 1834, got it right: 'Saint-Maximin is a miserable hole between Aix and Draguignan.' It hasn't changed. The general atmosphere of bricks and litter is reminiscent of some burnt-out inner-city in the Midlands or Midwest. It is hard to imagine a place remaining in such a state of total, lackadaisical decrepitude, in the midst of a prosperous region, without some effort of will on the part of its inhabitants.

But once upon a time, the Miserable Hole was a goal for the pious from all over France. According to legend, the site was the burial place of the Magdalene (*see* Stes-Maries-de-la-

Mer, p.128) and her companions St Maximin, the martyred first bishop of Aix, and St Sidonius. Their bodies, supposedly hidden from Saracen raiders in a crypt, had disappeared, and were conveniently 'rediscovered' in 1279 by the efforts of Charles II of Anjou, Count of Provence. Inconveniently, the body of the Magdalene was already on display at the famous church of Vézelay, in Burgundy. Nevertheless, an ambitious basilica and abbey complex was begun, and eventually the Pope was convinced or bribed into declaring St-Maximin's relics the real McCoy. The pilgrim trade made St-Maximin into a town; among the visitors were several kings of France, the last being Louis XIV. There were wild times during the Revolution; St-Maximin renamed itself 'Marathon', and was briefly under the command of Lucien Bonaparte, who was calling himself 'Brutus'. This most devoutly revolutionary of Bonapartes saved the basilica from a sacking. As the local legend tells it, an official from Paris came down to oversee its liquidation, but Brutus had him greeted with the *Marseillaise*, played all stops out on the church's great organ.

Basilica Ste-Marie-Madeleine

After its ramshackle, unfinished façade, on a desolate square decorated only by a faded Dubonnet sign, the interior seems an apparition: the only significant Gothic building in Provence. Despite the prevailing gloom, and the hosts of awful, neglected 18th- and 19th-century chapels and altars, the tall arches of the nave and the lovely apse, with its stained glass, leave an impression of dignity and grace.

The original decoration is spare: coats of arms and effigies of Charles of Anjou and Queen Jeanne on some of its capitals. Among the later additions, the most impressive is the enormous, aforementioned **organ**, almost 3000 pipes and all the work of one man, a Dominican monk named Isnard (1773). Another Dominican, Vincent Funel, was responsible for the lovely choir screen (1691). To the left of the high altar, don't miss the retable of the *Passion of Christ* (1520) by an obscure Renaissance Fleming named Ronzen: 22 panels of the familiar scenes with some surprising backgrounds: the Papal Palace in Avignon, the Colosseum and Venice's Piazzetta San Marco. Stairs lead down to the **crypt**, a funeral vault from the 4th or 5th century AD, where the holy sarcophagi remain with a host of eerie reliquaries.

The Couvent Royal

The monastery attached to Ste-Marie-Madeleine was a 'royal' convent because the kings of France were its titular priors. After losing it in the Revolution, the Dominican Order bought back the monastery and church in 1859. Apparently St-Maximin proved too depressing even for Dominicans; they bolted for Toulouse in 1957, leaving the vast complex in a terrible state. Restorations have been going on fitfully since the '60s. The buildings include the imposing **hospice** from the 1750s (now the town hall), to the left of the basilica's façade; the rest, behind it, now houses an institute for cultural exchanges. The best part is the **cloister**, with Lebanon cedars and a charming subtropical garden in the centre. One of the arcades is a Gothic original of 1295 (*guided tours of the cloister and basilica available, open all year; adm*).

The Massif de la Ste-Baume

If you're heading towards Marseille or the coast from here, you might consider a detour into this small but remarkable patch of mountains. Rising as high as 975m, and offering views over the sea and as far north as Mont Ventoux, the massif shelters a small forested plateau called the **Plan d'Aups**. This is a northern-style forest, including maple, beech and sycamore, as well as scores of species of wild flowers and other plants not often seen around the Mediterranean. They have remained in their primeval state because the massif is holy ground, the site of the cave (*Sainte-Baume*, or holy grotto) where according to legend the Magdalen spent the last years of her life as a hermit. The cave, furnished as a chapel, was part of the pilgrimage to St-Maximin since the Middle Ages, and can be seen today along the D 80. Monastic communities grew up around the site, and you may visit the 13th-century Cistercian **Abbaye de St-Pons**, near the loveliest part of the forests (the Parc de St-Pons).

Where to Stay and Eating Out

Les Arcs (✉ 83460)

Les Arcs, strategically located on the road to the Côte d'Azur, has spawned one exceptional hotel-restaurant. ★★★**Le Logis du Guetteur**, Place du Château, ✆ 94 73 30 82, 🖷 94 73 39 95, is located at the top of the old town, a lavishly restored castle dating in parts from the 11th century, with a garden and pool; some rooms have wonderful views. The restaurant serves ambitious *haute cuisine*: smoked salmon, stuffed sole, and elaborate desserts with menus at 125F, 165F, 248F and 355F.

Brignoles (✉ 83170)

Brignoles has plenty of inexpensive hotels, most of them dives; try the centrally located ★**Le Caramy**, over a simple restaurant at 11 Place Caramy, ✆ 94 69 11 08. Something more elegant can be found outside town: the ★★**Château de Brignoles-en-Provence**, Ave Dréo, ✆ 94 69 06 88, just on the eastern edge of Brignoles, offers peace and quiet in an old farm, with pool and tennis. A little further east, at the village of **Flassans-sur-Issole** (✉ 83340), is a gracious and friendly farm hotel, ★★**La Grillade au Feu de Bois**, with sixteen rooms and a restaurant with admirable home cooking (on the N 7, ✆ 94 69 71 20).

Dining in Brignoles' medieval centre, the best bet is **L'Assiette Gourmande**, on Rue Gradalet, ✆ 94 59 04 48; the cooking is both Italian and French—you can have *carpaccio* or pizza for starters, and there is a shady outdoor terrace; menus 67F and 120F. For a change, there is a good Vietnamese restaurant, the **Saigon** on Square St-Louis, ✆ 94 59 14 51; menus 55 –150F.

If you're compelled to stay in St-Maximin (✉ 83470), head for the wild orange shutters of the ★★**Hôtel Plaisance** on Place Malherbe, ✆ 94 78 16 74. Dining in this town is an adventure; the local speciality is limp pizza; finding anything else can be difficult.

St-Tropez

The beaches of the eastern Riviera are not renowned for their beauty. From Menton to Antibes the shore is rocky—beaches are shingle, or in some cases artificial pebble. Lack of sand is more than compensated for by the spectacular settings of many beaches, backed by 200m cliffs, palm trees and some of the world's most expensive real estate. But purists should head as far as Antibes, where the sand starts in earnest. There are two public beaches in Antibes: the best lie south of the town centre, just before the cap, with views back across the Baie des Anges to the Alps.

Juan-les-Pins, blessed with fine sand, is also cursed with countless private beach clubs. Public beaches exist here—try further west towards Golfe-Juan. Cannes has even more snooty beach clubs, but here too there is a public beach right in front of the Palais des Festivals. Further west towards Mandelieu the beach is beautifully sandy, and free.

The western Côte d'Azur region contains some of the most enticing beaches in France. From Cannes to St-Tropez the dramatic corniche road offers glimpses down to small sandy coves hiding between jagged rocks. This is above all a place to take your time, stopping where fancy dictates. The beaches of St-Tropez are actually 5km south of the town—Plage de Tahiti is the most infamous, Plage de Pampelonne the least spoiled. True aficionados head south to Plage de l'Escalet and round Cap Lardier to

Beaches on the Côte d'Azur

Gigaro. The footpath east of Gigaro takes you to a well-patronized nudist beach.

From St-Trop to Toulon the road climbs and falls along the Corniche des Maures. Some of the most revered beaches in Europe lie offshore—the

Ile de Porquerolles have national park status and offer unrivalled sand (catch a ferry from Hyères). West of Toulon, Sanary and Bandol have thin strips of beach, but these get very crowded in summer.

If you fancy a day-trip to a beach during your stay in Provence, here is a selection of the best, from Monaco on the eastern end of the Côte to Bandol and La Ciotat in the west. On p.138 you can find a list of the best beaches in the Marseille area.

Monaco: chic and sharp; safe swimming.

Beaulieu (Plage des Fourmis): backed by palms, view across to Cap Ferrat.

Villefranche-sur-Mer: the most happening beach in the region.

St-Jean-Cap-Ferrat (Plage du Passable): views to Villefranche.

Antibes: Port and south of centre on D 2559.

Cannes: Palais des Festivals and west to Mandelieu.

St-Aygulf: long sand, lots of space, but crowded in summer.

Les Issambres: as above.

Port Grimaud: long beach backing onto Spoerry's *cité lacustre*.

St-Tropez: Plage de Tahiti, Plage de Pampelonne, Plage de l'Escalet.

Gigaro: long beach, a favourite with families.

Cavalaire-sur-Mer: the long sandy beach of the bay, more popular with families than movie stars

St-Clair: just outside Le Lavandou; views across to the islands.

Cap de Bregançon: wilder coves, off the beaten track.

Ile de Porquerolles: Plage de Notre Dame, or any of the northern coastal beaches.

Ile du Levant: Héliopolis, premier nudist beach.

Hyères: large town beach.

Bandol/Sanary/La Ciotat: thin beaches, crowded in summer, restful off-season.

Abbaye	Abbey.
Anse	Cove.
Arrondissement	City district.
Auberge	Inn.
Aven	A sink-hole (a pre-Gallic word).
Bastide	A taller, more elaborate version of a *mas*, with balconies, wrought-iron work, reliefs, etc; also a medieval new town, fortified and laid out in a grid.
Beffroi	Tower with a town's bell.
Borie	Dry-stone shepherd's hut with a corbelled roof.
Buffet d'eau	In French gardens, a fountain built into a wall with water falling through levels of urns or basins.
Cabane	A simple weekend or holiday retreat, usually near the sea; a *cabane de gardian* is a thatched cowboy's abode in the Camargue.
Calanque	A narrow coastal creek, like a miniature fjord.
Caryatid	Column or pillar carved in the figure of a woman.
Cave	Cellar.
Château	Mansion, manor house or castle.
Chemin	Path.
Chevet	Eastern end of a church, including the apse.
Cirque	A round natural depression created by erosion at the loop of a river.
Cloître	Cloister.
Clue	A rocky cleft or transverse valley.
Col	Mountain pass.
Côte	Coast; on wine labels, *côtes, coteaux* and *costières* mean 'hills' or 'slopes'.
Cours	Wide main street, like an elongated main square.

Geographical and Architectural Terms

Couvent	Convent or monastery.
Crèche	Christmas crib with *santons*.
Donjon	Castle keep.
Ecluse	Canal lock.
Eglise	Church.
Etang	Lagoon or swamp.
Félibre	Member of the movement to bring back the use of the Provençal language.
Ferrade	Cattle branding.
Gardian	Cowboy of the Camargue.
Gare	Train station (SNCF).
Gare routière	Coach station.
Garrigues	Irregular limestone hills pitted with caves.
Gisant	A sculpted prone effigy on a tomb.
Gîte	Shelter.
Gîte d'étape	Basic shelter for walkers.
Grande Randonnée (**GR**)	Long-distance hiking path.
Grau	A narrowing, either of a canyon or a river.
Halles	Covered market.
Hôtel	Any large building or palace; a Hôtel de Ville is the city hall.
Mairie	Town hall.
Manade	A herd of cows or horses in the Camargue.
Maquis	Mediterranean scrub. Also used as a term for the French Resistance during the Second World War.
Marché	Market.
Mas	Farmhouse and its outbuildings.
Motte	Hammock, a raised area in a swamp.
Oppidum	Pre-Roman fortified settlement.
Pays	Region.
Pont	Bridge.
Porte	Gateway.

Predella	Small paintings beneath the main subject of a retable.
Presqu'île	Peninsula.
Restanques	Vine or olive terraces.
Retable	A carved or painted altarpiece, often consisting of a number of scenes.
Rez-de-chaussée (RC)	Ground floor.
Santon	A figure in a Christmas nativity scene, usually made of terracotta and dressed in 18th-century Provençal costume.
Source	Spring.
Tour	Tower.
Transi	In a tomb, a relief of the decomposing cadaver.
Tympanum	Sculpted semicircular panel over a church door.
Vieille ville	Historic, old quarter of town.
Village perché	Hilltop village.

BC

c. 1,000,000	First human presence, near Menton; use of bone as a tool
c. 400,000	Discovery of fire, as at Terra Amata in Nice
c. 60,000	Neanderthal hunters on the Riviera
c. 40,000	Advent of *Homo sapiens*; invention of art
c. 8000	Invention of the bow
c. 3500	Development of Neolithic culture; first villages built
c. 2000	First metallurgy; copper and tin at Vence and Caussols
c. 1800–1000	Worship at Mont Bégo, at Tende, and Vallée des Merveilles incisions
c. 600	Greek traders found Marseille
c. 380	Celtic invasions in Provence
218	Hannibal and elephants pass through region on the way to Italy
125	Roman legions attack Celto-Ligurian tribes that threaten Marseille
122	Founding of *Aquae Sextiae* (Aix)
118	Founding of Narbonne and *Provincia*, the first Roman province in Gaul
102	Marius and his legionaries defeat the Teutones
49	Marius' nephew, Julius Caesar, punishes Marseille for its support of Pompey
14	Augustus defeats Ligurian tribes in the Alpes Maritimes

AD

46	Arrival of the Boat of Bethany at Stes-Maries-de-la-Mer (traditional)
310	Emperor Maximian captured at Marseille by son-in-law Constantine
314	Constantine calls Church Council at Arles
410	Honorat founds Lérins monastery
413	Visigoths conquer Languedoc
476	Formal end of Western Roman Empire
535	Provence and Languedoc ceded to the Franks
719	Arab invasions

Chronology

737	Charles Martel defeats Arabs and crushes anti-Frank rebellions in Arles, Avignon and Marseille
759	Pépin the Short adds region to his Frankish empire
855	Creation of the kingdom of Provence for Charles the Bald, third son of Lothaire
879	At the death of Charles the Bald, the Duke Boson proclaims himself king of Provence
c. 890	More Arab raids and invasions
924	Magyars (Hungarians) sack Nîmes
949	Conrad of Burgundy inherits Provence and divides it into four feudal counties
979	Count William defeats Saracens at La Garde-Freinet, proclaims himself Marquis of Provence
1002	First written text in Provençal
1032	Death of Rudolph II, king of Burgundy and Provence; lands bequeathed to Holy Roman Emperor Conrad II
1095	Occitans join First Crusade under Raymond of St-Gilles, Count of Toulouse and Marquis of Provence; William of Aquitaine writes first troubadour poetry
1112	Marriage of Douce, duchess of Provence, with Raymond-Berenger III, Count of Barcelona
1125	Provence divided between the houses of Barcelona and Toulouse
1176	Pierre Valdo of Lyon founds Waldensian (Vaudois) sect
1186	Counts of Provence make Aix their capital
1187	Discovery of relics of St Martha at Tarascon
1208	Albigensian Crusade begins
1246	Charles I of Anjou weds Béatrice, heiress of Provence, beginning the Angevin dynasty
1248	St Louis embarks on Seventh Crusade from Aigues-Mortes
1266	Battle of Benevento gives Charles of Anjou the Kingdom of Naples
1274	Papacy acquires Comtat Venaissin
1276	Division of Aragon; Kingdom of Majorca founded with capital at Perpignan
1280	Relics of Mary Magdalene 'discovered' at St-Maximin-la-Ste-Baume
1286	First meeting of the Etats de Provence
1289	The school of medicine in Montpellier becomes a university

1297	Francesco Grimaldi the Spiteful, merchant-prince of Genoa, conquers Monaco (but is forced to abandon it in 1301)
1303	Boniface VIII founds University of Avignon
1309	Papacy moves to Avignon
1327	Petrarch first sees Laura
1340s	Sienese painters bring International Gothic style to Avignon
1348	Jeanne of Naples and Provence sells Avignon to the Pope; the Black Death strikes the South
1349	Jews expelled from France and take refuge in Comtat Venaissin
1362	Election of abbot of St-Victor as Pope Urban V
1363	The Grimaldis recover Monaco and hold it still
1377	Papacy returns to Rome
1380	Louis I d'Anjou adopted by Jeanne of Naples
1388	Regions of Nice, Barcelonnette and Puget-Théniers secede from Provence, join County of Savoy
1464	Founding of the Fair of Beaucaire
1481	Charles du Maine, Count of Provence, leaves Provence to the King of France
1496	Military port founded in Toulon
1501	French create Parlement of Aix to oversee Provence
1524	Provence invaded by the imperial troops of Charles V
1525	Jews in the Comtat Venaissin compelled to wear yellow hats
1539	Edict of Villars-Cotterêts forces use of French as official language
1540	Parlement of Aix orders massacre of Waldensians in the Lubéron
1559	Completion of the canal between the Durance and Salon
1562	Beginning of Wars of Religion: Protestant assembly at Mérindol
1577	First soap factory (Prunemoyr) founded in Marseille
1590–92	Carlo Emanuele of Savoy invades Provence
1598	Edict of Nantes ends the Wars of Religion
1603	Royal college founded at Aix
1639	Last meeting of the Etats de Provence before the Revolution
1646	Jews confined to ghettos
1680	Louis XIV enters rebellious Marseille
1685	Louis XIV revokes Edict of Nantes

1702–4	The War of the Camisards
1707	Toulon unsuccessfully besieged by the English and Duke of Savoy
1720–21	100,000 die of plague, mostly in Marseille
1731	Principality of Orange incorporated into France
1752	Last Protestant persecutions
1766	Tobias Smollett publishes his *Travels*, enticing the British to Nice
1779	Roman mausoleum and palace of the counts demolished, at Aix
1784	Hot air balloon goes up in Marseille
1787	The Edict of Tolerance
1790	France divided into *départements*
1791	France annexes Comtat Venaissin
1792	Volunteers from Marseille sing *La Marseillaise* to Paris
1793	Revolutionary tribunal in Marseille; Siege of Toulon makes Bonaparte famous
1795	Massacres in Marseille and Tarascon
1800	Marseille population around 100,000
1815	Napoleon escapes Elba and pops up again near Juan-les-Pins
1820	First signs of tourist industry at Hyères
1830	Revolution brings Louis Philippe to power
1831	Lord Brougham begins the vogue for wintering in Cannes
1839	Inauguration of Marseille–Sète railroad; birth of Cézanne
1840–8	Prime Ministry of Guizot, Protestant liberal from Nîmes
1851	Louis Napoleon's coup ends Second Republic; armed resistance in the south
1854	Founding of the *Félibrige* at the Château de Fontségugne
1859	Mistral publishes *Miréio*
1860	Plebiscite in County of Nice votes for union with France
1861	The prince of Monaco sells Roquebrune and Menton to France
1865	Silkworm industry destroyed by disease
1868–90	Phylloxera epidemic devastates vines
1869	Opening of Suez Canal brings boom times to Marseille
1888	Stephen Liégeard gives the Côte d'Azur its name
1888–90	Van Gogh in Provence
1900	Population reaches 500,000 in Marseille, 20% of which is Italian

1904	Frédéric Mistral wins the Nobel Prize for Literature
1906	Colonial *Exposition* at Marseille
1911	Diaghilev signs contract to bring the Ballets Russes to Monte Carlo
1924–5	Scott and Zelda Fitzgerald raise hell on the Riviera
1928	Creation of the Camargue Regional Park
1930	D.H. Lawrence dies in Vence
1930s	Marcel Pagnol films his *Marius, Fanny* and *César* trilogy in Marseille
1939	Founding of the Cannes Film Festival
1942	Sinking of the fleet at Toulon
1943	Formation of the Maquis resistance cells
1944	American and French landings around St-Tropez; Provence liberated in two weeks
1945	Creation of the Institut d'Etudes Occitanes
1947	Val de Roya incorporated into France
1956	Bardot and Vadim make *And God Created Woman* in St-Tropez
1962	Independence of Algeria: tens of thousands of French North Africans (*pieds-noirs*) settle in the south
1965	Last silk weaving company closed
1966	Steelworks founded at Fos
1970	Completion of Paris-Lyon-Marseille autoroute
1982	Regional governments created
1992	30 die in Vaison-la-Romaine floods

A working knowledge of French will make your holiday more enjoyable, but is hardly essential in the heartland of Provence, where you can always find someone working in travel offices, banks, shops, hotels, and restaurants who speaks at least rudimentary English. Venturing into the less-travelled hinterlands may well require an effort to recall your school French; a small travel phrase book and English-French dictionary can come in handy. Near the Alpine border you can try out your Italian.

Even if your French is brilliant, the soupy southern twang may throw you a curve. Any word with a nasal *in* or *en* becomes something like *aing* (*vaing* for *vin*). The last vowel on many words that are silent in the north get to express themselves in the south as well (*encore* becomes something like *engcora*). What stays the same is the level of politeness: use *monsieur*, *madame* or *mademoiselle* when speaking to anyone, from your first *bonjour* (and never *garçon* in restaurants!) to your last *au revoir*.

Many of the restaurants in this book don't translate their menus, so we've included the decoder below; try the section on regional specialities (*see* p.21) if an item isn't listed below.

Deciphering French Menus

Hors d'oeuvre et Soupes — Starters and Soups

Assiette assortie	Mixed cold hors d'oeuvres
Bisque	Shellfish soup
Bouchées	Mini vol-au-vents
Bouillon	Broth
Consommé	Clear soup
Crudités	Raw vegetable platter
Potage	Thick vegetable soup
Velouté	Thick smooth soup, often fish or chicken
Vol-au-vent	Puff pastry case with savoury filling

Language

Poissons et Coquillages (Crustacés)	Fish and Shellfish
Aiglefin	Little haddock
Anchois	Anchovies
Anguille	Eel
Barbue	Brill
Baudroie	Anglerfish
Belons	Rock oysters
Bigourneau	Winkle
Blanchailles	Whitebait
Brème	Bream
Brochet	Pike
Bulot	Whelk
Cabillaud	Fresh cod
Calmar	Squid
Carrelet	Plaice
Colin	Hake
Congre	Conger eel
Coques	Cockles
Coquilles St-Jacques	Scallops
Crabe	Crab
Crevettes grises	Shrimps
Crevettes roses	Prawns
Cuisses de grenouilles	Frogs' legs
Darne	Thin slice of fish
Daurade	Sea bream
Ecrevisse	Freshwater crayfish
Eperlans	Smelt
Escabèche	Fish fried, marinated, and served cold
Escargots	Snails
Espadon	Swordfish
Flétan	Halibut
Friture	Deep fried fish
Fruits de mer	Seafood
Gambas	Giant prawns

Gigot de mer	A large fish cooked whole
Grondin	Red gurnard
Hareng	Herring
Homard	Lobster
Huîtres	Oysters
Langouste	Spiny Mediterranean lobster
Languoustines	Dublin Bay prawns
Limande	Lemon sole
Lotte	Monkfish
Loup (de mer)	Sea bass
Maquereau	Mackerel
Merlan	Whiting
Morue	Salt Cod
Moules	Mussels
Oursin	Sea urchin
Pageot	Sea bream
Palourdes	Clams
Poulpe	Octopus
Praires	Small clams
Raie	Skate
Rascasse	Scorpion fish
Rouget	Red mullet
Saumon	Salmon
Saint-Pierre	John Dory
Sole (à la meunière)	Sole (with butter, lemon and parsley)
Stockfisch	Stockfish (wind-dried cod)
Telline	Tiny clam
Thon	Tuna
Truite	Trout
Truite saumonée	Salmon trout

Viandes et Volaille — **Meat and Poultry**

Agneau (de pré salé)	Lamb (grazed in fields by the sea)
Ailerons	Chickenwings

Andouillette	Chitterling (tripe) sausage
Biftek	Beefsteak
Blanc	Breast or white meat
Blanquette	Stew of white meat, thickened with egg yolk
Boeuf	Beef
Boudin blanc	Sausage of white meat
Boudin noir	Black pudding
Brochette	Meat (or fish) on a skewer
Caille	Quail
Canard, caneton	Duck, duckling
Carré	The best end of a cutlet or chop
Cervelles	Brains
Châteaubriand	Porterhouse steak
Cheval	Horsemeat
Chevreau	Kid
Civet	Stew of rabbit (usually), marinated in wine
Confit	Meat cooked and preserved in its own fat
Contre-filet	Sirloin steak
Côte, côtelette	Chop, cutlet
Cuisse	Thigh or leg
Dinde, dindon	Turkey
Entrecôte	Ribsteak
Epaule	Shoulder
Estouffade	A meat stew marinated, fried, and then braised
Faisan	Pheasant
Faux filet	Sirloin
Foie	Liver
Foie Gras	Goose liver
Frais de veau	Veal testicles
Fricadelle	Meatball
Gésier	Gizzard
Gibier	Game
Gigot	Leg of lamb

Graisse	Fat
Grillade	Grilled meat
Grive	Thrush
Jambon	Ham
Jarret	Knuckle
Langue	Tongue
Lapereau	Young rabbit
Lapin	Rabbit
Lard (lardons)	Bacon (diced bacon)
Lièvre	Hare
Maigret (de canard)	Breast (of duck)
Marcassin	Young wild boar
Merguez	Spicy red sausage
Museau	Muzzle
Navarin	Lamb stew with root vegetables
Noix de veau	Topside of veal
Oie	Goose
Os	Bone
Perdreau (perdrix)	Partridge
Petit salé	Salt pork
Pieds	Trotters
Pintade	Guinea fowl
Porc	Pork
Poularde	Capon
Poulet	Chicken
Poussin	Baby chicken
Queue de boeuf	Oxtail
Ris (de veau)	Sweetbreads (veal)
Rognons	Kidneys
Rôti	Roast
Sanglier	Wild boar
Saucisses	Sausages
Saucisson	Dry sausage, like salami
Selle (d'agneau)	Saddle (of lamb)

Steak tartare	Raw minced beef, often topped with a raw egg yolk
Suprême de volaille	Fillet of chicken breast and wing
Tête (de veau)	Head (calf's)
Taureau	Bull's meat
Tortue	Turtle
Tournedos	Thick round slices of beef fillet
Travers de porc	Spare ribs
Tripes	Tripe
Veau	Veal
Venaison	Venison

Légumes, Herbes, etc. — Vegetables, Herbs, etc.

Ail	Garlic
Algue	Seaweed
Aneth	Dill
Artichaut	Artichoke
Asperges	Asparagus
Aubergine	Aubergine (eggplant)
Avocat	Avocado
Basilic	Basil
Betterave	Beetroot
Cannelle	Cinnamon
Céleri (-rave)	Celery (celeriac)
Cèpes	Wild dark brown mushrooms
Champignons	Mushrooms
Chanterelles	Wild yellow mushrooms
Chicorée	Curly endive
Chou	Cabbage
Choufleur	Cauliflower
Choucroute	Sauerkraut
Ciboulettes	Chives
Citrouille	Pumpkin
Coeur de palmier	Heart of palm

Concombre	Cucumber
Cornichons	Gherkins
Courgettes	Courgettes (zucchini)
Cresson	Watercress
Echalote	Shallot
Endive	Chicory
Epinards	Spinach
Estragon	Tarragon
Fenouil	Fennel
Fèves	Broad beans
Flageolets	White beans
Fleur de courgette	Courgette blossoms
Frites	Chips (French fries)
Genièvre	Juniper
Gingembre	Ginger
Girofle	Clove
Haricots (rouges, blancs)	Beans (kidney, white)
Haricots verts	Green (French) beans
Jardinière	With diced garden vegetables
Laitue	Lettuce
Laurier	Bay leaf
Lentilles	Lentils
Maïs (épis de)	Sweet corn (on the cob)
Marjolaine	Marjoram
Menthe	Mint
Mesclum	Salad of various leaves
Morilles	Morel mushrooms
Moutarde	Mustard
Navet	Turnip
Oignons	Onions
Oseille	Sorrel
Panais	Parsnip
Persil	Parsley
Petits pois	Peas

Piment	Pimento
Pissenlits	Dandelion greens
Poireaux	Leeks
Pois chiches	Chick-peas
Pois mange-tout	Sugar-peas
Poivron	Bell pepper
Pomme de terre	Potato
Primeurs	Young vegetables
Radis	Radishes
Raifort	Horseradish
Riz	Rice
Romarin	Rosemary
Safran	Saffron
Salade verte	Green salad
Salsafis (with *ess*)	Salsify
Salé	Salted
Sarrasin	Buckwheat
Sauge	Sage
Seigle	Rye
Serpolet	Wild thyme
Thym	Thyme
Truffes	Truffles

Fruits, Desserts, Noix — **Fruits, Desserts, Nuts**

Abricot	Apricot
Acajou	Cashew
Amandes	Almonds
Ananas	Pineapple
Banane	Banana
Bavarois	Mousse or custard in a mould
Biscuit	Cake
Bombe	Ice-cream dessert in round mould
Bonbons	Sweets, candy
Brebis	Sheep cheese

Brioche	Light sweet yeast bread
Brugnon	Nectarine
Cacahouète	Peanut
Cassis	Black currant
Cérise	Cherry
Charlotte	Custard and fruit in almond biscuits
Chausson	Turnover
Chèvre	Goat cheese
Citron	Lemon
Citron vert	Lime
Clafoutis	Berry tart
Coing	Quince
Compote	Stewed fruit
Corbeille de fruits	Basket of fruit
Coupe	Ice cream
Crème anglaise	Custard
Crème Chantilly	Sweet whipped cream
Crème fraîche	Sour cream
Crème pâtissière	Thick cream pastry filling made with eggs
Dattes	Dates
Figues (de Barbarie)	Figs (prickly pear)
Fraises (de bois)	Strawberries (wild)
Framboises	Raspberries
Fromage (plateau de)	Cheese (board)
Fromage blanc	Yoghurty cream cheese
Fromage frais	Similar to sour cream
Fruit de la passion	Passion fruit
Gâteau	Cake
Génoise	Rich sponge cake
Glace	Ice cream
Grenade	Pomegranate
Groseilles	Red currants, gooseberries
Lavande	Lavender
Macarons	Macaroons

Madeleines	Small sponge cakes
Mandarine	Tangerine
Mangue	Mango
Marrons	Chestnuts
Merise	Wild cherry
Miel	Honey
Mirabelle	Mirabelle plum
Mûres	Mulberry, blackberry
Myrtilles	Bilberries
Noisette	Hazelnut
Noix	Walnuts
Oeufs à la neige	Meringue
Pamplemousse	Grapefruit
Parfait	Frozen mousse
Pastèque	Water melon
Pêche (blanche)	Peach (white)
Petits fours	Tiny cakes and pastries
Pignons	Pine-nuts
Pistache	Pistachio
Poire	Pear
Pomme	Apple
Prune	Plum
Pruneau	Prune
Raisins (sec)	Grapes (raisins)
Reine-Claude (La)	Greengage
Sablé	Shortbread
Savarin	A filled cake, shaped like a ring
Tarte, tartelette	Tart, little tart
Tarte Tropézienne	Sponge cake filled with custard and topped with nuts
Truffes	Chocolate truffles

Cooking Terms, Miscellaneous, Snacks

Addition	Bill
Aigre-doux	Sweet and sour

Aiguillette	Thin slice
A l'anglaise	Boiled
A l'arlésienne	With aubergines, potatoes, tomatoes, onions, rice
A la châtelaine	With chestnut purée and artichoke hearts
A la grecque	Cooked in olive oil and lemon
A la périgourdine	In a truffle and foie gras sauce
A la provençale	Cooked with tomatoes, garlic, olive oil
Allumettes	Strips of puff pastry
A point	Medium steak
Au feu de bois	Cooked over a wood fire
Au four	Baked
Auvergnat	With sausage, bacon, and cabbage
Baguette	Long loaf of bread
Barquette	Pastry boat
Beignets	Fritters
Béarnaise	Sauce of egg yolks, shallots and white wine
Beurre	Butter
Bien cuit	Well done steak
Bleu	Very rare steak
Bordelaise	Red wine, bone marrow and shallot sauce
Broche	Roast on a spit
Chasseur	Mushrooms and shallots in white wine
Chaud	Hot
Chou	Puff pastry
Confiture	Jam
Coulis	Strong clear broth
Couteau	Knife
Crème	Cream
Crêpe	Thin pancake
Croque-monsieur	Toasted ham and cheese sandwich
Croustade	Small savoury pastry
Cru	Raw
Cuillère	Spoon
Cuit	Cooked

Diable	Spicy mustard sauce
Emincé	Thinly sliced
En croûte	Cooked in a pastry crust
En papillote	Baked in buttered paper
Epices	Spices
Farci	Stuffed
Feuilleté	Flaky pastry
Flambé	Set aflame with alcohol
Forestière	With bacon and mushrooms
Fourchette	Fork
Fourré	Stuffed
Frais, fraîche	Fresh
Frappé	With crushed ice
Frit	Fried
Froid	Cold
Fromage	Cheese
Fumé	Smoked
Galantine	Cooked food served in cold jelly
Galette	Flaky pastry case or pancake
Garni	With vegetables
(au) Gratin	Topped with crisp browned cheese and breadcrumbs
Grillé	Grilled
Hachis	Minced
Hollandaise	A sauce of butter and vinegar
Huile (d'olive)	Oil (olive)
Marmite	Casserole
Médaillon	Round piece
Mijoté	Simmered
Mornay	Cheese sauce
Nouilles	Noodles
Oeufs	Eggs
Pain	Bread
Pané	Breaded

Parmentier	With potatoes
Pâte	Pastry, pasta
Paupiette	Rolled and filled thin slices of fish or meat
Pavé	Slab
Piquante	Vinegar sauce with shallots and capers
Pissaladière	A kind of pizza with onions, anchovies, etc.
Poché	Poached
Poivre	Pepper
Quenelles	Dumplings of fish or poultry
Raclette	Toasted cheese with potatoes, onions and pickles
Salé	Salted, spicy
Sanglant	Rare steak
Sel	Salt
Sucré	Sweet
Timbale	Pie cooked in a dome-shaped mould
Tranche	Slice
Vapeur	Steamed
Véronique	Green grapes, wine, and cream sauce
Vinaigre	Vinegar
Vinaigrette	Oil and vinegar dressing

Boissons	**Drinks**
Bière (pression)	Beer (draught)
Bouteille (demi)	Bottle (half)
Café	Coffee
Chocolat (chaud)	Chocolate (hot)
Demi	A third of a litre
Doux	Sweet (wine)
Eau (minérale)	Water (mineral, spring)
Eau de vie	Brandy
Gazeuse	Sparkling
Glaçons	Ice cubes
Infusion (or *tisane*)	Herbal tea

Lait	Milk
Moelleux	Semi-dry
Pichet	Pitcher
Pressé	Fresh fruit juice
Pression	Draft
Sec	Dry
Sirop d'orange/de citron	Orange/lemon squash
Thé	Tea
Verre	Glass
Vin blanc/rosé/rouge	Wine white/rosé/red

Ardagh, John, *France Today* (Penguin, 1987). One in Penguin's informative paperback series on contemporary Europe.

Barr, Alfred, *Henri Matisse: his Art and his Public* (Museum of Modern Art, New York, 1951).

Bishop, Morris, *Petrarch and His World* (Chatto & Windus, 1964).

Bonner, Anthony, *Songs of the Troubadours* (Allen & Unwin, 1973). An excellent introduction to the life and times of the troubadours, with translations of the best-known verses.

Cézanne, Paul, *Letters* (London, 1941).

Cook, Theodore A., *Old Provence* (London, 1905). A classic traveller's account of the region, out of print and hard to find.

Daudet, Alphonse, *Letters from my Windmill* (Penguin, 1982). Bittersweet 19th-century tales of Midi nostalgia by Van Gogh's favourite novelist.

Dumas, Alexandre, *The Count of Monte Cristo,* many editions; romantic fantastical tale of revenge, much of it set in Marseille and the Château d'If.

Durrell, Lawrence, *The Avignon Quintet* (Faber, 1974–85); lush wartime sagas that take place in Avignon and around.

Fitzgerald, F. Scott, *Tender is the Night,* many editions. 1920s Riviera decadence based on personal research.

Ford, Ford Madox, *Provence: From Minstrels to the Machine* (Allen & Unwin, 1935). A lyrical pre-war view of the region.

Fortescue, Winifred, *Perfume from Provence* (1935). Poor, intolerable Lady Fortescue's misadventures with the garlicky peasants near Nice.

Giono, Jean, *To the Slaughterhouse, Two Riders of the Storm* (Peter Owen, 1988). Giono is a major 20th-century novelist of Provence, whose deep pessimism contrasts with the sunnier views of his contemporary Pagnol.

Goldring, Douglas, *The South of France* (Macdonald, 1952). Travels and comments by another English resident.

Gramont, Sanche de, *The French: Portrait of a People* (Putnam, New York, 1969). One of the funnier attempts at the favourite French intellectual pastime: national self-analysis.

Greene, Graham, *J'Accuse: The Dark Side of Nice* (Bodley Head, 1982). The late Graham Greene, resident of Antibes, discovers the mafia connections and graft in the government of discredited mayor Jacques Médecin.

Further Reading

Hugo, Victor, *Les Misérables*, many editions. Injustice among the galley-slaves and basis for the hit musical.

Ladurie, Emmanuel Leroi, *Love, Death and Money in the Pays d'Oc* (Scolar, 1982).

de Larrabeiti, Michael, *The Provençal Tales* (Pavilion, 1988). Troubadours' tales, legends and stories told by shepherds around the camp fire.

Lyall, Archibald, *Companion Guide to the South of France* (Collins, 1978). Personal, well-written but dated guide of the entire Mediterranean coast.

Mayle, Peter, *A Year in Provence* and *Toujours Provence* (Sinclair Stevenson/Pan, 1989 and 1991). The entertaining bestsellers on ex-pat life in the Lubéron.

Mistral, Frédéric, *Miréio* and *Poème du Rhône*, epic poems by the Nobel prize-winning Félibre, widely available in French or Provençal.

More, Carey and Julian, *A Taste of Provence* (Pavilion, 1987). Father and daughter team up to evoke the countryside and gastronomy of Provence in words and photographs.

Morris, Edwin T., *Fragrance: The Story of Perfume from Cleopatra to Chanel* (Charles Scribner & Sons, 1984).

Pagnol, Marcel, *Jean de Florette* and *Manon of the Springs*, *The Days were too Short* (Picador, 1960). Autobiography by Provence's most beloved writer.

Petrarch, Francesco, *Songs and Sonnets from Laura's Lifetime* (Anvil Press, 1985).

Pope Hennessy, James, *Aspects of Provence* (Penguin, 1952). A fussy but lyrical view of the region in the '40s and '50s.

Raison, Laura, compiler, *The South of France: An Anthology* (Cadogan, 1985).

Smollett, Tobias, *Travels through France and Italy* (London, 1776). The irrepressible, grouchy Tobias 'Smellfungus' makes modern travel writing look like advertising copy.

Stendhal, *Travels through the South of France* (London, 1971).

Süskind, Patrick, *Perfume* (Penguin, 1989). Thrilling and fragrant murder in the 18th-century perfume industry in Grasse.

Van Gogh, Vincent, *Collected Letters of Vincent Van Gogh* (New York, 1978).

Vergé, Roger, *Cuisine of the Sun* (London, 1979). The owner of the Moulin de Mougins tells some of his secrets of nouvelle Provençal cooking.

Whitfield, Sarah, *Fauvism* (Thames and Hudson, 1991). A good introduction to the movement that changed art history.

Worwood, Valerie, *Aromantics* (Pan, 1987). An amusing look at aromatherapy.

Wylie, L., *Village in the Vaucluse* (Harvard University Press, 1971). The third edition of a very readable sociologist's classic based on the village of Roussillon.

Zeldin, Theodore, *France 1845–1945* (Oxford University Press, 1980). Five well-written volumes on all aspects of the period.

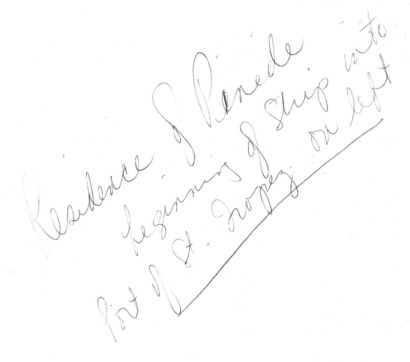

Residence of Penede.
beginnings of ship into
Port of St. Tropez on left